FAULKNER AND DOSTOEVSKY

by Jean Weisgerber
Translated by Dean McWilliams

Faulkner
and Dostoevsky

Influence and Confluence

Ohio University Press / Athens, Ohio

Faulkner et Dostoïevski: confluence et influence
© 1968 by Presses Universitaires
de Bruxelles

Faulkner and Dostoevsky
Copyright © 1974
Library of Congress Catalog Number 72-85537
ISBN 8214-0149-1
Manufactured in the United States of America by
Oberlin Printing Co. Inc.
Designed by Hal Stevens

Contents

Foreword

This is a curious book that will undoubtedly shock systematic minds.
First of all, the expression "comparative literature" is taken literally, my purpose being to juxtapose two writers, and more specifically to explain and evaluate Faulkner in the light of Dostoevsky. At first glance a long article would have seemed sufficient to record their factual relations, but, considered in such a narrow and positivistic spirit, the influences risk being confused with fortuitous convergences, and the more profound and interesting analogies might remain hidden. In the present case it is the secret confluences of sensibility and attitudes which, once established, will enable us to locate and list the borrowings. It is a matter then, first of all, of showing the ways in which the temperaments of these two men are akin and of constructing the perspective within which their relations take place. Because for the most part, it is a matter of *impregnation* rather than of direct and precise actions, the contributions of Dostoevsky and the accidental resemblances from which they are practically indistinguishable will be studied side by side. Isolated details are practically impossible to catalogue, all the more so because Faulkner often manipulates his sources to the point that they become unrecognizable. Only by accumulating our materials will we be able to attempt to measure and define the total influence. Our meandering progress will reflect the ambiguities of our subject. We will see above all that Dostoevsky furnishes Faulknerians with some extremely useful instruments: an observation post, a guiding theme, a detector indicating meanings and values.

vii

Needless to say, the slavicist will gain little from these pages. Moreover, I do not know Russian. But neither did Faulkner, and the translations and commentaries that I have consulted in five or six languages have somewhat remedied this deficiency.

Finally, I do not believe in the panaceas that are being offered from all sides for literary studies. Or rather, I believe them all good, in varying degrees and depending on the case, and reserve my own freedom to choose the tool appropriate to my work.

The project that I have conceived necessitates a multiplicity of viewpoints and methods, and this will inevitably cause a certain amount of repetition. The two parts of the book are fundamentally opposed in that the first describes the works of Faulkner and Dostoevsky as *phenomena*, either moral ("The Feelings: Forms and Norms of Conduct"), philosophical ("Between the Devil and the Good God"), political ("A Certain Conservatism"), or literary ("Questioning the Novelistic Tradition"), while the other, more technical in emphasis, traces the *history* of affinities and contacts from the Faulknerian perspective. It goes without saying that these points of view mix and blend one with the other. Thus the ideas analyzed in "An Attempt at Historical Explanation", which ends the first part, reappear in the diachronic investigation of the second part, but here they are studied in terms of their development and their interrelationship at a given moment.

Since we are concerned only with confluences and influences, I feel no obligation to exhaust the material in the novels under review. That would, of course, be quite unimaginable. However, after finishing the work, one will notice that few of the essential problems have been ignored, at least concerning Faulkner, on whom Dostoevsky casts some most revealing light. We will thus be able to devise, by means of the comparative method, the traditional evaluations and interpretations.

I would like to mention that the bibliography contains only the principal works consulted.

In conclusion let me thank the American Council of Learned Societies, whose generosity enabled me to complete my documentation in the United States, as well as my friends and colleagues Messrs. Albert Baiwir, Claude Backvis and Roland Mortier, who kindly read and corrected my manuscript. Finally, it is thanks to the constant aid of my wife that this work was possible.

THE PROBLEM

That Faulkner encountered Dostoevsky is in no way surprising. In a certain sense, the confrontation of these two writers appears inevitable. A man of the nineteenth century, Dostoevsky is defined in terms of the guiding ideas of the epoch: the slogans of '89, progress, the struggle of faith and science. From deep within the czarist empire shaken by the abolition of serfdom, he indicted the European bourgeoisie; inversely, during his travels in the west after his Siberian exile, he diagnosed the Russian malaise, the social and spiritual crisis that tore his country. Transforming the serial novel of Dickens and Sue, he launched a passionate appeal to future generations, sensing the coming of socialism, and dreaming of the reign of Christ the King. Turned completely toward the future, he speaks to us, announcing Nietzsche and the superman, Freud and psychoanalysis, German expressionism, existentialism and, in pages of brilliant clairvoyance, Hitler, Stalin and the world of the concentration camp. There are few men who could more justly be said to be ahead of their time. Moreover, Dostoevsky proposes to paint not fixed, sclerotic vestiges of the past, but reality in gestation, that from which a new world will emerge.[1] The eccentric is for him the carrier of the norms to come, the trailblazer of the path soon to be trod by everyone. With him the realist becomes a prophet and experimenter; life is a quest and an adventure: art as well. In many cases, history has proven him right. Therefore it is not so much the craftsman, the narrator, that posterity has admired and studies of Dostoevsky's influence have tended to neglect this aspect in favor of his "message". At first glance nothing distinguishes the composition of his narratives from the formula "to be continued in the next issue", and such themes as money, the family, adultery are similar to those of Balzac, Dickens and Flaubert. As a general rule, Dostoevsky has been seen only as the thinker haunted by God and Satan, the apostle of suffering and freedom. This philosopher, the inventor of situations and characters whose originality is universally acknowledged, was, all things considered, regarded as a rather traditional craftsman.

The idea of comparing him to Faulkner would apparently seem absurd. The worlds they have constructed are in immediate contrast by their geographic situation, their locale. Despite the fact that Faulkner has described the mirth of New Orleans during Mardi Gras, his favorite milieu remains the countryside. The majority of his novels take place in open air, in nature swept by the winds, eroded by rains and floods, illuminated by lightning or somnolent in the brutal heat of summer; even the town of Jefferson borders on the wilderness. In Dostoevsky, on the other hand, the background is essentially urban: the leprous and overpopulated hovels, sordid alleyways, garrets where those who have defied God and man torture themselves, with here and there a quick glimpse of a wealthy drawing room or a view of a snow-covered avenue. Man chokes in the Russian city, but the southern countryside, although limitless, offers little more than the illusion of freedom: on the banks of the Mississippi as in St. Petersburg, the setting is often a prison. We discover here, despite superficial differences, our first common ground.

There are many others, and more striking ones. Thus, Faulkner and Dostoevsky explore what is most intense in the real; their art prefers to render the extremes, the tensions and, above all, the tragic: sorrow, violence and horror. Lena Grove's peacefulness and Prince Myshkin's candor set the frightening tribulations of Christmas and Rogozhin in relief; the silences, the moments of joy and recollection provide a contrast for audacities as extravagant as those of the Gothic novel or Zola. In this universe, one encounters the unusual and freakish more often than the normal. "We are certainly all not infrequently like madmen, but with the slight difference that the deranged are somewhat madder," Zossimov affirms in *Crime and Punishment*, "a normal man, it is true, hardly exists."[2] The cult of the exceptional—here made into the rule—the taste for pathological cases and strong emotions also marks Faulkner's "dark" novels where idiocy, suicide, murder and incest are common occurrences. On the other hand, the themes treated by Dostoevsky and the traditional novelists are also found: "love and money and death are the skeletons on which the story is laid,"[3] Faulkner says while at the same time distinguishing these from the deeper aspirations which drive his heroes.

The brilliant formal manipulations of *The Sound and The Fury*, *As I Lay Dying* and *Absalom, Absalom!* are, in reality, always employed on top of the cliches of the realist novel. Modernism grafts itself onto the traditional: Faulkner creates new novels from ancient themes. What is the story of the Compsons, the Sartorises and the de Spains if not that of the Buddenbrooks where the heritage of Zola—family album and theory of heredity—is allied with the idea of decadence. Faulkner, the rival of Joyce and Virginia Woolf as a pioneer of the experimental novel, welds the nineteenth century to the twentieth. If he overturns the forms consecrated and exhausted by time, he continues to exploit the themes dear to naturalism and the *fin de siecle*. Thomas Hardy's Wessex prefigures Yoknapatawpha County, the imaginary countryside whose map Faulkner has carefully sketched. *La Comédie humaine* and *Les Rougon-Macquart* find themselves transplanted in Mississippi: from *Sartoris* (1929) to *The Reivers* (1962), the genealogical trees grow and mingle their branches, covering the 2400 square miles of Faulkner territory with an inextricable network. And the forces which bear down on the individuals here are those defined earlier by Zola, Hardy and Conrad. It is a curious fact that this innovator was, according to his own testimony, little interested in contemporary literature: the authors he loved belong, for the most part, to the preceding century: Dickens, Melville, Balzac, Flaubert, Conrad etc.[4] By the same token, he often turned in his own writing to the past. Faulkner has, however, scarcely written historical novels; he attaches importance to the past only to the degree that he recognizes its pressure on the present. Hence his predilection for recent history, a characteristic perhaps to be expected in a southerner born thirty years after the memorable fall of the Confederacy. The milieu as well as the writer's own temperament seems to have destined him to turn to the world of the past and confront it with that of today.[5] Such is the guiding theme of *Sartoris*, where Civil War heroes face the "lost generation" of 1918. Of the four moments in which the action of *The Sound and the Fury* takes place, one is 1910 while the three others are eighteen years later and coincide more or less with the time in which the novel was written (published in 1929). *Absalom, Absalom!* (1936) also carries us back to 1909-10; and it is in the first decade of the twentieth century that *The Hamlet* (1940)[6] and *The Reivers* take place. The period 1905-10 is precisely the period of the author's childhood. He returns there eagerly because of his nostalgia for it, because fundamentally he is one of those men who accept progress only because it is inevitable, less with the heart than with the reason, and who continue to long for the "good old days"[7] even though they were darkened by the sadness of conquered soldiers.

To summarize, Faulkner gazes in a direction diametrically opposed to that of Dostoevsky. The past with which the one is so taken is approximately the present or the near future of the other: the second half of the nineteenth century and the beginning of the twentieth. The first, a historian and chronicler, is haunted by what has been; the other, a prophet, by that which is to come. Their designs cross; in some ways, they are even complementary. Let us say, simplifying things a bit, that in Faulkner the "form" is more on the pitch of 1960 than the "substance"; in Dostoevsky, it is the reverse. The Russian adds the corrective of freedom to Faulknerian fatalism, the heritage of a late-blooming naturalism. It remains to be seen if Faulkner will fall under the spell of these rather old-fashioned portraits and attempt to restore them according to our modern tastes.

Circumstances have combined to render operative relationships that we have treated as purely virtual. Faulkner read and reread Dostoevsky. He discovered him during his youth and made him a friend for life. Thus he has many times listed *The Brothers Karamazov* as one of his favorite books.

Can we then conclude that Dostoevsky has influenced him? Before launching into a detailed comparison of their works, it is permissible to answer that, generally speaking, such an influence is possible and even very likely. In his discussions at the University of Virginia during 1957 and 1958 Faulkner maintained that the author drew on three sources of inspiration: imagination, observation and experience.[8] Let us pass over the first, which does not concern us here; the two others, however, deserve definition since they can easily be confused. Observation is concerned, above all, with the verification of particular facts, the spontaneous exercise of the senses at a given moment. Experience, larger and more profound, suggests a modification or, even better, an enrichment of knowledge through contact with life: it assumes memory. On the one hand: that which is seen; on the other: that which is remembered. These are the very terms used by Faulkner, who quite rightly includes books among the components of experience.

Despite their geographic specificity, the material thus collected is quite similar; beyond the colors and smells proper to each place, Faulkner sees the universal man. The South, he tells us, is scarcely different from the North, nor is America different from Russia or China.[9] This authorizes the writer to take material where he wishes, randomly from among his fancies, travels, or readings. Once the particularities of time and place are eliminated, nothing prevents a situation produced in Petersburg in 1880 to be reproduced in Jefferson a half-century later.

Not without a certain reverse snobbism, Faulkner displayed a scorn, too forced to be sincere, for all literary cuisine: did he not introduce himself as a farmer to his interviewers? We are all familiar with the amusing but slightly questionable legend, surrounding *Soldiers' Pay*, according to which Sherwood Anderson recommended the manuscript to his publisher on the condition that he not read it. In 1955, the Nobel laureate in literature confided to a contributor to the *Nouvelles Littéraires*[10] that he had read nothing since his youth: "I occasionally reread Shelley, Keats, Verlaine, Laforgue."[10] In such exaggeration allowances must be made for the desire to mystify, for the Anglo-Saxon's irreverent impatience with the cult of the Man of Letters. It is

more accurate to say that, if Faulkner was little interested in
the new generations, he nevertheless returned constantly to the
books with which he was taken in his youth.[11]

> I suppose I have about fifty that I read—I go in and out like you go
> into a room to meet old friends, to open the book in the middle and
> read for a little while, and I imagine over the course of every ten years
> I would have read all of them through.[12]

There is more: Faulkner considered reading as the best way
to learn how to write;[13] he advised it to his students, for the
writer, he pointed out, is a thief: "he robs and steals from everything he ever wrote or read or saw."[14]

In giving the lie to his posturing as an "ignorant" genius, he
justifies at the same time an investigation like this one. Richard
P. Adams has, moreover, called attention in a long article on "The
Apprenticeship of William Faulkner" (1962)[15] to all that the poet
and novelist owed to the teachings of Swinburne, Housman, Eliot,
Shakespeare, Keats, the Bible, Sherwood Anderson, Cézanne,
Conrad, Balzac, Proust, Joyce, Dickens, Mark Twain, Hawthorne,
Melville, Frazer, Bergson, etc. Little by little, the critics have
managed, more or less, to reconstruct Faulkner's intellectual baggage and to estimate its role in his work. In doing so they have
been able to build their case on three kinds of documents: direct
or indirect references contained within the prose fiction or verse;
oral or written commentaries of the author: recorded lectures,
interviews, essays, letters, the testimony of relatives or friends;
finally the catalogue of Faulkner's library, drawn up after his
death by Joseph Blotner (1964).

It is evident that he knew the Russian novel relatively well.
Of all the foreign language literatures, which he usually read
in English translations, it is to the French (Balzac, Flaubert,
Camus) and to the Russian that he refers most often. In 1927,
the characters of *Mosquitoes*, tireless salon philosophers who
seem copied from Aldous Huxley, allude to the latter in veiled
terms.[16] At the University of Virginia thirty years later he spoke
of Gogol[17]—whose *Dead Souls* is a kind of caricature prefiguration
of the hypocrisy of public opinion and the pettiness of the provincial backwaters painted in *Sanctuary*[18] and *Light in August*[19]—

of Tolstoy,[20] Chekov[21]—whose short stories he admired—of Artsy-bachev,[22] and especially of Dostoevsky.

Despite his disdain, studied and intermittent, for erudition, Faulkner occasionally embellishes his novels with quotations: Keats, Eliot, Shakespeare, etc. Although many are easily identifiable, his use of allusions betrays both a taste for culture as well as an Anglo-Saxon reticence about it. For example, he names Dostoevsky only once in his narratives. The single reference that one finds, in *Requiem for a Nun* (1951), the most Dostoevskian of his works, is indirect, periphrastic, and almost ashamed of itself. When in the midst of the scene at the governor's, Temple declares:

> What we came here and waked you up at two o'clock in the morning for is just to give Temple Drake a good fair honest chance to suffer—you know: just anguish for the sake of anguish, like that Russian or somebody who wrote a whole book about suffering, not suffering for or about anything, just suffering, like somebody unconscious not really breathing for anything but just breathing,[23]

it is certain that Dostoevsky is intended. As for the book in question, it is probably *The Brothers Karamazov*, where Dmitri expiates a crime of which he is innocent, taking upon himself a more or less gratuitous suffering. A case can be made elsewhere for short phrases, but one must, quite truthfully, be very indulgent to attribute to *Crime and Punishment* an expression as banal as "his crime and guilt, and his punishment."[24] We will discover—as Richard P. Adams has already noted in his essay—that far from quoting his Dostoevskian sources textually, Faulkner almost always disguises them in the process of subjecting them to his own purposes. Where to begin and where to end in such a case?

Since there are few irrefutable proofs within his stories, we must cull his lectures and interviews. And here Dostoevsky's name occurs at every turn, alongside those of Conrad, Dickens, Flaubert and Cervantes. The more guarded the artist, the more expansive the man, at least after the war. He spoke of the Russian novelist in 1955 to Cynthia Grenier[25] and to Annie Brierre,[26] the following year to Jean Stein, who questioned him for the *Paris Review*,[27] and several times between 1955-58 to university audiences in Japan and the United States.[28] We thus learn that he read Dostoevsky intensively at the ages of eighteen and nineteen (1915-16), that he remained faithful to him and was marked by him; he admires the craftsman, the psychologist, and underlines in passing his capacity of compassion for human suffering; in short, Dostoevsky was for Faulkner an example, one of those who has left his imprint on history. Here, as an illustration, is the complete text of his answer to a question asked of him on March 13, 1957, at the University of Virginia (Undergraduate Course in Contemporary Literature):

> Q. Sir, you mentioned some of the Russian authors before. What do you think of Dostoevsky? Do you consider him one of the best?
>
> A. He is one who has not only influenced me a lot, but that I have got a great deal of pleasure out of reading, and I still read him again every year or so. As a craftsman, as well as his insight into people, his capacity for compassion, he was one of the ones that any writer wants to match if he can, that he was one who wrote a good Kilroy Was Here.[29]

Among Dostoevsky's novels he mentions only *The Brothers Karamazov*,[30] his favorite. But we know that he had also read *Crime and Punishment*[31] and everything indicates that he knew others. Blotner's inventory reveals that at his death his library included English editions of Turgenev (1960), Chekov (1932 and 1956), and Pasternak (1958 and 1959), *War and Peace* (1931), three copies of *Anna Karenina* (1930 etc.), two of *Dead Souls* (1923 and 1936), and the following works of Dostoevsky:

The Brothers Karamazov. Translated from the Russian by Constance Garnett. New York: Grosset & Dunlap, n.d.

Autograph (with inscription): Wili Lengel/New York/November 16, 1931.

Autograph: William Faulkner/New York. 16 Nov. 1931.   L

———. Translated by Constance Garnett. Illustrated by Boardman Robinson. New York: Random House, 1933.

Autograph: William Faulkner/Rowan Oak. 1932.   L

———. Translated by Constance Garnett. Introduction by Marc Slonim. New York: The Modern Library, 1950.   C

Crime and Punishment. Translated from the Russian by Constance Garnett. New York: The Modern Library, 1932.   L

————. Translated from the Russian by Constance Garnett, with an introduction by Ernest J. Simmons. New York: The Modern Library, 1950.   C

Poor People. New York: Boni & Liveright, 1917.

Autograph: William Faulkner/Rowanoak/1 April 1932.   L

The Possessed. Translated from the Russian by Constance Garnett, with a foreword by Avrahm Yarmolinsky. New York: The Modern Library, 1936.   L

Autograph: Faulkner/ 917 Rugby Road.[32]   C

Dostoevsky is not only the Russian author with the largest representation: three copies of *The Brothers Karamazov*, two of *Crime and Punishment*, two of *The Possessed*, one of *Poor People*, but with Faulkner the presence of doubles and the inscription of his signature and address are always definite signs of esteem. In addition, he could read Dostoevsky wherever he was staying; one portion of his books (C) were at Charlottesville, Virginia, where he was writer-in-residence, the others (L) were at Rowan Oak, his property in Oxford. We should also note that the majority of the translations are by Constance Garnett and that the date of the editions or of Faulkner's signature are, according to Blotner, unimportant. Faulkner had read more books than he owned. Thus neither Swinburne nor D. H. Lawrence is included in the catalogue, although he mentioned them as early as April, 1925.[33] Nor does the year of publication or of his signature necessarily coincide with his first reading. As for Faulkner's silences, they are not signs of ignorance. When speaking of Tolstoy, he mentions only *Anna Karenina*[34] and not *War and Peace*. When questioned about the latter work, however, he discusses it and does not answer, as he had for Virgil—whose *Georgics* he owned!—that he did not remember reading him.[35]

The material conditions required by the comparatist thus seem to be fulfilled: more or less intimate relations between a writer and another writer's work which extend over nearly fifty years, an unequivocal confession of the influence he underwent. The reading of Dostoevsky was for the young Faulkner an experience rich in consequences; throughout his life, he returned with pleasure to him again and again.

The critics have not failed to exploit individual analogies, but they have studied them only in a fragmentary and hesitant manner, sometimes lingering on a detail and at other times confining themselves to prudent generalities. The majority of the interviews and studies of Faulkner date from after the war: he was a long time in breaking through, and his reputation was contested until 1939.[36]

The first interest directed to our problem dates from February, 1931, when John Chamberlain published an article on *Sanctuary* in the *New York Times Book Review* ("Dostoyefsky's Shadow in the Deep South").[37] Two years later, after the appearance of *Light in August*, F. R. Leavis posed the question in *Scrutiny*: "Dostoevsky or Dickens?"[38] With his usual perspicacity the English critic put his finger on an enigma which every comparatist concerned with Faulkner confronts sooner or later. Granted the universal success of Dickens and the more or less equal admiration accorded him in Russia and America, to what extent does an allegedly Dostoevskian element in Faulkner derive from Dostoevsky or from Dickens? The same problem is posed by Balzac and perhaps, in another vein, by Conrad who had read Dostoevsky without liking him.[39]

In 1939, George Marion O'Donnell alluded to Dostoevsky in his celebrated essay on "Faulkner's Mythology".[40] After the war, parallels and comparisons, always brief and superficial, followed one another at an accelerated rate. They are to be found in Irving Howe's monograph (1952),[41] in Jean-Jacques Mayoux's article (1952),[42] in the columns of the *Times Literary Supplement* (notably in 1953 and 1962),[43] in the studies by Philip Blair Rice (1954)[44] and by Delmore Schwartz (1955)[45] on *A Fable*, in those by John L. Longley (1957)[46] and by Alfred Kazin (1957)[47] on *Light in August*, in the works of Irving Malin (1957),[48] Michael Millgate (1961)[49] and Fredrick J. Hoffman (1961),[50] in the *New Statesman* (1962),[51] in the volume on Dostoevsky (1961) edited by René Wellek,[52] etc. Let us point out to complete our picture three analyses: Frederick L. Gwynn[53] on *Crime and Punishment* and *The Sound and the Fury* (1958), Edward Wasiolek on "Dostoevsky and *Sanctuary*" (1959)[54] and Robert W. Weber on "Raskol'nikov, Addie Bundren, Meursault" |1965)[55] as well as comparisons attempted by French critics[56] including, among others, Jean Pouillon.[57] Although the influence of Dostoevsky in England,

Germany and France has been studied, no synthesis on the United States exists at present, and in the article on the sources of Faulkner (1962) Richard P. Adams limits himself to posing a question mark.[58]

To summarize, the inventory is rather thin and disappointing: after more than thirty years of Faulknerian studies, the surface of the area that interests us has scarcely been scratched. With the exception of some remarks bearing principally on *The Sound and the Fury, Sanctuary, Light in August* and *A Fable*, the rest of the work remains to be done. It is this gap that we propose to fill in the present work.

NOTES TO THE PROBLEM

1. See Johannes van der Eng, *Dostoevskij romancier* (The Hague: Mouton and Co., 1957), pp. 14-15.
2. *Crime and Punishment*, p. 201.
3. *Faulkner in the University*, p. 198.
4. *Ibid.*, p. 50.
5. See Frederick J. Hoffman: *William Faulkner* (New York: Twayne Publishers, Inc., 1961), pp. 24-26.
6. See *Faulkner in the University*, p. 29.
7. See *ibid.*, pp. 68, 98.
8. *Ibid.*, p. 172.
9. *Ibid.*, p. 87.
10. Annie Brierre, "Faulkner parle," *Les Nouvelles Littéraires*, no. 1466 (October 6, 1955), 1, 6.
11. See *Faulkner in the University*, pp. 12-13.
12. *Ibid.*, p. 150. See also p. 202.
13. See *ibid.*, pp. 117, 172, 192.
14. *Ibid* p. 115. See also John Faulkner, *My Brother Bill* (London: Victor Gollancz Ltd., 1964), pp. 206-08.
15. Richard P. Adams, "The Apprenticeship of William Faulkner," *Tulane Studies in English*, XII (1962), 113-156.
16. *Mosquitoes*, pp. 183-84.
17. *Faulkner in the University*, pp. 50, 101.
18. *Sanctuary*, p. 221.
19. *Light in August*, pp. 64-65, 298, 345.
20. See *Faulkner in the University*, pp. 50, 55-56, 61, 101, 150.
21. See *ibid.*, pp. 24, 48, 50, 145, 207.
22. See *ibid.*, p. 50.
23. *Requiem for a Nun*, p. 133.
24. *Go Down, Moses*, p. 349.
25. Cynthia Grenier, "The Art of Fiction: An Interview with William Faulkner—September, 1955," *Accent* XVI, 3 (Summer, 1956), 168-169.
26. Brierre, *loc. cit.*.
27. Jean Stein, "William Faulkner: An Interview," *William Faulkner. Three Decades of Criticism*. (ed.) Frederick J. Hoffman and Olga Vickery (East Lansing, Mich.: Michigan State Univ. Press, 1951), pp. 67, 78.
28. *Faulkner at Nagano*, p. 42 and *Faulkner in the University*, pp. 12-13, 20, 69, 101, 150.

29. *Ibid.*, p. 69. The passage was originally published in 1957 in Fredrick L. Gwynn and Joseph L. Blotner, "Faulkner in the University: A Classroom Conference," *College English*, XIX 1 (October, 1957), 6.

30. *Faulkner in the University*, p. 150. See also Brierre and Grenier above and *Faulkner at Nagano*, p. 42.

31. Frederick L. Gwynn quotes this statement dated September 15, 1956, in his "Faulkner's Raskolnikov," *Modern Fiction Studies* IV, 2 (Summer, 1958), 170.

32. *William Faulkner's Library—A Catalogue* compiled by Joseph Blotner (Charlottesville, Va.: University of Virginia Press, 1964), pp. 81-82.

33. *Early Prose and Poetry*, p. 115.

34. *Faulkner in the University*, p. 55.

35. *Ibid.*, p. 150.

36. See *William Faulkner: Three Decades of Criticism*, p. 8.

37. John Chamberlain, "Dostoyefsky's Shadow in the Deep South," *The New York Times Book Review*, February 15, 1931, p. 9.

38. F. R. Leavis, "Dostoevsky or Dickens?," *Scrutiny* II, (June 1933), 91-93.

39. See René Wellek "A History of Dostoevsky Criticisms" in *Dostoevsky* (ed.) René Wellek (Englewood Cliffs, N. J.: Prentice-Hall, 1962), p. 10 and Walter Neushäffer *Dosotjewskijs Einfluss auf den englishchen Roman* (Heidelberg: Carl Winter, 1935), p. 24.

40. *William Faulkner: Three Decades of Criticism* p. 93. O'Donnell's study originally appeared in *The Kenyon Review* in 1939.

41. Irving Howe, *William Faulkner* (New York: Vintage Books, 1962), pp. 23, 80-81. Howe does not refer directly to Dostoevsky but compares the situation of the Southern writer at the beginning of the twentieth century to that of the Russian novelists of the nineteenth century.

42. *William Faulkner: Three Decades of Criticism*, p. 157.

43. "A Saga of the Deep South," *The Times Literary Supplement*, February 13, 1953, p. 104, and "The Last of William Faulkner" *ibid.*, September 21, 1962, p. 726.

44. *William Faulkner: Three Decades of Criticism*, pp. 375, 379.

45. Delmore Schwartz, "*A Fable* by William Faulkner" in *Perspectives USA*, 10 (Winter, 1955) pp. 134-135.

46. *William Faulkner: Three Decades of Criticism*, pp. 269, 276.

47. *Ibid.*, p. 261.

48. Irving Malin, *William Faulkner* (Stanford, Calif.: Stanford University Press, 1957), p. 11.

49. Michael Millgate, *William Faulkner* (London: Oliver and Boyd, 1961), p. 111.

50. Frederick J. Hoffman, *William Faulkner*, p. 117. Hoffman restricts himself to alluding to nineteenth century Russian literature.

51. V. S. Pritchett, "The Time and That Wilderness," *New Statesman*, September 28, 1962, pp. 405-06.

52. René Wellek (ed.) *Dostoevsky*, p. 13.

53. Gwynn, *loc. cit.*. Gwynn notes other parallels. See p. 169.

54. Edward Wasiolek, "Dostoevsky and *Sanctuary*," *Modern Language Notes* LXXIV, 2 (February, 1959), 114-17.

55. Robert W. Weber, "Raskol'nikov, Addie Bundren, Meursault. Sur la continuité d'un mythe," *Archiv fur das Studium der neueren Sprachen und Literaturen*, 202, Band 117. Jahrgang 2, Heft, 81-92.

56. See 'Configuration critique de William Faulkner I," *La Revue des Lettres Modernes* IV, 27-29, 2ᵉ Trim. 1957, p. 188. See also S. D. Woodworth, *William Faulkner en France (1931-1952)* (Paris: M. J. Minard, 1959).

57. Jean Pouillon, *Temps et roman* (Paris: Gallimard, 1946), pp. 233-34.

58. Adams, *loc. cit.*.

PART ONE

I

THE FEELINGS: FORMS AND NORMS OF CONDUCT

The works of Faulkner testify, as do those of Dostoevsky, to man's struggle with nature as it is given or imposed by existence. Both are idealists: they strive to adapt things, the flesh and brute matter to the schemes they elaborate. This, it might indeed be said, is the activity of the artist in particular and of man in general, for by the mere fact of being, thinking or acting we intervene in the spontaneous flow of things. How, for instance, are things to be defined without forcing them to adopt the order presupposed by the simple arrangement of words in a sentence and, *a fortiori*, by the structure of the work of art? Moreover, the transformation becomes even more complicated when it operates on the level of conduct. Morality is a construct whose purpose is to render existence supportable, despite the fact it frequently leads to the opposite result. It superimposes on blind matter, formless and empty of sense, an aggregate of concepts and rules, a signification fabricated by intelligence, the heart and the imagination. Thus Quentin Compson in *The Sound and the Fury* prefers sin to "amorality." When his sister Caddy is discovered to be pregnant by her lover he accuses himself of incest rather than be forced to recognize the triumph of instinct in his sister's "fault."[1] An ineffectual bit of trickery, to be sure, but one which denotes, nonetheless, a desperate attempt to reduce "animality" to an ethical system. The case of Quentin is exemplary. It reveals the limits within which nature can be sublimated, because this vital principle, indifferent to good or evil,[2] cannot be violated with impu-

3

nity. One must respect and love it, while at the same time controlling it. Nothing is more dangerous or vain than to smother it under theories and artifices created exclusively by the mind in isolation. The struggle of man and nature is marked by the same restraints as the sporting match; it is a matter of surmounting the adversary, not of suppressing him; to break the rules of the game would be to lose in advance. In our dealings with matter we do not listen just to the mind: the heart also has its word to contribute. Faulkner's *bête noire* is the anemic rigidity of the intellect, pure abstraction, the ignorance of the real. In this he resembles Tolstoy and that implacable adversary of scientific morality who created Raskolnikov. Dostoevsky places the logic of concrete facts well above that of reason: he always asked if his ideas were viable, if they squared with reality.[3] A Christian receptive in the highest degree to the mystery of life, he does not, for all that, repudiate intelligence:[4] like Faulkner he distrusts its excesses. In short, in both cases man engages himself entirely—heart, will, intuition and reason—in his duel with nature; he seeks not to annihilate it because it is himself, among other things, that he would destroy, but to contain it, to tame it and correct it. Raskolnikov and Thomas Sutpen fail because, staking everything on an idea, they scorn everything else, striving for a total victory, literally against nature. On the other hand, the spontaneous and passionate conversion of Dmitri Karamazov, which is also a deliberate renunciation of debauchery, represents the true—and difficult— conquest of ethics over the disorder of the senses.

The primacy of moral values expresses itself obsessively in the Faulknerian vocabulary by the repetition of certain words. The pair of pride and humility ("pride . . . through humility") appears as early as *Sartoris*.[5] This strange duo, to which are joined courage ("courage through adversity overcome") and patience ("sheer and vindictive patience"), are heard from one end of Faulkner's work to the other: in *Absalom, Absalom!* ("when you are proud enough to be humble")[6] and above all in *Go Down, Moses* ("the humility and the pride," "humility through suffering . . . pride through the endurance which survived the suffering," "humility and pride," "humbly and with pride")[7] where the initial pair of pride and humility is abruptly joined to a cluster of other no-

4

tions which gravitate around it, but from which it has heretofore remained separate. In subsequent utterances it draws in its wake a train of virtues, any one of which is sufficient to cause others to rise in a chain reaction:

pity and humility and sufferance and endurance ("The Bear," 1942)[8] humility and pity and sufferance and pride. . . . pity and humility and sufferance and endurance (ibid.)[9]

honor and pride and pity and justice and courage and love. . . . Courage and honor and pride, and pity and love of justice and of liberty (ibid.)[10]

love and honor and pity and pride and compassion and sacrifice. . . . the courage and honor and hope and pride and compassion and pity and sacrifice ("The Stockholm Address," 1950)[11]

compassion and honor and pride and endurance (University of Virginia, February 15, 1957)[12]

courage, honor, pride, compassion, pity (ibid., May 8, 1957)[13]

honesty and pity and responsibility and compassion (ibid. April 24, 1958)[14]

One could extend *ad libitum* the litany of what the author calls "the old verities and truths of the heart,"[15] those which have enabled man to survive, to escape the fate of the species obliterated by natural selection. We are dealing here, Faulkner believes, less with an aspiration for the good than with a vital necessity: in the final analysis, the worship of spiritual values assures the perenniality of the human race. "Man has endured despite his frailty because he accepts and believes in those verities . . . one must be honest not because it's virtuous but because that's the only way to get along."[16] It pertains to man to have a soul[17] and a moral conscience. Such is again, with greater reason, the personal conviction of Dostoevsky. In "The Meek One Rebels" (*The Diary of a Writer*, November, 1876) the narrator, studying his young sixteen-year-old wife, exclaims "And where . . . did this naive, this meek, this taciturn one learn all this? . . . what truth in her condemnation!" and concludes that "the whole truth rose from her soul."[18] Even the criminal—witness the case of Raskolnikov—cannot always succeed in smothering the voice of conscience.

The most remarkable feature in the catalogue of Faulknerian "verities" is, without a doubt, the marriage of pride and humility.

The union of opposites is a common occurrence in his works. He loves to wed elements which are mutually exclusive and which, in addition, represent extremes. In this way, the antithesis is intensified, setting off open or covert warfare, bringing a confrontation of enemies, but leaving, however, the possibility of peace overtures once the quarrel is finished. Walter J. Slatoff has devoted an entire volume to the polarity of the Faulknerian imagination, emphasizing the contrast between movement and repose, sound and silence, quietude and agitation, stressing the attraction of extremes and the oppositions of concepts, characters and style.[19] Slatoff observes[20] that *Absalom, Absalom!* ends with a kind of oxymoron in which Quentin Compson's devotion to his homeland is merged with his detestation. When his friend asks him why he hates the South, Quentin protests that "I don't hate it,"[21] a negation infinitely more nuanced and ambiguous than a declaration of love. Addie Bundren (*As I Lay Dying*) is able to communicate with others only by means of the suffering she inflicts; as is often the case in Dostoevsky, self-abandon mingles with sadism.[22] The same ambivalence is found in Linda Snopes (*The Town*), who sees in Flem a father and an adversary.[23] The idea of conflict completely dominates Faulkner's thought. Has he not on several occasions declared that his fundamental theme was man in conflict with himself, with others or with his environment?[24] He sings of "the courage and the cowardice, the baseness and the splendor" of the heart.[25] In the Mississippi, the Old Man River of song and the geographical background of his stories, he discerns simultaneously a tutelary presence and a force of destruction.[26] Each term calls into play its opposite, whether it be a question of virtues, sentiments or physical setting. Contrasts, tensions, shocks: we are at the sources of a dialectic and, at the same time, in the center of a novelistic world characterized by variety. An analogous and somewhat more emphatic dualism inspired Dostoevsky, the painter of the Grand Inquisitor and Father Zossima, poet—like Faulkner—of the love-hate relationship and subtle psychologist of the Double: haughty and submissive, hostile and loving, avid of pleasures and pains, suffering and inflicting suffering, torn between good and evil. After proclaiming his theories, Raskolnikov cries *"vive donc la guerre éternelle."*[27]

6

It is impossible to imagine a more adequate definition of the philosophical and artistic method of his spiritual father.[28]

When the poles are brought together and the spark flashes, there is always torment, scandal and, above all, outrage. The shock of opposing forces ordinarily is translated in this manner: the hero causes an outrage or feels himself outraged. Having said this, we can define the meaning of the conflict and the nature of the forces involved. It is obvious that the struggle is presented as an encroachment, a transgression, a shocking attack by one adversary on the legitimate rights of another. Infringement, insult, and a wound of the most painful kind: the feeling of outrage is displeasure pushed to the extreme, a violent form of it—as the etymology of the word indicates: *ultra*, beyond, excessive—and therefore intolerable. On one side are arranged the just and the good or what is taken to be the just and the good: a more or less coherent collection of opinions on the moral or physical universe; on the other side: all that breaks, in an extraordinary explosion, the equilibrium of the system and demolishes its foundations. Man, in this war, is anything but an observer: he identifies with one camp or both, sometimes a victim, sometimes an aggressor, more often the field of battle. In reality, the outrage results from the violation of the schemes with which we cover nature and to which we try to reduce her. But, indocile and whimsical, she resists them and amuses herself by demonstrating the fragility of these structures and their authors. At bottom, what provokes the outrage is the blinding proof of our weakness, of the imperfection of what we are and what we do: our codes and our knowledge which nature insultingly denies.

Thus, there is no law so good nor a regime so just that it can eliminate crime. The murderer takes his revenge on the "Thou shalt not kill": a revolt against human and divine law, against social imperatives, and, in many cases, against those which the individual has forced upon himself; murder is a sovereign decree of the will, then, and a victory of freedom, but one which isolates the self from others. For, in their eyes, homicide pulverizes the scale of values laboriously erected by civilization to stifle or sublimate our antisocial instincts. If murder for the criminal is sometimes equal to a liberation, opinion in general experiences it as an outrage: that by means of which freedom is achieved only makes the masses shockingly aware of their impotence. Crime, the supreme outrage, obsessed Dostoevsky; he ran the entire gamut from simple assassination to philosophical suicide, including even parricide. To his Raskolnikov, Kirillov and Smerdyakov correspond Faulkner's Mink Snopes, Quentin Compson and Christmas. In Jefferson as in Petrograd, blood cries vengeance, covers the guilty hand with opprobrium and draws the group's anathema. The techniques of the detective novel and the trial situation, both abundantly exploited, derive from this.

It is not just violent death which scandalizes; in this case, the target has not even had the chance to experience outrage and it is the community which takes his place. Regardless of whether or not the victim survives, our awareness of outrage always derives from an enormous, upsetting, suddenly discovered gap existing between things as they are and our idea of them, in short, the opposition between what is and what ought to be, between reality and our expectations. Faulkner treats outrages unknown by Dostoevsky: those, for example, caused by the physical world and the past. To be sure, the rough Russian climate and the immensity of the Russian plains and rivers can harm man as surely as those of America. But such was never the purpose of Dostoevsky, who always remained a city dweller at heart. Faulkner, a regionalist and an heir of naturalism, insists on the determinism of the soil and the insult inflicted on us by our milieu. The convict of *The Wild Palms*, fighting the flooding Mississippi and awaiting the second wave which could carry him away, feels no outrage when it breaks because this is perfectly consistent with his earlier —quite outrageous—experience.[29] Nature offends us only when she seems to cheat and breaks the rules the mind had believed it had deduced from observation.[30] Faulkner goes so far as to describe the country itself as a result of an ancient outrage inflicted on the land by telluric forces.[31] The earth is thus personified, humanized. Faulkner establishes tight relations between it and history: the milieu weighs on Man and with it, the accumulated burden of the past. Quentin Compson sees the South, dead since 1865, as populated by garrulous, frustrated, outraged ghosts;[32] he is one of them himself since he bears the wreckage of their defeat in his blood.[33] Although he does not deny the influence of heredity,[34] this determinism is alien to Dostoevsky; the similarities with Faulkner are situated in other areas—not in what ties man to the soil and his past, but in the relationships formed between persons or between the individual and the group. Nonetheless, since the group's norms are developed in the course of time; we will be forced to return to the problem of history. What are, then, the kinds of outrage common to these novelists? Let us, first of all, state that this feeling does not necessarily tell us what value the writer places on the system that is under attack. The Snopes, abominated by Faulkner, can feel it as well as others. Outrage betrays nothing more than the notion of good and evil to which the characters are committed. With these reservations in mind we will distinguish, according to the case, individual and collective aspects. Sometimes nothing more is shaken than one's opinion of oneself: pride and vanity or, better, self-respect. The wound suffered translates as humiliation. Both Faulkner and Dostoevsky have welded them to their opposites: pride to humility, and vanity—which Pascal, Rousseau and Vauvenargues link with selfishness—to compassion. Other kinds of outrage concern the attitudes or feelings associated with social life and tradition, such as honor, decorum and propriety, whose violation result in an explosion, a scandal.

Generally speaking, we have defined outrage as a result of a violent deviation of events away from the expectations possible within the system. *"Perhaps that is where outrage lies,"* Joe Christmas tells himself, *"Perhaps I believe I have been tricked, fooled."*[35] The term recurs incessantly in Faulkner, often coupled with the word "rage."[36] It is an outrage which inspires the vain and perverse ambition of Sutpen, the hero of *Absalom, Absalom!*. Here tragedy comes from a child's brutal initiation to social injustice, that is to say, a humiliation. Sent dressed in rags to the home of a rich planter, young Sutpen is snubbed by a black servant who orders him to use the back door:[37] the next night he leaves his family determined to search his fortune. The unexpected and shocking event marks him for the rest of his life: from the camp of the offended Sutpen will pass to that of the offenders. That he uses the arms of the adversary, that his plans are morally reprehensible, matters little: the essential, for us, is his obsessive desire to remove the ignominy with which he has been covered. Humiliation, which according to Dimitri Karamazov is a "degradation,"[38] has been made by Dostoevsky into one of the most important elements in his psychology: one has only to think of *The Insulted and the Injured* and, above all, of *Notes from the Underground* whose protagonist is devoured by the desire to render evil for evil.[39]

> There in its nasty, stinking, underground home our insulted, crushed and ridiculed mouse promptly becomes absorbed in cold, malignant and, above all, everlasting spite. For forty years together it will remember its injury down to the smallest, most ignominious details, and every time will add, of itself, details still more ignominious, spitefully teasing and tormenting itself with its own imagination.[40]

Walking along Nevsky Prospect he feels

> innumberable miseries, humiliations and resentments; but no doubt that was just what I wanted. I used to wriggle along in a most unseemly fashion, like an eel, continually moving aside to make way for generals, for officers of the Guard and the Hussars, or for ladies. At such minutes there used to be a convulsive twinge at my heart, and I used to feel hot all down my back at the mere thought of the wretchedness of my attire, of the wretchedness and abjectedness of my little scurrying figure. This was a regular martyrdom, a continual, intolerable humiliation at the thought, which passed into an incessant and direct sensation that I was a mere fly in the eyes of all this world, a nasty disgusting fly— more intelligent, more highly developed, more refined in feeling than any of them, of course, but a fly that was continually making way for every one, insulted and injured by every one.[41]

In extreme cases, humiliation becomes the object of a cult: rather than bandaging his wound, the hero irritates and deepens it by "gloating over [the idea] and playing with it with vindictive pleasure."[42] We are not deceived: this bathing in infamy which appears to be the annihilation of pride is actually its apogee. We have here one of the paradoxes of psychology. Gide said that humiliation opens the doors of hell: "if humility is a renunciation of pride, humiliation on the other hand leads to a reinforcement of pride"[43] And again, "the man who has been humiliated seeks to humiliate in his turn."[44] The sick man immured in the underground and the demoniacal and wretched Sutpen with his puritanical intransigence and naivete react in this way. The proud are legion in the work of these two novelists: from book to book they file past, bent under their torment, like the sinners of Purgatory before Dante. For extreme pride brings unhappiness and can even drive one to death. The arrogant Orlov and Raskolnikov, who believed himself the imitator of Napoleon, end in prison; the proud Nastasya Filippovna is assassinated, Kirillov kills himself, etc. If Dostoevsky endows his doubles with a humility which sometimes saves them, the will to affirm oneself and dominate makes veritable monsters, asocial beasts, of the proud. "All is for me," Valkovsky declares, "the whole world is created for me."[45] Sutpen could have maintained a similar position, but Faulkner does not open such dizzying perspectives on this problem. The pride of the Sartorises, as imperious as it is, is situated somewhat lower: aristocratic arrogance, military vainglory and a rather infantile masculine vanity. It does not approach the destructive, delirious and omnipotent fury of the criminal, although the effects are strangely similar. Faulkner recounts in *The Unvanquished* how the patriarch, a Civil War hero, causes himself to be struck down by the man he had snubbed; and in *Sartoris* how his descendants, heirs of his violence and *grandezza*, expiate the family weakness.[46] This kind of pride is a curse because it attacks others and culminates in annihilation for everyone.

Weakness, a curse? "Sin" would be more exact, for pride such as we have described implies a perverse intention, an act of illwill. Faulkner and Dostoevsky denounce it for the same reasons as the Christian moralists and, like them, contrast it to the virtue of humility. One can ask, however, if it is always to be condemned. Is it not numbered among the "verities of the heart" by the American novelist? And is there not a legitimate pride, one born out of an objective evaluation, fair-minded about one's merits and excluding neither a sense of the relative nor humility? Rather than judging oneself superior to others in order to crush them, one looks back upon one's conduct, and the satisfaction of a duty fulfilled stimulates one to persevere in that path. Faulkner explains that to take pride in something is to say: "I did well, I did nothing that I was ashamed of, I can lie down with myself and sleep."[47] The *libido dominandi* is transformed into presumption if the praises one bestows on oneself are excessive. The ambivalence of pride, both a sin and the sign of virtue, is reflected in Ratliff's words in 1959 when he says that the old families of the South would have been too proud to mishandle the money of others:[48] the scorn for others expands to include a scorn of the harm we could do them: it is equivalent in the final analysis to a rejection of evil. To see how this rehabilitation is effectuated it is sufficient to refer to *Intruder in the Dust*, where Chick Mallison demonstrates that the superiority conferred by social rank is accompanied by an obligation to serve; it is this *noblesse oblige*, the motto of the Southern aristocracy, that is illustrated by Horace Benbow's ineffectual gesture in *Sanctuary*. More particularly, *Absalom, Absalom!* compares the praiseworthy pride which consists in bearing up under one's fate to the false pride which reacts to the unexpected with disdain and outrage and which expresses itself in aggression:

> that true pride, not that false kind which transforms what it does not at the moment understand into scorn and outrage and so vents itself in pique and lacerations, but true pride which can say to itself without abasement *I love, I will accept no substitute; something has happened between him and my father; if my father was right, I will never see him again, if wrong he will come or send for me; if happy I can be I will, if suffer I must I can.*[49]

To be proud in the best sense of the word is to be conscious of one's virtues, to pay homage to oneself, of course, but also to others, since the feeling of our elevation comes finally from the esteem we have of them in our search for the good. It is, in short, a matter of simply recognizing the dignity of Man. Zossima does this[50] and Lucas Beauchamp, who wants to be treated as an equal by the whites, as a man and not a Negro, demands it in *Intruder in the Dust*.

Seen from this angle, pride is no longer in opposition to humility. Does not the Gospel speak of the glory of the elect? "Whosoever shall exalt himself shall be abased; and he that shall humble himself shall be exalted." To be sure, Christ's promise of glory at the price of humility is to be fulfilled only in the beyond; this is simply a reversal of values coincidental with the entry into eternal life. In Faulkner the two overlap, coexisting in the conscience of the individual. The merits which man attributes to himself, he owes, among other things, to the stoic acceptance of existence: we have stated that the pair pride-humility almost automatically evokes the idea of courage, of effort, of sacrifice. This is the modest pride that Faulkner finds in the blacks, the mule, and, sometimes all in the same breath, in woman: "pride through humility."[51] This formula which appeared in 1929 becomes the subject of a gloss in *Go Down, Moses*. The blacks, he wrote, have learned humility by suffering and pride by the endurance which enabled them to survive suffering.[52] It follows that one may justifiably be proud of having been able to grit one's teeth, bear up under the lashes like the mule, and in so doing prove not only one's own tenacity but also that of the species. Pride testifies less to our personal virtues than to the instinct for the preservation of the race. Humility also flows from suffering: it is attached to it directly, while pride or, rather, pride without arrogance assumes an intermediary: the conviction of having victoriously resisted. Taken together, they are the salt of the earth: "the best, the best of all breathing, the humility and the pride."[53] If the adjective "proud," psychologically derived from "enduring," marks the *will* to survive, "humble" denotes the renunciation of all revolt against adversity, an abandonment which is not an avowal of defeat but a simple consenting to the inevitable. Humility necessitates a stripping, an almost mystical detachment: before seeing the bear, that is to say, before being able to communicate with nature, Isaac McCaslin must give up one by one all of the attributes of the civilized man: his rifle, his watch and his compass.[54] Ratliff points out in *The Mansion* that humility, if it implies an admission of our limits, also constitutes a means of forcing them back. For it goes hand in hand with patience: "That was humility, the only kind of humility that's worth a hoot: the humility to know they's a heap of things you don't know yet but if you jest got the patience to be humble and watchful long enough, especially keeping one eye on the

13

back trail, you will."[55] Faulkner teaches us to bear affliction valiantly, without the vain rebellion of false pride, without provoking destiny into a senseless battle from which we, the weaker party, must inevitably emerge vanquished: we must rather accept our fate in order to evade it and, who knows, perhaps discourage it by our perseverance. This type of humility, this invincible humility,[56] does not prevent us from feeling, like the wolf in De Vigny's poem, a "stoic pride" our "long and heavy task" having been accomplished. In the end, pride and humility are reconciled whenever the former evolves from a tyrannical egoism into a respect for man. Modesty, we are told, implies a regard for the self-respect of others or, in the language of certain psychologists, for the "self-feeling" of each creature.[57] In this manner, one passes from *amor sui* to *amor fati*.

Nothing is more common in Dostoevsky than this binomial, but where Faulkner tends to blur the disparity between these terms, Dostoevsky sets them in relief. He has, more than Faulkner, a taste for dissonances, shocks and unresolved conflicts. At first glance, any synthesis would seem excluded: in most cases, the encounter ends in the momentary annihilation of one of the poles. At the moment when Raskolnikov is about to denounce himself to the police, he abandons the pride of the conqueror and prostrates himself in the dust. Katerina Ivanovna also alternately dominates Dmitri Karamazov and lowers herself before him. As long as these forces are actively present, there is no other possible relation but war, no other conclusion but the triumph of one and the disappearance of the other. Rather than to the "doubles" tossed between eternally opposed impulses, let us direct our attention to the heroes who finally surmount their contradictions or to those who *a priori* incarnate only humility (Sonia Marmeladov, Myshkin) or pride (Valkovsky, Kirillov). A virtue or a vice, pushed to the extreme, can join its opposite. We read in *Notes from the Underground* how supreme pride takes pleasure in abjection. We repeat, however, that this is not humility but a travesty: a voluptuous pleasure which knows only the self and which considers others as a kind of erotic accessory. For Dostoevsky, pure pride cannot reverse itself. Unless it is accompanied from the beginning by its contrary, as is the case with Raskolnikov, it remains to the end tantamount to the will to power. Faulkner also knows "the arrogance of false humility and . . . the false humbleness of pride,"[58] the attitude of "formal abjectness"[59] which denotes pride. Authentic humility, whose malign excrescences Dostoevsky has outlined better than any other, is quite different. It comprises, Gide tells us, "a kind of voluntary submission; it is freely accepted."[60] As a general rule, the will limits itself to repressing any intention of meddling in the course of things: Sonia, the prostitute of *Crime and Punishment*, and Prince Myshkin are passive beings, slaves to divine decisions. They exert, however, considerable influence on those around them: Sonia convinces Raskolnikov to confess his crime, and the Idiot sows disquiet and unhappiness in his path. Blind obedience to Providence, in fact, constitutes a "great force," because it immunizes those who practice it. Humility renders one invulnerable, free, as we are told in *The Diary of a Writer* (August 1880).[61] Let us reread the confession of Terentiev:

> Let me tell you, there is a limit of ignominy in the consciousness of one's own nothingness and impotence beyond which a man cannot go, and beyond which he begins to feel immense satisfaction in his very degradation. . . . Oh, of course humility is a great force in that sense, I admit that—though not in the sense in which religion accepts humility as a force.[62]

At this level, humility becomes confused with despotism: it is sovereign because nothing can touch it, tyrannical because it imposes its inertia on others. We recognize here the "invincible" humility which Faulkner makes one of the guarantors of the perenniality of man. Obviously the value of the word varies from one author to the other. What Terentiev regards as an excess contrary to the duties of a believer (although Dostoevsky also has Bishop Tikhon say that "the most defamed cross has become a great glory and the greatest force if the humility of the deed was sincere."[63]) Faulkner erects into a cardinal virtue. Despite these differences, the affinities are incontestable.

Outrage affects not only pride: at a lower level, it also touches self-respect. It is no less wounding. Quite to the contrary, because, instead of aiming at an excessive self-esteem, the attack is di-

15

rected against a reasonable and natural attitude towards oneself. Seen from the outside, the outrage seems all the more unjust. All things considered, there is little difference between self-respect and the true pride of which Faulkner speaks. Self-respect is to the vanity (*amour-propre*) of La Rochefoucauld and Pascal as true pride is to false. The common denominator of this vanity, which afflicts, among others, Luzhin,[64] Kolya Krassotkin[65] and Smerdyakov,[66] and blameworthy pride is to be found in selfishness, the hateful ego. Vauvenargues says of vanity that "it is itself its only object and its only end;" it wishes, he adds, "that things give themselves to us and makes itself the center of all," a definition which applies *a fortiori* to dominating and destructive arrogance. In contrast, self-respect takes others into account for the same reason that "good" pride does. It is distinguished above all by the approbation with which the individual contemplates himself: the weaker notions of regard, attention and consideration are substituted for that of adulation. One selects for praise only those qualities of which one believes oneself worthy—we find once again the idea of dignity mentioned earlier. Consideration, more tolerant, closes its eyes on imperfections and addresses itself to the entire being. In both cases the individual ego expands until it coincides with the universal ego: I recognize myself in the other. Among the forces which assail self-respect, Dostoevsky has insisted from the beginning on social inequality and the prejudices attached to it. Dyevushkin, the hero of his first novel, is a poor and humble person whose "disastrous position" comes, according to his own testimony, as much from a lack of consideration as from his misery. Others scorn him, and, affected by this, he falls in his own esteem: "I carefully hide everything from everyone, and I edge into the office sideways, I hold aloof from all."[67] However, he is all the more sensitive for feeling disinherited.

Poor people are touchy—that's in the nature of things. . . . The poor man is exacting; he takes a different view of God's world, and looks askance at every passer-by and turns a troubled gaze about him, whether they are saying that he is so ugly, speculating about what he would feel exactly, what he would be on this side and what he would be on that side, and everyone knows, Vavrinka, that a man is worse than

16

a rag and can get no respect from anyone; whatever they may write, those scribblers, it will always be the same with the poor man as it has been. And why will it always be as it has been? Because to their thinking the poor man must be turned inside out, he must have no privacy, no pride whatever![68]

Dyevushkin does not speak only in his own name but as a representative of a class. The narrator of *The House of the Dead* makes a similar remark about the prisoners: "Every one, whoever he be and however down-trodden he may be, demands—though perhaps instinctively, perhaps unconsciously—respect for his dignity as a human being,"[69] an opinion echoed by Marmeladov in *Crime and Punishment*.[70] In *The Diary of a Writer* (December, 1877) this "social" ego is finally transformed into a quasi-"national" ego when Dostoevsky recalls that Pushkin considered "the lofty feeling self-respect"[71] as a distinctive trait of the Russian people.

Like pride, the vanity or *amour-propre* of the seventeenth century alternates with its opposite. Self-contempt is not truly in opposition to the selfishness denounced by Pascal, for it is only a negative form of interest in oneself, an attenuated form of voluntary humiliation which, as we well know, does not contradict false pride. Here the contradictory feeling is compassion. In fact, the latter performs a complementary function in relation to self-respect. Beneath the spheres of pride, emotional tensions relax and the contrasts become blurred. The shock of humility and pride, already dampened by the mutations performed by Faulkner on the latter, is hardly felt at this level. There is no gap between the consideration that I have for myself and for others, the regard I accord man in spite of his faults and the compassion which leads me to share his sufferings. Perhaps one can speak of a shift of focus: far from simply being another consideration, misfortune requisitions all of my attention, appeals to my charity. Thus crime, synonymous with "misfortune" in the language of the muzhiks, excites the compassion of the people.[72] Mercy, the Christian virtue par excellence, plays a capital role in Dostoevsky's thought: it is one of the keystones, supported on one side by suffering and on the other by forgiveness.[73] Faulkner, for his part, eloquently preaches compassion and pity, particularly beginning with *Go Down, Moses*. It is advisable to recall at the

17

outset the subtle difference which sometimes distinguishes these two feelings. Both have in common receptivity to the misfortunes of others, the *Mitleiden*, but while compassion evokes a relation between equals and therefore the feeling that the same misfortune could strike the person who is compassionate, pity, sometimes more limited, addresses itself—according to certain commentators —particularly to inferiors: unlike compassion, pity strikes at one's self-respect. Faulkner seems to have established this *distinguo* in his vocabulary; nonetheless, the two words often overlap in practice, such that pity becomes synonymous with compassion: as always with Faulkner, allowance must be made for rhetoric, the magic of the word. The same mixture, moreover, can be observed in *The Brothers Karamazov*.[74] In the short story "Ad Astra" one of the characters declares: "I believe in the pitiableness of man," thus suggesting that all men are worthy of pity and are therefore brothers.[75] Moreover, Faulknerian pity demands courage—"the courage it takes to pity"[76]—the bravery which takes upon itself a sadness not its own, which says no—for and with others —to enemy forces, repairs the damages and enables the species to survive. In brief, it expresses a reaction to a situation in which all feel engaged. During a discussion, after having enumerated the "verities of the heart" ("courage, honor, pride, compassion, pity"), the writer gave a summary definition of them, but, arriving at the last two, he confuses them under the same rubric: "if people didn't practice compassion there would be nothing to defend the weak until they got enough strength to stand for themselves."[77] This kind of weakness attracts less pity than compassion, provided that one keeps in mind the precariousness of existence: this debility was formerly ours in childhood and can at any moment return. For Faulkner, the human race has maintained itself *despite* its fundamental fragility.[78] We have not cited an example of self-respect in his work precisely because he presents it in conjunction with compassion. The Virginia discussions leave no doubt on this point. Pity, he said in commenting on "A Rose for Emily," and he is here once again speaking more of compassion, pity is raised not so much by particular situations or states of soul as by the universal conflict discerned within them: the struggle of man against himself, his peers, or the physical environ-

18

ment, a fundamental opposition, one remembers, in the novelist's philosophy.[79] In this case, the heroine shows how man sullies his nature, his own conscience or, better, how he violates his ego and scorns the respect he owes himself and others. By the same token Faulkner believes Sutpen merits compassion to the degree that he misunderstands man and excludes himself from the human family.[80] It is this that renders him authentically tragic, worthy of Aristotelian "pity."[81] One sees then that for both writers, the outrage made to self-respect extends to the entire human family and in reaction provokes compassion in others.

In conclusion, Faulkner resolves the antagonism of pride and humility, of vanity and compassion by a dialectical step parallel to Hegel's, lifting the first term from the level of selfishness to altruism. Thus turned outwards, pride and vanity coincide respectively with the cult of human dignity and simple human respect; their enemies, humility and compassion, in this way become friends. Despite its theoretical and fragmentary character, this reconstruction enables us to determine the direction in which this synthesis is achieved: one which goes from instinct to its sublimation, from matter to spirit, from "I" to "We." Such is also the path taken by Dostoevsky, but he is an extremist who rejects accomodations, adopting the rule of all or nothing: for the combatants there is no other issue than victory or death.

What has been said should be adequate to indicate that it is impossible to separate the individual aspects of outrage from their repercussions in the collectivity. Thus whoever wounds my self-respect attacks not only me: it is humanity he assails through me or, at least, my idea of it. However, the value under attack emanates from the individual. In other cases, it is rooted in the group. Honor, for example, sets ideas of dignity and respect elaborated by the individual on a social basis: it creates a kind of collective awareness of them, although it reflects less the ideal of the community than of one of its parts. In obeying it the individual affirms his solidarity with a social class, proclaims its preeminence as a cell of the whole and his adherence to its values. "The reciprocal penetration of the individual by society" has been described as "an essential element of honor:"[82] imposed from the outside, it is, however, subservient to the conscience which re-

19

turns it, modified, to the group. Traditions are not immutable. A patrimony transmitted by society, they are constantly modified by the individual. Originally honor belonged by right to the nobility, to the knight and the gentleman:[83] it guaranteed the social contract established between the lord and his vassal. The feudal code, highlighted so well by Calderon and Corneille, naturally conquered other strata of society. It habitually characterized the ruling classes, even if they were not technically of noble blood. In the nineteenth century one finds it in the Virginia planters, the country gentry with their nostalgia for the English squire, and even in a frontier area like Arkansas among simple farmers and clerks.[84] Their jealous concern for the reputation of the women of the family, their sensitive pride and mania for duels, their hospitality and even their taste for the magnificent; none of this would be out of place in a *comedia* of the Spanish Golden Age.[85] It is an attitude of the elite to be sure, but also a model for their inferiors. On the other hand, in crossing centuries and jumping national and social boundaries, honor frequently loses its primitive justification, which consisted (see Vico on duels) in containing brute force.[86] Without its historical justification and unless it be regenerated, honor hardens, formalizes and freezes in ritual. It has humorously been called "the right of the dead over the living"[87] and this explains its fascination for Faulkner, who denied the death of the past. We do not, however, all admit their right in the same way or to the same degree; we can mock it. There is room for an infinity of nuances between unconditional allegiance to an outmoded morality and pure and simple rejection of honor. The Church, to cite only one example, accomplished a remarkable conversion of honor and renewed its meaning. The love and humility that it taught conflicted with the chivalric code, and it is of the soldier's culpable vanity that Pascal is thinking when he quotes Livy: "*Ferox gens, nullam esse vitam sine armis rati.*" On the other hand, there is also a Christian honor rewarded by glory in heaven, which adheres not to a worldly code but to the commandments of Christ. The latter, of course, also belong to tradition: the believer rejects what is sanctioned by the warrior and vice versa. Contrary to popular opinion, tradition is not an homogeneous block, and each finds in it something that suits his purposes. The knight turned hermit, in renouncing the world, gives proof of an attachment to the ideal of his class as tight as when he was dueling with his neighbors.

The metamorphosis of honor has been studied with particular care by Dostoevsky. It survives in its feudal, warlike form, void of substance and reduced to a few cliches, in the Russian nobleman. In the *Diary of a Writer* he dwells on it several times,[88] linking it to original sin[89] and to the Europeanization of the elite.[90] He contrasts the concern for reputation with the praiseworthy honor that comes from a pure heart—in short, the Russian honor preserved by the people. The same contrast generates a series of scenes and excursuses in the novels. There is, first of all, in *The Idiot* the story of Ganya's slapping of Myshkin that young Kolya interprets in these terms:

> I can't endure those ideas. Some madman, or fool, or scoundrel in a fit of madness, gives you a slap in the face and a man is disgraced for life, and cannot wipe out that insult except in blood, unless the other man goes down on his knees and asks his pardon. In my opinion it's absurd and it's tyranny.[91]

Innocent of the prejudices of the nobility, Myshkin kisses his offender. Then there is the scandal provoked by Nastasya Filippovna and the intervention of the prince who, while protecting her, exposes himself to the blows of an officer.[92] Everyone expects a duel except Myshkin to whom the idea does not even occur: called to account by Aglaia he confesses that, although not a coward, he would be very frightened . . . but "perhaps" he would not flee.[93] Finally, two hundred pages later, he delivers a speech on the duty of the nobility which resides, in his opinion, in the pardon of offenses.[94] Honor, evoked again in *Crime and Punishment* and *A Raw Youth*,[95] is spotlighted in *The Brothers Karamazov* where Dostoevsky reveals its workings with unprecedented skill. One of the motivating forces of the plot, it is incarnated principally in three characters: Dmitri Karamazov, Captain Snegiryov and Father Zossima. All are gentlemen and retired officers, but of modest means: Snegiryov wallows in the sordid misery dear to Dickens and Balzac. The impetuous and inconstant Dmitri, although engaged to Katerina Ivanovna, falls in love with

Grushenka. When the first gives him three thousand rubles to send to Moscow, he eagerly squanders half of it with his new conquest, then breaks into the rest to run off with her again on the night of his father's assassination. Between his two sprees with Grushenka he carries Katerina's fifteen hundred rubles sewn into a cloth pouch like a hair shirt on his chest. As long as they are not spent he does not believe he has truly stolen; he has merely been slightly dishonest. The nuance is specious, but important. Beyond this limit begins dishonor, which is a breach of a tacit agreement, an authentic abuse of trust: the "mutual confidence between educated, well-bred people, who have the common bond of noble birth and honour"[96] are Mitya's words. He repeatedly alludes to this detail which is of capital importance to him.[97] Stricken with shame, he omits it at the beginning of the investigation, the fear of exposing his turpitude winning out over the desire to save himself: "I wanted to pay a debt of honour, but to whom I won't say":[98]

> I won't speak of that, gentlemen, because it would be a stain on my honour. The answer to the question where I got the money would expose me to far greater disgrace than the murder and robbing of my father, if I had murdered and robbed him. That's why I can't tell you.[99]

Dmitri, despite his indelicacies, poses as a "man of honour"[100]: true, he has made a *faux pas*, but he intends to set it straight. In his eyes the pouch containing the money is only the sign of a temporary and reparable mistake. He might at any moment make restitution to Katerina, although he doubts this eventually— with good reason, as we know—and even admits that he has divided the sum only that he might carry Grushenka off, should the occasion arise.[101] This division was perhaps not even an excuse against dishonor, despite what he has said about it, because, in the light of his hidden intention, saving the money was as reprehensible as spending it. In the final analysis, it is possible that Dmitri accepts his condemnation as much to expiate his theft and his hidden purpose and the other "filthy things"[102] he has done, as for having *wished* to kill his father. The concept of honor includes for him not only the usual integrity but also fidelity to his image of himself, less as an individual than as an officer and a gentleman. When they prepare to search him, he mutters to himself: "he treats me not as an officer but as a thief";[103] in prison he is indignant because, "they speak to [him] rudely."[104] In addition to respect for the law, Dmitri's honor includes those obligations taken for granted in the customs of his class. Intentions touch him as deeply as acts: "Oh, gentlemen, the purpose is the whole point!"[105] His honor assumes, in addition, sincerity, truth to oneself.[106] Dostoevsky, far from repudiating honor, finds in it the foundation of the moral values which will lead his hero to salvation. It is, among other things, to recover his honor that Dmitri goes to Siberia:

> I've sworn to amend and every day I've done the same filthy things. I understand now that such men as I need a blow, a blow of destiny to catch them as with a noose, and bind them by a force from without. Never, never should I have risen of myself! But the thunderbolt has fallen. I accept the torture of accusation, and my public shame, I want to suffer and by suffering I shall be purified.[107]

Similarly, in the epilogue Alyosha praises the conduct of Ilyusha, the son of Captain Snegiryov: "he was a fine boy, a kind-hearted, brave boy, he felt for his father's honour and resented the cruel insult to him and stood up for him."[108] Ilyusha avenges Dmitri's insult to his father by biting the hand of Alyosha (there is much to be said about biting, a frequent act of aggression in Dostoevsky). Alyosha, who is ignorant of the law of revenge, does not abandon his gentleness and asks of what he is guilty . . . and the child runs away in tears. Like *The Idiot*, young Karamazov preaches forgiveness of sins.[109] Snegiryov, for his part renounces challenging Dmitri to a duel because of his poverty.

> What will become of them? And worse still, if he doesn't kill me but only cripples me: I couldn't work, but I should still be a mouth to feed. Who would feed it and who would feed them all? Must I take Ilyusha from school and send him to beg in the streets? That's what it means for me to challenge him to a duel. It's silly talk and nothing else.[110]

He points out immediately that it is, in any case, a sin to make an attempt on the life of another, wise counsel which sublimates his son's thirst for vengeance to pardon.[111] Finally, when Alyosha offers him money the captain first shows an overwhelming joy and then savagely tramples the notes. As Alyosha explains, "he is one of those awfully sensitive poor people"[112] and one who would give them charity must assuage their honor, say "excuse us" to them and, reversing the roles, treat them "not only on an equal, but even on a higher footing."[113] True honor implies, therefore, that one pardons both insults and kindnesses, words often synonymous: a reciprocal pardon of the offended and the offender, each being responsible for everything to everyone.[114] The very notion of outrage is suppressed and we find the adversaries enlaced in an orgy of charity. The idea is developed in the stories of Father Zossima, in which the evangelical notion of honor wins out over the spirit of vendetta. Once, about to fight a duel, Zossima realized in a sudden moment of illumination the unworthiness of his motives and the perverse absurdity of his acts: abruptly converted, he asked his rival's pardon while respecting the customs of his class. We will come back to this scene. In the meantime, let us note that for the bloody honor of the braggart soldier and the duellist, Dostoevsky, like Tolstoy in *Anna Karenina*, substitutes Christian honor, a much larger concept because it is tied to universal moral values rather than to the specific reflexes of a group. He does not condemn this sentiment, this norm of conduct: he opens it to love of one's neighbor. On the one hand, he underlines in *The Possessed* that revolutionaries openly advocate the "right to be dishonourable"[115] and, on the other hand, he makes honor, thus Christianized, dependent on both the people and on a certain idea of nobility.[116] On these different points, he is in astonishing agreement with Faulkner. The feudal honor, the honor of the great families, to which the latter has devoted numerous pages, is represented both by the bellicose Colonel Sartoris and by Quentin Compson who is obsessed, not by his sister's body, but by the idea of family honor concretized by Caddy's virginity.[117] In the first case, in the Civil War hero, it is allied with *virtù*, an energy which Quentin, it must be admitted, totally lacks. In both cases, however, it contains a poison whose effect will be fatal. The colonel perishes a victim of his arrogant violence, while Quentin takes a futile stand as the defender of a "membrane"[118] as fragile as it is empty of value, instead of undertaking practical and efficacious action: his virus is the lucid but impotent intelligence, hyperconsciousness joined to the impossibility of accepting reality, which paralyzed Hamlet. Devoured by pride, undermined by the fever of self-imprisoning thought, this kind of honor constitutes an encumbering and dangerous heritage for modern man: Quentin dies of it, and Rosa Coldfield stigmatizes the same flaw in speaking of *"honor's empty sake."*[119] Nonetheless, honor, like most of the Faulknerian abstractions, covers such a vast semantic range that it excites alternately, and sometimes one would say simultaneously, approbation and censure. Worthy of condemnation (Drusilla, Houston, Mink Snopes) when it reinforces the destructive instinct, a sterile vestige when it is transformed into an obsession, it rests on values to which the American novelist remains passionately attached. The gesture of Quentin, the redresser of imaginary wrongs, is according to Faulkner "comical and a little sad," but he also says "it is a very fine quality in human nature. I hope it will always endure."[120] Exalting the old cavalier spirit of the South, he identifies it with the disinterested cult of honor and integrity.[121] The term which designates the latter is honesty, a term whose sense is akin to the Roman *honestum,* that is, the moral good seen from the point of view of man's relationship to himself. Honesty shifts the accent from the group which sustains honor to the individual and is tinged with a distinctly ethical coloring. It enjoins respect for the imperatives of the conscience, emphasizes their moral excellence and evokes rectitude and purity. This concept is best described as "integrity" as the line from Horace—*"Integer vitae sclerisque purus"*—quoted in *Soldiers' Pay*[122] suggests. Irving Howe, after stressing the equivocal nature of Faulknerian honor, states its progressive effacement in favor of this new concept.[123] Honor, Howe notes, relates "to what one is in the world," integrity "to what one is in oneself." But perhaps more important than the shift from the collective to the individual is the introduction of ethical norms: in Faulkner honor tends to become individualized and moralized at the same time. The modification which it undergoes through contact with integrity, implied by the alliance of the two within the cavalier spirit,[124] appears particularly around 1938. During the period of *Light in August* (1932), *Absalom, Absalom!* (1936) and *The Unvanquished* (1938) the writer becomes a more and more severe judge of the Southern tradition in which the aristocratic code of honor plays a preponderant role. In "Delta Autumn" (*Go Down, Moses*, 1942), honor again contradicts the elementary exigencies of love and justice because it forces a white to repudiate his black mistress: one finds here the ancient prejudices of class and, what is worse, of race.[125] But in "The Bear", the central episode of the volume, the same word expresses, on the contrary, one of the "verities" of the human heart:

> *Truth is one. It doesn't change. It covers all things which touch the heart—honor and pride and pity and justice and courage and love. . . . Courage and honor and pride, and pity and love of justice and liberty. They all touch the heart, and what the heart holds to becomes truth, as far as we know truth.*[126]

This time it is unquestionably an attribute of the species and, consequently, of each member: rich or poor, black or white. In addition, it is a quality that the author glorifies and sets on the same footing as compassion, justice or love. Honor, therefore, loses its social prerogatives. Already present in the Bundrens, the poor whites of *As I Lay Dying*, it is also often found among the blacks who become its most jealous guardians. Elnora, the black servant of the Sartorises, knows the duties it prescribes as well as old Miss Jenny, sister of the colonel, and infinitely better than Narcissa, who confuses them with the rites of respectability ("There Was a Queen"). Other blacks, Lucas Beauchamp in *Intruder in the Dust*, Uncle Parsham in *The Reivers*, are paragons of honor and integrity in the highest sense. Elsewhere, honor belongs to Indians,[127] prostitutes[128]—see Sonia Marmeladov[129]—convicts,[130] and even Snopeses.[131] As a rule, these qualities confer an eminence and authority on their possessors which, independent of social and economic status, is derived essentially from their moral value. Thus, alongside of the aristocracy of birth, is formed an aristocracy of the heart among whom are figured Miss Jenny, Elnora, Dilsey (the black servant of *The Sound and the Fury*), Lucas Beauchamp and Chick Mallison, but from which are excluded Jason Compson and Narcissa. The white narrator of *The Reivers* describes Uncle Parsham as a patrician: "the aristocrat of us all and judge of us all."[132] He is himself one, both by blood and by soul, and the novel, following a typically American schema, tells how a child raised in the gentlemanly tradition is initiated into evil, passing suddenly from innocence to experience. From this book, the last published by Faulkner (1962), we can extract the henceforth unchanging image of honor in its final stage of evolution. Here it is no longer a matter of the consensus of one's peers or milieu. Before meeting Uncle Parsham, young Lucius, thrown into the picaresque world of prostitutes and scoundrels, is its only champion. Deprived of the example and support of his family, he remains nonetheless faithful to their principles: the important thing for him is not the reputation—rather dubious in this context—that his acts might earn in his new entourage, but virtue itself, "integrity": "that inviolable and inescapable rectitude concomitant with the name I bore, patterned on the knightly shapes of my male ancestors as bequeathed —nay, compelled, to me by my father's word-of-mouth, further bolstered and made vulnerable to shame by my mother's doting conviction."[133] Dishonorable and immoral are indecency,[134] lying, breaking one's word or the rules of good conduct.[135] If one is not taken in by superficial similarities, the ethic of the gentleman, thus defined, is seen to be diametrically opposed to that of the warrior. One must go back to *The Unvanquished* to see the contrast between these attitudes and the triumph of the former. The story entitled "An Odor of Verbena" describes a situation parallel in every detail to that of Zossima's duel: the hero also refuses to obey the senseless dictates of homicidal honor and listens to his conscience, but he nonetheless makes obeisance to the prevailing customs. If human life is something sacred for him, as it is for Snegiryov and the holy man,[136] why shock opinion when one can win it over? Better to respect etiquette while, at the same time, avoiding the duel. The episode, announced by similar passages in *As I Lay Dying*[137] and *Light in August*,[138] illustrates the ethical and even frankly Christian code of honor advocated by Faulkner. Flem Snopes, the traitor par excellence, has little sense of honor, and that of Quentin and the warriors is falsified;

The Unvanquished, on the other hand, announces its correct formulation, founded on moral duty: individual insofar as it departs from local customs, but essentially universal since it postulates the inviolability of all life. As in Dostoevsky, the notion abandons the conscience of the social group to take refuge in that of individual persons; it thus becomes capable of extension to all of humanity. In addition, it allows the possibility of forgiveness ("Honor") and applies to the descendants of slaves and masters alike.

Another form of outrage concerns propriety, decorum and civility, in short, the public marks of altruism which, at first sight, seem less to pay homage to human dignity than to respect the common feeling of what is "proper" in day to day relationships. Any infraction of what is acceptable indicates a lack of concern for others; it wounds all the more sharply where the group's life style is coherent. But deference to etiquette, a pre-established and collective psychic fact which each person accepts while at the same time subjecting it to his own interpretation, is easily confused with esteem for one's personal dignity and for that of man in general. Decorum, we have been told, is "a kind of moral sense."[139] Particularly in a homogeneous society the "proper" and the "good" may seem bound inextricably together. Take Faulkner's patricians: the manners of the true gentleman, far from being an illusion, have their roots in the *ethos*. Quentin Compson believes, not without irony, that "God is not only a gentleman and a sport; He is a Kentuckian too."[140] Horace Benbow affirms peremptorily in *Sanctuary*: "God is foolish at times, but at least he is a gentleman;"[141] such is again the opinion of Gavin Stevens, the corresponding figure in *Requiem for a Nun*: "He—if there was one—would at least play fair, would at least be a gentleman"[142] and *The Mansion*: "God was anyhow a gentleman."[143] Dostoevsky confers this title on the devil of Ivan Karamazov;[144] in Faulkner, on the other hand, the very principle of good is identified with the norms of propriety. The idea, repeated continually by the Southern aristocrats, first appears in 1926 in *Soldiers' Pay*, where the author surprisingly attributes it to Januarius Jones, a libidinous and cynical pedant who in no way resembles a gentleman. The God of the new age need be neither merciful nor very intelligent, "But he must have dignity."[145] In other words, the sovereign Good ought to act in a manner appropriate to the position it occupies, that is, with due decorum. One notices thus a curious interpenetration of morality and civility to which the equivocal term "dignity" bears testimony. For if, on the ethical level, one means by dignity respect for oneself and, by extension, for the human person, from the point of view of etiquette the word designates nothing more than the nobility or gravity which ornaments a certain manner of acting or speaking. Faulkner employs it often and in both meanings. The moral world is so steeped with the notion of propriety that it is possible to sin gracefully. Charles Bon, Frenchified dandy and decadent Catholic of New Orleans, practices an *art* of living which shocks the barbarous puritans of Yoknapatawpha. Without wishing to exonerate himself, he suggests that a sin committed elegantly and according to the rites of etiquette offends God less grievously than the bestial debauchery of the Anglo-Saxons:

> And perhaps when God looks into one of these establishments like you saw tonight, He would not choose one of us to be God either, now that He is old. Though He must have been young once, surely He was young once, and surely someone who has existed as long as He has, who has looked at as much crude and promiscuous sinning without grace or restraint or decorum as He had to do, to contemplate at last, even though the instances are not one in a thousand thousand, the principles of honor, decorum and gentleness applied to a perfectly normal human instinct which you Anglo-Saxons insist upon calling lust and in whose service you revert in sabbaticals to the primordial caverns.[146]

The brute makes the beast with two backs; man makes love which is still a way—heterodox perhaps—of loving one's neighbor. Sin, as Charles understands it, remains within the limits of the human, which coincide with those of decorum. To summarize, the idea of decorum can be said to constitute a synthesis of the ethical and the aesthetic: translating the idea of the good on the level of gestures, it transposes it at the same time into the realm of the beautiful. One sees in "The Bear", for example, how the hunter learns to kill according to the rules, that is, as the writer specifies, "with the nearest approach you can to dignity and to decency."[147] Thus is explained Faulkner's interest in all activities governed by a code which makes superiority dependent on a ceremonial: hunting, chess, riding, defense and prosecution of criminals and even the preparation of a cold toddy. He takes something from the English public school spirit, something that reminds us of Kipling: the taste for the game well played, executed with fair play and elegance, whether it be on the cricket field or the stock exchange, and also the virile sense of comradeship in the physical test, a certain misogyny that is proper both to the clubman and to the puritan. To be a man is, then, to adopt a form of behavior that aims both at the good and the beautiful:[148] Faulkner thus attaches himself to the Platonic tradition.[149] Bertrand Russell has quite judiciously compared the pedagogical program of the *Republic* to the education of the Victorian gentleman,[150] one of the great human types imagined by the West along with Castiglione's courtier, Méré's *honnête homme* and the eighteenth century philosopher. Just as Plato wished to develop the body and soul harmoniously by a reasonable dosage of gymnastics and fine arts and to inculcate in the child self-mastery, hatred of vice and ugliness, gravity and temperance, steadfastness and courage ("firm in the ranks and resolute, he repulses the attacks of fate"), Faulkner defines his human ideal as follows:

> I would say that a first-rate man is one—is a man that did the best he could with what talents he had to make something which wasn't here yesterday. And also to—that never hurt an inferior, never harmed the weak, practiced honesty and courtesy, and tried to be as brave as he wanted to be whether he was always that brave or not.[151]

The Faulknerian image of the gentleman drawn in *The Reivers* corresponds rather faithfully to the Platonic model, although the author modifies it slightly at several points. The gentleman respects his neighbor,[152] confronts adversity—"A gentleman can live through anything. He faces anything."[153]—and accepts the consequences of his acts bravely.[154] But when Faulkner adds that he takes care not to label his peers according to race or religion,[155] he is speaking very much as a man of his time.[156]

The *ethos* of the gentleman, a survival of the colonial period and before that of Renaissance Platonism,[157] poses a problem that we must explore further. For if Faulkner, as a true humanist, makes of the past a ferment for renewal, if he chooses his destiny

30

by following historic examples and regenerating himself by contact with the past, as Heidegger would wish us to do, his attitude toward tradition is not always so favorable. Tradition is, like many of the notions we have reviewed, a sword that cuts both ways, at the same time both the best and worst of things. Fecund when it provides a generous ethic capable of adaptation to historic conditions, it can also smother us in an outmoded corset and reduce etiquette to a shaky facade. It is the same with decorum as with honor, which Faulkner accepts or discards according to whether it is identified with integrity or with the fossils of a feudal regime. Traditionalism properly understood—the form approved by Faulkner—always submits the patrimony to a critical examination; it destroys the slag and searches only the purest mineral. We have just seen what is preserved; let us now look at what is rejected. The living tradition, André Varagnac writes,[158] requires the active collaboration of the individual insofar as it forces him to remodel the historic example in applying the latter to his situation. It constitutes a source of creative inspiration which makes it possible to dominate the present by a reflective act, and not a model to be slavishly copied. Routine sounds the death knell for the traditionalist because it betrays either the impotence of the mind to interpret the past in terms of the present or, what is worse, the sterility of the precedents cultivated before a radically different reality. Faulkner condemns two kinds of traditionalism without appeal. Hightower, the preacher of *Light in August*, lives among the dead: his existence stopped twenty years before his birth[159] during the Confederacy; he is, moreover, impotent in every sense of the word[160] and obstinately refuses to play a part in the drama of Joe Christmas; when he finally decides to save Christmas, he is too late. The cult of the past is a curse that cuts Hightower off from the community, paralyzes him and relegates him to a spectral world, plunging the present into the shadows. What is more, the value of the past itself is cast in doubt. In this case it is tantamount to a kind of hero worship, the object of which is an insult to the intelligence. The heroism which so obsesses Hightower is little more than an adolescent exploit: his paladin, we are told, fell during a hundred-mile ride in enemy territory while raiding a hen house.[161] This was an act

31

of absurd and destructive courage, for it sowed nothing but ruin. The episode evokes another "hero" who, in *Sartoris*, braves a Yankee army to carry a plate of anchovies to a prisoner.

"No gentleman has any business in this war," the major retorted. "There is no place for him here. He is an anachronism, like anchovies. At least General Stuart did not capture our anchovies," he added tauntingly. "Perhaps he will send Lee for them in person."

"Anchovies," repeated Bayard Sartoris, who galloped near by, and he whirled his horse.[162]

Challenged, Bayard charges head lowered to assault the enemy kitchens and is felled. *Sartoris* precedes *Light in August* by three years, but the novelist's scepticism, although indecisive, is nonethe less striking. While expressing admiration for the daredevil's chivalric bravura, Faulkner describes the act as a "harebrained prank."[163] This aspect of the tradition is, therefore, corrupted at its base. The nostalgia for romantic spectacle which impregnates *Sartoris* (1929)[164] soon gives way during the period of 1932-38 to a painstaking criticism of the concept; then, the sorting operation completed, to a defense of that which is salutary in the tradition offered by the past to future generations. In this way the notion of tradition is clarified and leads to the glorification of the gentleman. Among the things that are scrapped are: immobility ("A Rose for Emily"), unrestrained and unmotivated violence, the point of honor and respectability based on nothing more than empty formalism. The respectability portrayed successively in Jason Compson (*The Sound and the Fury*),[165] Narcissa Benbow (*Sanctuary*, "There Was a Queen"), Gowan Stevens and Temple Drake (*Sanctuary*) and Flem Snopes (*The Town, The Mansion*) is denounced once more during the Virginia conferences as an obstacle to the development of the individual.[166] Charles Anderson has noted that where Colonel Sartoris acts spontaneously in light of clear and undisputed principles, his descendants meditate on each decision, wasting in debate energy needed for action.[167] Perhaps, but there is a definite gain. The criticism of traditional morality flows, as we shall see, from changes precipitated by economic and social factors which daily widen the gap between archetypes and modern reality. The historic interval does

32

not prevent the latter from being shaped by the former, although it prevents the literal repetition of these models. When the gap in time is too narrow, it favors the copy; when too wide, it risks suppressing any relationship; as it is during the period of Faulkner's writing it invites a purification of the tradition, a process which testifies to the vitality of the past and its heirs. As Gavin Stevens says in *Intruder in the Dust*, "no man can cause more grief than that one clinging blindly to the vices of his ancestors,"[168] a maxim that summarizes admirably the novelist's hatred of the automaton and of the demons lurking in the ancestral home.

Dostoevsky has also dealt with tradition. However, the example he recommended to remedy the Russian malaise is apparently quite distant from the Faulknerian gentleman. His human type is the muzhik, the peasant, the people he discovered in Siberia, whose faith, humility and "dignity, their true and seemly dignity"[169] should, according to Zossima, save the homeland. The discourses of the holy man demonstrate that it is a matter of returning to the past or rather to the constants of the national character which have been contaminated by the adoption of Western mores. While Faulkner withdraws from a supposedly living tradition which is being cultivated indiscriminately (notably by the Agrarians), Dostoevsky executes the opposite maneuver: he attempts to restore an eclipsed tradition to a world which has come to care less and less about it. The first redefined, improved, purified something that was allegedly powerful; the other sought to rehabilitate almost forgotten values. In addition, the Dostoevskian popular ethic sounds a Christian note that is heard only faintly in Faulkner. Finally, Faulkner demystifies the heroes, while Dostoevsky idealizes the people. Any parallel between the Russian muzhik and the Anglo-Saxon gentleman seems, at first glance, forced and even ridiculous. On closer inspection, however, they share an essential quality: dignity. Zossima insists:

I've been struck all my life in our great people by their dignity. I've seen it myself, I can testify to it, I've seen it and marvelled at it, I've seen it in spite of the degraded sins and poverty-stricken appearance of our peasantry. They are not servile, and even after two centuries of serfdom, they are free in manner and bearing, yet without insolence,

33

and not revengeful and not envious. "You are rich and noble, you are clever and talented, well be so, God bless you. I respect you, but I know that I too am a man. By the very fact that I respect you without envy I prove my dignity as a man."[170]

There is, obviously, a world of difference between this freedom in "manner and bearing," Zossima's "be wise and ever serene,"[171] and the decorum analyzed above. With the Russian the accent falls less on the refinement of forms than on their religious infrastructure. If the acts of the muzhik also have their beauty, it resides above all in their moral aura: purity of the soul, spontaneity, sensibility, goodness, in short, all the romantic fibers of simple hearts from Goldsmith to George Sand. The distinction of the peasant is rough and naive in comparison with the more studied manner of the gentleman whose good taste restrains effusions and dries tears. The muzhik's beauty is a product of his goodness, the esthetic in this case is subservient to the ethical, while the gentleman combines them on a level of near equality. The ideal of decency, the feeling of what is proper, which mixes the beautiful with the good is also found in Dostoevsky, but it is rather the property of certain noblemen. When Dmitri Karamazov rejoins Grushenka, who is in the company of her first lover, she asks the hero to take her away. Despite her drunkenness, however, she also tells him:

> "Don't touch me, till I'm yours. . . . I've told you I'm yours, but don't touch me . . . spare me . . . With them here, with them close, you musn't. He's here. It's nasty here . . ."
> "I'll obey you! I won't think of it . . . I worship you!" muttered Mitya. "Yes, it's nasty here, it's abominable."
> And still holding her in his arms, he sank on his knees by the bedside.
> "I know, though you're a brute, you're generous" Grushenka articulated with difficulty. "It must be honourable . . . it shall be honourable for the future . . . and let us be honest, let us be good, not brutes, but good . . . take me away, take me far away, do you hear? I don't want it to be here, but far, far away . . ."[172]

Like Faulkner (one thinks of Charles Bon in *Absalom, Absalom!*), Dostoevsky underlines that, since evil is inevitable, the authentic man surrenders to it with moderation, in contrast with the animal governed by his glands. As indelicate as he is, Dmitri recognizes those limits. When the prosecutor reproaches him for not having asked Katya for the money necessary to take Grushenka away he explodes:

> to tell her of my treachery, and for that very treachery, to carry it out, for the expenses of that treachery, to beg for money from her, Katya (to beg, do you hear, to beg), and to go straight from her to run away with the other, the rival, who hated and insulted her—to think of it! You must be mad, prosecutor.[173]

And adds: "That would have been filthy beyond everything"[174] after his arrest he is shocked by the familiarity of his guards.[175] Versilov in *A Raw Youth* proclaims himself an aristocrat: *"Je suis gentilhomme avant tout et je mourrai gentilhomme."*[176] The definition that he gives of his rank is both social and spiritual. Nobility constitutes an elite but also incarnates an idea: the faculty of "world-wide compassion for all"[177] which is, at bottom, a Russian interpretation of the Southern patrician's motto *"noblesse oblige."*[178] Noblemen—Versilov estimates that there are perhaps a thousand of them—are "bearers of the idea"[179] par excellence, examples of "the highest culture never seen before,"[180] which is specifically national in its character. In his discussion with Prince Sergei (II, 2, ii) he even dreams of opening up his "class" to anyone who has distinguished himself by honor (for him synonymous with "duty"), science or courage and thus to make "an assembly of the best in a true and literal sense." In short, nobility, for him, represents the traditional qualities of the Russian character—but intensified, in full bloom: they are thus an extension of the people. In the final analysis, the extremes of the social ladder touch in this curious novel[181] whose conclusion praises nobility as a style of life. Unfortunately *A Raw Youth* portrays its decadence rather than its grandeur. Except for the Idiot, none of Dostoevsky's aristocrats succeed as models of behavior, none possess the virtues of their class in a pure state, not even the sense of propriety, since all, Myshkin included, provoke a scandal. Here Dostoevsky and Faulkner are at some distance: for the first the outrage to decorum often comes from those whom the second makes the most zealous protectors of civility.

This does not prevent there being, even in this area, a number of correspondences. In both cases propriety is based on the ethical, and, in different degrees, on a sense of the beautiful. In *Crime and Punishment* mention is made of "vice and aesthetics."[182] The moneylender's murderer insists, moreover, that "the fear of [unattractive] appearances is the first symptom of impotence,"[183] contrary to the author's own credo. Here are the common bases of ideal conduct. There is more: our novelists take their models from the national tradition while repudiating mere conformity: they take them from the gentleman and the muzhik whose qualities are on occasion reflected in other social strata.

It remains before concluding to localize the power that dictates our conduct. For Faulkner, an enthusiastic reader of Keats,[184] the "verities" emanate from the heart; as for Dostoevsky, he found a similar attitude in Schiller—"Das Herz nur gibt davon Kunde" ("Die Worte des Glaubens"). Both celebrate love as the supreme virtue. Zossima defines Hell as "the suffering of being unable to love"[185]; according to Razumihin, Raskolnikov "loves no one"[186] and it is a woman who will save him. For the Russian, love is fundamentally an expression of a free acceptance of life, an active and concrete will to exist in harmony with God and his creatures, even in suffering and far from any *amor sui*. In its spiritual form, love is the very foundation of the moral law. "The Dream of a Strange Man" (*The Diary of a Writer*, April, 1877) could not be more explicit on this point: "they, however, knew how to live even without science"[187] because paradise is made of love. *Caritas* crowns the respect and esteem we bear for others; it extends solidarity to its limits. It is this that Stavrogin and Ivan Karamazov, cut off from others by their intellects, lack. If life and love are also married in Faulkner, their alliance is not sealed in quite so Christian a setting. Faulknerian love is less opposed to Satan than to the logic and abstract teachings of the Protestant church. Quentin Compson, a victim of his Presbyterian training, is "incapable of love"[188] and kills himself. As for Addie Bundren, her pagan devotion to life would surely have incurred the wrath of the Russian novelist. Once again, misconduct, misfortune and death frequently result from the incapacity to love. Jason, Quentin's brother, is a "cold man"[189] and therefore a reprobate; the gangster Popeye and Flem Snopes, who loves only himself, are respectively a sexual pervert and impotent: both come to a bad end.

Caritas guards the gates to domains more secret than those we have visited: before asking the keys, let us glance back over the path we have traveled. Faulkner and Dostoevsky cast behavior, feelings and morality in a homogeneous block. The instinctual appetites, the inclinations of the heart are, with them, always evaluated in terms of the innate values of good and evil. But seeing existence from an ethical perspective, remodeling the material world, is a common phenomenon. The kinship of these writers is seen clearly only in the light of the tensions that animate their psychology and which are exteriorized in outrage. The analysis of pride and self-respect brings all this into striking relief. In both cases egoistic tendencies are extroverted and spiritualized in order to be joined on the level of *caritas* with either humility or compassion. The same movement can be seen in the evolution of honor, which is transformed from the prerogative of class into a "moral" concept applicable to all. In general terms, the final stage is the same although the processes often describe divergent curves. While Faulkner purifies pride, softening its impact with humility and assigning them a common basis in courage and effort, Dostoevsky pushes them to their breaking point or alternates them. He has, moreover, a thirst for God not found in Faulkner. In addition, despite certain similarities, the gentleman, a prototype both esthetic and moral, is scarcely comparable to the muzhik, unless the latter is disguised as a nobleman. And one must admit finally that tradition differs according to whether it is considered from a Russian or American point of view. Be that as it may, the analogies take precedence over the disparities, and it is incontestable that we are dealing with congeneric spirits whose affinities will be even more evident, we hope to show, on the level of philosophical speculation.

NOTES TO CHAPTER I

1. *The Sound and the Fury* and *As I Lay Dying*, pp. 98 and 167. See p. 195: "you wanted to sublimate a piece of natural human folly into a horror."

See also George Marion O'Donnell, "Faulkner's Mythology" in *William Faulkner: Three Decades of Criticism*, (ed.) Frederick J. Hoffman and Olga Vickery. (East Lansing, Mich.: Michigan State University Press, 1960), p. 85.

2. See *Faulkner at Nagano*, p. 51.
3. See Reinhard Lauth, *Die Philosophie Dostojewskis* (München: R. Piper Verlag, 1950), pp. 38-39.
4. See *ibid.*, pp. 67, 135.
5. *Sartoris*, p. 278.
6. *Absalom, Absalom!*, p. 328.
7. *Go Down, Moses*, respectively pp. 233, 295, 351.
8. *Ibid.*, p. 257.
9. *Ibid.*, pp. 258-59.
10. *Ibid.*, p. 297.
11. *William Faulkner: Three Decades of Criticism*, p. 348.
12. *Faulkner in the University*, p. 5.
13. *Ibid.*, p. 133.
14. *Ibid.*, p. 242.
15. "The Stockholm Address" in *William Faulkner: Three Decades of Criticism*, p. 348 and *Faulkner in the University*, p. 133.
16. *Faulkner in the University*, p. 133.
17. See *ibid.*, p. 245: "That is the young writer's dilemma as I see it. Not just his, but all our problems, is to save mankind from being desouled as the stallion or boar or bull is gelded; to save the individual from anonymity before it is too late and humanity has vanished from the animal called man."
18. *The Diary of a Writer*, pp. 508-09.
19. Walter J. Slatoff, *Quest for Failure* (Ithaca, N. Y.: Cornell University Press, 1960). See also Frederick J. Hoffman, *William Faulkner* (New York: Twayne Publishers, Inc., 1961), pp. 28, 73, 116.
20. Walter J. Slatoff, "The Edge of Order: The Pattern of Faulkner's Rhetoric," in *William Faulkner: Three Decades of Criticism*, p. 191.
21. *Absalom, Absalom!*, p. 378. See also *The Sound and the Fury* (Appendix, p. 10).
22. *The Sound and the Fury* and *As I Lay Dying*, pp. 461-63.
23. *The Town*, p. 324.
24. *Faulkner in the University*, p. 19: "I'm interested primarily in people, in man in conflict with himself, with his fellow man, or with his time and place, his environment." See also pp. 88, 132, and John Faulkner, *My Brother Bill*, p. 212.
25. *Faulkner in the University*, p. 103.
26. *Ibid.*, p. 178.
27. *Crime and Punishment*, p. 232.
28. See Donald Fanger, *Dostoevsky and Romantic Realism* (Cambridge, Mass.: Harvard University Press, 1965), pp. 223-24, 256.
29. See *The Wild Palms*, p. 175: "So when it happened he was not surprised. He heard the sound which he knew well (he had heard it but once before, true enough, but no man needed hear it but once) and he had been expecting it; he looked back, still driving the paddle, and saw it, curled, crested with its strawlike flotsam of trees and debris and dead beasts and he glared over his shoulder at it for a full minute out of that attenuation far beyond the point of outragement where even suffering, the capability of being further affronted, had ceased, from which he now contemplated with savage and invulnerable curiosity the further extent to which his now anaesthetised nerves could bear, what next could be invented for them to bear, until the wave actually began to rear above his head into its thunderous climax."
30. See *ibid.*, pp. 145-46: "The bow began to swing back upstream. It

turned readily, it outpaced the aghast and outraged instant in which he re-
alised it was swinging far too easily . . . the boat which had threatened him
and at last actually struck him in the face with the shocking violence of a
mule's hoof now seemed to poise weightless upon it like a thistle bloom,
spinning like a wind vane while he flailed at the water and thought of, envisioned, his companion safe, inactive and at ease in the tree with nothing
to do but wait, musing with impotent and terrified fury upon that arbitrar-
iness of human affairs which had abrogated to the one the secure tree and
to the other the hysterical and unmanageable boat."
  31. See *ibid.*, p. 144: "He was now in the channel of a slough, a bayou,
in which until today no current had run probably since the old subterranean
outrage which had created the country."
  32. See *Absalom, Absalom!*, p. 9.
  33. See *ibid.*, p. 12. See also *Knight's Gambit*, p. 46: "there it was, inherited from the earth, the soil, transmitted to him through a self-pariahed
people—something of bitter pride and indomitable undefeat of a soil and the
men and women who trod upon it and slept within it."
  34. See the common traits shared by Fyodor Karamazov and his sons.
  35. *Light in August*, p. 99.
  36. See for instance the numerous occurrences in the "Flem" section of
The Mansion.
  37. *Absalom, Absalom!*, pp. 229, 233, 237-38.
  38. *The Brothers Karamazov*, p. 109.
  39. *White Nights and Other Stories*, pp. 56-57.
  40. *Ibid.*, p. 57.
  41. *Ibid.*, p. 89.
  42. *Crime and Punishment*, p. 244.
  43. Andre Gide, *Dostoïevsky* (Paris: Plon, 1923), p. 135. See also pp.
132-33.
  44. *Ibid.*, p. 140.
  45. *The Insulted and the Injured*, pp. 245-46.
  46. See *Sartoris*, pp. 373-76. See also *Go Down, Moses*, p. 111: "Then
one day the old curse of his fathers, the old haughty ancestral pride based
not on any value but on an accident of geography, stemmed not from courage and honor but from wrong and shame, descended to him."
  47. *Faulkner in the University*, p. 134.
  48. See *The Mansion*, p. 153: "all them generations of respectability and
aristocracy that not only would a been too proud to mishandle other folk's
money."
  49. *Absalom, Absalom!*, p. 121.
  50. *The Brothers Karamazov*, pp. 330-31.
  51. *Sartoris*, p. 278. On this point see William R. Taylor, *Cavalier and
Yankee* (Garden City, N. Y.: Doubleday and Co., 1963), pp. 153, 155.
  52. See *Go Down, Moses*, p. 295: "a people who had learned humility
through suffering and learned pride through the endurance which survived
the suffering."
  53. *Ibid.*, p. 233.
  54. *Ibid.*, p. 207.
  55. *The Mansion*, p. 157.
  56. See *A Fable*, p. 5: "irresistible in that passive and invincible humility."
  57. Edward Westermarck, *L'origine et le developpement des idées morales*
(Paris: Payot, 1928-29), Vol. 11, p. 139.
  58. *Go Down, Moses*, p. 309.
  59. *Light in August*, p. 265.
  60. André Gide, *Dostoïevsky*, p. 133.
  61. *The Diary of a Writer*, p. 970.

39

62. *The Idiot*, p. 393.
63. *The Possessed*, p. 726.
64. *Crime and Punishment*, p. 318.
65. *The Brothers Karamazov*, pp. 589-90.
66. *Ibid.*, p. 276.
67. *The Gambler and Other Stories* (*Poor People*), p. 204.
68. *Ibid.*, p. 197.
69. *The House of the Dead*, p. 106.
70. *Crime and Punishment*, p. 13.
71. *The Diary of a Writer*, p. 941.
72. *The House of the Dead*, p. 52.
73. See the words of Marmeladov in *Crime and Punishment*, p. 20: "Yes! There's nothing to pity me for! I ought to be crucified, crucified on a cross, not pitied! Crucify me, oh judge, crucify me but pity me! And then I will go of myself to be crucified, for it's not merry-making I seek but tears and tribulation! . . . but He will pity us Who has had pity on all men, Who has understood all men and all things, He is the One, He too is the judge. He will come in that day and He will ask: ". . . Where is the daughter who had pity upon the filthy drunkard, her earthly father, undismayed by his beastliness? And He will say, 'Come to me! I have already forgiven thee once . . . I have forgiven thee once . . . thy sins which are many are forgiven thee for thou hast loved much.'"
74. *The Brothers Karamazov*, p. 779.
75. *Collected Stories*, p. 410.
76. *A Fable*, p. 45. See "When you stop to pity, the world runs over you."
77. *Faulkner in the University*, p. 134.
78. See *ibid.*, p. 133: "Man has endured despite his fraility."
79. See *ibid.*, p. 59: "I don't think that one should withhold pity simply because the subject of the pity, object of pity, is pleased and satisfied. I think the pity is in the human striving against its own nature, against its own conscience. That's what deserves the pity. It's not the state of the individual, it's man in conflict with his heart, or with his fellows, or with his environment—that's what deserves the pity. It's not that the man suffered, or that he fell off the horse, or was run over by the train."
80. See *ibid.*, p. 80: "To me he is to be pitied, who does not believe that he belongs as a member of a human family, of the human family, is to be pitied."
81. See Aristotle, *Rhetoric*, Book II, Chapter VIII.
82. Eugène Terraillon, *L'honneur. Sentiment et principe moral*, (Paris: Felix Alcan, 1912), p. 77.
83. See *ibid.*, p. 161: "the least relaxation of the feudal bond or, as it was called, the *félonie*, compromised the entire regime and all of the society. That is why the respect for the oath of homage and of every pledge, the scrupulous accomplishment of the mission each individual must accept and fulfill to worthily occupy his place in society, was, in the name of honor, the most serious of obligations." (Translated by D.McW.)
84. See Clement Eaton, *The Growth of Southern Civilization, 1790-1860*, (London: Hamish Hamilton, 1961), p. 2.
85. See *ibid.*, pp. 13, 275-77, 320.
86. Terraillon, *op. cit.*, p. 126.
87. *Ibid.*, p. 227.
88. *The Diary of a Writer*, p. 514.
89. *Ibid.*, p. 686.
90. *Ibid.*, pp. 701-702.
91. *The Idiot*, p. 111.
92. See *ibid.*, p. 334.
93. *Ibid.*, p. 337. See also pp. 342-43.

94. See *ibid.*, p. 527.
95. *A Raw Youth*, pp. 238-39.
96. *The Brothers Karamazov*, p. 499.
97. *Ibid.*, pp. 153, 410-11, 719-20.
98. *Ibid.*, p. 496.
99. *Ibid.*, p. 509.
100. *Ibid.*, p. 502.
101. *Ibid.*, p. 523.
102. *Ibid.*, p. 539.
103. *Ibid.*, p. 512.
104. *Ibid.*, p. 808.
105. *Ibid.*, p. 521.
106. *Ibid.*, pp. 502, 809.
107. *Ibid.*, pp. 539-40.
108. *Ibid.*, p. 819.
109. *Ibid.*, p. 207.
110. *Ibid.*, p. 211.
111. *Ibid.*, p. 213.
112. *Ibid.*, p. 223.
113. *Ibid.*, p. 224. See also p. 218.
114. *Ibid.*, pp. 169-70, 300-301.
115. *The Possessed*, p. 394. See also p. 378.
116. See *A Raw Youth*, pp. 238-39.
117. *The Sound and the Fury and As I Lay Dying*, p. 9.
118. *Ibid.*.
119. *Absalom, Absalom!*, p. 150.
120. *Faulkner in the University*, p. 141.
121. See *ibid.*, p. 80: "By cavalier spirit, I mean people who believe in simple honor for the sake of honor, and honesty for the sake of honesty."
122. *Soldiers' Pay*, p. 57.
123. Irving Howe, *William Faulkner* (New York: Vintage Books, 1962), pp. 146-48.
124. "Honor," "honesty" and "integrity" are associated several times. See *Faulkner in the University*, p. 132: "the honor which he hopes that he can always match. The honesty, the courage which he hopes that he can always match." See also *A Fable*, pp. 177, 231.
125. See *Go Down, Moses*, pp. 361, 363.
126. *Ibid.*, p. 297.
127. *Collected Stories*, pp. 316, 323.
128. *The Reivers*, pp. 159-60.
129. *Crime and Punishment*, p. 354.
130. *The Wild Palms*, p. 166.
131. *The Hamlet*, p. 35.
132. *The Reivers*, p. 176.
133. *Ibid.*, pp. 50-51.
134. See *ibid.*, pp. 157-59.
135. See *ibid.*, p. 218.
136. See *The Unvanquished*, p. 249: "since we had talked about it, about how if there was anything at all in the Book, anything of hope and peace for His blind and bewildered spawn which He had chosen above all others to offer immortality, *Thou shalt not kill* must be it."
137. See *The Sound and the Fury and As I Lay Dying*, p. 508.
138. *Light in August*, p. 241.
139. L. Jeudon, *La morale d l'honneur* (Paris: Felix Alcan, 1911), p. 12.
140. *The Sound and The Fury and As I Lay Dying*, p. 110.
141. *Sanctuary*, p. 337.
142. *Requiem for a Nun*, p. 164.

41

143. *The Mansion*, p. 131. See also the story entitled "The Leg" in *Collected Stories* p. 838: "God is at least a gentleman."

144. *The Brothers Karamazov*, p. 677.

145. *Soldiers' Pay*, p. 58: "But we of this age believe that he who may be approached informally, without the intercession of an office-boy of some sort, is not worth the approaching. We purchase our salvation as we do our real estate. 'Our God.' continued Jones, 'need not be compassionate, he need not be very intelligent. But he must have dignity.' "

146. *Absalom, Absalom!*, pp. 115-16.

147. *Faulkner in the University*, p. 54.

148. For the black see *The Sound and the Fury and As I Lay Dying*, p. 105, and for the Yankee see *The Unvanquished*, p. 127.

149. See Jean-Jacques Mayoux, "The Creation of the Real in William Faulkner" in *William Faulkner: Three Decades of Criticism*, p. 172.

150. Bertrand Russell, *History of Western Philosophy* (London: George Allen and Unwin Ltd., 1948), p. 130.

151. *Faulkner in the University*, p. 269. See also *Go Down, Moses*, pp. 117-18.

152. *The Reivers*, p. 245.

153. *Ibid.*, p. 302.

154. See *ibid.*: "A gentleman accepts the responsibility of his actions and bears the burden of their consequences, even when he did not himself instigate them but only acquiesced to them, didn't say No though he knew he should."

155. See *ibid.*, p. 143.

156. On the code of the gentleman see *The Wild Palms*, p. 300, and *The Mansion*, p. 212. Before killing himself Quentin Compson equips himself with a clean handkerchief, brushes his teeth and puts on his hat (see *The Sound and the Fury and As I Lay Dying* p. 197.)

157. See Clement Eaton, *The Growth of Southern Civilization 1790-1860*, pp. 113-14.

158. André Varagnac *Civilisation traditionelle et genres de vie*, (Paris: Albin Michel, 1948), pp. 302-303.

159. *Light in August*, p. 452.

160. *Ibid.*, p. 54.

161. *Ibid.*, pp. 457-59.

162. *Sartoris*, p. 16.

163. *Ibid.*, p. 9.

164. See *ibid.*, p. 380: "The music went on in the dusk softly; the dusk was peopled with ghosts of glamorous and old disastrous things. And if they were just glamorous enough, there was sure to be a Sartoris in them, and then they were sure to be disastrous."

165. See *The Sound and the Fury* and *As I Lay Dying* p. 207: "I've got a position in this town, and I'm not going to have any member of my family going on like a nigger wench."

166. See *Faulkner in the University*, p. 35: "Mr. Faulkner, you have said that you regarded respectability as one of the prime enemies of individualism." See also pp. 112-13 on the absurdity of certain obligations and conventions.

167. See Charles Anderson, "Faulkner's Moral Center," *Études anglaises* VII, 1 (January, 1954), 58.

168. *Intruder in the Dust*, p. 49.

169. *The Brothers Karamazov*, pp. 330-31.

170. *Ibid.*.

171. *Ibid.*, p. 337.

172. *Ibid.*, p. 467.

173. *Ibid.*, p. 525.

174. *Ibid.*
175. *Ibid.*, p. 808.
176. *A Raw Youth*, p. 507.
177. *Ibid.*, p. 510.
178. See *The Sound and the Fury and As I Lay Dying*, p. 110.
179. *A Raw Youth*, p. 507.
180. *Ibid.*, p. 510.
181. See *ibid.*, p. 331: "My uncle, my grandfather, tilled the soil with their own hands. We have been princes for a thousand years, as aristocratic and ancient a name as the Rohans, but we are beggars.
And this is how I will train my children: 'Remember always all your life, that you are a nobleman, that the sacred blood of Russian princes flows in your veins. But never be ashamed that your father tilled the soil with his own hands . . . he did it like a prince.' "
182. *Crime and Punishment*, p. 415.
183. *Ibid.*, p. 457.
184. See Richard Adams, "The Apprenticeship of William Faulkner," *Tulane Studies in English* XII (1962), p. 120.
185. *The Brothers Karamazov*, p. 338.
186. *Crime and Punishment*, p. 191.
187. *The Diary of a Writer*, p. 683.
188. *The Sound and the Fury and As I Lay Dying*, p. 10.
189. *Ibid.*, p. 225.

II

BETWEEN THE DEVIL AND THE GOOD GOD

Faulkner, unlike Dostoevsky, has no talent for philosophy. Ideas come to life for him only after being transmuted into novelistic material; divorced from the concrete, left to themselves, they crush or derail the narrative. Without exception, he fails in his attempts to integrate the exposition of ideas into the action, a talent of which Dostoevsky can justifiably boast. Dostoevsky, however, always combines the thought with the lived experience. He describes one of his heroes as "a man possessed by *an idea*," but adds that the idea has "*become embodied* in his person, becoming a part of his nature."[1] The remark applies to all of his characters: although a philosopher, he prefers to express himself in situations rather than treatises. This is an obvious fact that critics have often forgotten in their absorption in artistically irrelevant theoretical constructs and variations. Such an approach does violence to the work and, if we give the impression of having in turn fallen into the same mistake, let it be attributed to a desire to cut directly to the heart of the matter.

Much has been written about evil in Dostoevsky's thought. He is obsessed with it, from the troubling ruminations of the man from the underground to the hallucinations of Ivan Karamazov. It is unnecessary here to recount the history of this notion: it will suffice to indicate the aspects of it found in Faulkner. In *Notes from the Underground* evil is presented as a deliberate choice, in contradiction to the utilitarian doctrine which maintains that man, enlightened as to his interests, automatically

44

chooses the good because he sees that it is to his advantage.[2] In denouncing rationalist meliorism, which he regarded as one of the most naive myths of his century, Dostoevsky at the same time underscored our freedom. Reason and the lights of science cannot determine our acts because we can very easily choose evil even though we know that we cannot profit from it. Choice does not operate on this level:

And how do these wiseacres know that man wants a normal, a virtuous choice? What has made them conceive that man must want a rationally advantageous choice? What man wants is simply *independent* choice, whatever that independence may cost and wherever it may lead. And choice, of course, the devil only knows what choice.[3]

Freedom, of which evil is the touchstone,[4] thus asserts itself in opposition to reason on the vital level of "desire," feeling and the heart: "You see, gentlemen, reason is an excellent thing, there's no disputing that, but reason is nothing but reason and satisfies only the rational side of man's nature, while will is a manifestation of the whole human life including reason and all the impulses."[5]

Dostoevsky rehabilitates evil in the name of man's most precious privileges: his liberty and responsibility which are, as the Grand Inquisitor tells us, the gifts of Christ.[6] Following Goethe, he insists on the utility of evil, but the devil who converses with Ivan Karamazov contrasts with Mephistopheles in that, wishing good, he is compelled to do the opposite.[7] Dostoevsky takes pride in having reversed the Goethean definition—"Ein Teil von jener Kraft, Die stets das Böse will, und stets das Gute schafft"—tainted in his eyes with eighteenth century optimism, in order to preserve the demon's catalytic power. For if the devil also sings "hosanna," evil disappears and free will becomes inoperative. To be sure, the devil is and remains an imposture, a travesty of the good, "the father of lies" (John, 8:44), but while deceiving us he can aid in our salvation. In the final analysis, despite whatever Dostoevsky might think, he obtains results rather similar to those of Mephistopheles:

Then I shall have attained my object, which is an honourable one. I shall sow in you only a tiny grain of faith and it will grow into an oak-tree—

and such an oak-tree that, sitting on it, you will long to enter the ranks of 'the hermits in the wilderness and the saintly women,' for that is what you are secretly longing for. You'll dine on locusts, you'll wander into the wilderness to save your soul.

"Then it's for the salvation of my soul you are working, is it you scoundrel?"

"One must do a good work sometimes. . . ."[8]

. . . my destiny though it's against the grain—that is, to ruin thousands for the sake of saving one.[9]

Mephistopheles and Ivan's devil share, in addition, the function of denial, with the difference that Goethe's character justifies this function eloquently while Dostoevsky's does so only grudgingly. In *The Brothers Karamazov*, demoniacal nihilism is presented as an indispensable stimulus, sowing doubt, initiating criticism and engendering the irrational: it is the salt of life, even when it causes suffering.[10] This negative spirit already animates most of the heroes of *The Possessed*, a novel which could be said to constitute the reversal of the *Imitation of Christ*[11] and in which Shatov forcefully asserts that: "Reason has never had the power to define good and evil, even approximately."[12] The proposition is illustrated paradoxically by the theoreticians and analysts of crime whose too rigorous logic is a sign of abnormality or even of madness. Raskolnikov not only acts outside of all *ratio* and all *caritas*, he falls squarely into the irrational. To these two qualities of evil, beneficient and irrational, is added a third: its character of being innate. In accordance with Christian tradition, Dostoevsky connects evil with the very nature of man. We bear it within us as an original weakness, Ivan tells his *alter ego*: "You are my hallucination. You are the incarnation of myself, but only one side of me"[13]—"you are I and nothing more."[14] Father Ferapont's visions, parodies of Ivan's, corroborate this remark: according to this fanatic ascetic, the other monks are possessed; he has even seen a demon "settled in the unclean belly of one."[15] Ivan, in his turn, accuses Alyosha of having "a little devil sitting in [his] heart" for "in every man, of course, a demon lies hidden."[16] Evil, like good, is a part of being; at any moment it is possible to choose one or the other. Dostoevsky's last novel, however, goes beyond this dilemma. For example, the Roman church which is the work of man frankly claims kinship with Satan through the mouth of the Grand Inquisitor; like Ivan's devil, it dreams of doing good for humanity but only institutes tyranny, that is to say, evil. Which, in reaction, leads to good, since Alyosha sees his brother's poem simply as a panegyric of Christ, made in reverse.[17] Satan can do nothing against Christ; in reality he can only destroy himself: an impotent guest of the soul, he pushes it on the road to Damascus.[18]

Faulkner has expressed convictions rather close to these. Raised in a Puritan climate, he believes a fortiori that evil is imposed on us with life: "Evil is a part of man, evil and sin and cowardice, the same as repentance and being brave. You got to believe in all of them, or believe in none of them."[19] During his dark period from The Sound and the Fury to Absalom, Absalom! he describes man as a victim of a demon, groping for the good but irremediably lost in the dark. He preserves from his Protestant background only the torturing obsession of universal evil and the conscience of a fall so acute that it dismisses any hope of redemption. His faith, at this point, is virtually dead. In Sanctuary, Popeye sings the litanies of the Evil One. Faulkner points out in this novel that, according to the chronology of Genesis, the serpent was created before Adam; he preceded him in his fall[20] so that he might cause him to fall in his turn, in other words, to plunge man into History, into time that is, for the author of Sanctuary, the warehouse of our defeats, the arena of our damnation.

> She watched the final light condense into the clock face, and the dial change from a round orifice in the darkness to a disc suspended in nothingness, the original chaos, and change in turn to a crystal ball holding in its still and cryptic depths the ordered chaos of the intricate and shadowy world upon whose scarred flanks the old wounds whirl onward at dizzy speed into darkness lurking with new disasters.[21]

The evil to which the serpent introduced us is closely tied to time: "of the tree of the knowledge of good and evil you shall not eat," God tells Adam, "for the day you eat of it you shall die." (Genesis 2:17) Evil is a specific cancer which, like the devils of Ivan and Father Ferapont, is lodged in us from birth and gnaws at us until death—an irrevocable decree which causes de-

47

spair in the man who grasps its infallible mechanism. Faulkner
and Dostoevsky, with very different mental reservations to be
sure, agree that the supreme perversity is the one which wears
the mask of cold reason:

> Perhaps it is upon the instant that we realize, admit, that there is a logical
> pattern to evil, that we die. . . .[22]

> (Stravrogin's anger) was a calm, cold, if one may so say, *reasonable* anger,
> and therefore the most revolting and most terrible possible.[23]

Christian doctrine, reduced to the fall and deprived of the
counterweight of redemption, culminates in nothingness. In *Sanctuary* evil makes a void around itself: it neutralizes the good,
sullies, corrupts and ruins even its instrument—Popeye. One of
Faulkner's most pessimistic works, it dates from 1931; evil, innate
as in Dostoevsky, remains an all-powerful, purely negative force
whose unadulterated nihilism eventually seems to have revolted
the author, since he returns to these characters twenty years later
with the intention of saving them according to the precepts of
the Russian novelist. *Requiem for a Nun* (1951) is the "progressivist" correction of *Sanctuary*. Popeye is dead, but the evil he
sowed continues. To root it out, Nancy, Gowan's and Temple's
servant, kills their child, preventing her mistress from leaving her
husband and falling into her old ways. Nancy's act violates what
is right and moral, and she expiates this, but evil, committed
this time for a good purpose, provokes a catharsis. Temple public-
ly confesses her wrongs, makes an act of contrition in the manner
of Raskolnikov and Dmitri Karamazov, and reveals her perversity,
carefully concealed in *Sanctuary*. And we see once again how
evil tests free will: Nancy chooses her crime; Temple decides
to acknowledge her past mistakes. Between 1931 and 1951, Faulkner's attitude changed completely. Not only does freedom become
operative, exorcising the spell of Fate, but it exerts itself, no matter what happens, in the direction of the good. Nancy is not as
far removed from Ivan's devil as one might think. Willing good,
she does evil to achieve her ends: "good can come out of evil."[24]
This is also the approach of Rosa Millard, who in *The Unvanquished* prays to God in these terms:

I have sinned. I have stolen, and I have borne false witness against my neighbor, though that neighbor was an enemy of my country. And more than that, I have caused these children to sin. I hereby take their sins upon my conscience. . . . But I did not sin for gain or greed . . . I did not sin for revenge. I defy You or anyone to say that I did. I sinned first for justice. And after that first time, I sinned for more than justice; I sinned for the sake of food and clothes for Your own creatures who could not help themselves.[25]

The utility of evil as experience will be featured even more importantly in *The Reivers*, where we read that nothing that we have lived is forgotten because "it is too valuable."[26] Finally, Temple, the repentant sinner, specifies that it is not enough to combat evil in full knowledge of the facts. We must, she explains, prepare ourselves for the struggle even before seeing the adversary, the choice operating, as in Dostoevsky, in an extra-rational domain beyond cognition:

It's not that you must never even look on evil and corruption; sometimes you can't help that, you are not always warned. It's not even that you must resist it always. Because you've got to start much sooner than that. You've got to be already prepared to resist it, say no to it, long before you see it; you must have already said no to it long before you even know what it is.[27]

Unfortunately Faulkner does not dwell on the question. Nonetheless, the level on which he situates the choice is vaguely evocative of Shatov's opinions. We notice once again that his ideas, although developed in less detail than those of Dostoevsky, have, around 1938, moved singularly close to them. One might say that, little by little, he has joined what Reinhard Lauth calls Dostoevsky's "*positive Philosophie.*" If Cash Bundren still believes, like the hero of *Notes from the Underground*, that we do not necessarily desire "the safe things,"[28] if Popeye is the devil personified, dangers and spells vanish with the years. *A Fable* scarcely gives the devil any more of a chance than *The Brothers Karamazov*: "Man is full of sin. . . . Someday something might beat him, but it won't be Satan."[29] The evil that the heart perceives better than the mind and that man carries in him ordinarily joined to the good[30] submits itself to the latter and promotes its growth.

Flem Snopes lets himself be killed by Mink, and the author of *The Reivers* prefers the more euphemistic expression "non-virtue" to the word "evil."

Evil is, in a word, the enemy of *caritas*. Because it loves the material, it easily seduces those who are avid of worldly pleasure: because it is an isolating illusion, it leads minds so inclined to stray away from life, the heart and others in pursuit of their own infinite arabesques.

From evil to sin is a very short step in a world view so suffused with Christianity. Popeye lives on the fringes of nature which *Genesis* repeatedly tells us is good. He is a voyeur, a robot; his pale complexion seems flooded by electric light and his thin body seems stamped out of sheet metal;[31] he spits in the spring and is ignorant of the bird singing in the tree. Likened to evil in *Sanctuary*, alienation—the absence of *caritas*—becomes synonymous with sin in the later works. Beginning with *Light in August* the black race is identified with God's curse on the whites for their sins,[32] an idea also developed in *Absalom, Absalom!*. The South drew divine anger and was defeated, Quentin believes, because it was built not on morality but on slavery.[33] It is *Go Down, Moses* which joins the notion of sin introduced earlier to the conception of evil in *Sanctuary*. Isaac McCaslin accuses the whites of having enslaved creation and of having destroyed the natural state intended by God. They have made it the arena of their violence and have divided among themselves the common heritage of all mankind.

> The woods and the fields he ravages and the game he devastates will be the consequence and signature of his crime and guilt, and his punishment.[34]

> He told in the Book how He created the earth, made it and looked at it and said it was all right, and then He made man. He made the earth first and peopled it with dumb creatures, and then He created man to be his overseer on the earth and to hold suzerainty over the earth and the animals on it in His name, not to hold for himself and his descendants inviolable title for ever, generation after generation, to the oblongs and the squares of the earth, but to hold the earth mutual and intact in the communal anonymity of brotherhood.[35]

It is of this destructive madness and this cupidity that Isaac is purged by contact with the forest; it is the white's original sin from which he thinks he is disentangling himself by repudiating his heritage. In short, the tyranny exercised over the land merges with the tyranny exercised over man. Such a definition of sin could only be born, one suspects, in a still feudal agrarian society only recently imposed on nature, that is, on a never forgotten and often missed wilderness. Let us remark here before pursuing the question in depth that Dostoevsky has evinced similar views in his journal (April 1887).[36]

Evil and sin, omnipresent in Faulkner, are equally so in Dostoevsky. For both men the whole problem is to eliminate, or at least channel, them. They believe or end up believing in this possibility inherent in their conception of evil. But to say that evil can engender good is to state a postulate and not to demonstrate a mechanism. How does man disengage himself from evil? By what miracle is the chaff turned into wheat? We know Dostoevsky's answer: by suffering. The path of salvation follows the way of the cross. Redemption, offered to the soul by the death of the God-Man, is modelled on his passion: it is imitation as defined by Christian tradition. "Per hominem Christum . . . ad Deum Christum." Suffering builds a bridge between evil and redemption. Caused by evil and, beyond that, by the fall, it testifies to the persistence of virtue in the heart of the sinner, but at this stage it is not sufficient for salvation; to achieve this end, it must be accepted with gratitude, loved and sought as a means of expiation. The decisive factor is the way in which we receive it. Dostoevsky, carried away in his enthusiasm, makes suffering the object of a cult, an idolatry which betrays an inveterate masochism. Dyevushkin writes already in *Poor People*: "I suffer for you, yet it eases my heart to suffer for you."[37] Faced with suffering, the brothers Karamazov become its priests: each worships it in his own way. Alyosha's vocation, Zossima prophesies, is "in sorrow [to] seek happiness";[38] Ivan, like the novelist obsessed by the tears of children, does not resign himself and reproaches God;[39] Dmitri finally personifies the conversion to suffering necessary for salvation:

> I punish myself for my whole life.[40]

> I want to suffer and by suffering I shall be purified. Perhaps I shall be purified, gentlemen? But listen, for the last time, I am not guilty of my

51

father's blood. I accept my punishment, not because I killed him, but because I wanted to kill him, and perhaps I really might have killed him.[41]

It's for the babe I'm going. Because we are all responsible for all. For all the "babes," for there are big children as well as little children. All are "babes." I go for all, because some one must go for all. I didn't kill father but I've got to go. I accept it. . . . Oh yes, we shall be in chains and there will be no freedom, but then in our great sorrow, we shall rise again to joy, without which man cannot live nor God exist, for God gives joy: it's his privilege—a grand one.[42]

Dmitri repeats the example of Christ, he embraces his cross to redeem the sin of Adam. An analysis of suffering shows that it accompanies knowledge—see the myth of original sin—as well as the love of God and his creatures: it is the very condition of man chased from the Garden of Eden. *Patior, ergo sum.* To aspire to life's torments is to purge the punishment inflicted by God. To do so is to lessen the distance that separates us from our lost Paradise. Such is also the meaning of the *caritas* and forgiveness prescribed by God which restores the solidarity of the wretched isolated on earth.

Dostoevsky erects his personal thirst for suffering into the foundation of the national character,[43] which for him embodies so much of the spirit of the Gospels. But ideas blaze across national boundaries: did not the Idiot predict the universal reign of the Russian Christ? Thanks to Faulkner, his prophecy is partially accomplished: if Dostoevsky's God has not conquered mankind he at least found a disciple, and not an insignificant one, in Mississippi. For his idea of redemption by suffering, Faulkner was inspired during the last twenty years of his life by *The Brothers Karamazov.* This time we can exclude any notion of convergence or parallelism: it is a matter of a true influence as Temple's allusion in *Requiem for a Nun* proves.[44] The revaluation of suffering, proposed by Dostoevsky, interested Faulkner at the precise moment that the "old verities and truths of the heart" were being developed and moved to the foreground. From 1926 to 1936, from *Soldiers' Pay* to *Absalom, Absalom!,* he etches a portrait of the two post-war periods, that of 1918, and especially that of 1865. With *The Unvanquished* he finally breaks the circle of evil: the dissector of the South begins to wish to revive the corpse whose corruption he has exposed, the painter of decadence adds rose to his palette without improving, however, his narrative talent. Bearer of a "message" he prepares—without suspecting it?—his candidacy for the Nobel prize. We shall see that Dostoevsky contributed decisively to this evolution, for he showed how to pass from damnation to salvation. Obviously the process required many years, hampered as it was by relapses into the old manner of viewing things. The epilogue to the story of the lovers in *The Wild Palms* (1939) in which Wilbourne renounces suicide preferring suffering to nothingness[45] is something that truly suggests the exclamation of Dmitri Karamazov: "I'm tormented on the rack —but I exist! I see the sun, and if I don't see the sun, I know it's there."[46] Suffering thus means: to participate in existence, to know that one is alive; vitality is measured by resistance to suffering: "I am I through bereavement and because of it,"[47] the hero of "Beyond" (1933) tells us. By the same token, the value of love is deduced from the pain it provokes: "Love and suffering are the same thing."[48] The idea exists even earlier in germ but without a clear formulation in the primacy accorded to life.[49] In 1942 *Go Down, Moses* signals the fecundity of affliction, which thus develops into something active and positive.[50] Suffering, presented as a test of energy and, more, as an instrument of knowledge,[51] leads to redemption. This will be once again the directing idea of *Requiem for a Nun* (1951), a long variation on this Dostoevskian theme after the echoes of *Intruder in the Dust*[52] and *Knight's Gambit*.[53] That suffering should be cultivated for its own sake and can serve as an act of expiation, that it can bring sinners together and culminate in forgiveness, all of these theses bear Dostoevsky's mark. Faulkner's attitude towards suffering rests on another common trait which, far from being borrowed, springs from the deepest parts of his personality. Without scorning the intellect, our writers always reason with their hearts. This is why Dostoevsky's expositions shake with passion; this is also what makes Faulkner's so dull and obscure. The heart is in both of them, to be sure, but Dostoevsky reinforces it with an intelligence that Faulkner does not possess in the same degree. To give priority to feeling over understanding is finally a matter of temperament, a postulate that reveals a manner of being which is found in all periods although the vogue for it varies according to time and place. In the man from the underground, for whom two and two make five, in the Idiot who is closer to a child than to an adult, in Alyosha who loves "life more than the meaning of it,"[54] even in Ivan, it is basically a romantic survival, although the exaltation of the irrational, the condemnation of positivism and the anathema cast against scientific determinism announce Nietzsche, Bergson and existentialism. We must do, we read in *The Diary of a Writer*, only what the heart commands, even if it should enjoin us to give away our fortune.[55] For the heart, which is love, is not mistaken and can only lead us to virtue: a personal conviction, unprovable and frequently contradicted by actual events, to which Faulkner also enthusiastically adheres. He confided to students on several occasions a distrust of thought and an ignorance of ideas[56] that is sufficiently borne out by his excursions into this area. It is difficult to resist the urge to note here the dichotomy between theory and practice. Must we attribute the discursive grandiloquence of his latter years to a desire to rival Dostoevsky in a genre which turned, in his hands, into pompous bombast? It is possible. In any case, the best, the true Faulkner is the one who writes under the dictates of the heart[57] and pours his precepts into the mold of the narrative without preaching. The fourth chapter of "The Bear," so precious for exegesis, so painful to read, forcefully insists on the subjective, intuitive, illogical character of choice and truth, the latter term designating all that moves the heart:

> I know what you will say now: That if truth is one thing to me and another thing to you, how will we choose which is truth? You don't need to choose. The heart already knows. He didn't have His Book written to be read by what must elect and choose, but by the heart . . . there is only one truth and it covers all things that touch the heart.[58]
>
> the heart knows truth, the infallible and unerring heart[59]
>
> *Truth is one. It doesn't change. It covers all things which touch the heart —honor and pride and pity and justice and courage and love.*[60]

We recognize here one of the seeds from which existentialism springs, a current that Faulkner also evokes by his hatred of bourgeois respectability, his awareness of the absurd and, as we shall see, by his feeling of guilt.

Faulkner's cult of suffering is normally limited to courage, firmness, endurance in adversity, the traditional values of the English public school. The stoicism that underlies his entire philosophy probably favored his conversion to the headier ideas of *The Brothers Karamazov*. In a less ethereal and passionate context than that of love of suffering, simple courage also saves man, even if only in preserving him physically: it permits him to endure, it assures the perenniality of the species. Faulkner sees courage, at bottom, as an admirable faculty of adaptation to the environment[61]–"man can bear anything"[62]–thereby agreeing with the narrator of *The House of the Dead*: "Man is a creature that can get accustomed to anything, and I think that is the best definition of him."[63] The value of courage is not, however, measured by its end: Faulkner also glorifies it for its own sake. But since courage guarantees existence, praising it comes down to asserting oneself. Vitality, instinct of preservation, constancy under suffering, courage: so many synonyms. It is the supreme mark of quality that one can bestow on an individual, for it concerns his faculty of being; from this point of view, existence and the way in which one exists, end and means, are merged. Derived from this is the admiration for the gratuitous courage which is, in a certain sense, an extension of biological resistance, the stubborn will to survive of the mule, the black and the woman which, from a certain perspective, borders on the cult of suffering. Faulknerian courage, which is not to be confused with the temerity which tempts fate, consists essentially in bearing up under the blows unflinchingly, and by its victories saying no to the void, maintaining life, and continually surmounting new tests, thereby opening the door to salvation. The novelist incarnates this effort in *Soldiers' Pay* in the character of Mrs. Powers; he remains faithful to the motto of the R.A.F.–"Per ardua ad astra"–to the manly philosophy of Conrad,[64] to what he had found particularly striking in Thomas Mann,[65] to what was for him, in sum, a fundamental doctrine whose praises he sings right up until *The Mansion*[66] and *The Reivers*.[67] Whether it be stoic self-sacrifice without practical result but precious as discipline, asceticism or purification as in 1926, or determination never to give up once the battle is joined as in 1962, courage signifies man's decision to surpass himself, to triumph over his innate weakness. "A man conquers himself."[68] For it does not operate automatically, it assumes on the contrary the intervention of the will. Thus it takes the form of effort: "I would say if there is one truth of the human heart, it would be to believe in itself, believe in its capacity to aspire, to be better than it is, might be. That it does exist in all people."[69] One is at first reminded less of Dostoevsky than of the Puritan pioneers, the sailors, soldiers and merchants who built the Empire, of the stoics of antiquity, of Kipling and Conrad. Let us point out, however, that the courage recommended by Faulkner is not directed toward a will to power. The only conquest it seeks is that of the self, that of the cowardice which saps us from within; purely defensive, it limits itself to containing the enemy which assails us from without. Have not Faulkner and Dostoevsky, as of one voice, stigmatized the bravado associated with feudal honor? On the other hand, as Charles Anderson suggests,[70] in extolling effort Faulkner resolutely rejects *laisser-faire* humanitarianism, that smug and indolent optimism which renounces the forging of character and flatters our vices. In this he is in sympathy with the author of *The Brothers Karamazov*, who glorifies monastic obedience because it chastises the "proud and wanton will,"[71] and leads to self-mastery, to freedom.[72] But their meeting takes place at an even more precise spot which Gide locates when he says that "Dostoevsky's heroes enter into the kingdom of God only by resigning their intelligence, by abdicating their personal will, by their renunciation of self."[73] Once again, salvation—a term we have yet to define—crowns effort: to resign, abdicate, renounce, is in effect to conquer oneself. The tergiversations of Raskolnikov before he denounces himself, those of Temple when she confesses in *Requiem for a Nun*, prove that redemption is not given to us: it is earned by suffering, by the courage which endures suffering. In both cases there is a conflict: less between man and others than between man and himself, and it is this that makes his world so profoundly tragic. There is more. During the terrifying fake execution of December, 1849, Dostoevsky also discovered the relationship between courage and the *élan vital*, the will to live of all men. Immediately afterwards he wrote to his brother Michael:

> I am not dismayed, I have not lost heart. Life is everywhere life, life is in ourselves, not in outward things. There will be people beside me, and to be a *man* among men, and remain a man forever, not to falter or fail in any misfortune whatever—that is what life is, that is where its task lies. I have come to know this. The idea has become part of my flesh and blood.[74]

In him, hatred of the void, carried to its culmination, denies the death of the soul and takes refuge in a spiritual beyond; Faulkner, on the other hand, is content to transmit this same hatred from father to son.

Raskolnikov, we remember, chose to declare his guilt and Temple to admit her errors. In both cases the inner conflict resolved itself by a free acceptance of suffering. To approach the problem of freedom, of capital importance for our study, it is best to take the detour of responsibility, or, rather, of guilt. Dostoevsky says we are guilty because he believes us free. He revolts, for instance, against any positivistic justification of crime which would deprive the criminal of his free will. He who excuses the act, degrades the agent, makes him the plaything of social and biological pressures. Once again Dostoevsky sets sail against the current and rebels against the scientific humanitarianism of his century in the name of human dignity.[75] The idea of responsibility implies the solidarity of the agent with his acts only insofar as he has been able to foresee them and has really willed them. *The Brothers Karamazov* goes much further. For Dostoevsky, obsessed by original sin, man is punishable in any case, even before acting, and responsibility degenerates into total and unconditional culpability. In virtue of the Fall, the fault precedes the act. This belief which insults our reason and which has been popularized in our time by Kafka, the existentialists and Faulkner, was already announced by Zossima: "For know, dear ones, that every one of us is undoubtedly responsible for all men and everything on earth, not merely through the general sinfulness of creation, but each one personally for all mankind and every individual man."[76] The holy man concludes that individual salvation is necessarily mediated by expiation of all of the sins of humanity according to Christ's example: "There is only one means of salvation, then, take yourself and make yourself responsible for all men's sins,"[77] advice that Dmitri does not hesitate in putting into practice.[78] This is not the place to detail the debt contracted by Faulkner in this matter.[79] Nancy in *Requiem for a Nun* repeats almost textually the words of Zossima and of Dmitri.[80] Nothing is more common in contemporary thought and literature than to make existence equivalent to suffering, human disgrace to some original and universal taint, redemption to an effort of solidarity. But, of all the variables that can enter into this equation, it is precisely those of Dostoevsky that Faulkner takes during his mature years: suffering as the last hope, the taint as sin, solidarity as guilt and as love.

Thus a fairly coherent conception of choice takes shape. We have seen that Faulkner and Dostoevsky refuse to link virtue exclusively to rational knowledge or action to intellectual understanding. Proponents of a morality of feeling, they make the decision proceed from either "desire" as with the man from the underground or—ordinarily—from the "heart" which renounces all analysis and knows from the start what it wants. It is necessary to think and act less as a man of science than as a man of the heart, as one who loves and who serves life. The decisive proof of the indissoluble union of choice and the *élan vital* is found in the refusal of nothingness; the first choice which is also the most spontaneous and the least reflective, the choice of existence, is dictated to us by the instinct for preservation. But, deprived of the light of science, every decision carries risks, even carries more doubts than certitudes. To choose, even when one obeys the innate sentiment of good and evil, is—objectively—always a leap into darkness.[81] Man, Faulkner writes, decides first, reasons later: "he thought of man who apparently had to kill man not for motive or reason but simply for the sake the need the compulsion of having to kill man, inventing creating his motive and reason afterward so that he could still stand up among men as a rational creature."[82] Of Byron in *Light in August*, he says: "already his decision was made, without his even being aware of it."[83] Nancy—

and Sonia Marmeladov—so sure of the path to follow, are uneducated.

The freedom that Dmitri Karamazov and Nancy exploit to assume the suffering of others is conceived as a normative term. In other words, it "designates an ideal state, in which human nature is governed exclusively by what is best in it."[84] Furthermore, even when this freedom permits us to choose evil, the operation results, in the final analysis, in good. Does it invariably turn out this way? Does the idealistic alchemy suffer no exceptions? Neither of our writers is so naive or simplistic. They have understood fairly well the degrees of freedom, the multiplicity of its significations and effects, its traps and its limits.

In *The Brothers Karamazov* perfect freedom, for Zossima, merges with self-mastery: it is "freedom from self"[85] obtained by obedience and asceticism; it results from an imitation of Christ and is, moreover, something we owe to Him. Ivan explains that Rome has discarded this present from God in order to make man happy.[86] The legend of the Grand Inquisitor poses this dilemma: freedom or happiness in servitude, and pronounces itself in favor of happiness. There is, according to Dostoevsky, a fundamental incompatibility between the two, at least on earth. For freedom, as it is understood here, always draws in its wake suffering, the condition of redemption; moreover, choice is anguish since it is by definition sacrifice, and is always accomplished in the dark. "Nothing is more seductive for man than his freedom of conscience, but nothing is a greater cause of suffering."[87] To connect freedom with the God-Man means that one assumes its excellence. To choose is to open oneself to the Supreme Good. Like Christ in the desert, Dmitri and Alyosha willingly forsake the shadowy world of terrestrial happiness for their goal: the Kingdom of God. This freedom, triumphant over the ego and directed towards the good, has also been depicted by Faulkner: in *Soldiers' Pay* (Mrs. Powers), "Ad Astra," *Intruder in the Dust* (Chick Mallison), *Requiem for a Nun* (Nancy), etc. He relates it to Christ, however, only in *Requiem for a Nun* and *A Fable* and there by the intermediary of a character.[88] It is impossible, therefore, to enter this idea in Faulkner's ledger of debts. The most that can be said is that, if in Dostoevsky the exercise of freedom leads to salvation of the soul, in Faulkner it assures the immortality of the race.[89] The identity of views on the pangs of choice is, on the other hand, quite clear as these Faulknerian texts show:

> No one needs freedom. We cannot bear it.[90]
>
> No man is ever free and probably could not bear it if he were.[91]
>
> apparently no man can stand freedom.[92]
>
> I did have a choice between could and would, between shall and must and cannot, between must and dare not, between *will do* and *I am afraid to do*: had that choice, and found myself afraid.[93]

From *Mosquitoes* to *A Fable* it is always the same song. The residue of the readings? Nothing is less certain. The history of slavery, particularly that of the South, undoubtedly furnished abundant illustrations of this Dostoevskian theme.

From another angle, freedom can be regarded as an indifferent free will, as Descartes defines it: "*Indifference* seems to me to properly signify that state in which the will finds itself when it is not carried by knowledge of what is true or good to follow one direction or the other." Let us eliminate the word "knowledge" which is inappropriate in our context; let us substitute intuition, feeling, instinct; and we transform liberty into a power to choose or not to choose an act, whatever its moral value. It is an indeterminate, unattached will, still unconcerned about God, good and evil, or any principle and ready for any adventure whatever; metaphysical freedom, absolute, anterior to any choice and, therefore, to the other form, "liberty under a chosen principle."[94] Without it, tyranny might triumph. By itself, however, it apparently engenders "the total independence"[95] of blasphemers and rebels: it pushes man to escape the laws of his nature and will and demands that he indulge its caprices; it attempts to realize itself thoroughly. The participation in the divine which rewards the man attentive to the voice of the heart, and, thereby, to the Spirit of God, finds its counterpart in luciferism whose terrible but seductive grandeur is revealed in *The Possessed*. And it is not just Stavrogin—who neither understands nor feels good or evil[96]—nor Verkhovensky, nor Kirillov: the prophets of demoniacal freedom are legion in Dostoevsky, from Orlov and Petrov, the convicts of *The House of the Dead* to Ivan Karamazov for whom "everything is lawful." Violent men, murderers; they kill or kill themselves. In *The House of the Dead* murder appears as the instrument *par excellence* of this freedom which is finally only the unbridled licence of pride, self-glorification, pure will to power.[97] Such also is the meaning of Raskolnikov's[98] crime and of the philosophical suicide, planned by Terentiev in *The Idiot* and committed by Kirillov in *The Possessed*. Total freedom expresses itself as a challenge to God:

> Nature has so limited any activity by its three weeks' sentence, that perhaps suicide is the only action I still have time to begin and end by my own will. And perhaps I want to take advantage of the last possibility of *action*.[99]

> There will be full freedom when it will be just the same to live or not to live. . . . Life is pain, life is terror, and man is unhappy. Now all is pain and terror. Now man loves life, because he loves pain and terror, and so they have done according. Life is given now for pain and terror, and that's the deception. Now man is not yet what he will be. There will be a new man, happy and proud. For whom it will be the same to live or not to live, he will be a new man. He who will conquer pain and terror will himself be a god. And this God will not be.[100]

The reign of the Man-God, Kirillov tells us again, will be followed by that of the God-Man[101]: freedom spinning wildly, choosing only itself, a slave of itself, provokes a monstrous hypertrophy of the ego and attempts to annihilate God and to usurp his throne. Here we find the sin of Lucifer and, beyond it, the ancient motif of deicide linked in Dostoevsky, among others, with parricide. This type of rebel occurs so often it is impossible not to see a projection of the artist in it: Dostoevsky must have felt the vertigo of Raskolnikov before resigning himself to suffering. His Christian faith must, in order to triumph, have passed through the crucible of doubt. We do not expect Faulkner's criminals to attain this metaphysical paroxysm. In their attempts to follow the "possessed" on their tightrope of speculation, the Mississippi farmers unfailingly stumble. Only Quentin Compson—a student—risks it, but his suicide has nothing in common with Kirillov's. However, Joe Christmas of *Light in August* also kills to proclaim his freedom, his dignity as a man; and Mink Snopes in *The Mansion* frees himself through murder. But how to compare the reactions of an animal at bay to the experimental, calculated and sovereign act of Raskolnikov? The latter can choose (to kill or not); at this stage he can imagine other solutions: to give lessons or borrow money, for example, and he actually does so.[102] Christmas, on the other hand, runs up against the bars of fate at every step; he is from the beginning the prisoner of a single alternative. We can measure here the distance separating the two novelists. Hypnotized by freedom, the Russian from the start places it in the foreground without pausing to consider the complementary problem of determinism; the American, extracting freedom little by little from the pressures which smother it, ends up where the other begins. There is nothing surprising in the fact that Faulkner, who initially shrank the range of free will to the point of making evil a quasi-obligation, seems unaware of its indeterminate variety. Quentin Compson can only deny the undeniable evidence—his sister's pregnancy—and stifle himself. His freedom is one of chimeras and despair.[103]

One easily sees why. During the period of *The Sound and the Fury* and *Light in August*, evil, almost omnipotent, is still seen in a naturalist's perspective,[104] as fatality. The last chapter of *Sanctuary*, a deterministic flashback on the heredity and antecedents of Popeye, confirms this hypothesis: it proves the kinship of Faulkner and Zola. Freedom wilts in this atmosphere. If he wants the good (Horace Benbow), man is beaten before he starts; if he wants evil (Popeye), he does not want it more than fate does. Destiny, fate, doom are the leitmotifs of Faulkner's works. Yoknapatawpha, a condemned land bewitched by Calvin's God, withers under the weight of the past. The elect are rare—the Mac-Callums, Dilsey, Lena Grove, the "simple people" who do not question their condition. The doctrine of predestination magnifies tenfold the malediction with which Zola, Hardy and Conrad[105] have struck man. Fate, which is ordinarily only the object of a belief, dominates the novelistic world from without; it develops into an objective law because it obsesses the author as much as his characters. An error or illusion that one imposes on oneself, it loses its hold as soon as one begins to analyze it. It is not surprising then that it begins to fade when Faulkner becomes attracted by ideas. There is a world of difference between the pessimistic opinions of Mr. Compson (1929)—"a man is the sum of his misfortunes . . . time is your misfortune"[106] and the interview of 1959-60: "after all, man is never time's slave."[107] In the earlier narratives one is at the antipodes of the Dostoevskian position that Faulkner will later espouse. Around 1935, weary, it would seem, of the atrocities he had exposed, he found the philosopher's stone in Dostoevsky: evil leads to good, suffering is metamorphosed into redemption, the dungeon of Fate is cracked. Freedom, once discovered, does not cease to grow while the determinism of blood, history and environment is proportionally attenuated. The two men, starting from opposite premises, end by offering each other their hand. For Faulkner evil is first identified with constraint, for Dostoevsky with free choice. But the basic principle of the Faulknerian philosophy imperceptibly loses its rigor. Faulkner, to be sure, could no more conceive the limitless freedom of Kirillov than Dostoevsky could admit the determinism of Popeye. They meet half way on the terrain of a moral freedom directed towards the good.

I think that man's free will functions against a Greek background of fate, that he has the free will to choose and the courage, the fortitude to die for his choice, is my conception of man, is why I believe that man will endure. That fate—sometimes fate lets him alone. But he can never depend on that. But he has always the right to free will and we hope the courage to die for his choice.[108]

Dostoevsky also speaks of fate; he discusses it even in *Crime and Punishment* where he integrates it into the psychology of his protagonist, in contrast to the young Faulkner who submits the whole world to it. And it is from this that his interest in Raskolnikov undoubtedly derives. "I should have done that. *There is no free will, fatalism,*"[109] we read in the notebooks of *Crime and Punishment*. Although exalting freedom, Dostoevsky does not leave it without restraints: total independence, as the case of Raskolnikov testifies, is purchased at the price of violence and slavery; scorn of the Savior and freedom *in God* eventually leaves no other issue than that of subjection to the natural laws. Dostoevsky recognizes the existence of a necessity: physical na-

ture, economic conditions, even heredity and past time. But its
limits are vague and remote in comparison to the omnipresent
destiny of *Light in August*. The very delicate problems of God and immortality remain.
For the Russian, God is the basis of the entire system. Suppress
Christ, and suffering immediately becomes absurd and revolting,
freedom breaks down, the moral order gives way to anarchy, to
"everything is lawful." Moreover, Dostoevsky's militant nationalism rests, essentially, on the idea of God. Dostoevsky conquered
faith at the end of an exhausting dialogue[110] in which the angelic
choir of Sonia Marmeladov, the Idiot and Alyosha barely cover
the bass notes of the demons. What power among the atheists:
Kirillov, Verkhovensky, Ivan Karamazov; and how dull is Zossima's
bland piety after the Grand Inquisitor's indictment! The last
works, centered with growing insistence on the quest for God,[111]
illustrate one of the major themes of the nineteenth century: the
conflict of faith and science. Dostoevsky is in this very much a
man of his times, although in his approach to this problem he
anticipates contemporary philosophy. After weighing both the
pros and cons faith wins out, but without diminishing the apos-
tates' very rigorous, robust and attractive arguments. Moreover,
Dostoevsky's attack is directed less against the rebels whom he
understands very well and with good reason, than against the
indifferent who are infinitely more dangerous for religion. "The
complete atheist," Bishop Tikhon says in *The Possessed*, "stands
on the next to top step of the most perfect faith (he may step
over or not)."[112] Versilov, who in *A Raw Youth* describes the
return of the pagan golden age then turns right around and installs Christ in a paradise from which he was absent,[113] proceeds
more or less in this manner. The characters to whom we should
devote ourselves here are neither the fanatics nor the born believ-
ers—these also file past in Faulkner—but the converts and the
consciences still torn between the heart and the reason, between
certitude and scepticism. Shatov, for instance, hesitates on the
threshold of faith. Called to account by Stavrogin, he proclaims
that he believes in "Russia," "her orthodoxy," "the body of Christ"
etc. But when the other insists "And in God? In God?", Shatov
can only answer "I . . . I will believe in God"[114]—an incomplete

faith, a projected faith, willed, but for the moment dormant and homeless. We should point out that its object is, by definition, inaccessible to human understanding. Zossima himself has declared: "Credo, but I don't know in what"[115] echoing Tertullian's "Credo quia absurdum" and, even more, Saint Augustine and Kierkegaard. No need to understand to believe: to love is sufficient. Approaching the unknowable demands the abdication of reason: it is to risk the leap, not of death, but of Life. For others God is the hypothesis or rather the postulate supporting any explanation of existence. This is the position of Ivan Karamazov who, paraphrasing Voltaire, declares that he "admits" God, but does not love him, condemns his Creation, sullied by suffering, and gives him back his ticket:[116] without this "invention" there would have been no civilization.[117] It is again that of young Kolya: "I've nothing against God. Of course, God is only a hypothesis, but . . . I admit that He is needed . . . for the order of the universe and all that . . . and that if there were no God he would have to be invented."[118] Even Kirillov recognizes the necessity of God and in committing suicide seeks to identify with him.[119] To summarize, there are in Dostoevsky moments when faith in God is reduced to a will to believe, others where it is equivalent to love of the unknown. Elsewhere, the apologist assumes God as an indispensable premise to account for the universe or "proves" the immortality of the soul by the utility this belief offers for life on earth: to deny God is to call for death (*Diary*, December, 1876).[120]

These lessons, essential for Dostoevsky, were learned by Faulkner late in life. Until 1942 (*Go Down, Moses*) nothing in his work betrays any adherence to Christian principles. If an occasional element—religious symbolism, the sense of sin—could perhaps suggest a future conversion, none made it necessary. Quite to the contrary. The young novelist took with one hand what he parsimoniously gave with the other. The Christmas peace in *Sartoris* is described as an illusion[121] and God—or Fate—is compared to a chess player moving men like pawns.[122] *Sanctuary* and especially *Light in August* and *Absalom, Absalom!* pillory puritanical hypocrisy and cruelty. It is continually repeated that man is a fallen creature, but when is redemption to come? Hightower vilifies clerical tyranny[123] as Dostoevsky does that of Rome; for Gavin Stevens, religion is only a chimera—"a blind faith in something read in a printed Book;"[124] Mr. Compson, Quentin's father, likens the Anglo-Saxon God to a jealous and sadistic Jehovah.[125] The first novels are rife with attacks on the Puritanism with which they are saturated: a double movement of absorption and repulsion develops between the artist and the milieu. But soon the tide of hate ebbs back. Having settled his accounts with the fanatics, Faulkner yields, little by little, to the religiosity with which he had been impregnated since childhood.[126] In this area the evolution seems to follow, but only slightly, the metamorphoses studied above. At least we have no evidence anterior to "The Bear" where Isaac McCaslin takes Christ for his model[127] and in which the Bible becomes the receptacle of all the "heart's truth."[128] The dominant Christian note which blends mutations developed over several years is accentuated in *Intruder in the Dust* (1948), *Requiem for a Nun* (1951) and *A Fable* (1959). Faulkner is, nonetheless, no more a subscriber to an official doctrine than Dostoevsky: "Bill," says his brother, "had not belonged to any church."[129] But there are sharper resemblances. The unconditional faith, blind to its object, unquestioning, unmurmuring faith, the "Credo, but I don't know in what" of Zossima, was not difficult to reconcile with the instinctive endurance of the Negro and the mule, the invincible tenacity in suffering, the effort at any price on which the durability of the species depends. Thus a fundamentally similar love of life is expressed: life in God who is its principle in Heaven as well as on earth, or simply on earth across the infinite chain of generations. This is the faith that animates Henry Sutpen,[130] Chick Mallison and the runner in *A Fable*,[131] although in them it is not centered on God but on man. It borders, moreover, on the will to believe:[132] "*I will believe.*"[133] *Requiem for a Nun*, on the other hand, poses the same question (*Believe? Believe what?*) on the religious level:

NANCY
. . . All you need, all you have to do, is just believe . . . .
STEVENS
Believe what?
NANCY
Just believe.[134]

Nancy does not know if God exists, but plunges like Zossima into the unknown.[135] It is, in Faulkner, a borderline case well beyond the range of his own convictions; he himself remains closer to Gavin Stevens. In explaining Temple's past to the governor, Stevens constantly refers to God, but he speaks only in the conditional: "God—if there was one—".[136] The nuance is important. For Stevens, who sees in Calvin's God the only justification of man's downfall,[137] for Temple, who is lost *if* Heaven is empty, the universe sinks into the absurd without the—conjectural—notion of God. This is, textually, the point of view of Kolya in *The Brothers Karamazov*. Faulkner has explained himself in public on the point several times.

> To me, a proof of God is in the firmament, the stars. To me, a proof of man's immortality, that his conception that there could be a God, that the idea of a God is valuable, is in the fact that he writes the books and composes the music and paints the pictures. They are the firmament of mankind. They are the proof that if there is a God and he wants us to see something that proves to him that mankind exists, that would be proof.[138]

> I think that no writing will be too successful without some conception of God, you can call Him by whatever name you want.[139]

> . . . within my own rights I feel that I'm a good Christian—whether it would please anybody else's standard or not I don't know.[140]

> "Probably you are wrong in doing away with God in that fashion. God is. It is He who created man. It you don't reckon with God, you won't wind up anywhere. You question God, and then you begin to doubt, and you begin to ask 'Why? Why? Why?'—and God fades away by the very act of your doubting him." . . . .

> "Naturally," he continued, "I'm not talking about a personified or a mechanical God, but a God who is the most complete expression of mankind, a God who rests both in eternity and in the now." When I asked if he were thinking of the God of Bergson, he said, "Yes, a deity very close to Bergson's. Listen, neither God nor morality can be destroyed."[141]

Dostoevsky's God tortures and enraptures him at the same time. Faulkner's impersonal creator, an *élan vital* operating in humanity, the architect of nature, the guarantor of the fine arts and, probably, the source of morality, does not provoke such exclusive or disinterested passions. The arguments in his favor spring from the physico-theological proofs; furthermore, they rest on a kind of reasoning by a *reductio ad absurdum*. On the one hand, the existence of God can be deduced from the coherence of the world as it is perceived by the aging writer; on the other hand, nothing has sense without the hypothesis of a *deus ex machina* who, with a wave of the wand, solves the puzzle, explains everything but settles nothing, except a certain vaguely comforting feeling. What role did Dostoevsky play in this conversion? Was it accomplished under his direct influence? Could it not have resulted from the interaction of other forces? One thing is certain: at the end of his life, Faulkner repeats the formulas that he read and reread in *The Brothers Karamazov*.

We should point out, however, that the two writers present man's immortality, an idea they both dearly cherish, in a different light. For Dostoevsky it is inscribed within the Christian tradition. It is tantamount to the survival of the individual soul in the beyond,[142] while Faulkner, rejecting all transcendence, is content to affirm the perenniality of the species by virtue of its capacity for adaptation and aptitude for compassion and suffering. The Stockholm Address gives no other meaning to the soul: "a soul, a spirit capable of compassion, sacrifice and endurance."[143] Immortality is only an unceasingly renewed victory over hostile forces, passed from father to son by the hereditary virtues of the race—"man . . . enduring not because he is immortal but immortal because he endures."[144] The qualities which assure the indestructibility of the race are undoubtedly spiritual as well as physical, but this continuity which is synonymous with progress— "man will not merely endure: he will prevail"[145]—does not extend into the atemporal and is not concerned with individuals, with the possible exception of the artist,[146] but with the vital principle of humanity.[147] God and salvation are secularized; the Marshal who regards Christian eternity as an illusion[148] is a heretic, like the author. The old Faulkner was right in doubting his orthodoxy. On this particular point he clearly contradicts Dostoevsky, more of a conformist than himself. But the analogy of a certain vitalism, remote from the idea of immortality and situated, so to speak, at its periphery, remains. For the Russian novelist, to believe in God, the Eternal Father, implies a love of the earthly life created by him. The belief in a future existence tightens man's ties to earth, he explains in *The Diary of a Writer* (December, 1876),[149] as it makes him conscious of his vocation in this world. Ivan Karamazov suggests that this belief is the "living force maintaining the life of the world."[150] But is this not, word for word, the opposite of what the Nobel laureate says: "immortal *because* he endures?"

Whether it be in his conception of evil, of redemption through suffering, of guilt, effort, choice, freedom or God, Faulkner in the thirties initiates a movement that draws him closer to Dostoevsky. Considered in isolation, any of these parallels could seem simply an accident. It is easy to blame chance, but does it ever show such regularity in its effects? It seems certain, therefore, that despite fortuitous kinships, Faulkner's thought assimilated over a period of time a substantial amount of Dostoevskian material.

NOTES TO CHAPTER II

1. *The Notebooks for The Possessed*, ed. Edward Wasiolek and trans. Victor Terras (Chicago: Chicago Univ. Press, 1968), p. 174.
2. *White Nights and Other Stories* ("Notes from the Underground"), pp. 64-65.
3. *Ibid.*, p. 69.
4. See N. Berdjajew, *Die Weltanschauung Dostojewskijs*, (München: C. H. Becksche Verlagsbuchhandlung, 1925) p. 79.
5. *White Nights and Other Stories* ("Notes from the Underground"), p. 71.
6. *The Brothers Karamazov*, pp. 267-68.
7. *Ibid.*, pp. 686-87.
8. *Ibid.*, p. 684.
9. *Ibid.*, p. 687.
10. See *ibid.*, pp. 680-81: "by some decree which I could never make out, I was predestined 'to denie' and yet I am genuinely good-hearted and not at all inclined to negation. . . . Well, they've chosen their scapegoat and they've made me write the column of criticism and so life was made possible. We understand the comedy; I, for instance, simply ask for annihilation. No, live, I am told, for there would be nothing without you. If everything were sensible in the world, nothing would happen. There would be no events without you, and there must be events. . . . They suffer, of course . . . but then they live, they live a real life, not a fantastic one, for suffering is life. Without suffering what would be the pleasure of it?"
11. See René Girard, *Dostoïevski. Du double à l'unité* (Paris: Plon, 1963), p. 117.
12. *The Possessed*, p. 254.
13. *The Brothers Karamazov*, p. 676.
14. *Ibid.*, p. 681.
15. *Ibid.*, p. 175.
16. *Ibid.*, pp. 252, 250.

17. *Ibid.*, p. 270.
18. *The Diary of a Writer*, pp. 689-90.
19. *A Fable*, p. 203.
20. *Sanctuary*, p. 181.
21. *Ibid.*, pp. 180-81.
22. *Ibid.*, pp. 265-66.
23. *The Possessed*, p. 206.
24. *Requiem for a Nun*, p. 208.
25. *The Unvanquished*, p. 167.
26. *The Reivers*, p. 302. See also *The Mansion*, p. 230: "Man ain't really evil, he jest ain't got any sense."
27. *Requiem for a Nun*, p. 134. See also pp. 150-51: "because the bad was already there waiting, who hadn't even heard yet that you must be already resisting the corruption not only before you look at it but before you even know what it is, what you are resisting."
28. *The Sound and the Fury and As I Lay Dying*, p. 431.
29. *A Fable*, p. 180, and *Essays, Speeches and Public Letters*, pp. 137-38.
30. It seems that this not always the case. See *A Fable*, p. 285.
31. *Sanctuary*, p. 2.
32. *Light in August*, pp. 239-40.
33. *Absalom, Absalom!*, pp. 11, 221, 260.
34. *Go Down, Moses*, p. 349.
35. *Ibid.*, p. 257.
36. *The Diary of a Writer*, pp. 526-27.
37. *The Gambler and Other Stories* (New York: MacMillan, 1917), p. 224.
38. *The Brothers Karamazov*, p. 77.
39. *Ibid.*, pp. 250-55.
40. *Ibid.*, p. 427.
41. *Ibid.*, p. 540.
42. *Ibid.*, p. 627.
43. *The Diary of a Writer*, p. 36.
44. See *Requiem for a Nun*, p. 133: "you know: just anguish for the sake of anguish like that Russian or somebody who wrote a whole book about suffering, not suffering for or about anything, just suffering, like somebody unconscious not really breathing."
45. See *The Wild Palms*, p. 324: "between grief and nothing I will take grief."
46. *The Brothers Karamazov*, p. 628.
47. *Collected Stories*, p. 796.
48. *The Wild Palms*, p. 48.
49. *The Sound and the Fury and As I Lay Dying*, p. 121, and *Collected Stories*, p. 584 ("Doctor Martino").
50. See *Go Down, Moses*, p. 186: "Think of all that has happened here, on this earth. All the blood hot and strong for living, pleasuring, that has soaked back into it. For grieving and suffering too, of course, but still getting something out of it for all that, getting a lot out of it, because after all you don't have to continue to bear what you believes is suffering: you can always choose to stop that, put an end to that. And even suffering and grieving is better than nothing; there is only one thing worse than not being alive, and that's shame. But you cant be alive forever, and you always wear out life long before you have exhausted the possibilities of living. And all that must be somewhere; all that could not have been invented and created just to be thrown away. And the earth is shallow; there is not a great deal of it before you come to rock. And the earth dont want to just keep things, hoard them; it wants to use them again."
51. See *ibid.*, p. 286: "Apparently they can learn nothing save through suffering, remember nothing save when underlined in blood."

52. See *Intruder in the Dust*, pp. 154-55, 204, 210.
53. *Knight's Gambit*, p. 49.
54. *The Brothers Karamazov*, p. 239.
55. *The Diary of a Writer*, p. 622.
56. See *Faulkner in the University*, p. 6:
"Q. Mr. Faulkner, what do you think is man's most important tool—the mind or the heart . . . ?
A. I don't have much confidence in the mind. I think that here is where the shoe fits, that the mind lets you down sooner or later, but this doesn't." See also pp. 10, 19.
57. See *ibid.*, p. 26: "it's the heart that makes you want to be better than you are. That's what I mean by to write from the heart. That it's the heart that makes you want to be brave when you are afraid that you might be a coward, that wants you to be generous, or wants you to be compassionate when you think that maybe you won't. I think that the intellect, it might say, Well, which is the most profitable—shall I be compassionate or shall I be uncompassionate? Which is the most profitable? Which is the most profitable—shall I be brave or not? But the heart wants always to be better than man is."
58. *Go Down, Moses*, p. 260.
59. *Ibid.*, p. 261.
60. *Ibid.*, p. 297.
61. See *Faulkner in the University*, p. 5: "man will prevail, will endure because he is capable of compassion and honor and pride and endurance." See also p. 133 and "The Stockholm Address" in Frederick J. Hoffman and Olga W. Vickery (eds.), *William Faulkner: Three Decades of Criticism* (East Lansing, Mich.: Michigan State Univ. Press, 1960), pp. 347-48.
62. *A Fable*, p. 203.
63. *The House of the Dead*, p. 7. See *Light in August*, p. 401: "It seems like a man can just about bear anything."
64. See Richard P. Adams, "The Apprenticeship of William Faulkner," *Tulane Studies in English* XII (1962), pp. 134-35.
65. Thomas Mann, *Ausgewählte Erzählungen* (Stockholm: Bermann-Fisher Verlag, 1945), p. 464: "sein Lieblingswort war "Durchhalten" ("Der Tod in Venedig").
66. See *The Mansion*, p. 307: "Just to hate evil is not enough. You—somebody—has got to do something about it."
67. See *The Reivers*, pp. 279, 302.
68. *Collected Stories*, p. 419. See also *Light in August*, p. 372: "He approached the bed. The still invisible occupant snored profoundly. There was a quality of profound and complete surrender in it. Not of exhaustion, but surrender as though he had given over and relinquished completely that grip upon that blending of pride and hope and vanity and fear, that strength to cling to either defeat or victory, which is the I-Am, and the relinquishment of which is usually death."
69. *Faulkner in the University*, p. 78.
70. Charles Anderson, "Faulkner's Moral Center," *Études anglaises* VII, 1 (January, 1954), p. 50.
71. *The Brothers Karamazov*, p. 329.
72. *Ibid.*, pp. 24-25.
73. André Gide, *Dostoievsky* (Paris: Plon, 1923), p. 148.
74. Cited in Jesse Coulson, *Dostoevsky: A Self Portrait* (London: Oxford University Press, 1962), pp. 56-57.
75. *The Diary of a Writer*, p. 460. See also *The Brothers Karamazov*, pp. 612-13.
76. *The Brothers Karamazov*, p. 194. See also pp. 301-02, 335.
77. *Ibid.*, p. 335.

78. *Ibid.*, pp. 627-28.
79. In our opinion, a much stronger debt than that owed to Conrad. See Richard P. Adams, "Apprenticeship," p. 134.
80. See also *Faulkner in the University*, p. 236: "That no man can be an island to himself, that you have a responsibility toward mankind" and p. 242.
81. See *The Reivers*, p. 155.
82. *Intruder in the Dust*, pp. 116-17. See also *Go Down, Moses*, p. 349.
83. *Light in August*, p. 374.
84. *Vocabulaire technique et critique de la philosophie*, André Lalande (ed.), (Paris: Presses Universitaires de France, 1960), p. 562.
85. *The Brothers Karamazov*, p. 24. See also pp. 271, 329.
86. *Ibid.*, p. 260.
87. *Ibid.*, p. 264.
88. *Requiem for a Nun*, p. 278, and *A Fable* p. 278.
89. See Jean Stein "William Faulkner: An Interview," in *William Faulkner: Three Decades of Criticism*, p. 70: "Man is indestructible because of his simple will to freedom."
90. *Mosquitoes*, p. 243.
91. *Go Down, Moses*, p. 281.
92. *Intruder in the Dust*, p. 149.
93. *A Fable*, p. 329.
94. Paul Evdokimov, *Gogol et Dostoïevsky ou la descente aux enfers* (Paris: Desclée de Brouwer, 1961), p. 260.
95. *Ibid..*
96. *The Possessed*, p. 712.
97. See *The House of the Dead*, pp. 102-03: "The man is, as it were, drunk in delirium. It is as though, having once overstepped the sacred limit, he begins to revel in the fact that nothing is sacred to him; as though he had an itching to defy all law and authority at once, and to enjoy the most unbridled liberty, to enjoy the thrill of horror which he cannot help feeling at himself.
98. See *Crime and Punishment*, p. 292: "Freedom and power, and above all, power! Over all trembling creation and all the antheap! . . . That's the goal."
99. *The Idiot*, p. 395.
100. *The Possessed*, p. 114.
101. *Ibid.*, p. 241.
102. *Crime and Punishment*, p. 48.
103. See Jean-Jacques Mayoux, "Le temps et la destinée chez William Faulkner," *La profondeur et le rythme*, (Grenoble-Paris: B. Arthaud, 1968), p. 330.
104. On heredity see: *The Sound and the Fury*, p. 122; on the determinism of the soil and the climate see: *As I Lay Dying*, p. 369, *Collected Stories*, p. 170 ("Dry September"), *Go Down, Moses*, p. 118, *Intruder in the Dust*, p. 151; on the determinism of the past: *The Sound and the Fury*, p. 142, *Light in August*, passim, *Absalom, Absalom!*, pp. 9, 12, *Intruder in the Dust*, p. 12, *Requiem for a Nun*, p. 92, and *Faulkner in the University*, pp. 48, 84.
105. See Joseph Conrad, *Nostromo*, (New York: Dell Publishing Co. 1961), p. 94: "God looked wrathfully at these countries," and p. 378.
106. *The Sound and the Fury and As I Lay Dying*, p. 123.
107. Loic Bouvard, "Conversation with William Faulkner," *Modern Fiction Studies* V, 4 (Winter, 1959-60), p. 362.
108. *Faulkner in the University*, pp. 38-39. See also *The Reivers*, p. 114; "my definition of intelligence: which is ability to cope with the environment: which means to accept environment yet still retain at least something of personal liberty."
109. *The Notebooks for Crime and Punishment*, p. 79.

110. See René Girard, *Dostoïevski. Du double a l'unité*, p. 163: "It is not as a child that I believe in Christ and confess him. My hosanna is passed through the crucible of doubt." (Translated by D.McW.)
111. See Ernest Simmons, *Dostoevsky* (London: Oxford Univ. Press, 1940), p. 344.
112. *The Possessed*, p. 698.
113. *A Raw Youth*, pp. 512-14.
114. *The Possessed*, p. 256.
115. *The Brothers Karamazov*, p. 141.
116. See *ibid.*, pp. 243-44, 253-54, 271-72.
117. See *ibid.*, p. 140.
118. *Ibid.*, p. 585.
119. *The Possessed*, p. 626.
120. *The Diary of a Writer*, pp. 541-42.
121. *Sartoris*, p. 347.
122. *Ibid.*, p. 380.
123. See *Light in August*, p. 461: "He seems to see the churches of the world like a rampart, like one of those barricades of the middleages planted with dead and sharpened stakes, against truth and against that peace in which to sin and be forgiven is the life of man."
124. *Ibid.*, p. 425.
125. *Absalom, Absalom!*, p. 109.
126. See *Faulkner in the University*, p. 86: "the writer must write out of his background. He must write out of what he knows and the Christian legend is part of any Christian's background, especially the background of a country boy, a Southern country boy. My life was passed, my childhood, in a very small Mississippi town, and that was a part of my background. I grew up with that. I assimilated that, took that in without even knowing it. It's just there. It has nothing to do with how much of it I might believe or disbelieve."
127. *Go Down, Moses*, p. 309.
128. See *ibid.*, p. 260.
129. John Faulkner, *My Brother Bill* (London, Victor Gollancz Ltd., 1964), p. 8. See also *Essays, Speeches and Public Letters*, pp. 75, 99-100, 210.
130. *Absalom, Absalom!*, pp. 90, 111.
131. *A Fable*, p. 203.
132. See *Intruder in the Dust*, p. 72: "*Believe? Believe what?*" and p. 126: "to believe truth for no other reason than that it was truth, told by an old man in a fix deserving pity and belief, to someone capable of the pity even when one of them really believed him. 'Which you didn't at first,' his uncle said to him, 'When did you really begin to believe him? . . . . 'I don't know,' he said. Because he didn't know . . . . it seemed to him that he had never really believed Lucas."
133. *Absalom, Absalom!*, pp. 90, 111.
134. *Requiem for a Nun*, p. 273. See also pp. 281-283.
135. *Ibid.*, p. 283.
136. *Ibid.*, p. 163.
137. *Ibid.*, p. 286.
138. *Faulkner at Nagano*, p. 29.
139. *Faulkner in the University*, p. 161.
140. *Ibid.*, p. 203.
141. Loic Bouvard "Conversation with William Faulkner," p. 362.
142. *The Diary of a Writer*, p. 419.
143. "The Stockholm Address" in *William Faulkner: Three Decades of Criticism*, p. 348.
144. *A Fable*, p. 260.

73

145. "The Stockholm Address" *loc. cit.*.
146. *Essays, Speeches and Public Letters,* pp. 83, 182.
147. See *Intruder in the Dust,* p. 202: "Pity and justice and conscience too—that belief in more than the divinity of individual man . . . but in the divinity of his continuity as Man."
148. *A Fable,* p. 352.
149. See *The Diary of a Writer,* pp. 541-42.
150. *The Brothers Karamazov,* p. 69.

III

A CERTAIN CONSERVATISM . . .

Admittedly, the political opinions of a Petersburger or a Muscovite at the end of the imperial regime and those professed in our times by a citizen of Mississippi ought not to have a great deal in common: they are defined in terms of historic and geographical factors so disparate that they defy comparison. However, the attitudes—the relationship of the mind to milieu, the manner of posing problems, the lines of force regulating the judgements or feelings expressed on public life—these attitudes are apt to repeat themselves despite the diversity of circumstances.

The moral vision of the world in our novelists, as absorbing as it is, does not disdain politics: it englobes them.

Faulkner worshiped tradition. He believed in the perenniality of the race because moral and physical virtues are transmitted biologically. In his late novels, heredity which earlier, following Zola's example, was equated with the powerful spell of Fate, is transformed into a process, an ascension. Traditionalism, we repeat, does not mean immobility. Fascinated by time and attached to the earth and life, Faulkner could only conceive existence as growth and action.[1] Seen from a pessimistic perspective, the movement leads to misfortune and death, as in *Sartoris, The Sound and the Fury, Sanctuary, Light in August* and *Absalom, Absalom!*. After this period, Faulkner reverses direction and heads back upstream.[2] From this point on, faith in progress colors the tone, determines the conclusion, supports the message of his stories, and becomes the leitmotif of the public declarations in which he acknowledges improvements in the areas of economics and society.[3] But it is hardly as a materialist that he praises this step forward. Far from it. He misses the South of his childhood, denounces the invasion of nature by a barbarous technology, deplores the substitution of steel for the horse, a symbol of the cavalier spirit.[4] He rejects simultaneously the industrialism of the North, modern economic controls and marxism. Although hostile to economic liberalism of the industrial type,[5] he praises nonetheless the patriarchal and agrarian variety ("The Tall Men", 1941). We are reminded of D. H. Lawrence and also of Conrad, who has one of the heroes of *Nostromo* say: "There is no peace and rest in the development of material interests. They have their law and their justice. But it is founded on expediency, and is inhuman; it is without rectitude, without the continuity and the force that can be found only in a moral principle."[6] Faulknerian progress has as its primary objective the moral good in relation to which physical well-being is only an accidental corollary. To compare the progress of 1950 to the fate of 1930 is also to stress the elevation of freedom. Faulkner's later characters are not obliged to plod after the good; they do not obey, bound hand and foot, the writer's meliorism in the same way that Joe Christmas obeys his defeatism. The movement toward the heights has nothing to do with will-destroying necessity, but depends on an individual choice, on an effort of the soul, which makes itself felt on the level of action. This is precisely the point where politics merges with ethics. Chick Mallison chooses freely and acts practically to save the Negro. Faulkner himself reproaches Isaac McCaslin for limiting himself to turning his back on a game of which he disapproves. It is not sufficient to will the good; one must do it.

there are some people in any time and age that cannot face and cope with the problems. There seem to be three stages: The first says, this is rotten, I'll have no part of it, I will take death first. The second says, This is rotten, I don't like it, I can't do anything about it, but at least I will not participate in it myself, I will go off in a cave or climb a pillar to sit on. The third says, This stinks and I'm going to do something about it. McCaslin is the second. He says, This is bad, and I will withdraw from it. What we need are people who will say, This is bad and I'm going to do something about it, I'm going to change it.[7]

Attachment to tradition or, more accurately, the intuition of the value of certain historical models, the sense of continuity, of organic evolution, of the gradual purification of man, a movement transmitted by a moral elite, the priority of the spiritual over the material, all denote a circumspect reformism as distant from revolutionary iconoclasm as from the absurd and reactionary worship of the past.

Dostoevsky arrived at a rather similar compromise. His political thought, more dynamic, audacious and complex than the American's, knew all of the extremes. His revolt against western liberalism and revolutionaries of every kind after his Siberian exile is well established. But his fervent defense of holy Russia preserves and extols the new and dynamic that is latent within the national past. To be sure, it can be said that he came to hate the scientifically-based progress of the utilitarians, that "necessity of doing good"[8] in which he quite correctly recognized one of the masks of determinism. It is once more because he loves freedom that he castigates and mocks this obsession of his age and its zealots, Chernyshevsky and Buckle in *Notes from the Underground*[9] and Luzhin in *Crime and Punishment*.[10] Man's renovation depends in his eyes neither on self-interest nor reason; it will not be achieved according to the ineluctable logic of a system of abstractions. But is this to say that Dostoevsky rejects all possibility of improvement? Assuredly not. Nothing is more fallacious than political terminology. Razumihin, for instance, does not deny progress: he proposes a definition of it diametrically opposed to materialistic and utopian formulas and thus recalls Faulkner's ideas on organic evolution: "Human nature is not taken into account, it is excluded, it's not supposed to exist! They don't recognize that humanity, developing by a historical living process, will become at last a normal society, but they believe that a social system that has come out of some mathematical brain is going to organize all humanity at once and make it just and sinless in an instant, quicker than any living process!"[11] For the progress rejected by Dostoevsky does not include that form suggested by Faulkner at Stockholm which is primarily derived from the choices and works of the individual, that is to say, by the activation of the eternal "verities of the heart." If there is a dream to which Dostoevsky clings, it is surely of the restoration of the golden age. And whether this coincides with the coming of God's Kingdom on earth, as Zossima thinks,[12] or whether it be imagined in the manner of the pagan paradise envisioned by Versilov,[13] the common denominator remains the passage from isolation— or alienation as we would say today—to love of one's neighbor. Let it be pointed out in passing that it is Versilov's vision inspired by Claude Lorrain's *Acis and Galatea* which most clearly approaches the Faulknerian view of the immortality and moral development of the race:

> "Tomorrow may be my last day," each one would think, looking at the setting sun, "but no matter. I shall die, but all they will remain, and after them their children." And that thought that they will remain, always as loving and as anxious over each other, would replace the thought of meeting beyond the tomb.[14]

As for the parallel passage in the "Biography" of Father Zossima, it accents even more heavily the spiritual change, independent of all positivistic process, from which the millenium will issue.

> Believe me, this dream, as you call it, will come to pass without doubt; it will come, but not now, for every process has its law. It's a spiritual, psychological process. To transform the world, to recreate it afresh, men must turn into another path psychologically. Until you have become really, in actual fact, a brother to every one, brotherhood will not come to pass. . . . You ask when it will come to pass; it will come to pass, but first we have to go through the period of isolation.[15]

Basically, Dostoevsky, a chronicler of a decadent world, simply spiritualizes the revolutionary *élan* of the radicals: he replaces the material upheavals by a spiritual rebirth that is to spring from the Russian nation, particularly the masses who kept its virtues intact. In so doing he both opposed and joined the right and the left. At least, in principle. For does a political program which would abolish the scandals on earth by a conversion still deserve the name? It reduces itself to a kind of ethics or theology. This utopia which subordinates today to tomorrow, time to eternity, the collectivity to individuals, matter to the soul is often nothing more than an excuse for reactionaries. However, in *The*

Brothers Karamazov, love, the leaven of renewal, is translated into action. Alyosha, the "monk", unhesitatingly puts himself at the service of others: he hurries untiringly from one to the other, spreading the benefits of charity around him. In contrast to Sonia Marmeladov, the paragon of passivity, or to McCaslin who, repudiating the established order, withdraws from the world, Alyosha makes the decision advocated by Faulkner. He is one of those who say: "This is bad and I'm going to do something about it, I'm going to change it."[16] From Sonia's inertia to Alyosha's charitable zeal, from Horace Benbow's impotence to Chick Mallison's salutary labors, the two novelists seem to march in step. They join voices at the end of their lives to recommend the creative intervention of well-born souls in the course of history, in their judgement, the proper act for leading humanity towards an ideal type.

It is the belief in progress, the value placed on action, in short, the organic and constructive dynamism professed by the Russian and the American, despite individual nuances, that enables one to situate their political attitude outside any ossified conservatism. Another common conviction, the primacy of the individual, is derived from the characteristics of action. For action here does not emanate from the mob; it is played out either in solitude or in the less austere setting of friendship; it is always seen from the angle of the individual, his choices and difficulties. A unique and therefore isolated mind, entirely absorbed by the problems of the soul, Dostoevsky willingly projects himself into characters escaping any classification: Kirillov or the narrator of *Notes from the Underground.* Faulkner for his part vehemently protests the crushing of man by society[17]: "if I ever become a preacher, it will be to preach against man, individual man, relinquishing into groups, any group. I'm against belonging to anything."[18] If they rise up against parties and doctrines, it is not simply because of their eclecticism, the conflicts to which they are prey and their disgust of ready-made slogans; it is also and above all in the name of individuality stifled by abstractions.

Among the latter, "humanity," as opposed to individuals, disturbs them supremely. It is a collective notion to which one frequently has recourse in industrial societies where mechanization has, in reaction, provoked the growth of communal action groups. Concepts such as "class," "bloc," and "coalition" are, in addition to "humanity," among the most important generalizations; the community splits into employers and employees, exploiters and exploited, and the disequilibrium of the camps encourages the search for a better organization of the state by the application of a variety of theories. In general, the accent falls more and more on the whole to the detriment of its parts as each theory, coalition or class attempts to impose itself on society. Does not the Internationale aspire to become "the human race?" Even liberalism, the obvious advocate of the rights of the individual, indulges in these vague terms which designate everyone and no one. The hatred of slogans in Dostoevsky and Faulkner can, as we shall see, be explained by their historical situation. They both witness the conquest of a feudal—or post feudal—mode of life based on technology, competition and capital; and both were profoundly marked by the ideological struggles which followed. Sometimes they pretend to pay homage to the industrial ethic—its faith in progress, its veneration of action—but in fact they shamelessly appropriate it to themselves. At other times they condemn it without appeal, for example when they explode the myth of philanthropy. Zossima reports the comments of a friend:

> 'I love humanity,' he said, 'but I wonder at myself. The more I love humanity in general, the less I love man in particular. . . . I become hostile to people the moment they come close to me. But it has always happened that the more I detest men individually the more ardent becomes my love for humanity.'[19]

and Ivan Karamazov tells us at the beginning of his long discussion with Alyosha:

> I must make you one confession. . . . I could never understand how one could love one's neighbours. It's just one's neighbours, to my mind, that one can't love, though one might love those at a distance.[20]

One can love one's neighbors in the abstract, or even at a distance, but at close quarters it's almost impossible.[21] One must exercise care in reading Ivan's remarks, however, for he often argues *ex contrario*. Abstract and general "humanity" veils living

reality: it slides, like a mirror infinitely multiplying our own reflection, between us and others and blinds us. For Dostoevsky,
who always embodies his ideas in characters, love of one's neighbor does not begin on the level of concepts but rather on that
of individual existence and the concrete situations in which it
is engaged.[22] This is also what Faulkner teaches when he reproaches Yankees for loving the idea of the Negro rather than
a particular black. "Negro" and "nigger" are for many whites simply labels empty of any human content, cabalistic signs, like "humanity", "Jew", "Kraut" etc., which crystallize love or hatred.

> they [the Northeners] love the Negro in theory, but they don't want much
> to do with him. I've noticed that the Southener, he don't love the Negro
> in quantities, but he will defend some particular Negro—it may be the
> Negro just owes him money—but anyway, whatever the reason is, he will
> defend him.[23]

> We done invented ourselves so many alphabets and rules and recipes that
> we can't see anything else; if what we see can't be fitted to an alphabet
> or a rule, we are lost.[24]

Henry Adams has said, rather disdainfully, that the South did
not know how to handle ideas (but it gets along rather well without them by substituting social instinct.)[25] His judgement, although rather hasty, is perfectly apt in relation to Faulkner, so
different in this area from Dostoevsky. And yet, even the latter,
as experienced as he is in dialectical acrobatics, does not hesitate
for a minute between the airy structures of the mind and the
pulsations of the heart. It matters little to us today that in preferring a moral point of view to the economic and social solutions
of politics the two men were, each in his turn, echoing opinions
found elsewhere among their contemporaries. The manners of
thinking, the resistance to groups and abstractions, and the equally existential value placed on the concrete being, match up point
for point when abstracted from their historical context.

Dostoevsky and Faulkner particularly abominate—the first
more than the second—the great republican motto: "Liberty,
equality and fraternity." While discarding the "humanity" of
party manifestoes, they open themselves to the people met in
the street. Thus the anonymous fraternity of the mobs disappears

before the active love of one's neighbor. Similarly, freedom finds its social and political meaning only after having been tested and tempered by conscience. As for the rather ambiguous ideal of equality, it is replaced by the clearer notion of an elite, a minority to which anyone with the requisite virtues can accede.[26] The movement outlined earlier in relation to pride, vanity and honor is repeated. The existing concepts, far from being discarded, disassociate themselves from the material world and find a home in the soul. Although these concepts are made more specific, individualization and spiritualization in no way restrict their field of application. One has only to reread Myshkin's attack on socialism: "That too, is freedom through violence, that too, is union through sword and blood. 'Don't dare to believe in God, don't dare to have property and individuality, *fraternité ou la mort,* two millions of heads' "[27] and Shigalov's thesis in *The Possessed*: "starting from unlimited freedom, I arrive at unlimited despotism."[28] Such are the baleful effects of fraternity and liberty conceived by "scientific" doctrines. Dostoevsky draws the "true" politics from the Gospel.[29] For his part, Faulkner thinks it vain to impose democracy by force of a decree on a society that is not spiritually prepared to accept it. Gavin Stevens in *Intruder in the Dust*[30] censures that mechanical, abstract and artificial means of governing, that of the North toward the South. The South *farà da sé*. They will achieve the integration that the North would impose immediately one day—but when?—and they will do so by means of growth and expiation.[31] To see history as an organic development and moral purification is to stress the futility of all neatly formulated claims. How can one believe in the ancient promises of "Liberty, equality, fraternity" which are constantly postponed and contradicted by facts.[32] And what value can political freedom have when men do not know what to do with it because of a lack of civic education,[33] and when they hasten to unload it on the first tyrant who comes along.[34] Faulkner, to be sure, does not spare democracy but he does not hate it either. It is for him something quite different from the paradise of the shopkeeper or the blueprints of the philosophers and lawmakers. He sees it only as an objective realizable in the distance, an end rather than a reality and always the fruit of an effort.

Laws are also numbered among the abstractions that are questioned. These literary criminologists, raised outside the Roman legal traditions, do not portray the tribunals with an impartial pen. In general, the condemned are the victims of an error or else they are only accessories or instruments, in any case, trial is a parody, punishment an absurdity. Who is guilty, Goodwin or Popeye? Dmitri Karamazov or Smerdyakov? However, it is the first whom men punish, while the narrator leaves no doubt about their innocence. There is an incompatibility between our concrete and unique acts and the rules that measure them all by the same yardstick. Mindful of the sermons of Christ (Matthew 7: 1-3) and of Zossima[35] Alyosha abstains from judging because "no one can judge a criminal, until he recognizes that he is just such a criminal as the man standing before him, and that he perhaps is more than all men to blame for that crime."[36] The notion of universal guilt renders the juridical decision relative, but the representatives of the law are unaware of this fact. No sooner do they suspect Dmitri than they humiliate him and banish him from society. Justice substitutes abstract relations for individual relations and an administrative code for a living ethic.[37] We find here the old distinction between the letter and the spirit, between legal truth and goodness and moral truth and goodness which in *The Brothers Karamazov* is rewarded only by the good will of the novelist. In *Sanctuary* the law reveals itself equally inept at punishing evil and it is again the novelist who does so. The hero of *Intruder in the Dust*, armed with virtue, does succeed in guiding the law in the way of the good; but *Requiem for a Nun* still opposes the "meek and bloody" cross of Christ and Nancy to the scales, blindfold and sword of Justice.[38]

TEMPLE
. . . all you can say when they ask you to answer to a murder charge is, Not Guilty. Otherwise, they can't even have a trial . . . So they asked her, all correct and formal among the judges and lawyers and bailiffs and jury and the Scales and Sword and the flag and the ghosts of Coke upon Littleton upon Bonaparte and Julius Caesar and all the rest of it, not to mention the eyes and the faces which were getting a moving-picture show for free since they had already paid for it in the taxes, and nobody really listening since there was only one thing she could say. Except that she didn't say it: just raising her head enough to be heard plain—not loud:

just plain—and said 'Guilty, Lord'—like that, disrupting and confounding and dispersing and flinging back two thousand years, the whole edifice of *corpus juris* and rules of evidence we have been working to make stand up by itself ever since Caesar. . . . when they finally explained to her that to say she was not guilty, had nothing to do with truth but only with law, and this time she said it right, Not Guilty, and so then the jury could tell her she lied and everything was all correct again and, as everybody thought, even safe, since now she wouldn't be asked to say anything at all any more.[39]

The same or virtually the same note is sounded in *A Fable*[40] and *The Town*[41]. For in Faulkner, despite the attraction of legal ceremony, morality supplants legality: "There's somewhere the Law stops and just people starts."[42] And it has been said[43] that Gavin Stevens in *Requiem for a Nun* explains rather than judges.

Let us point out finally that abstraction includes, in addition to liberal and radical humanitarianism, the doctrines of the "totalitarian" churches. The matter is too evident to need discussion here.[44]

Whichever way one turns—politics, justice, religion—one finds the same will to seize the world through the concrete, lived, existential experience of the individual. Do Dostoevsky and Faulkner finally refuse any idea of the group? Quite to the contrary. This point of view, in them, blends surprisingly well with the idea of the nation, ambiguous as that term may be. On what facts is the Dostoevskian nation founded? What are its meaning and distinctive traits? *The Idiot, The Possessed, A Raw Youth, The Brothers Karamazov* and the *Diary* treat this question with an unaccustomed abundance of detail. At the base of the Russian nation, Dostoevsky tells us in rhapsodic tones, there is the Russian God, the Christ of the Orthodox Church who proclaims love, freedom, suffering and mercy, that is, the exact opposite of Rome, the seat of violence and authority. The romantic—and German—doctrine of the chosen people thus takes on an exclusively Christian coloring; but substantially the same idea is found in Bonald. "The people," Shatov responds heatedly to Stavrogin when the latter accuses him of annexing God to the nation, "is the body of God. Every people is only a people so long as it has its own god and excludes all other gods on earth irreconcilably; so long as it believes that by its god it will conquer and drive out of the world all other gods."[45] Actually, Shatov wishes to annul the divorce of the spiritual and the temporal by integrating the latter into the former,[46] an idea taken up again in *The Brothers Karamazov* by Father Paissy:

> the Church is not to be transformed into the State. That is Rome and its dream. That is the third temptation of the devil. On the contrary, the state is transformed into the Church, will ascend and become a Church over the whole world—which is the complete opposite of Ultramontanism and Rome, and your interpretation, and is only the glorious destiny ordained for the Orthodox Church.[47]

Stated differently, the political nation serves only religious ends: it even strives to disappear, transforming the state into a theocracy, inaugurating the reign of the Orthodox Church over "the whole world." To see the state give way to the Church is not simply the dream of the slavophile Shatov nor that of a fanatical monk; their creator who, both in his *Diary* (August, 1880)[48] and by means of his characters accuses Europe of having secularized the Word, also desires it. The Russian nation, thus exalted as the city of God, is necessarily the best. "Only one nation is 'god-bearing'," Shatov declares, "that's the Russian people."[49] Like many nationalists, but without their will to power, Dostoevsky refuses coexistence with other nations; he is aware of their struggle and exhorts his to absorb the others. Sublimated, this is the spirit of conquest proper to those who claim membership in a large nation: such a pretension which might possibly be acceptable in extreme circumstances in a Russian, American or a Frenchman would seem ridiculous in a Dutchman or a Hungarian. On the other hand, Dostoevsky's politics are situated within the context of the national struggles which extended, more or less, from the French Revolution to the Treaty of Versailles. Around 1870 panslavism was in fashion in Russia, coloring the writings of the slavophiles and even of Bakunin.[50] But, whatever the influences, historical factors clarify nothing if one fails to take into account the writer's temperament and, particularly, the crises, lacerations and shocks which form the texture of his life. His psychological conflicts naturally are reflected in his international schema. Russia and Europe are opposed to each other like good and evil, God and Satan, the poles of a spiritual dualism. And the sometimes clear-cut, sometimes nuanced opinions of the nationalist are a response to the indecisions of moral choice, for the man who makes evil an instrument of redemption likewise needs the imperialist West, the atheistic, protestant or Catholic West to define his orthodox panacea. The Dostoevskian nation aims, of course, at planetary supremacy. But it desires only to reign over the hearts of the conquered people without enslaving them. Its weapon is love; its battle plan: peaceful conversion,[51] evangelization, apostolization; its ultimate objective: not the hegemony of a group, but the renaissance of man, the Kingdom of (the true) God. The universality claimed by the large nations generally comes from the belief in the absolute excellence of one or more material criteria on which they are allegedly founded: race, language, culture, etc. Thus they practice cosmopolitanism to their own advantage, loving others only insofar as they recognize themselves in them or after subjugating them. For Dostoevsky the Christian foundation of the nation, which includes, among other things, charity and freedom, excludes all dominating selfishness on principle, and the great political theme of his last writings, the harmony of souls under the law of Christ, is in fact a transposition of the radical dream of brotherhood that had earlier cost him a prison term.[52] Versilov affirms already in *A Raw Youth*:

> Only to the Russian, even in our day, has been vouchsafed the capacity to become most of all Russian only when he is most European. . . . Only Russia lives not for herself, but for an idea, and you must admit, my dear, the remarkable fact that for almost the last hundred years Russia has lived absolutely not for herself, but only for the other states of Europe![53]

Obviously, there is another side to this beautiful medallion: Christian love, it seems, stops at the frontiers of Christianity. Dostoevsky built his utopia for the "great Aryan races"[54] and it is unlikely that he would have extended it to Jews and Turks.[55] As personal as his vision is, it respects many of the taboos of his contemporaries. Thus the sublimation of nationalism into evangelical internationalism is not so complete as to rid its nationalism of all of its romantic and imperialist baggage. Dostoevsky prescribes the use of Russian rather than French to the ruling class

since Russian is the language of the masses[56] and, as the slogan
of the age has it, salvation will come from the people. No one
has, according to Dostoevsky, better guarded the ancestral faith
than the muzhik. The latter is thus essential both to the preservation of those qualities which are uniquely Russian and, in light
of the mission assigned to Russia, to the redemption of the
world.[57] Indirectly, by means of its religious origins and implications, nationalism is linked to the primitivism of Rousseau, to
the myth of the noble savage and his cousin, the pure and simple-
hearted peasant. The imitation of Christ is largely equivalent to
the imitation of the common people thus idealized. To go to the
people is not simply to bridge "the great gulf between all educated Russia and the original native springs of Russian life,"[58]
to dam up the excesses of atheism, socialism, and the western
heresies, to recuperate the Russian conscience, virtues and faith,
in short, to save the fatherland. It is also to save Europe by hast-
ening the building of the Christian city: is not Russia the crucible
of nations? Although Dostoevsky exorcises the specter of revolution, although he asks a spiritual lesson of the people and refuses
the aid of their hammers and sickles, the "bucolic" tendencies
in his thought differ less than one might expect from that of the
left.[59]

Before *Absalom, Absalom!* Faulkner gives no hint of convictions of this kind. At the most, he betrays his attachment to his
native land (*Heimatliebe*), a patriotism centered on southern traditions and stimulated by the glorious or painful memories of
Chancellorsville or Appomattox. Being totally absorbed by decadence, he could scarcely conceive a passion as conquering or a
doctrine as militant as nationalism. However, the diagnosis of
a local sickness in *Absalom, Absalom!* leads him to it without
his suspecting it. While going back to the origins of tradition
and putting the past on trial, he hazards several conjectures about
the future, as much about America as about the South. One notices, for instance, that Quentin Compson succeeds in reconstructing the story of Sutpen only while engaged in a dialogue with
his Canadian friend Shreve. Can one infer that the South must
appeal for aid from its Northern brothers[60] to solve its problems?
The idea should not be rejected. Moreover on the last page

Shreve predicts the inevitable multiplication of half-breeds and the conquest of Western civilization by the mulatto. Stupen, vanquished by racial prejudice, leaves no white descendants; the only member of his house to survive in 1910 is his great-grandson Jim Bond, and this man of mixed blood is also the only victor in the novel—because he is alive. According to Shreve the future belongs to the mulatto—read also: to the black—because he can stand fast against all of the storms of fortune:

> I think that in time the Jim Bonds are going to conquer the western hemisphere. Of course it won't quite be in our time and of course as they spread toward the poles they will bleach out again like the rabbits and the birds do, so they won't show up so sharp against the snow. But it will still be Jim Bond; and so in a few thousand years, I who regard you will also have sprung from the loins of African kings.[61]

The epilogue of *Absalom, Absalom!* clashes with the narrators' lamentations over the downfall of the hero. The prophetic tone, the perspective opened on the future, the promise of survival, although disappointing, perhaps, for the hopes of the whites, marks a turning point. Faulkner's submission to the seduction of ideas, his desire to meditate on, rather than describe, history is also to be inferred from the unusual confrontation of barbarous, Anglo-Saxon, puritan Yoknapatawpha and the Catholic and Latin refinements of New Orleans. The concept of the nation, however, only enters the picture with *Go Down, Moses.* Faulkner, like so many others, describes America—in this case, the Mississippi delta[62]—as a racial melting pot. The fourth chapter of "The Bear" specifies in fact that the white man had, in discovering America after so many centuries of pillaging, usurpation and fratricidal struggle over the land, obtained a second chance from God[63] to found a nation on the "verities" of the heart: "humility and pity and sufferance and pride of one to another."[64] It matters little at this stage that the land, given in order that these truths might reign, has been defiled from the very beginning by the vices of the Old World or that whites have driven off the Indians, enslaved the blacks, and chained themselves to the very soil they had seized: Faulkner's nation draws the whole of its support from a spiritual reality, a dream less imbued with religious fervor than in Dostoevsky, to be sure, but also harking back to a biblical context. For one as for the other, the nation is a goal to be sought, rather than an observable fact, an ethical norm before being a political entity. However, Faulkner, to whom all dreams of a universal crusade remain foreign, is interested in the idea of the nation only in relation to the United States and insofar as it is tied to the wound of the South: interracial relations. His weakness —somewhat mitigated, to be sure[65]—for the "Southern" nation often wins out over his adherence to the American nation, although during the period from 1948 (*Intruder in the Dust*) to the Charlottesville discussions (1957-58) his attitude was perhaps modified. Faulkner is convinced that the South possesses a personality distinct from that of the North. In his rambling monologues in *Intruder in the Dust*, Gavin Stevens underlines its homogeneity, a quality he denies to the other regions of the United States,[66] which flows essentially from the adherence to the same values. Faulkner's South is obviously less a territory than a spiritual vision, "an emotional idea."[67] Is there any other refuge than the immaterial for a nation which a military defeat and the assaults of technology have deprived of tangible foundations? The defeat had prevented the Southern "nation" from materializing into a State. It had consecrated the supremacy of federal power and facilitated the progress of industrialization, which tended to destroy local particularities and the "agrarian" heritage of the South, in favor of a civilization symbolized by the radio, the automobile and social legislation. Faulkner finds the innermost character of the South in its principle of freedom.[68] It is the ideal nation in contrast with the United States, the Leviathan of the Agrarians, a real but impure nation riddled with materialism: love of money,[69] atrophy of the soul,[70] the cult of the successful shopkeeper. However, Faulkner chastises only out of love as "Shall Not Perish" (1943) shows. Writing the history of Yoknapatawpha in *Requiem for a Nun*, he sees in it an exemplary microcosm, the archetype of Western expansion, and the aspiration to individual freedom, reserved until then to one region, becomes an attribute of all regions.[71] The feeling of alienation in relation to the North gives way to solidarity, to a sense of the American unity—"One nation . . . ; one universe, one cosmos: contained in one America"[72]—born out of the memory of common suffering and the standardization of modes of life under the sign of the machine.[73] The North-South contrast underscored in *Intruder in the Dust* begins to blur several years later. Why? Because the problem is posed differently. The sharp criticism, the diatribes directed against the "aberrant" humanitarianism of the North on the question of racial integration, a burning question where Mississippi was involved, were no longer appropriate when it was a matter of celebrating the saving power of suffering. Faulkner's "anti-americanism" is tempered in passing from the local to the universal, from a situation conditioned by geographical factors to a strictly ethical problem. Nancy Mannigoe's negritude in no way modifies the significance of her act, while that of Lucas Beauchamp constitutes the mainspring of the action. One finds the same moderation in the lecturer at the University of Virginia for whom America is a great country, hostile to servitude but inspired by doubtful values.[74] The American nation that he calls for is a South on a grand scale, a kingdom of the soul where the spirit takes precedence over matter and where political freedom depends on moral freedom. Such is indeed the *idea* that supports the southern "homogeneity" which, Gavin Stevens tells us in a passage which evokes *The Diary of a Writer* (August, 1880),[75] produces all that is good and durable in a people: literature, art, science, the form of government and national character.[76] It is clear that the difference with Dostoevsky is less a matter of quality than of quantity. In spite of the fact that Faulkner did not share the enthusiastic messianism of the Russian, the essence of the nation remains the same in both. The parallel can be pursued further. Dostoevsky, in the final analysis, does not fail to situate the city of Christ on a terrestrial base, the redemption of the universe being achieved by a return to the muzhik. Faulkner is not far from this line of reasoning. Blacks and whites, despite injustices, are inextricably mixed[77] in the South, in "his" South: tied in many cases by blood and the memories of childhood and always by the expiation of the sin committed by the one against the others.[78] It is because he formulates the political problems of slavery and integration in moral terms that Faulkner wishes to leave the initiative of freeing the blacks to the whites. Coming from the

North, imposed by law, it would not coincide with the catharsis that he anticipates and which alone can cure the South: freedom will be paternalistic, granted by the autochthons, the ruling class, the whites, under the pressure of their conscience or it will not be.[79] To summarize, the Southern personality is composed of traits borrowed from two races, and in this combination, the contribution of the blacks—a class still oppressed—assumes capital importance. While the blacks can profit from the white heritage, for example from the *ethos* of the gentleman, they, on the other hand, furnish the nation its substrata, its perenniality, its aptitude to suffer and to conquer suffering. For Faulkner, the descendants of Ham are related to the Earth and to Woman; the Gaea of the ancients, a symbol of eternal fecundity, is revived among them: they "preserve the world"[80] Raskolnikov would say.[81] In exchange for giving them their freedom, the whites will gain their robustness and—who knows—perhaps even the Negro's pure and simple mores, his love of the household gods who contrast with the tinsel of industrial America:

> (the black) who has a better homogeneity than we have and proved it by finding himself roots into the land where he had actually to displace white men to put them down: because he had patience even when he didn't have hope, the long view even when there was nothing to see at the end of it, not even just the will but the desire to endure because he loved the old few simple things which no one wanted to take from him: not an automobile nor flash clothes nor his picture in the paper but a little music (his own), a hearth, not his child but any child, a God a heaven which a man may avail himself a little of at any time without having to wait to die, a little earth for his own sweat to fall on among his own green shoots and plants. We—he and us—should confederate: swap him the rest of the economic and political and cultural privileges which are his right, for the reversion of his capacity to wait and endure and survive. Then we would prevail; together we would dominate the United States.[82]

The gain is certain, history proves it: "the whole chronicle of man's immortality is in the suffering he has endured, his struggle toward the stars in the stepping-stones of his expiations."[83] The Southern nation, exactly like the Russian, is erected on the spiritual resources of the disinherited: the negro plays a role similar to that of the Dostoevskian peasant, but his crown does not glow with the same intensity. Dostoevsky, more passionate on this question, embellishes his muzhik almost to the point of making him a paragon;[84] there is none of this in Faulkner's black, whom the Christian "school" of suffering[85] has not sanctified to the same degree. The white patrician, in offering his hand to his former slaves, does not display such a generous altruism: he would never mistake himself for one of them. One may as well say that the Russian muzhik corresponds simultaneously to the Negro and his master, the Southern gentleman.

The sin expiated by the South would seem to be a double offense against God, for the white oppresses creation, the land, as much as its creatures. To enslave the black and to seize the soil is fundamentally the same thing. Faulkner, although a self-proclaimed farmer in his latter years, always protested against private property. In *Soldiers' Pay* the fact of possession is described—by a clown and in passing, but that does not matter— as a curse and slavery.[86] In *Absalom, Absalom!* the idea becomes clearer. Thomas Sutpen comes from the frontier where the soil, still intact, belongs to everyone; his innocence is, among other things, his ignorance of private property and the social hierarchy it supports: "he didn't even know there was a country all divided and fixed and neat with people living on it all divided and fixed and neat because of what color their skins happened to be and what they happened to own."[87] Sutpen is an unscrupulous climber who repudiates the pioneer's egalitarian credo to perpetrate, with a neophyte's zeal, the crimes of the South. *The Unvanquished* and then *Go Down, Moses* assert that the earth, a public domain, does not belong to individuals; quite the contrary, it is man who must put himself at her service, and the earth tolerates his presence only insofar as he respects her:[88] God wished it thus.[89] Little by little and culminating in *Requiem for a Nun*, a philosophy of American history, based on the Bible, Rousseauism and the pioneer spirit, is sketched. In the beginning there was the virgin land, created at the dawning of the sixth day, which God saw as "good." Then came man placed by God in nature like Adam in the Garden of Eden: to till it and keep it in his name. This is the precolumbian period of America, the origins of a lost paradise whose legitimate guardians were the Indians, although, Faulkner points out, they held it in common.[90] Private property appears only with the whites for whom God had planned a second chance after the fiasco of the Old World. But the fall does not occur immediately, a fact that weakens the theory that the whites perverted the entire continent simply by landing.[91] Between the innocence of the early ages and the pestilence of civilization—that is: the usurpation and parcelling of the soil as well as the institution of slavery—the novelist seems to grant the immigrants a certain respite, at least to the rude settlers of the frontier who, lost in the immensity of the land, were able to conciliate nature and society: "these were frontier, pioneer times, when personal liberty and freedom were almost a physical condition like fire or flood."[92] Misfortune strikes the South as soon as the conquest is organized, when the freedom of the great wild spaces gives way to fences, to the marking out of plantations and to the color bar. The white race has botched its chance. America is the theater of its second failure, of a new fall that must be expiated. But the earth herself remains good, even impeccable; she is the mother of man[93] and the one who loves her and is suckled by her, though he be fallen, is stronger and happier: Emmy in *Soldiers' Pay*, Lena Grove in *Light in August*. The nostalgia for the primitive earth, the moral and esthetic protest against the cult of Mammon and the machine[94] reflect on the affective level the ideal of liberty of Faulkner's final period.

To see nature, lovely, good and unfettered, ravaged in a few years by the cupidity of man is, we have been told,[95] an experience unknown in Europe. Perhaps. But the rhythm of degradation matters less than its effects and, above all, the opposition of reality with the dream, of the present with the past. Kraft in *A Raw Youth* also denounces the deforestation of the country—"they are stripping Russia of her forests . . . turning the country into a waste"[96]—and Dostoevsky, in a more mystical key than Faulkner, intones the canticle of the earth, the Magna Mater who suffers from a fall in which she has not participated.[97] Marya Timopheievna Lebyadkin, the idiot married by Stavrogin, introduces this theme—liturgical as Evdokimov shows[89]—at the beginning of *The Possessed*:

> God and nature are just the same thing. . . . the mother of God is the great mother—damp earth, and therein lies great joy for men. And every earthly woe and every earthly tear is a joy for us; and when you water the earth and your tears are a foot deep, you will rejoice at everything at

once, and your sorrow will be no more, such is the prophecy. . . . Since then when I bow down to the ground at my prayers, I've taken to kissing the earth. I kiss it and weep.[99]

Taken up a little later by Shatov,[100] it is echoed again at the end: "the man who loses connection with his country loses his gods, that is, all his aims."[101] The prostrations of Raskolnikov, who soiled the earth in killing and the unexpected gesture of Alyosha Karamazov in "Cana of Galilee" is best explained in the light of these extracts. Returned to the monastery after the death of Zossima, surmounting the disarray into which his faith had been thrown by this death and perhaps remembering Dmitri's Schillerian quotation:

> Dass der Mensch zum Menschen werde,
> Stift' er einen ew'gen Bund
> Gläubig mit der frommen Erde,
> Seinem mütterlichen Grund . . .
> ("Das Eleusische Fest")

Alyosha in a dream once again sees his beloved master at the table of Christ and is reminded by him of the terrible majesty of the Lord, equal to that of the sun, and his infinite mercy. God became man out of love for his creatures; he not only created the earth: he wished to walk it and suffer as we do. The earth is thus doubly holy:

> The silence of earth seemed to melt into the silence of the heavens. The mystery of earth was one with that of the stars. . . .
> Alyosha stood, gazed, and suddenly threw himself down on the earth. He did not know why he embraced it. He could not have told why he longed so irresistibly to kiss it, to kiss it at all. But he kissed it weeping, sobbing and watering it with his tears, and vowed passionately to love it, to love it for ever and ever.[102]

This moment of mystic communion mediated by the earth, a crisis which will fortify Alyosha through the rest of his life, joins, in the same ecstatic outpouring, Schiller's enthusiasm, the Christian cult of suffering and romantic primitivism, the *agape* and the love of *physis*, the foster Mother of the humble peasant renounced by the rationalists. According to *The Diary of a Writer* (July-

94

August, 1876), the earth and the people, the earth and the political and social order, form an indissoluble whole; even spiritual values depend on the land and the system of land tenure.[103] But there still exist in Russia agrarian communities where the use or ownership of the land is collective: the *obscina* which Dostoevsky, and many slavophiles and socialists cite as an example. In a passage originally expurgated by the czarist censor, he, like the slavophiles and socialists, sees in them the seeds of the renewal awaited during this period, and he attacks the unequal distribution of the land, the original sin which he believed to be perhaps the source of all the ills that beset humanity.[104] From this point to the renunciation of the very principle of property is only a step which Dostoevsky easily makes when he sketches the idyllic spectacle of a Garden belonging to everyone, in contrast with the monstrous cities of industrial and bourgeois civilization. The passage deserves quotation *in extenso* since it curiously ties the ancient pastoral dreams to the marxist theories of class struggle:

> Mankind will be regenerated in the Garden, and the Garden will restore it—such is the formula. You see how all this happened: at first, there were castles, and beside them—mud huts. The barons lived in the castles —and the vassals, in the mud huts. Thereupon the bourgeoisie began to rise behind fenced towns—slowly, on a microscopic scale. Meanwhile, the castles came to an end, and the kings' capitals came into existence—big cities with kings' palaces and court hotels; this has lasted up to our century. In our century a dreadful revolution took place, and the bourgeoisie came out victorious. With the bourgeoisie there arose horrible cities which were never even dreamed of. Cities, such as sprang up in the Nineteenth Century, mankind had never seen before. These are cities with crystal palaces, with international exhibitions, banks, budgets, polluted rivers, railway platforms, with all kinds of associations—and, around them, factories and mills. At present people are awaiting the third phase: the bourgeoisie will expire and a regenerated mankind will come in its wake. It will distribute the land among communes, and will start living in the Garden. 'It will be regenerated in the Garden, and the Garden will restore it.' Thus—castles, cities and the Garden.[105]

It is significant that it is in "The Dream of a Strange Man," under the cover of a "fantasy" (*Diary*, April, 1877), that the magazine writer risks overtly describing the distinction of mine and yours and slavery as alienation and imputes them to man's fallen nature.[106]

It is all highly speculative, as Dostoevsky himself was well aware. As for Faulkner, he scarcely dares imagine the healing of the South; in any case it is not about tomorrow's happiness that he talks. But dreams, that some have called empty, are full of meaning and therein the two men differ significantly. For the Russian, although the fall is irreversible, suffering humanity trudges between two paradises: the one he lost and the millenium. Fascinated by his utopia, Dostoevsky continues to hope where Faulkner more or less resigns himself to the fate of an exile and gives up building castles in the air. This does not prevent them both from believing in the excellence of nature as God created it and in the sin committed by man when he divided it up. In both cases, the ugliness of technology is stigmatized, the agrarian tradition is honored, private property and social injustice are condemned. On this point certain pages of *The Unvanquished* and the *Diary*, "The Bear" and *A Raw Youth* might even be called communist. Our authors are, moreover, aware of this:

> Father said they (Uncle Buck and Buddy) were ahead of their time; he said they not only possessed, but put into practice, ideas about social relationships that maybe fifty years after they were both dead people would have a name for. These ideas were about land. They believed that land did not belong to people but that people belonged to the land.[107]

When Makar, the wanderer of *A Raw Youth*, paints a seductive portrait of a world where love of one's neighbor will have replaced that of money:

> Now we gather and have not enough and squander senselessly, but then there will be no orphans or beggars, for all will be my people, all will be akin. I have gained all, I have bought all, every one. . . . Then thou wilt attain wisdom, not from books alone, but wilt be face to face with God Himself, and the earth shine more brightly than the sun, and there shall be no more sorrow nor sighing, nothing but one priceless Paradise,[108]

the young Dolgoruky exclaims: "Why, it's communism, absolute communism, you're preaching!"[109] Let us add: a spiritualistic communism at the antipodes of Marx, Engels and Lenin and which, in both cases, calls as witness Christ's answer to the young rich man: "sell all that you have, give it to the poor, and you will have riches in heaven."[110]

NOTES TO CHAPTER III

1. See *The Mansion*, unnumbered page after table of contents: "Since the author likes to believe, hopes that his entire life's work is a part of a living literature, and since "living" is motion, and "motion" is change and alternation and therefore the only alternative to motion is unmotion, stasis, death."

2. See *Faulkner in the University*, p. 5: "I said only that man will prevail and will—in order to prevail he has got to . . . (try to be good). As to whether he will stay on the earth long enough to attain ultimate goodness, nobody knows. But he does improve, since the only alternative to progress is death." See also pp. 6, 98, 151.

3. See *ibid.*, pp. 5-6: "And we can see the little children don't have to work, a merchant can't sell you poisoned food. They are minor improvements but they are improvements. Nobody is hanged for stealing bread any more. People are not put in jail for debt." See also p. 6, 98, 151.

4. See *Sartoris*, pp. 3, 113-14; *Light in August*, p. 70, and *Go Down, Moses*, pp. 340-41.

5. See *The Wild Palms*, pp. 187-88.

6. Joseph Conrad, *Nostromo* (New York: Dell Publishing Co., 1961), pp. 435-36.

7. *Faulkner in the University*, pp. 245-46. See also in the remark about Ratliff, one of the heroes of *The Hamlet*, *The Town* and *The Mansion*, p. 253: "he's in favor of change, because it is motion and it's the world as he knows it, and he's never one to say, I wish I had been born a hundred years ago, or I'm sorry I was born now and couldn't have put it off a hundred years. Ratliff will take what's now and do the best he can with it." See the author's remarks quoted by Frederick J. Hoffman: *William Faulkner* (New York: Twayne Publishers, Inc., 1961), p. 98: "Well, I think a man ought to do more than just repudiate. He should have been more affirmative instead of shunning people."

8. *White Nights and Other Stories* ("Notes from the Underground"), pp. 64-65.

9. *Ibid.*, pp. 67-68.

10. *Crime and Punishment*, pp. 133-34.

11. *Ibid.*, p. 227.

12. *The Brothers Karamazov*, pp. 316-18.

13. *A Raw Youth*, pp. 513-14.

14. *Ibid.*.

15. *The Brothers Karamazov*, p. 317.

16. See *The Diary of a Writer*, p. 622.

17. See *Faulkner in the University*, p. 33.

18. *Ibid.*, p. 269. See also p. 100 and *Essays, Speeches and Public Letters*, p. 198.

19. *The Brothers Karamazov*, p. 56.

20. *Ibid.*, p. 245.

21. *Ibid.*, p. 246.

22. See Dmitri Chizhevsky, "The Theme of the Double in Dostoevsky" in *Dostoevsky* (ed.) René Wellek (Englewood Cliffs, N. J.: Prentice Hall, 1962), pp. 126-27.

23. *Faulkner in the University*, p. 220. See also *Intruder in the Dust*, pp. 22, 48-49, and John Faulkner, *My Brother, Bill* (London: Victor Gollancz Ltd., 1964), pp. 51-52.
24. *Collected Stories*, p. 59. ("The Tall Man").
25. Quoted by Clement Eaton, *The Growth of Southern Civilization 1790-1860* (London: Hamish and Hamilton, 1961), pp. 295-96.
26. See *Essays, Speeches and Public Lectures*, p. 105: "there is no such thing as equality *per se*, but only equality *to*: equal right and opportunity to make the best one can of one's life within one's capacity and capability, without fear of injustice or oppression or violence."
27. *The Idiot*, p. 519.
28. *The Possessed*, p. 409.
29. *The Diary of a Writer*, pp. 622-24. Also *The Brothers Karamazov*, p. 82.
30. See *Intruder in the Dust*, p. 155: "Someday Lucas Beauchamp can shoot a white man in the back with the same impunity to lynch—rope or gasoline as a white man; in time he will vote anywhen and anywhere a white man can . . . But it won't be next Tuesday. Yet people in the North believe it can be compelled even into next Monday by the simple ratification by votes of a printed paragraph."
31. See *ibid.*, p. 204. See also *Essays, Speeches and Public Letters*, p. 86.
32. See *Go Down, Moses*, p. 279: " 'We are seeing a new era, an era dedicated, as our founders intended it, to freedom, liberty, and equality for all, to which this country will be the new Canaan—' . . . What corner of Canaan is this?"
33. See *ibid.*, p. 289.
34. See *Intruder in the Dust*, p. 149.
35. See *The Brothers Karamazov*, pp. 336-37.
36. *Ibid.*, p. 336.
37. See *ibid.*, p. 511 and following. See also p. 699: "the lawyers . . . were more interested in the legal than in the moral aspects of the case."
38. *Requiem for a Nun*, p. 105.
39. *Ibid.*, pp. 199-200.
40. *A Fable*, p. 164.
41. See *The Town*, p. 175.
42. *The Reivers*, p. 243.
43. See Frederick J. Hoffman: *William Faulkner* (New York: Twayne Publishers, Inc., 1961), p. 108.
44. See V. V. Zenkovsky, "Dostoevsky's Religious and Philosophical views," in *Dostoevsky* ed. René Wellek, p. 138, and *Faulkner in the University*, p. 73.
45. *The Possessed*, p. 255. See also p. 254.
46. See *ibid.*, p. 255: "I raise the people to God."
47. *The Brothers Karamazov*, p. 66. See also p. 62.
48. *The Diary of a Writer*, p. 1003.
49. *The Possessed*, p. 255.
50. See Ettore Lo Gatto, *Storia della Russia* (Firenze: G. C. Sansoni, 1946), p. 615.
51. See *The Idiot*, pp. 520-21: "Show him (the Russian) the whole of humanity, rising again, and renewed by Russian thought alone, perhaps by the Russian God and Christ, and you will see into what a mighty and truthful, what a wise and gentle giant he will grow, before the eyes of the astounded world, astounded and dismayed, because it expects of us nothing but the sword, nothing but the sword and violence, because, judging us by themselves, the other peoples cannot picture us free from barbarism."
52. See *The Diary of a Writer*, pp. 961-62, 979-80. See also Ernest J. Simmons, *Dostoevsky* (London: Oxford U. Press, 1940), pp. 288-89; Irving

A CERTAIN CONSERVATISM . . .

Howe, "Dostoevsky: The Politics of Salvation" in *Dostoevsky* ed. René Wellek, pp. 56-57.
53. *A Raw Youth*, pp. 511-12.
54. *The Diary of a Writer*, p. 979.
55. See Irving Howe, *op. cit.*, p. 55.
56. See *The Diary of a Writer*, pp. 399-400.
57. See *The Brothers Karamazov*, pp. 330-31.
58. "Letter to Grand Duke Alexander Alexandrovitch," in Jesse Coulson, ed., *Dostoevsky: A Self Portrait* (London: Oxford Univ. Press, 1962), p. 202.
59. See Ernest J. Simmons, *op. cit.*, pp. 298-99.
60. See *Absalom, Absalom!*, pp. 258, 294, 334.
61. *Ibid.*, p. 378.
62. See *Go Down, Moses*, p. 364: "This Delta. *This land . . . where . . . Chinese and African and Aryan and Jew, all breed and spawn together until no man has time to say which one is which nor cares.*"
63. See Frederick J. Hoffman *op. cit.*, p. 98. See also William R. Taylor, *Cavalier and Yankee* (Garden City, N. Y.: Doubleday & Co., 1963), p. 238.
64. *Go Down, Moses*, p. 259.
65. See *Essays, Speeches and Public Letters*, p. 36.
66. See *Intruder in the Dust*, p. 153: "we alone in the United States . . . are a homogenous people. I mean the only one of any size."
67. *Ibid.*, p. 152.
68. See *ibid.*, pp. 153-54: "We are defending not actually our politics or beliefs or even our way of life, but simply our homogeneity from a federal government to which in simple desperation the rest of this country has had to surrender voluntarily more and more of its personal and private liberty in order to continue to afford the United States. . . . That's why we must resist the North: not just to preserve ourselves nor even the two of us as one to remain one nation because that will be the inescapable by-product of what we will preserve: which is the very thing that three generations ago we lost a bloody war in our own back yards so that it remain intact: the postulate that Sambo is a human being living in a free country and hence must be free. That's what we are really defending: the privilege of setting him free ourselves."
69. See *ibid.*, p. 156.
70. See *ibid.*, pp. 202, 238-39.
71. See *Requiem for a Nun*, p. 10: "the United States, the power and the will to liberty, owing liegence to no man, bringing even that still almost pathless wilderness the thin peremptory voice of the nation which had wrenched its freedom from one of the most powerful peoples on earth and then again within the same lifespan successfully defended it." See also *Essays, Speeches and Public Letters*, pp. 62, 127-29.
72. *Ibid.*, pp. 246-47.
73. See *ibid.*, pp. 244-45.
74. See *Faulkner in the University*, pp. 161-62.
75. *The Diary of a Writer*, pp. 1000-1001.
76. *Intruder in the Dust*, p. 154.
77. See *ibid.*, pp. 12, 194.
78. See *ibid.*, p. 210: "one expiation since expiation must surely be."
79. See *ibid.*, p. 154. See also *Faulkner in the University*, pp. 79-80, 210, 211: "So we alone can teach the Negro the responsibility of personal morality and rectitude . . . What he must learn are the hard things—self-restraint, honesty, dependability, purity; to act not even as well as just any white man, but to act as well as the best of white men."
80. *Crime and Punishment*, p. 231.
81. See *Absalom, Absalom!*, pp. 116, 200.
82. *Intruder in the Dust*, pp. 155-56.

83. *Ibid.*, pp. 154-55.
84. See *The Diary of a Writer*, pp. 203, 945.
85. *Ibid.*, p. 983.
86. See *Soldiers' Pay*, p. 60.
87. *Absalom, Absalom!*, p. 221. See also p. 220.
88. See *The Unvanquished*, p. 54: "They believed that land did not belong to people but that people belonged to land and that the earth would permit them to live on and out of it and use it only so long as they behaved and that if they did not behave right, it would shake them off just like a dog getting rid of fleas."
89. See *Go Down, Moses*, p. 257: "He made the earth first and peopled it with dumb creatures, and then He created man to be his overseer on the earth and the animals on it in His name, not to hold for himself and his descendants inviolable title for ever, generation after generation, to the oblongs and squares of the earth, but to hold the earth mutual and intact in the communal anonymity of brotherhood, and all the fee He asked was pity and humility and sufferance and endurance and the sweat of his face for bread."
90. See *Faulkner in the University*, p. 43.
91. See *Go Down, Moses*, p. 259.
92. *Requiem for a Nun*, p. 6.
93. See *Collected Stories*, p. 900 ("Carcassonne") and *A Fable*, p. 404.
94. See *Faulkner in the University*, p. 277: "if all the destruction of the wilderness does is to give more people more automobiles just to ride around in, then the wilderness was better."
95. See Ursula Brumm, "Wilderness and Civilization: A Note on William Faulkner," *William Faulkner: Three Decades of Criticism*, ed. Frederick J. Hoffman and Olga W. Vickery (East Lansing, Mich.: Michigan State U. Press, 1960), p. 130.
96. *A Raw Youth*, p. 65.
97. See Reinhard Lauth, *Die Philosophie Dostojewskis* (München: R. Piper Verlag, 1950), p. 473.
98. See Paul Evdokimov *Gogol et Dostoïevsky ou la descente aux enfers* (n. p.: Desclée De Brouwer, 1961), p. 217.
99. *The Possessed*, p. 144.
100. See *ibid.*, p. 258: "Kiss the earth, water it with your tears, pray for forgiveness."
101. *Ibid.*, p. 686.
102. *The Brothers Karamazov*, pp. 380-81. See also *The Diary of a Writer*, p. 418.
103. See *ibid.*, pp. 418-420.
104. See *ibid.*, p. 416.
105. *Ibid.*, pp. 417-18.
106. See *ibid.*, pp. 526-27.
107. *The Unvanquished*, p. 54.
108. *A Raw Youth*, p. 419.
109. *Ibid.*
110. Matthew 19: 21;Mark 10: 21; Luke 18: 21. See *A Raw Youth*, p. 419,

100

IV

QUESTIONING THE NOVELISTIC TRADITION

Let us not look for a realistic and effective
political program from these novelists.
Rather let us question them about something they know: their
craft. In this area, the similarities in procedures and situations
are quite intriguing.

Dostoevsky does not usually pass for a skilled artisan. Ideas,
portraits, conflicts, sensational scenes follow one another in an
avalanche, and it is all so rich. so unexpected that the architecture escapes us. Most critics still forget that the best way to define
an artist's thought is to approach it on the formal level: plot structure, narrative point of view, psychological methods, etc. And
it is only very recently that the traditional opinion according to
which Dostoevsky's philosophy, so modern in many ways, was
hidden under the banal exterior of the serialized novel, has been
seriously questioned. It might, at first glance, seem strange to
ask what Faulkner, a renovator of the narrative art, could have
learned reading such apparently traditional stories. This is, however, precisely the question to pose, all the more because Faulkner
saw in Dostoevsky an extraordinary "craftsman."[1]

Rather than recounting the events himself, Faulkner willingly
turns this job over to one of his characters. Thus the plot, situated
most often in the past, is revealed through a narrator who recon-
structs it *a posteriori*, based either on his own experience or on
what others have told him. With a few exceptions, the author
makes neither himself nor the reader a direct witness of the facts.
He is no omniscient demiurge—the chorus of a tragedy—but a

101

simple reporter; and we, separated from the events by the voice which retraces them, listen to time past: we hear only the story, or the story of a story, recited after the fact. We will never know if things took place as we are told: the subjectivity of the story-teller or storytellers, the distance in time, all cause us to doubt the veracity of the account. In *Sartoris*, it is the old woman, Virginia Du Pre who, singing—more than a half-century afterwards—the fabulous exploits of warriors, reactivates through this ritual the primordial time of myth. But let us rather reread Faulkner's commentary:

> It was she who told them of the manner of Bayard Sartoris' death prior to the second battle of Manassas. She had told the story many times since (at eighty she still told it, on occasions usually inopportune) and as she grew older the tale itself grew richer and richer, taking on a mellow splendor like wine; until what had been a hare-brained prank of two heedless and reckless boys wild with their own youth had become a gallant and finely tragical focal point to which the history of the race had been raised from out the old miasmic swamps of spiritual sloth by two angels valiantly fallen and strayed, altering the course of human events and purging the souls of men.[2]

Absalom, Absalom! is a veritable historical study consisting of oral declarations which are synthesized in the course of the spoken reconstructions, discussions and dialogues recorded by the author. Published in 1936, the novel takes place in 1910, just before the suicide of Quentin Compson described in *The Sound and the Fury* (1929); but the stories dealing with Sutpen encompass the whole of the nineteenth century, such that they fit one inside the other. For example, the stories told by Sutpen about his youth to Quentin's grandfather, who repeated them to Quentin, who repeats them to Shreve are passed down by word of mouth and culminate in the resuscitation of the horrors and splendors of the old South a hundred years later amidst the snows of Massachusetts. But what certitude do they offer? Faulkner's last book, *The Reivers* (1962), revealingly subtitled "A Reminiscence," relates a story which begins with these words: "Grandfather said. . . ." The procedure recalls the memories and legends Faulkner had heard in his childhood[3] and, on the literary level, the American tradition of the storyteller which inspired Mark Twain in the preceding century. It also reminds us of the sophisticated manner of Joseph Conrad who had the story of *Lord Jim* told by the narrator Marlow. However, these retrospective narratives, told by the actors, eye witnesses or hearers of the drama, are common occurrences in *The Brothers Karamazov*. Here it is Dmitri who reports his antecedents to Alyosha ("The Confession of a Passionate Heart," III, 4 and 5); there, Ivan who gives the same "listener" the first recitation of the poem of "The Grand Inquisitor" (V,5). But the best specimens are encountered in Book VI entitled "The Russian Monk." At this point the colorless "I" who is writing—*The Brothers Karamazov* is an *Ich-Erzählung*—interrupts himself to incorporate in his account the manuscript in which Alyosha recorded rather freely, it seems, the last conversation of Father Zossima. It is a long two-part allocution: an autobiography (VI,2) followed by a sermon (VI,3). The first is an oral narration—and a flashback—of a quite traditional sort. Zossima expatiates on his youth, the death of his brother Markel, his career as an officer, his near duel, and also on a "mysterious visitor" whose ideas and confession are sometimes quoted textually, sometimes summarized by the speaker. In short, this episode is presented as a narrative at the third degree: the "I" who writes the novel includes in his work Alyosha's written account of the holy man's conversations which repeat the story of a third person which Zossima gathered from the latter. At this point the novel, which provides a view of several narrative levels, limits itself to presenting in writing, by means of the traditional technique of the found manuscript, oral accounts which in turn refer to other accounts. The action gains temporal depth in this manner, but the ambiguity grows proportionally. Spoken—and retrospective—narratives are legion in Dostoevsky: Dolgoruky's "memoires" in *A Raw Youth* are full of them, and the autobiography that a drunken Marmeladov retraces for Raskolnikov (*Crime and Punishment*, I, 2) is another one. Often even the subject matter is eclipsed by the narrator, and his manner of speaking—the tics and clichés in which one indulges while speaking—takes precedence over the thing said. To be sure, Faulkner had at his disposal more characteristic and therefore more instructive models: but he would have found in *The Brothers Karamazov* the technique that he probably learned from Conrad and the American story-tellers.

Dostoevsky does not confer on the past the immediacy of the present that is possible today with cinematic flash-backs, the evocations of pure duration and the disruption of chronology. He wrote before the discoveries of the Lumière brothers, Bergson, and Joyce. Since the narrator in his work is always situated at a fixed point within the chronology, and since he never authorizes his heroes, no matter how free, to think, so to speak, "entirely without his control," the past, even the psychological past, cannot become present, and any representation of lived time is translated necessarily by the recollection of memories, not by the resurrection of the experience as it was at the very moment of occurrence. Nothing is more revelatory than the beginning of the second part of *Notes from the Underground*, a flash-back introduced by these sentences: "*At that time* I *was* only twenty four. My life *was even then* gloomy, ill-regulated, and as solitary as that of a savage."[4] Similarly, in the major novels the story is always recounted from the point of view of a single period: that of the crime of Raskolnikov, the arrival of Myshkin at Petersburg, Verhovensky's conspiracy, etc. In *The Possessed, A Raw Youth* and *The Brothers Karamazov*, the novelist gets rid of a portion of the exposition in the first pages in order to be better able to confine himself to the period of the action. Elsewhere he casts us *in media res*, and the exposition thus loses its place as the overture or curtain-raiser that it occupied in, for example, *Eugenie Grandet*. And since, even when it comes at the beginning, he never gives it to us immediately in its entirety, it is fragmented, held back, unveiled in bits and pieces at the same time that main elements of the action are developed. One expects then neither rectilineal development in time nor rigorous succession of causes and effects: Dostoevsky rejects strict scientific causality in practice as well as in theory. On the contrary, the plot jumps from one moment to another, violating the logical order of acts and motives and thus creating a pervasive aura of mystery. Moreover, Dostoevsky teases us with facts whose explanation he postpones, consequently leaving them obscure and confusing. Thus *Crime and Punishment* prefigures the detective novel where the discovery of the murder precedes its reconstruction. It is only well after the preparation of the murder (I,1) and the death of the money lender (I,7) that Raskolnikov sets forth his famous theory of the "mob" and superior men (III,5) a motive suggested by brief and enigmatic insinuations in the first chapters (I,4;[5] I,5;[6] I,6[7]). But the assassin had "suggested" these crucial questions six months earlier in an article that was published several weeks before the crime;[8] still the reader does not learn this until well into the middle of the book, when it is summarized by Raskolnikov. Similarly, Svidrigailov retraces the story of his life only at the end of the novel (VI,4) thus completing the letter of Pulcheria Raskolnikova reproduced at the beginning (I, 3). In *The Brothers Karamazov* there is the same back and forth movement between the past and the moment of the action, the same scattering of the exposition. Although the novel opens with a regular *status quaestionis*, "The Confession of a Passionate Heart" (III, 4 and 5), to cite only one example, supplies information that completes the short biography of Dmitri contained in Book I (2). Faulkner does not proceed differently but, fortified by the lessons of Conrad, Proust and Joyce, he raises to a rule what was only an experiment in Dostoevsky. The outline of *Light in August* resembles in its general contours that of *Crime and Punishment*: the analysis of motives follows the crime, the chronological order is reversed. In chapter 4 Byron recounts in detail how the body of Miss Burden was found, but, although the novel turns around Joe Christmas, the murderer who also is a prisoner of the racial question, we do not know of what parents he was born until chapter 16. Moreover, it is this essential piece of information that completes—and explains—his *curriculum vitae* (chapters 6-12) as it is presented by the author. Here temporal development and artistic logic are no longer limited to just avoiding common experience: they run counter to it. The Faulknerian exposition is not just disjointed and delayed; it is atomized throughout the plot (*The Sound and the Fury, Absalom, Absalom!*) or arrives at the tail end: in *Sanctuary*, part of it comes in the epilogue (chapter 31). The interior monologues of Benjy, Quentin and Jason Compson also plunge us into the middle of the subject, for they emanate from a psychological time, they unravel in a continuum in which all of the past states and the present mutually interpenetrate. Here the shifts forward and backward in the chronology, whose rhythm would be difficult to hurry, proceed from an immobile point of focus enclosed within pure duration. The cause and effect relationship between phenomena gives way to psychological associations, and Dostoevskian mystery becomes hermeticism. The first three chapters of *The Sound and the Fury* represent, in any case, an extreme example whose audacities result from the interiorization of time.

To reveal the premises of the plot progressively and stingingly and, at the same time, to remodel the temporal and logical succession according to the caprices of the imagination, condemns to its very foundations the traditional image of reality formed by the science of the time: Dostoevsky's method poses enigmas for the reader to solve, it promises him pleasures and pains. From the confusion of the initial surprises one eventually arrives, through carefully constructed and distributed revelations, at a state of relative order and clarity, a classical ideal that Dostoevsky never achieved and never really sought. He installed ambiguity in the novel, substituting the equivocal and the polyvalent for the quasi-scientific certitude with which Balzacian narration completely fills our minds. To what degree are his loquacious heroes, his prolix "I"'s worthy of our confidence when they report the accounts of others? What were the true motives of Raskolnikov's murder? One does not really know. The chronicler of *The Possessed*—another "I"—confesses his ignorance more than once.[9] The novelistic world has lost that unpitying, blinding clarity that Balzac normally projected on it. The reader's feeling of possessing the single unique truth is replaced by the murky shadows of doubt, a malaise resulting from the intrusion of the narrators and the hidden, irrational meanderings of the plot. To these causes one can add the autonomy, still relative, of the protagonists in relation to the novelist. Dostoevsky is too much of a realist to display an unbelievable omniscience; man created in the image of God is himself a mystery. He has too great a respect for creatures, even fictional ones, and for their liberty to enslave them to himself. In a given situation several opinions are possible and even equally valuable. The trial of *The Brothers Karamazov*, a marvel of the genre, alternately sees Dmitri's case from the points of view of the prosecution and the defense, and the narrator notes their divergent interpretations with equal detachment. Faulkner, for his part, takes delight in the variety of opinions. "Each man his truth" is the implicit epigraph of *As I Lay Dying*, a "polyphonic" novel, an album of snapshots which applies literally the formula sketched by Dostoevsky. The author here is totally invisible and the situations can be seized only through the deformations that the individuals freely impose on them. No commentary, no central point of view nor bias: it is all action, dialogue and, above all, flux of the conscious and the unconscious. In *Sartoris*[10] and *Sanctuary*[11] Faulkner describes the same facts through the eyes of several characters; in *Absalom, Absalom!* the testimonies of the speakers contradict each other without the author specifying his preference for one or the other: they are, moreover, conjectures, the imprecise accounts of accounts, sometimes heard by an inattentive ear:

> And Bon may have, probably did, take Henry to call on the octoroon mistress and the child, as Mr. Compson said, though neither Shreve nor Quentin believed that the visit affected Henry as Mr. Compson seemed to think. In fact, Quentin did not even tell Shreve what his father had said about the visit. Perhaps Quentin himself had not been listening when Mr. Compson related it that evening at home; perhaps at that moment on the gallery in the hot September twilight Quentin took that in stride without even hearing it just as Shreve would have, since both he and Shreve believed—and were probably right in this too—that . . . etc.[12]

One is already lost in the "notlanguage"[13] which tallies with only a part—or a shadow, the illusion—of reality. If the perfect ambiguity of a Robbe-Grillet, an Uwe Johnson, a Hugo Claus already reigns in Faulkner, it is also announced in Dostoevsky: "we find it difficult in many instances to explain what occurred,"[14] he writes in *The Idiot*.

The more the novelist abandons chronology and causality, the more he is deprived of the proven methods of insuring the plot's cohesion. The old schemas based on the mechanical juxtaposition of a before and after, as in the picaresque novel, on the rational machinery of cause and effect, as in Racinean tragedy, all give way to the more supple, intuitive unity that distinguishes poetry

107

and music. In Dostoevsky, repetition, parallelism and the opposition of themes, scenes and images smooth the breaks in the traditional narrative. A motif, introduced almost without our knowing, will be developed long afterwards. There are numerous examples. For instance, the gentleman that Raskolnikov indignantly watches circle about a drunken young girl (I, 4). The man has a countenance and demeanor whose sketch anticipates several of the major episodes of *Crime and Punishment*: the hero's meeting with Svidrigailov (IV, 1; V, 3 and 4), who fancies adolescent girls and who is also in love with Raskolnikov's own sister; then the unforgettable scene between Dounia and her ignoble suitor (VI,5). The role of the first episode, apparently gratuitous, is only understood later. The hasty sketch that introduces the mysterious gentleman: "The gentleman was a plump, thickly-set man, about thirty, fashionably dressed, with a high color, red lips and moustaches" (I, 4)[15] prefigures the full length portrait of Svidrigailov:

> He was a man about fifty, rather tall and thickly set, with broad high shoulders which made him look as though he stooped a little. He wore good and fashionable clothes, and looked like a gentleman of position. He carried a handsome cane, which he tapped on the pavement at each step; his gloves were spotless. He had a broad rather pleasant face with high cheek-bones and a fresh colour, not often seen in Petersburg. His flaxen hair was still abundant, and only touched here and there with grey, and his thick square beard was even lighter than his hair. His eyes were blue and had a cold and thoughtful look; his lips were crimson. He was a remarkably well-preserved man and looked much younger than his years, (III, 4)[16]

a passage that will twice more be echoed:

> he was a man no longer young, stout, with a full, fair, almost whitish beard. (III, 6)[17]

> his face, which had impressed him before. It was a strange face, like a mask; white and red, with bright red lips, with a flaxen beard, and still thick flaxen hair. His eyes were somehow too blue and their expression somehow too heavy and fixed. There was something awfully unpleasant in that handsome face, which looked so wonderfully young for his age. Svidrigailov was smartly dressed in light summer clothes and was particularly dainty in his linen. He wore a huge ring with a precious stone in it. (VI, 3)[18]

108

The unknown personage's corpulence, his dapper air and, above all, the freshness of his complexion which clashes with his lewd behavior: these images are insinuated from the beginning, recalled insistently as the novel progresses, and are finally woven into a unifying and directing theme. The method of thematic composition, the recourse to the leitmotif and association usurp the place of the logical and temporal articulations of causality and chronology.

The cane with which the unknown man threatens Raskolnikov[19] is obviously not the switch which Svidrigailov used to whip his wife, who died well before the action begins;[20] the young lass with whom Svidrigailov becomes engaged and whom he caresses "paternally"[21] is in no way connected with the drunken girl pursued by his double, no more than this slatternly wench resembles Dounia. Despite the fact that the overture (I, 4) and the developments that it prefigures take place on different levels at different times, the heterogeneous elements are combined in the reader's mind by virtue of their kinship. In this instance visual impressions, the scene formed by their sequence and the theme they suggest (innocence hunted and abused by lewdness) are knit together in a unit which is reproduced in almost similar forms. But it is also possible to contrast the elements of the plot: the story of Svidrigailov, a gentleman whose rosy cheeks contradict his black designs, stands in jarring contrast with that of Sonia, the prostitute with a heart of gold. The dualism of Raskolnikov, pulled between the devil and the good God, obviously reflects this antithesis. Dostoevsky, himself a torn man, is fond of oppositions. See in particular Books V ("Pro and Contra") and VI ("The Russian Monk") of *The Brothers Karamazov*. Without insisting, doing nothing more than juxtaposing it to the discussions of Zossima, the author implicitly refutes the legend of the Inquisitor. The structure and psychology of his polyphonic narratives are a subtle play of theme and counterpoint, of voices which sometimes dialogue back and forth and sometimes unite in the mind as in the outer world. To the shocks of Svidrigailov and Sonia, of Ivan and Zossima, the Karamazovs and the Snegiryovs, correspond the conflicts which devour the souls of the "doubles" Raskolnikov, Katerina Ivanovna etc.

Faulkner pushes the principle of thematic composition to its final consequences, all the more since Thomas Mann, Virginia Woolf and Huxley had prepared the literary climate in the interim. The unity of *The Sound and the Fury* and of *As I Lay Dying* rests primarily on the repetition and contrast of leitmotifs: images, episodes and themes. In addition to witnessing the same incidents several times from several points of view, the reader can apprehend the swirls and meanderings of each psychological flux as a whole, thanks to the associations that it contains. For Benjy Compson, Caddy is linked to the fresh odor of trees ("She smelled like trees"), their brother Quentin is obsessed by the sensuous perfume of honeysuckle, Vardaman Bundren by the sight of a fish, etc. In *Absalom, Absalom!* it is objects as insignificant as a letter or a pipe which wrench us from the old South and return us to the present of the speakers. Even *Sanctuary*, one of the most traditional works of the young Faulkner, uses techniques that Dostoevsky employed in presenting Svidrigailov and the idea he incarnates. The contrast between being and seeming, the lewdness and evil dissimulated under a fresh appearance, is no longer expressed by the reddened lips of a fifty year old, but by those of a sexually precocious teenager. From the outset, Faulkner aims his camera on the face and particularly the mouth of Temple Drake: "She looked at him, her mouth boldly scarlet, her eyes watchful and cold beneath her brimless hat, a curled spill of red hair."[22] Once the theme is presented, the development operates more or less as in *Crime and Punishment*. In chapter 19, Horace Benbow encounters some female students whom we will not see again any more than the stranger observed by Raskolnikov. Their rouged lips are described as "savage": "He stood there while on both sides of him they passed in a steady stream of little colored dresses, bare-armed, with close bright heads, with that identical cool, innocent, unabashed expression which he knew well in their eyes, above the savage identical paint upon their mouths."[23] The detail, seemingly without significance at first glance, leads to the application of the same epithet to Temple, first when Horace visits her in Memphis, then when she gives perjured testimony during the trial of Goodwin:

110

two spots of rouge on her cheekbones and her mouth painted into a savage cupid's bow.[24]

Her face was quite pale, the two spots of rouge like paper discs pasted on her cheekbones, her mouth painted into a savage and perfect bow, also like something both symbolical and cryptic cut carefully from purple paper and pasted there.[25]

She turned her head . . . , her eyes blank and all pupil above the three savage spots of rouge.[26]

On the other hand, Joe Christmas' adventures in *Light in August* develop parallel to two subplots: Hightower's past and the journey of Lena Grove. Lena's story, while framing that of the murder, serves at the same time as a contrast; it adds a note of the comic and serene, for if Christmas can call himself a man only by killing, the good and peaceful Lena has only to wait peacefully to achieve her ends. The events prove her right: while Christmas seeks to live and finds only death, the daughter of the Earth seems born under a lucky star and everything works out successfully for her. Alyosha in *The Brothers Karamazov* listens alternatively to Ivan and Zossima, linking the poles to one another; similarly, Faulkner plants Byron Bunch as an intermediary between Christmas and Lena. The opposition of milieus which evokes the contrasted tableaux of the Marmeladov and Svidrigailov and the Karamazov and Snegiryov families or the contradicting accounts of Ivan and Zossima, is carried to its culmination in *The Wild Palms*, a contrapuntal novel where the episodes of the convicts' odyssey alternate systematically but without any rational necessity or chronological relationship with those of a love story.[27] Let us add finally that the repetition of episodes is sometimes reduced to a simple parallelism, accented in such a way as to reinforce the guiding theme. Thus Calvin Burden thunders against his son with the same violence as McEachern against Christmas;[28] similarly, in *The Brothers Karamazov* "A Laceration in the Cottage" and "And in the Open Air" (IV, 6 and 7) echo "A Laceration in the Drawing Room" (IV, 5): in both cases we assist at the convulsions of the offended. All of these techniques—literal or slightly varied repetitions, parallelisms or contrasts—concern not only the individuals, social milieux, and the elements of the plot

111

but also the tone of the work, since the two authors combine irony and the serious, farce and melodrama in a tightly woven fabric.

The young Faulkner often transposes the plot from the chronological level to the level of pure duration. From the tangible world of which the realists rendered only the commonly accepted public image, he raises the reader to the level of interiority, an eminently subjective point of view. *The Sound and the Fury* culminates—at least, temporarily—a movement found in all the areas of art and introduced in the novel by Proust, Joyce and Virginia Woolf following the discoveries of William James and Bergson. It is above all the interior monologue which enables the novelist to substitute for the direct painting of things the reflection preserved in the psyche and to jump from clock time to lived time. Faulkner is not, however, able to do without the former: he clips its wings, but he does not forget that man, who develops in history, must adopt a conventional representation of it. After breaking his watch, Quentin Compson measures the progress of the hours by the shadows. In addition, the frame of *The Sound and the Fury*, the days during which the author allows the Compson brothers to think, feel and dream aloud, the very chassis of the book, is borrowed from chronology. Without wishing to minimize the contributions of French and English literature, perhaps one ought to point out here the lesson of Dostoevsky whose daring Gide has already indicated.[29] *Crime and Punishment* abounds in "indirect" interior monologues, snapshots of the hero's consciousness that the author, without exception, introduces by a "he thought to himself,"[30] "he said to himself,"[31] "he asked himself,"[32] etc. Dostoevsky uses these anchoring devices to maintain control of the minutest details of the narrative, an intention denoted, moreover, by the deliberate choice of the third person form. Raskolnikov thinks with an open soul, to be sure, but at no time does the novelist leave the scene as Faulkner does in the first three chapters of *The Sound and the Fury*. When Raskolnikov says "I," the flow of his reflections is reported in quotation marks. The leash kept on the character by the novelist is seen in this passage where Dostoevsky protects his prerogatives as the stage-manager, while slipping into the skin of the actor:

112

He thought of nothing. Some thoughts or fragments of thoughts, some images without order or coherence floated before his mind—faces of people, he had seen in childhood or met somewhere once, whom we would never have recalled, the belfry of the church at V., the billiard table in a restaurant and some officers playing billiards, the smell of cigars in some underground tobacco shop, a tavern room, a back staircase quite dark, all sloppy with dirty water and strewn with egg shells, and the Sunday bells floating in from somewhere . . . The images followed one another, whirling like a hurricane. Some of them he liked and tried to clutch at, but they faded and all the while there was an oppression within him.[33]

The essential elements are the incoherence, the disparity and discontinuity, the free association of memories. Let us detach them from the author and whisk him away and we obtain what is virtually the "direct" interior monologue of *The Sound and the Fury* and *As I Lay Dying*:

A quarter hour yet. And then I'll not be. The peacefullest words. Peacefullest words. *Non fui. Sum. Fui. Non Sum.* Somewhere I heard bells once. Mississippi or Massachusetts. I was. I am not. Massachusetts or Mississippi. Shreve has a bottle in his trunk. *Aren't you even going to open it.* Mr. and Mrs. Jason Richmond Compson announce the *Three times. Days. Aren't you even going to open it* marriage of their daughter Candace *that liquor teaches you to confuse the means with the end.* I am. Drink. I was not. Let us sell Benjy's pasture so that Quentin may go to Harvard and I may knock my bones together and together. I will be dead in. Was it one year Caddy said.[34]

In both cases, we penetrate into lived time. But Faulkner stretches and tangles the threads that link the hero's thoughts to the chronological present of the action, that minute or second on June 2, 1910, when Quentin dies; Dostoevsky, on the other hand, solidly fixes reminiscences in a strict temporal succession. The extract from *Crime and Punishment* immediately follows the appearance of the person who accuses Raskolnikov of being a murderer; in addition, it is specified that the student returns to his room and remains standing there for ten minutes, and then lies down and "so he lay for half an hour."[35] After these thirty minutes have passed—that is, are summarized—we are plunged again into the chronological development. The novelistic time of Dostoevsky is still supported by clock and calendar time; his derogations from the traditional norms are negligible in comparison with the extravagances of *The Sound and the Fury*. Nonetheless, it seems that the Russian had had the intuition of pure duration well before Bergson and Faulkner. The use of the soliloquy and first-person narration (*Notes from the Underground*, "The Meek One Rebels," etc.) bear witness to this. To revive the past on the basis of personal, highly questionable testimony and not by means of certitudes bestowed by an omniscient author is to affirm its subjective quality, to underscore the fact that it exists only as lived, enclosed in a myriad of different forms in many different consciousnesses. In addition, let us recall the laconic, but very characteristic, passage of the notebooks of *Crime and Punishment*: "What is time? Time doesn't exist; time is numbers; time is the relationship of existence to nonexistence."[36] There exists, in sum, only the individual experience, and consequently, the concrete duration within which it is organized; as for non-being, or the non-lived, consciousness seizes it, masters it as best as it can by means of artificial dates, by the game of centuries, years and hours, in short, by "numbers." Kirillov has read the Book of Revelations, and has said: "There are moments, you reach moments, and time suddenly stands still, and it will become eternal. . . . Time is not an object."[37] Myshkin, an epileptic like the author, knew seconds of vision characterized by "an extraordinary quickening of self-consciousness . . . and at the same time of the direct sensation of existence,"[38] moments worth the whole of life. It is interesting to note that *The Wild Palms* describes a vaguely comparable experience: "for that one second or two seconds you were present in space but not in time."[39] Dostoevsky himself emphasizes the time proper to his work by cramming the days with incidents: a frenzied rhythm, jerky, careless of the regular and monotonous circumvolutions of the hands of a clock. Every plot reflects a conception of time, and the study of Dostoevskian structures proves that the reader of Balzac, Dickens and Eugene Sue had set philosophy and narration in the direction that Faulkner was going to follow.

Despite all of this, young Faulkner's concept of time is still a long way beyond that of Dostoevsky. For the Russian, it is very simply "the external milieu" in which the liberty of the free agent is exercised. Pouillon goes so far as to speak of a "disqualification" of time.[40] Neither the novelist nor his characters, with the exception of Raskolnikov, sees Fate in any way involved; the first does not insert it as such into the workings of the plot, the others do not submit to its yoke. In *Sartoris, Light in August* and *Absalom, Absalom!*, Faulkner, on the contrary, casts the entire universe into the grip of destiny. The past molds the present, the future is fixed.

> old Bayard sat and mused quietly on the tense he had unwittingly used. Was. Fatality; the augury of a man's destiny peeping out at him from the roadside hedge, if he but recognize it.[41]

> Quentin Compson who was still too young to deserve yet to be a ghost, but nevertheless having to be one for all that, since he was born and bred in the deep South.[42]

The admission of freedom will lessen the distance between the two men, without the weight of the Faulknerian past being entirely reduced. The formula of *The Sound and the Fury*, "Non fui. Sum. Fui. Non sum*" is paraphrased in "Beyond" (1933), in these terms: "what I have been, I am; what I am I shall be until that instant comes when I am not. And then I shall have never been."[43] and echoes through *The Wild Palms* (1939),[44] "Shall Not Perish" (1943)[45] and even *Requiem for a Nun* (1951): "The past is never dead. It's not even past."[46]

It is only a short step from the composition of the plot to the characters and situations: they are, after all, aspects of one and the same thing.

The structure "against the grain," the delayed and gradual revelation of the basic elements, in short the book's enigmas are compensated partially by the sixth sense which is bestowed on several heroes. Prince Myshkin, a brilliant idiot and an epileptic, is able to bare the deepest secrets, he reads souls with that sudden and acute intuition that Alyosha Karamazov will inherit. Hypersensitive, he has a premonition of the ills that await him: here, it is the eyes and knife of Rogozhin that pursue him, there Aglaia's warnings about the Chinese vase that he will nonetheless break. But his presentiments are explained by illness; he does not perceive the signs of an ineluctable destiny, while Faulkner's Mc-

115

Eachern[47] and Hines[48] are visionaries and prophets by virtue of their bigotry which has familiarized them with the predestined movement of evil.

The fate of a character is sometimes written in his name and revealed there from the beginning. But rather than the old adage *nomen est omen*—which could scarcely be applied to Dostoevsky —the technique evokes allegory and the morality plays. The hero tends to exceed the realistic framework of the "character," the individual who is the subject under study in the psychological novel, to be transformed into the mouthpiece of ideas, to personify a certain element in the scale of values upon which the novel's architecture is based. Individuals are confused with their conceptual role. Without reducing the action of *Sanctuary* to an allegorical pattern in the way that O'Donnell has done one can detect a tendency toward symbolization in the names. *Temple* Drake alludes—ironically, of course—to the title of the work; *Good*win betrays his innocence just as Morose, Volpone and Mosca indicate their humours in Ben Jonson, and his name is not without irony since Good*win* wins only an unjust death; finally *Gowan* Stevens, Temple's "attending knight" parodies the Arthurian champion. Gawain reappears in the guise of *Gavin* Stevens in *Intruder in the Dust, Requiem for a Nun, The Town* and *The Mansion,* but endowed this time with his traditional titles: defender of the Right, paladin of the old South, platonic lover of Eula Varner and her daughter. Ikkemotubbe, the Indian chief to whom the Compsons owe their fortune, is called "l'Homme" or "de l'homme" by the Louisiana French; anglicized, the expression is changed into *Doom* and prefigures both Quentin's suicide and the curse which strikes the land. Equally obvious are the meanings of *Christmas, Hightower* and Lena *Grove,* surnames which define respectively the victim sacrificed for the sins of society, the isolation caused by blind worship of the past and the spirit of the earth. One of the characters of *Light in August* explains himself on this point:

a man's name, which is supposed to be just the sound for who he is, can be somehow an augur of what he will do, if other men can only read the meaning in time. It seemed to him that none of them had looked especially at the stranger until they heard his name. But as soon as they heard

116

it, it was as though there was something in the sound of it that was trying to tell them what to expect; that he carried with him his own inescapable warning, like a flower its scent or a rattlesnake its rattle.[49]

In the patriarchal community portrayed by Faulkner, first and last names are all the more significant because they tie the individual to the family: they reflect a solidarity of blood and class. But we are concerned with a very different link here: that which exists between man and his destiny or, more accurately, his significance, the role that he plays in the story. Shreve, the Canadian student who with Quentin imagines the story of Sutpen, is an outsider: he is not even an American citizen and we know nothing of his surroundings. His name, however (cf., to shrive) very exactly denotes his function as a confessor in *Absalom, Absalom!*. Dostoevsky also uses emblematic names which announce the tribulations of their possessors. Raskolnikov, the example that is always cited, derives from *raskolnik*; even before he develops his ideas, we know that the hero of *Crime and Punishment* will, in his fashion, be a schismatic, a rebel. His sister Dounia (short for Avdotya) represents, in effect, virtue, honor and discernment (cf., *eudoxia*). *Stavrogin* recalls the word used in the Gospels to designate the instrument of the crucifixion (*stauros*, the cross): this character who, by his own admission, "is seeking a burden"[50] is the Christ of Evil. Alyosha, the youngest of the Karamazovs is simultaneously "the man of God" and he who brings aid (*alexis*) while Smerdyakov, born of a foul wench, displays his perfidy in his name as in a coat of arms. The game could be prolonged indefinitely: Dostoevsky lends himself to it better than Dickens. The technique renders the long ceremony of introductions superfluous, a label henceforth taking the place of the minute description of the character and his past history. If the author of *Everyman* can dispense with the descriptions of Death, Good Deeds or Beauty, heroes such as Hightower and Raskolnikov require much less laborious and urgent explanations than do Goriot and Grandet. The novelist characterizes merely by naming; he can thus postpone exposition and stimulate our curiosity, while, at the same time, beginning to satisfy it.

The intimate relationship between the character and the ideas that he represents is particularly striking when the individual patterns his actions ritualistically rather than acting pragmatically on the concrete level of phenomena. In Faulkner and in Dostoevsky, there is an abundance of ritual gestures which make the world sacred by replacing spontaneous action, the direct response to facts, by a symbolic act. The latter takes place within a network of similar acts and gives shape to the beliefs—or vestiges of beliefs—which the author usually shares with those around him. As his name suggests, Joe Christmas was found on Christmas Day. He will be arrested on a Friday and it is again on a Friday that Nancy is executed in *Requiem for a Nun*. But these details— like the choice of the feast of Easter for the epilogue of *The Sound and the Fury*—concern the texture of the plot rather than the heroes. On the other hand, the rite accomplished by Christmas when he kills a lamb and soils his hands with blood in order to accept a phenomenon as "outrageous" as menstruation is one that reveals him personally. The historic situation gives way to a symbol, the choice is elevated to a ceremony. Narcissa Benbow, the widow of young Bayard Sartoris, indulges in authentic ablutions after the stolen letters have been returned to her in exchange for her body ("There Was a Queen"). As for the hunt, it is characterized by a quantity of initiatory rites, carefully recorded in "The Bear." The tendancy to stylize and ritualize gestures, the will to transcend the confusion of phenomena in order to impose order and meaning on them is seen even more clearly in Dostoevsky. We have only to recall the kissing of the earth, a scene repeated in *Crime and Punishment, The Possessed* and *The Brothers Karamazov*. First Raskolnikov, counselled by Sonia, kisses the earth stained by his crime;[51] then Marya Lebyadkin, Shatov,[52] and Alyosha[53] in turn imitate or speak of imitating him. As one might expect, the ritual act is here in a closer relationship with Christianity. Sonia slips a cross of cypress wood, around Raskolnikov's neck when he decides to confess, while she keeps the copper cross that had belonged to Lizaveta, the murderer's victim. And Raskolnikov states; "It's the symbol of my taking up the cross."[54] The episode is foreshadowed at the moment of the crime, for Raskolnikov finds two similar objects suspended with the purse from the old lady's neck and throws them on her body after pocketing the money.[55] Much later we learn that Sonia had received a copper cross from Lizaveta and that she intends her own cypress wood cross for Raskolnikov: "Take it . . . it's mine! It's mine, you know," she begged him. "We will go to suffer together, and together we will bear our cross!"[56] In *The Idiot*, Rogozhin and Myshkin indulge in a similar trade,[57] the exchange of crosses solemnly sealing before God their brotherhood in suffering. Religion or liturgy are also suggested by Raskolnikov's prostration at Sonia's feet, Christ's kiss of the Inquisitor in Ivan's poem and, in a kind of inversion, the sacrilegious destruction of the icon in *A Raw Youth*.

The prescience of events and the emblematic names sketch the pattern of the action in advance; in another regard, certain acts extract the characters from the tangible world, even more than do their allegoric names or the background of symbolic colors and elements against which they move, in order to introduce them into a value system. From these techniques, which concern as much the arrangement of the narrative as the portrayal of character, let us pass to the human types and relationships depicted by the two novelists.

Both are specialists in alienation, a sickness that is today endemic. Their patients are isolated by their savage temperament or by banishment, the maladjusted in search of a place in society or an identity which evades them, idiots and, above all, criminals. The divorce between the individual and a social order that is changing or decadent and incapable of accepting him often culminates in rebellion and violence. Thus Raskolnikov and Christmas. The first breaks with the world following a crime which is itself the product of empty theories. The pure intellect rejects the warm presence of life; it is both a prison and also the antechamber of hell. The problem, already raised in *Notes from the Underground*, is taken up again in *The Possessed*—Stavrogin has lost his moral sense, Shatov says, because he has lost touch with his own people[58]—and finally in *The Brothers Karamazov* where "Recollections of Father Zossima's Youth" defines the period as that of human isolation:

the isolation that prevails everywhere, above all in our age—it has not fully developed, it has not reached its limit yet. For every one strives to keep his individuality as apart as possible, wishes to secure the greatest

119

possible fullness of life for himself; but meantime all his efforts result not in attaining fullness of life but self-destruction, for instead of self-realisation he ends by arriving at complete solitude. All mankind in our age have split up into units, they all keep apart, each in his own groove; each one holds aloof, hides himself and hides what he has, from the rest, and he ends by being repelled by others and repelling them. He heaps up riches by himself and thinks, 'how strong I am now and how secure,' and in his madness he does not understand that the more he heaps up, the more he sinks into self-destructive impotence. For he is accustomed to rely upon himself alone and to cut himself off from the whole; he has trained himself not to believe in the help of others, in men and in humanity, and only trembles for fear he should lose his money and the privileges that he has won for himself. Everywhere in these days men have, in their mockery, ceased to understand that the true security is to be found in social solidarity rather than in isolated individual effort.[59]

Social alienation and, more important, moral alienation, since the collectivity, according to Dostoevsky, owes its cohesion less to legal, political or economic ties than to a spiritual contract: a communion of souls, a reciprocal love of creatures united in the love of God. Thus it is by a conversion that Raskolnikov ends his solitude: the love of his neighbor—that is, of Sonia—resuscitates him,[60] restores the "schismatic" to the human race. It is not sufficient to expiate the legal crime: only a sudden reorientation of the soul can expel the sinner from his shell and reconcile him with his peers. The *amor sui* which expresses itself in his obsession is succeeded by *caritas* when the young intellectual contemplates "the vast steppe, bathed in sunshine"[61] and throws himself weeping at the prostitute's feet. The prodigal son at the same time reestablishes contact with nature, the people and the heart. The earth, the crowds, love: three sources of morality that draw men together. There is no doubt that in this story of a hunted man, Faulkner found several of his pet ideas. The alienation of Joe Christmas is also defined in relation to the earth, that is to say to the Mother and, subsidiarily, to the black race. One who discards the earth, the eternal Woman who patiently awaits our fertilization[62] is, by definition, a matricide: Christmas, moreover, literally killed his mother, who died in childbirth. Christmas feels stifled in Freedman Town,[63] the negro section of Jefferson, as soon as he arrives there, and the fields where he takes refuge offer him no peace.

It is as though he desires to see his native earth in all its phases for the first or the last time. He had grown to manhood in the country, where like the unswimming sailor his physical shape and his thought had been molded by its compulsions without his learning anything about its actual shape and feel. For a week now he has lurked and crept among its secret places, yet he remained a foreigner to the very immutable laws which earth must obey. For some time as he walks steadily on, he thinks that this is what it is—the looking and seeing—which gives him peace and unhaste and quiet, until suddenly the true answer comes to him. He feels dry and light. 'I don't have to bother about having to eat anymore,' he thinks. 'That's what it is.'[64]

The theme is already more than a mere sketch in *Sanctuary*: Pop-eye, an *outcast* and *outlaw*, has nothing of the natural about him. And in *As I Lay Dying*, man seeks to return to the native soil from which he has been separated: to reunite the umbilical cord, to curl up in the primordial womb. Faulkner confuses nature and the native land. Such regionalism—think of his concept of the nation—is foreign to Dostoevsky. Raskolnikov could be regenerated anywhere, in the Siberian steppe or elsewhere; but the community from which Christmas feels excluded does not exceed the borders of a county. The muzhik, for the Muscovite and the Petersburger, is *the* Russian peasant, while Faulkner's negroes all inhabit Jefferson or the surrounding area. The American's community does not extend to aggregates as vast and as vague as the "people" or the "nation"; the word designates, in its etymological sense, the *Vaterland*, land of one's ancestors and family, or the *Heimat*, the one where one was born and where, very often, one lives. It reflects a system of precise coordinates in relation to which the individual can easily determine his position. That is why Addie wishes to be buried at Jefferson and that is also the reason for the isolation of Christmas, an orphan knowing nothing of his fathers, his parents, his rank nor his race, therefore of himself, since in small towns, in the Yoknapatawpha country, contrary to what happens in metropolitan and industrial areas, man defines himself less by his work and his individual choices than by his roots: "that to me" Faulkner said, "is the most tragic condition that an individual can have—not to know who he was."[65] *Light in August* is the great novel of alienation (Christmas, Joanna Burden, Hightower) but it is not just that: Lena

Grove, who is so easily integrated into the group and can, therefore, count on the aid of all,[66] gives the lie to such a simplifica-
tion. In short, left to himself, the individual is on the fringes
of madness and crime. Existence makes no sense. Alone, how
do we define ourselves? We can only invent ourselves gratuitously. One truly knows and realizes oneself only within a group.[67]
Dostoevsky and Faulkner both recommend extraversion: love,
solidarity, respect of creatures. Turning one's back on others always draws the gravest disorders in its wake: the suicides of
Kirillov and of Quentin, the murders by Raskolnikov and Christmas, the sexual aberrations of Svidrigailov and Popeye, the fran-
tic ruminations of the man from the underground, Ivan Karamazov and Hightower, the scandalous ascension of Verhovensky and
Flem Snopes. From this point of view, what is real and good
are others. The recluse encloses himself in the abstract—or what
is, in effect, the same thing—in evil. "The whole object of my
'idea'," the ambitious Dolgoruky writes, "is . . . isolation":[68]

> I conclude that having something fixed, permanent, and overpowering
> in one's mind in which one is terribly absorbed, one is, as it were, re-
> moved by it from the whole world, and everything that happens (except
> the one great thing) slips by one. . . . The "idea" comforted me in dis-
> grace and in insignificance. But all the nasty things I did took refuge, as
> it were, under the "idea." So to speak, it smoothed over everything, but
> it also put a mist before my eyes.[69]

Alienation is the sister of madness. It is unnecessary to insist
once again on that constant of Dostoevskian psychology, the splitting of personality. Let us content ourselves by calling attention
to its traces in Faulkner. It is essential to point out at the outset
that this trait, predominant from *The Double* to *The Brothers
Karamazov*, appears here in a much more discrete form. Despite
the tensions that mark the Faulknerian hero's dual nature, they
rarely cause a permanent splitting of the ego. He is not, in fact,
"alternating between two characters."[70] When Temple Drake,
driven into a panic by the bootleggers, momentarily watches herself run out of her body and flee, the scene only denotes a simple
lag between the impulse and the act, produced and exaggerated
by anxiety—a simple "slow motion" between the moment of rest

in which the decision is made and the moment in which it is executed.[71] The same can be said of the passage in *Light in August* where Christmas, in the throes of a violent emotion, watches himself act.[72] Under the effects of a shock, the ego splits not into two antagonists, but into two aspects: the spectator and the agent. But sometimes authentic doubles in the Dostoevskian sense do appear. Thus, temporarily, Joanna Burden: "the two creatures that struggled in one body like two moongleamed shapes struggling drowning in alternate throes upon the surface of a black thick pool beneath the last moon."[73] Thus Temple, hungry for caresses and respectability (*Sanctuary*), heavy of heart and light of morals (*Requiem for a Nun*), a woman *bifrons:* Temple Drake and Mrs. Gowan Stevens.[74] Quentin Compson shows such a propensity toward disintegration that he throws himself into the water. *Absalom, Absalom!* juxtaposes the man of the present, born in Jefferson in 1891, a student in Cambridge, Massachusetts, and a phantom sprung from the past;[75] this second self, stronger than the other, already wanders in the realm of the dead: Quentin has been, rather than is, and his suicide abolishes his laceration by uprooting him from the here and now. In all of these cases, the splitting does not last long: Miss Burden only wants to make up lost time before the critical turn of life; the episode in the Memphis bordello is equally fleeting and, if Mrs. Gowan Stevens remembers her adventures as a young girl with nostalgia, her longings end with Nancy's sacrifice; as for Quentin, he kills himself at the age of nineteen. In Dostoevsky the cleavage is durable and the conclusion of the conflict ambiguous: although one double (Raskolnikov) does give in to his good side, what about the others? The Faulknerian hero is no more successful in solving his problems;[76] however, the forces of which he is the battleground crystallize less easily into two autonomous enemy beings. One notices that schizophrenia sometimes affects even the composition of the work: Raskolnikov recalls Svidrigailov as much as Sonia, Kirillov and Shatov are projections of Stavrogin and, similarly, Quentin and Shreve are confused—simultaneously—with Henry Sutpen and Charles Bon.[77]

The situational affinities are not limited to a few psychological particularities. Among all the possible relations between people,

Faulkner and Dostoevsky often chose the same ones—without necessarily questioning literary tradition.

The struggle between father and son, for instance, exercised a fascination on the Russian that is usually explained by his biography. There are indeed few sympathetic fathers and submissive and loving sons to be found in his novels. Take Stepan Trofimovitch and Verhovensky in *The Possessed*; Versilov and Dolgoruky in *A Raw Youth*; Karamazov and Ivan, Dmitri or Smerdyakov. In *The Brothers Karamazov*, hostility turns to amorous competition and then to parricide. We hate only what touches us, that is, that which resembles us or outrages us. Identity and opposition, hatred of the father both as a model and as a rival, both as himself and as another: this is revealed in the attitude of Dmitri, bracketed with old Karamazov under the denomination of "the sensualists" (III, 9). Verhovensky evokes by his very failures the father he scorns, and Dolgoruky, the bastard, competes with his father while wishing his recognition. The situation reappears in *Absalom, Absalom!*. For Quentin, Mr. Compson is still an example: a confidant, a counselor; Charles Bon, on the other hand, sees Sutpen, above all, as a force that must be conquered: they converge and diverge at the same time.[78] His mother, repudiated by Sutpen, made Charles the instrument of her revenge and, yet, far from hating him, the son—it seems—asks of his father only that he recognize him as such. But Sutpen's refusal makes Bon, against Bon's wishes, the cause of his father's ruin and death. A *Fable* presents the opposite case: an infanticide accomplished on the father's orders. The Marshal and his son, the corporal, complement one another,[79] for each affirms in his own way the immortality of man. Nonetheless, they repel each other even more since Authority causes the rebel's death. What remains in all this of the duel of Dmitri and Fyodor Pavlovitch Karamazov? Not a great deal, to be truthful.

In *A Raw Youth* and *The Brothers Karamazov*, father and son became enamored of the same girl; in *The Town* and *The Mansion* we see Gavin Stevens yearning first for the mother, Eula Varner, and then for her daughter, Linda Snopes, probably an accidental correspondence. Let us rather analyze the variations of love: frustrated, tempestuous, impossible loves. With few exceptions, the triangle does not arrange itself into the comfortably bourgeois form of the *ménage à trois.* Eula Varner establishes an equilibrium between Flem Snopes and Manfred de Spain, so also does Laverne (*Pylon*) between Shumann and Jack, the "eternal husband" adapts to being a cuckold. Yes, but what about the others? The others must choose: does Mrs. Powers (*Soldiers' Pay*) prefer Donald to Joe? Charlotte (*The Wild Palms*), Harry to Rat? Temple Drake (*Requiem for a Nun*), Gowan to Pete? Let us note in passing that the decision in Faulkner is less tormenting than to the Idiot, torn between Aglaia and Nastasya Filippovna, or to Dimitri Karamazov or Katerina Ivanovna. In all these stories there are few which finish better than *Madame Bovary* or *Anna Karenina.* Moreover, the sexes remain isolated; their communion when it takes place is at best ephemeral—the contact of two skins—and it leads to disaster. Charlotte and Harry, Temple and Red, Temple and Pete, Christmas and Miss Burden, Bayard Sartoris and Narcissa Benbow, Addie Bundren and Whitfield: they are all, in one way or another, unhappy lovers. Dostoevsky's are no more fortunate; they scarcely sleep together. The love-affairs between Rogozhin and Nastasya, of Lisa and Stavrogin, of Dmitri and Grushenka are pitiful messes. And what is to be said of the marriage of Mrs. Powers and Donald Mahon, an impotent amnesiac, of Raskolnikov and Sonia, a disincarnate and sexless soul despite her profession, if not that none of them taste either the ecstasies or the sweetness of the bed? Men and women seek and often torture each other, but never find each other. Love does not bring happiness—not that kind of happiness. It has other virtues: it bears witness to life, it causes suffering. It is not usually as *eros* that it triumphs in the novels of Faulkner and Dostoevsky, but as the seed of life, the heart's flight towards another (*agape*). Natasya, the heroine of *The Insulted and the Injured,* says that she loves Alyosha "as though (she) were mad," but she also knows that she has "gone out of (her) mind" and that she doesn't "love him in the right way."[80] Passionate love is equated with mad, selfish, violent, and passive love. Hence, as a general rule, the primacy of the soul over the body. The sister tends to replace the mistress, and the brother, the lover. Vanya, Natasya's chaste suitor who is prepared to sacrifice everything and who regards love as a school for virtue, practices the *Minnedienst* of the troubadours. Gavin Stevens worships Eula Varner and Linda Snopes in practically the same way; he neither succeeds nor wishes to succeed in his purposes.[81] *Requiem for a Nun* shows how ethics eliminates sex, and with Quentin Compson the Dostoevskian idealism that was content to sublimate instinct goes awry, disdaining all women with the exception of the sister: incest, taking amorous cartharsis literally, cannot be consummated for Quentin does not love his sister's body but the notion of honor he attaches to it.

A quasi-manichean conception of woman emerges from these examples. Angel or devil, woman attracts either the most glowing or the most insolent commentaries. She is, for our novelists as for many others, an enigma. Dmitri Karamazov, neither a fool nor a novice since he claims to have been destroyed by women, is constantly musing about their nature. To believe him, they are as perverse as they are indispensable:

> For a woman-devil only knows what to make of a woman: I know something about them, anyway. But try acknowledging you are in fault to a woman. Say, 'I am sorry, forgive me,' and a shower of reproaches will follow! Nothing will make her forgive you simply and directly, she'll humble you to the dust, bring forward things that have never happened, recall everything, forget nothing, add something of her own, and only then forgive you. And even the best, the best of them do it. She'll scrape up all the scrapings and load them on your head. They are ready to flay you alive, I tell you, every one of them, all these angels without whom we cannot live![82]

Dimitri, it is true, deals with "doubles"—Grushenka, Katerina Ivanovna—and it is no easy matter to deal with them. One fools him and the other testifies against him at the trial. That does not prevent Grushenka from accompanying him into exile, emulating the example of Sonia Marmeladov or Daria who follows in Stavrogin's wake. The two aspects balance each other: there are, in the final analysis, as many examples of abnegation as of selfishness. The *Diary of a Writer* (May and July-August 1876) goes much further. Women, courageous, heroic without ostentation,[83] are the author's great hope; they will perhaps one day be the saving plank of Russia.[84] Faulkner accentuates "that mixed

beauty of a woman's face" which Proust describes as one of Dostoevsky's greatest gifts to the world,[85] but which is also part of
the attraction of Anna Karenina. As early as *Soldiers' Pay* the
vampire is set off against the guardian angel: young Cecily, pretty
as a picture, but filled with self-love, artificial, dangerous, contrasts with Mrs. Powers, the symbol of disinterested sacrifice, pity
and constancy, as well as with Emmy, a child of the Earth.[86]
It is the verities of the heart and nature which Cecily repudiates.
A bourgeois coquette, a flirt tantalized by sex but incapable of
giving herself, concealing wantonness beneath the garments of respectability: such also is the Temple Drake of *Sanctuary*. Faulkner has unquestionably inherited something of the Puritan's misogyny, for his grievances go further. Following Milton's description of Dalila as "manifest Serpent," he attributes a natural affinity for evil to woman. Let us first listen to Quentin in *The Sound
and the Fury*:

> *Women are like that they dont acquire knowledge of people we are for
> that they are just born with a practical fertility of suspicion that makes a
> crop every so often and usually right they have an affinity for evil for sup-
> plying whatever the evil lacks in itself for drawing it about them instinc-
> tively as you do bedclothing in slumber fertilising the mind for it until the
> evil has served its purpose whether it ever existed or no.*[87]

and then to the novelist himself in *Light in August* where his
antipathy is expressed with unusual violence: "her natural female
infallibility for the spontaneous comprehension of evil."[88] Woman,
always linked with the earth, actually cannot subscribe to the
rules invented by man to control, indeed, to violate nature. She
cannot apply a code: pragmatic—the "plans" of Raskolnikov are
masculine sins—she adapts to the facts and her reactions therefore remain "unpredictable."[89] Women generally are little concerned about man's theories, morality and honor: "just a person
that don't look at things the same way a man has learned to
do. Don't have the same ideas about what is decent and what
is not."[90] It is precisely at the moment when this misogyny hits
its peak that Faulkner reverses direction and makes vice a virtue.
Although amoral in man's eyes, women are innocent of the excesses, extravagances and vainglory to which abstractions drive

127

men. In dealing with evil, they adapt to it and survive; in addition, they instinctively know all that the "innocent" male learns at the price of a painful initiation. Compare Lena Grove to Christmas or Miss Jenny (*Sartoris*) to the violent men around her. Faulkner, on this point, confirms the views of Dostoevsky's *Diary*. He has, in his turn, made of these heroines an instrument of salvation, for, like the black, they obstinately and unostentatiously resist, they endure and cause others to endure, on them depends the immortality of the race: "that indomitable spirit . . . she thought how much finer that gallantry which never lowered blade to foes no sword could find; that uncomplaining steadfastness of those unsung (ay, unwept too) women than the fustian and useless glamour of the men that obscured it."[91] Faulkner glorifies woman to the degree that, channelling nature, she purifies it without betraying it. She knows better than man, who dreams of being an angel and often acts like an animal, how to take advantage of her double nature: to adjust to evil and transform it into the good. Life triumphs with her, and that is the essential. Lena Grove leaves the hell of Jefferson quite unharmed. She is invulnerable. And here is the response to the castigations of the Puritans: "Woman . . . : the Passive and Anonymous whom God had created to be not alone the recipient and receptacle of the seed of his body but of his spirit too, which is truth or as near truth as he dare approach."[92] Salome or Beatrice? Neither Faulkner nor Dostoevsky offer a final answer. In their equation, the unknown always conceals two opposed values.

It remains to point out the role played by characters like the idiot and the child. The thinking child is seen in Nelly of *The Insulted and the Injured*, Kolya in *The Brothers Karamazov*, Chick Mallison in *Intruder in the Dust* who further relates, and comments upon, his memories in *The Town*, as Lucius Priest will also do later in *The Reivers*. Even the simple-minded are given to discourse: Prince Myshkin reasons with enviable eloquence and, if Benjy Compson does not have the gift of speech, Faulkner aids him in wording his impressions. The frequency of such examples is easily explained by the rehabilitation of irrational values: the child, the idiot, the negro, the muzhik are all equally the sons of the Earth.[93] Finally, one can refer to the preceding chapters for matters touching situations like the trial and the duel.

NOTES TO CHAPTER IV

1. *Faulkner in the University*, p. 69.
2. *Sartoris*, p. 9.
3. See John Faulkner *My Brother Bill* (London: Victor Gollancz Ltd., 1964), p. 90.
4. *White Nights and Other Stories* ("Notes from the Underground"), p. 81. Emphasis added.
5. *Crime and Punishment*, p. 41.
6. *Ibid.*, pp. 54-55.
7. *Ibid.*, pp. 59-60.
8. *Ibid.*, p. 229.
9. *The Possessed*, pp. 64, 89, etc.
10. *Sartoris*, pp. 154-57.
11. *Sanctuary*, Ch. VII and pp. 94, 196.
12. *Absalom, Absalom!*, p. 336.
13. *Ibid.*, p. 9.
14. *The Idiot*, p. 546.
15. *Crime and Punishment*, p. 43.
16. *Ibid.*, p. 217.
17. *Ibid.*, p. 247.
18. *Ibid.*, p. 412.
19. *Ibid.*, p. 43.
20. *Ibid.*, p. 249.
21. *Ibid.*, pp. 423-24.
22. *Sanctuary*, p. 42. See also p. 32.
23. *Ibid.*, p. 206.
24. *Ibid.*, p. 256.
25. *Ibid.*, p. 341.
26. *Ibid.*, p. 347.
27. See Jean Stein, "William Faulkner: An Interview," *William Faulkner: Three Decades of Criticism*, eds. Frederick J. Hoffman and Olga W. Vickery (East Lansing, Mich.: Michigan State University Press, 1960), pp. 75-76.
28. *Light in August*, pp. 232-33, 191-92.
29. Rather erroneously, for Gide confuses the confessional form of *Notes from the Underground*, a first person narrative, with the interior monologue. See André Gide *Dostoïevsky* (Paris: Plon, 1923), p. 237.
30. *Crime and Punishment*, p. 459.
31. *Ibid.*, p. 477.
32. *Ibid.*.
33. *Ibid.*, p. 242.
34. *The Sound and the Fury and As I Lay Dying*, pp. 192-93.
35. *Crime and Punishment*, p. 242.
36. *The Notebooks of Crime and Punishment*, p. 195.
37. *The Possessed*, p. 239.
38. *The Idiot*, p. 214.
39. *The Wild Palms*, p. 139.
40. Jean Pouillon *Temps et roman* (Paris: Gallimard, 1946), p. 228.
41. *Sartoris*, p. 92. See also pp. 126-27.
42. *Absalom, Absalom!*, p. 9.
43. *Collected Stories*, p. 792 ("Beyond").
44. *The Wild Palms*, p. 137.
45. *Collected Stories*, p. 104 ("Shall Not Perish").
46. *Requiem for a Nun*, p. 92.
47. See *Light in August*, pp. 188-89.
48. *Ibid.*, p. 355.
49. *Ibid.*, p. 29.
50. *The Possessed*, p. 295.

51. *Crime and Punishment*, pp. 370, 463.
52. *The Possessed*, p. 144.
53. *The Brothers Karamazov*, pp. 380-81.
54. *Crime and Punishment*, p. 461.
55. *Ibid.*, p. 71.
56. *Ibid.*, p. 372.
57. *The Idiot*, p. 209.
58. *The Possessed*, p. 259.
59. *The Brothers Karamazov*, pp. 317-18.
60. *Crime and Punishment*, p. 481.
61. *Ibid.*.
62. See Reinhard Lauth, *Die Philosophie Dostojewskis* (München: R. Piper Verlag, 1950), pp. 388, 473-79.
63. *Light in August*, p. 107.
64. *Ibid.*, p. 320.
65. *Faulkner in the University*, p. 118.
66. See Cleanth Brooks, *William Faulkner: The Yoknapatawpha Country* (New Haven, Conn.: Yale Univ. Press, 1963), p. 68.
67. See George Lukacs, "Dostoevsky" in *Dostoevsky*, ed. René Wellek (Englewood Cliffs, N. J.: Prentice Hall, 1962), p. 151.
68. *A Raw Youth*, p. 90.
69. *Ibid.*, pp. 100-101.
70. *Crime and Punishment*, p. 190.
71. *Sanctuary*, p. 109.
72. *Light in August*, p. 114.
73. *Ibid.*, p. 246. See also p. 248.
74. See *Requiem for a Nun*, p. 116.
75. *Absalom, Absalom!*, p. 9.
76. See Walter Slatoff, *Quest for Failure* (Ithaca, N. Y.: Cornell Univ. Press, 1960), pp. 131-32.
77. *Absalom, Absalom!*, p. 351.
78. Cleanth Brooks calls Charles Bon "a mirror image, a reverse shadow of his father," *op. cit.*, p. 302.
79. See *A Fable*, p. 348: "No, they are not inimical really, there is no contest actually; they can even exist side by side together in this one restricted arena." See also p. 349: "A fate, a destiny in it: mine and yours, one and inextricable."
80. *The Insulted and the Injured*, p. 39.
81. See Cleanth Brooks, *op. cit.*, p. 196-206.
82. *The Brothers Karamazov*, p. 630. See also p. 425.
83. See *The Diary of a Writer*, p. 409.
84. *Ibid.*, p. 335.
85. Marcel Proust, *A la recherche du temps perdu*, XII (Paris: Gallimard, 1947), p. 220.
86. *Soldiers' Pay*, p. 120.
87. *The Sound and the Fury and As I Lay Dying*, pp. 115-16. See also p. 124.
88. *Light in August*, p. 117. See also *The Unvanquished*, p. 262.
89. *Light in August*, p. 149. See also p. 157.
90. *Collected Stories*, p. 558 ("Honor"). See also *The Town*, p. 289.
91. *Sartoris*, pp. 357-58.
92. *Light in August*, pp. 441-42.
93. See the parallel between Faulkner and Wordsworth drawn by Cleanth Brooks *op. cit.*, p. 36, and Konstantin Mochulsky, *Dostoevsky* (Princeton, N. J.: Princeton Univ. Press, 1967), p. 559.

V

AN ATTEMPT AT HISTORICAL EXPLANATION

Faulkner and Dostoevsky are men who think and feel by antithesis. In them there are few ideas, emotions, attitudes which do not call forth their contrary or are not born of the marriage of water and fire. A matter of temperament, probably. But is this explanation sufficient? The writer is different from other men, and art has its own universe, to be sure, but are they not, just the same, a part of reality? The man who writes finds himself in a situation, a concrete relationship with the here and now from which flow all his choices, literary or otherwise; and we are very mistaken to neglect the ties which always exist between economics and aesthetics, society and literature. In short, it is here a matter of explaining literature through history and sociology while keeping in mind the unique character of the materials studied and the separation between them and lived events.

We have seen that neither Faulkner nor Dostoevsky resigns himself to his lacerations. Both writers usually attempt to resolve conflicts, to build bridges, to leap from the level of contradictions to that of synthesis. Their approach consists, we recall, in a judicious sublimation of the instincts, in an adequate submission of raw matter to the spirit, to the heart, to the moral sense. Thus charity wins out over *amor sui*, ethics over social pride, the freedom of the agent over the constraint of events, spiritual progress over technical progress, etc. Creation is good, to be sure, since it comes from God, but it is so only in principle, in its origins, for Adam's sin continues to contaminate it. It is for man to expiate, to purify what he has sullied—a restoration which operates according to formulas proper to Christianity, the soul of the sinner finding itself blessed with free will and a sense of the good. One would like to know, however, with exactly what materials the process operates: the direction is easy to define, but it is not the same for the terms, thesis and antithesis, which are our starting point. The labels "circumspect reformism" and "conservative reformism" which we have stuck on our authors are well suited to their fundamental dialectic. In all areas, they perceive an opposition between what is or has been and what perhaps tomorrow will be, a prospect for which they feel little attraction. Hence the dilemma. To choose the past is to deny that which is to come, that is, life. And to follow "the trend of history" is apparently to allow oneself to be consumed by what Bonald calls the "devouring cancer" of matter. An alternative that will avoid these dangers must be found. To settle the question, Faulkner and Dostoevsky elevate politics to the moral level, a technique which allows them to reconcile contraries with a minimum of sacrifices. Preserving all that is useful in the established order, they poach at the same time on the land of the progressivists. It is better to say that they recuperate or revalorize, for they change the nature of that which they keep from the past and that which they borrow from the left by considering it in an ethical perspective. Spiritualization allows them to run with the hare and hunt with the hounds, although it also renders the former less tasty and the latter less swift. We have already said that by disassociating social problems from their economic and political infrastructure, that is, by dematerializing them, one ends up a conservative. To make social mutations dependent on those of the soul is to postpone them indefinitely or at least to allow them to languish in some vague utopia. Recuperated rather than denounced, the evil inherent in the organization of the state—the debasement of the blacks and the poor—is transformed into a saving grace, into participation in a collective—but unequally distributed—expiation of a universal sin. We are taught to be patient, to accept, nay, to love suffering rather than seek to end it; we are lured by the bright prospects of either the stoic grandeur of the immortal race or an even less tangible beyond; and what do a Chick Mallison or an Alyosha Karamazov, solitary champions of charity, mean compared with the multitudes of the insulted and injured? The preaching of a spiritual revolution does not even have the excuse of being supported by a naive optimism, by an enthusiastic, contagious and unshakeable conviction that humanity will soon rediscover its lost paradise. We are confronted here with the traditional argument for eschatological politics, a politics which destroys itself, for it renounces collective action in the name of spiritual values, believes it is renewing the whole by improving the parts, remedies injustice while advising us to accept it, sets suffering up as a virtue and puts the golden age off into some hazy neverland. On closer examination, it seems that Faulkner and Dostoevsky strive above all to reevaluate the past and that part of it which survives in their time. Pride and honor are aristocratic attributes that they lift from destructive selfishness to the altruistic awareness of the dignity of man. In the same manner, patriarchal faith is saved, while, at the same time, being liberated from dogmatic formalism. Faulkner claims the support of no church, and Dostoevsky preaches an orthodoxy that is his own unique distillation. The nineteenth century nation is praised but projected into a world of ideas, disencumbered of any material substrata, linked with the virtues of hypothetical paragons: the black, the gentleman and the muzhik. Let us point out in passing that if the Faulknerian Negro, a symbol of endurance, can accede to the dignity of the white, Dostoevsky also attributes qualities of the people to the nobility. Even feeling, under attack by technology, is rehabilitated. Whether it be the verities of the heart or love of one's neighbor, it is directed toward the *élan vital* which it helps to sustain; associated with the primitive, the virginal, it gives off an authentically romantic perfume. If inequality, pride and honor, faith and the nation, the very stirrings of the heart constitute different facets of a heritage to which these writers remain loyal despite their clairvoyance, if they judge the existing order perfectible rather than detestable, they nonetheless borrow some of the principles of its adversaries. The salvage of the progressivist doctrines, although less concerted, is achieved in the same way as the salvage of tradition to which, moreover, it is subordinate. The mechanistic dogma of progress, applied to the spir-

133

itual, helps to germinate the good grain stored within the granaries of the past. The dynamism of industrial civilization is transformed into "good acts," acts of charity, inspired by the values of the past. The example of the West and the North can, in sum, only reanimate the sclerotic organism of Holy Russia or the Old South, permitting the exploitation of its hidden riches. Disassociated from humanitarian abstractions, the ideal of liberty universalizes the free will of the individual, formerly the prerogative of the propertied class. It is the same for brotherhood which, prefigured by the intimate relations of agrarian communities and the old plantations, transcends its outmoded boundaries and, without being confused with the vague precepts of the "liberals," englobes all souls in a reciprocal love. As for the "people" of the democrats, they play a role of primary importance in this synthesis, although Faulkner and Dostoevsky substitute a model of conduct for the anonymous masses. They open, however, the circle of the elite to the Negro and the peasant; in principle, spiritualism leads to the recognition of equality, it also abolishes with equal force the injustices of the past and the class struggle from which a better future is presumably to be born. Finally, the condemnation of private property bridges the gap between marxist communism and the Word.

These are, in general, the conclusions of our first three chapters, but the examination of novelistic forms probably permits a better definition of the causes and the nature of the process sketched above.

Can the decomposition of the traditional narrative announced by Dostoevsky and realized by Faulkner be compared to the decomposition of the accepted values of the nineteenth century? The enterprise is dangerous, even debatable. But, if we are careful not to make art the slave of environment, it is legitimate to compare areas where, under different aspects, the same human progress is developing. Let us remark at the outset that the expression "traditional narrative" is at best an approximate designation, which must be understood as referring to an *a posteriori* relation of events organized according to empirical or logical models, perceived by the omniscient and prescient eye of a God, and charged with a preordained meaning. Having said this, let us see in what direction the form develops from Dostoevsky to

Faulkner, or better, according to what lines of force do the reforms of the former and the audacities of the latter organize themselves. The problem of intelligibility poses itself from the very beginning. From 1880 to 1930—one thinks of Henry James, Conrad, Joyce, Proust, Kafka, Virginia Woolf—ambiguity slowly undermines the once unquestionable testimony of the narrator. Where certitude and common sense once reigned and where all was clear, "true," explainable and explained, the author is now no longer sure of what he reports and because of his scruples cedes his place to a third party, as if ashamed to display his ignorance. He indicates by this, finally, that there is every reason to question the narrator's veracity, all the more so because the latter also hesitates in his turn. Between us and the events described there is a screen of consciousness which doubts its own good faith and implicitly prohibits us from taking the narrative at face value. Fiction, rather than being imposed on us as something true (aesthetically speaking, of course), submits itself to our judgement as a conjectural representation. Already in Dostoevsky it has lost its innocence: the age of suspicion has begun. And yet, the novel does not turn away from the portrayal of reality: Dostoevsky sees himself as a "realist." His carefully documented realism focuses on the marginal case and the depths of the soul; it is remote from all that is banal and conventional.[1] One must, then, acknowledge that the relations between reality and the artist have changed. While the universe created by Flaubert, Turgenev and Tolstoy does not, despite their originality, differ essentially from the world inhabited by their readers, Dostoevsky's work is located on the fringes of the literature of his time and still today exhales an odor uniquely its own. To what is this to be attributed? To the temperament of the writer, his health, his ordeals? To be sure. But this line of reasoning only postpones the question. To explain a man's point of view by his psychology, his constitution and his experiences does not tell us how it varies from the norm; approached from this perspective, there is no norm, we are all exceptions. We must find a better explanation of Dostoevsky's fundamental strangeness in relation to the consensus of his contemporaries. Unlike those who naively accept the world—even if they subsequently reshape it as they please—Dostoevsky questions reality. He is one of the rare novelists of the nineteenth century who is fundamentally disturbed by reality, one of the first who cannot enter it easily and simply. The ambiguity which hovers over his narratives projects his personal malaise before the real world into the imaginary world: the feeling that things are more complex than is usually admitted, that the schemas we use to interpret them are artificial, simplified, outmoded—all the more since they are undergoing a radical upheaval at this time— and that one must explain all or nothing, encompass in the same glance the smallest insect and God, the money-lender's chest and Raskolnikov's mad gamble . . . A superhuman ambition which was nearly realized, but which in its haste jumps obstacles and rushes past question marks. In Dostoevsky, the obscurity testifies, in the final analysis, as much to the difficulty that he experienced in remaking the world to suit his unique vision as to his dissatisfaction with the order that exists and the image commonly made of it. Did he not reproach the Russian realists for painting only fixed types, situations already outmoded? What was needed, according to him, was "the latest news, red-hot,"[2] the premonitory signs of tomorrow, the Russia of crimes, conspiracies and suicides, "the carriers of degeneration and renewal."[3] "In times such as ours it would be strange," he writes in the preface to *The Brothers Karamazov*, "to require clarity of people. . . . For not only is an eccentric 'not always' a particularity and a separate element, but, on the contrary, it happens sometimes that such a person, I dare say, carries within him the very heart of the universal, and the rest of the men of his epoch have for some reason been temporarily torn from it, as by a gust of wind."[4] Dostoevsky was a prophet, then, and like all prophets spoke in sibylline terms, enclosed within a vision that is sometimes too gratuitous to allow posterity to recognize itself in it. Faulkner's case is much simpler, for his hermeticism, far from contrasting with his age, reflects its preoccupations. This is because the crisis predicted by Dostoevsky had been accomplished in the meantime, whether history has confirmed his views or not. Corresponding to the crumbling of the old economic, social and philosophical systems, there is a growing individualization of the methods of expression, although Faulkner, aware of his ties to patriarchal society, only occasionally falls into excesses. If Dostoevsky is "in advance" of Zola, Faulkner does not entirely reject the heritage of Medan. Among the contested and finally repudiated values, we may cite the spatial concept of time and the law of succession. The manner in which Dostoevsky's plots develop prefigure the Bergsonian notion of *durée* implicit in the monologues of *The Sound and the Fury*. Time is interiorized, spiritualized, to use a term that has already occurred in these pages. Chronological succession, whose systemization leads to the principle of causality, is eclipsed by a purely aesthetic principle. The interplay of leitmotifs succeeds the empirical unit based on the passage from one moment to another and the logical coherence which postulates the meshing of cause and effect. The novel, in avoiding the vulgar experience of existence as well as the laws of reason, betrays its mistrust of them. Beginning with *Crime and Punishment*, it seeks to communicate a more authentic vision of the world, that is to say, one more intuitive and less tainted with common sense than the one then prevailing. In the school of Comte and Claude Bernard, Dostoevsky tells us, we cram our heads full of superfluous, inexact fundamentals which separate us from the real —two times two is four. Nietzsche, Bergson, Freud and Einstein soon proved him right.

With Dostoevsky, not only does the novelist lose his self-confidence, his candor and his credulity, but he is hypnotized by phenomena which few people would view with such alarm. Turgenev was probably as interested in the conflict of father and son, and many others before Faulkner have analyzed the forces which sap a family. Dostoevsky sees further. Here society disintegrates; maniacs and criminals, the maladjusted, the "unhappy" that we will meet again in Faulkner withdraw into isolation. The unusual and the trivial, the grotesque and the melodramatic, in short, the murky and mysterious, none of this is new. It is already to be found in Hoffmann, Poe, Dickens and Balzac. But to enclose them all together within the soul and thus underline the strangeness of a problematic character in relation to others: this is proper to Dostoevsky.[5] In Faulkner as well, solitude manifests itself by means of soliloquies, and even by the splitting of the personality or idiocy and by love that is often sad and occasionally tragic.

The harmony between the individual and the community, between man and woman, is broken. It ought also to be pointed out that it is from this conflict with reality that ideas and art arise.[6] The contact is, however, occasionally reestablished: is not woman simultaneously a tomb and a mother? Alienation, although extensive, never achieves the amplitude found in Europe in the 1950's; it is restrained by the survival of the past and our novelists' desire to redress the situation.

Once public values are set aside and the ancient edifice demolished, the problem of constructing a new one remains. Dostoevsky and Faulkner made psychology an accessory: for them it is only a means of portraying the human condition, of translating a meditation on existence. We know, of course, that every narrative reflects a metaphysics, but in these two cases the all too powerful ideas more than once dispense with story telling. The Russian expatiates willingly, and so does the American beginning with Soldiers' Pay and Mosquitoes. But there he merely indulges in a bit of ironic and paradoxical juggling. In contrast, in Intruder in the Dust, Requiem for a Nun and A Fable he throws himself wholeheartedly into the discursive mode: less gifted than Dostoevsky, he falls into flatulence. Even if one sets aside the philosophic passages, these works are so informed by the notion of an alternative system in opposition to a dubious, outmoded system that the characters are transformed into bearers of ideas, anemic and empty of individuality. When one wishes to convince those who think differently rather than merely describe what everyone accepts, no trick is overlooked. Hence the emblematic names, the ritualized gestures which disassociate the hero from the vulgar illusion of the material world and link him with the only truth that matters: that which the artist wishes to inculcate in us.

Let us see if history can account for this extreme spiritualism, an attitude alternately critical and benevolent toward tradition, and, above all, hostile to the materialistic radicalism of the European and the Yankee. Perhaps history will tell us why these men attempt simultaneously to conserve and to go ahead, but in a manner that betrays both what they save and that which they anticipate? What is the source of this eclecticism which draws from right and left, more from the right than the left, to be sure, but from wherever it chooses? To what finally are these tensions, this hermeticism, these doubts about the validity of so many certitudes to be attributed?

The parallelisms pointed out in Faulkner and Dostoevsky result from the fact that, congenial spirits, they have had to make similar choices.

There is no lack of correspondences between the Russia of Alexander II and the ante-bellum South. They have been noted more than once from the point of view of the landowner: the same sense of hospitality, the same presumption, the same entourage of indolent and devoted servants, the same portraits of ancestors on the walls of old dwellings, the same relaxed atmosphere, the same hunting parties and visits, etc. In both cases, we are dealing with an economic system based on agriculture, landed estates and the serfdom or slavery of the manual laborers, that is to say, a regime surpassed by the societies that developed after the industrial revolution in France, England, and the northern United States. Well into the nineteenth century, Russia and the South feature vestiges of feudalism, the signs of a backward and isolated world.[7] But, as Irving Howe notes,[8] their "backwardness" gives these writers the proper perspective required for the critic. Their marginal position explains the lucidity with which Dostoevsky and Faulkner have been able to analyze industrial society.

Vestiges of feudalism: it is much more than a figure of speech. Considered as a type of regime outside all historic and geographic context, feudalism is defined by a set of characteristics, several of which are found around 1860 in Russia and in the South. A hierarchy subordinating the peasantry—serfs or slaves—to an aristocratic minority; a union of power and the earth: "the condition of the earth implies that of man;"[9] personal ties of obedience and protection between vassal and lord, a contract passed at the beginning prescribing rights and duties; dematerialization of property and the State which are replaced respectively by the *right* to demand the services of the tenant and the *notion* of devotion of man to man; decentralization and division of powers combined with the idea of the "moral mission" of the king; the importance of the guilds, of family kinship and of the home; the cult of honor and fidelity; such are, generally speaking, the salient characteristics of an organization[10] of which the Empire of Alexander II and the Confederate States sometimes offered only a caricature. Regimes also change. Honor becomes a facade, the terms of the contract fall into oblivion, the protection owed by the lord gives way to arbitrary power. The feudal pyramid is, in principle, crowned by the king, supreme sovereign whom anointing raises to a lieutenant of God: the hierarchy of servants and protectors in Christian feudalism is extended by the service and protection of God, a religious foundation which guarantees the excellence of the political order. But in the West, the King long ago freed himself of this humility, when he did not, in fact, disappear altogether as in France and the United States. The two keystones of medieval society—God and the king—later sealed in the divine right monarchy, underwent the assaults of deicides and regicides. The secularization of power was further accelerated by the industrial revolution. Mutilated, indeed decapitated, the feudal regime lost its social and moral equilibrium, but it did not immediately crumble. The discarding of God, in particular, deprived it of any spiritual sanction and permitted the substitution of the code of the jungle for the Gospels. The king questioned or dethroned, the nobles emancipate themselves, free themselves of their obligations toward the higher powers, but jealously guard their privileges regarding those lower. Feudalism, based on a system of mutual aid, thus turns into the exploitation of the weak by the strong. Having to account to no one, the powerful serve and protect only themselves.[11] That is why, among other reasons, Faulkner describes slavery as a sin and why Dostoevsky proposes the orthodox Christ as a model. In theory, social abuses result from a scorn for the virtues of the Gospels, which disfigures institutions in which faith plays an essential role, reduces Negroes and peasants to the level of objects, suffocates the sense of duty among the propertied class. The ideas of these writers are best understood in the light of history. They are intimately connected with their attitude toward the past, but they are so, one might say, in opposite directions. For Faulkner seems to pose God only as an hypothesis in order to sublimate a corrupt tradition, while Dostoevsky rehabilitates the peasant tradition in order to save God.

Before pursuing the parallel, it is well to underline the differences which we will then pass over. Situations are, to be sure, never identical, and history repeats itself only metaphorically. How is czarist despotism, its bureaucracy, and the strictly stratified Russian society to be compared to American democracy where the whites were in principle equal and where they could rise socially, if they had ambition and talent?[12] Mobility, the spirit of freedom and competition are in contrast to Russian rigidity, although the latter did relax little by little. In addition, the conquest of the West, which corresponds in part to the expansion into central Asia, marked the South decisively, inspiring its dynamism.[13] Let us add that slavery and serfdom are not synonymous, and that in America servitude was a function of the blackness of one's skin, a "blemish" which the muzhik did not share.[14] In any case, it was easier for the poor to raise themselves where there was no racial prejudice. In short, in the South democracy was allied with the oligarchic notion of the elite, and the methods of modern commerce rested on a life style closer to feudalism than industrial capitalism. In addition to a minority of rich planters, a white proletariat and millions of black slaves, this region possessed an important middle class of small farmers,[15] a group nonexistent in Russia, where the sparse bourgeoisie saw itself relegated to the towns and cities and assigned to commerce and industry. Finally, if the American intellectuals ordinarily felt themselves tied to the ruling class by virtue of the racial segregation,[16] the Russian intelligentsia on the eve of the reforms was recruited from the clergy, the common people and the nobility: they were "émigrés of the interior."[17]

In the countries which interest us, the decomposition of the feudal order attained its critical moment in the second half of the eighteenth century, a period during which the crown dispensed the nobility from obligatory service without depriving them of their serfs (1762) and which also witnessed the Declaration of Independence of the North American colonies (1776). The evolution was precipitated by the abolition of serfdom (1861) and slavery (1862), which undermined the bases of the established order. Dostoevsky lived until 1881 and was able to paint first hand the upheaval which followed; Faulkner's lot was, on the other hand, to study it from a greater distance. The first is an eyewitness, the second primarily a historian. It is the past, the time of the Civil War and Reconstruction, that Faulkner explores to define a present which he situates, as we know, around 1905-1910.

Shortly after 1850, the South and Russia went through crises characterized by military defeats, the diffusion either of Yankee materialism or of western positivism and extremist doctrines, industrialization, the appearance of new social classes and the liberation of the slaves and serfs. Centuries of evolution were condensed into a few decades: the modern spirit marched, one might say, double time to make up for the delay and the organic harmony of the eighteenth century disappeared before the idea of conflict.[18]

In both cases, servile manual labor constituted the very foundation of the regime. Emancipate the serfs and slaves and, on paper, the aristocracy loses its prerogatives and fortune, it evaporates as a political power. The abolitionist laws, however, scarcely sin by an excess of generosity. At the very most, they grant a theoretical freedom transforming legal servitude into economic slavery. The true reform in 1861-1862 would have consisted in transferring to the newly emancipated full ownership of the land they formerly cultivated. No one dared go so far, particularly in the United States, and freedom quickly saw itself encumbered by redemption annuities, required labor, tenant farming and debts. On the other hand, there was a disappearance of the personal ties of feudal paternalism, that is, the protection owed by the free man, a moral obligation which compensated, for better or worse, social inequality. Gone was the lord: in his place was the boss. The condition of the blacks and the muzhiks was, then, scarcely improved. But what about their former masters? As early as 1881, Leroy-Beaulieu noted that in Russia it was "the latter whose habits, mores and life style was most changed by emancipation;"[19] he also pointed out "the decay of the patriarchal mores."[20] The same remark is made by Pierre Belperron about the Southern planters.[21] The landowning class, generally jealous of its prerogatives, already frequently neglectful of its responsibilities to its inferiors, is abruptly dispossessed of its sovereign rights and of a portion of its resources. The bell has begun to toll for them unless they become involved in industry or business. In short, the reform, while accomplishing little more than a modification of the nature of abuses, also abolished the last benefits of the regime. Everyone lost in the process: the lord, his theoretical power and money; the slave, the help he could still expect of the lord. The "fraternal" and concrete relations of individual to individual are supplanted by the legal, administrative, anonymous relations between citizens, between boss and workers.[22] We pass simultaneously from the realm of free will and moral choice to an area where ethics tend to become confused with obedience to the Law.

Feudalism dies under the blows of a force which is doubly foreign. First in a literal sense, since it is the West and the North which sponsor liberalism; and then because liberalism is closely connected with the industrial economy which slowly but surely dethrones the old agrarian economy. The intrusion of mechanization into a regime founded on agriculture causes a social and moral disequilibrium. It has been observed, for instance, that it causes the decline of the family, reducing the extended family to the married couple.[23] In addition, industrialization reshapes the social map: it overthrows the existing hierarchy, for it permits the previously unpropertied groups to make their fortune. In the second half of the nineteenth century, Russia witnessed the emergence of a working class proletariat and the ascension of a third estate—the capitalist bourgeois, whose machines the abolition of serfdom provided with abundant labor. A comparable phenomenon was produced in the South, beginning before the Civil War,[24] then evident around 1880 and in 1920, when the industrial expansion raised the protests of the Agrarians. Consequently the *ethos* of the past was rejected in favor of the cult of money, until the moral and social evolution overtook the technical evolution and an "industrial" morality was elaborated. Science develops more quickly than our concepts of good and evil. It incessantly poses questions which conscience cannot immediately answer. This creates a void into which the outlaws are more than willing to move. It is the hunting grounds of parvenus, speculators and the greedy, who are joined by unscrupulous aristocrats: actual or potential usurpers, homeless adventurers who are morally, if not financially, bankrupt.

143

The works of Dostoevsky and Faulkner reflect all of these more or less analogous historical transformations, although it must be recognized that the Russian was directly involved in much that the American knew partially through hearsay. On the other hand, Faulkner, arriving later, was able to measure the complete extent of the disasters the other could only predict. It is often said that Dostoevsky's characters exist outside social categories.[25] This is false. Although this criterion is of secondary importance to him, it is nonetheless a factor in his world.[26] The problems debated by Tolstoy in *Anna Karenina*, for example—the consequences of emancipation, the scandals of capitalism, the unequal distribution of the land, etc.—are evoked both in his novels and his *Diary*.

In *Crime and Punishment* (1866) Svidrigailov, an example of the corrupted nobleman, boasts of having been spared by the abolition of serfdom.[27] "Raskolnikov," we read in *The Notebooks of Crime and Punishment*, "is a good name, even though your father was a teacher; the Raskolnikov's have been known for two hundred years."[28] Gaganov, the rich landowner of *The Possessed*, escapes ruin, but the imperial proclamation of February 19, 1861, strikes him to such a degree that he leaves the army: he belongs to "that strange section of the nobility" who "set an extreme value on their pure and ancient lineage" and he feels "himself personally insulted by the proclamation."[29] Other landowners, less fortunate, are left impoverished or without resources by the crisis.[30] Some are so undone that they dispose of their goods and emigrate, as Dostoevsky explains in his response to Gradovsky in *The Diary of a Writer* (August, 1880).[31] Stavrogin is guilty of being separated from the earth, and the intelligentsia of being cut off from the people.[32] Even more terrible is the shock which jolts the Southern aristocracy, for it is accompanied by war, surrender and an occupation painted in somber tones in *Absalom, Absalom!* and *The Unvanquished*: black and white founder in the same misery.[33] The Compson genealogy added to the second edition (1946) of *The Sound and the Fury*, emphasizes the decay of the patricians between 1865 and 1910. The family properties remain intact until the Civil War and then crumble little by little: mortgaged in 1866 to a Yankee carpetbagger after Union troops burned the town; partially dismembered and parcelled out until

1900 to meet the mortgage payments; sold around 1910 with the exception of the house, kitchen garden and out-buildings to a golf club. The governors and generals are succeeded by indolent lawyers, intellectuals haunted by death, "deserters" or idiots. The house becomes a boarding house, and the golf course a series of jerry-built bungalows.[34] *Sic transit.* The Sartorises and the de Spains, however, far from abdicating, adapt to the new economy. The planters become bankers; but young Bayard Sartoris loves death above everything, and Flem Snopes replaces de Spain as president of the bank. The political power of the great families diminishes from generation to generation. The prestige of Gavin Stevens depends in the later novels almost exclusively on the moral qualities which characterize the elite of his class, but the patricians have no monopoly on virtue. In losing their material power, some of the descendants of the aristocracy are elevated spiritually and fraternize with people their fathers would have snubbed. In the course of time the cutting memory of catastrophes is dissipated, and as Faulkner's desire for redemption grows, his patricians once more take the lead. From *Go Down, Moses* to *The Reivers*, they are the most eloquent preachers—and the guinea pigs—of "sublimation." Their decadence culminates in *The Sound and the Fury.* It is there that their social status and the situation of their fortune most recall the Karamazovs: landowners, aristocrats of the old stock, provincial notables, but brought to ruin. See the Compson home:

> the weedchoked traces of the old ruined lawns and promenades, the house which had needed painting too long already, the scaling columns of the portico where Jason III . . . sat all day long with a decanter of whiskey and a litter of dogeared Horaces and Livys and Catulluses.[35]

and that of the Karamazovs:

> the drawing room . . . was the largest room, and furnished with old-fashioned ostentation. The furniture was white and very old, upholstered in old, red, silky material. In the spaces between the windows there were mirrors in elaborate white and gilt frames, of old fashioned carving. On the walls, covered with white paper, which was torn in many places, there hung two large portraits—one of some prince who had been governor of the district thirty years before, and the other of some bishop, also long since dead.[36]

145

or better yet the hovel where Captain Snegiryov, another noble-man, starves with a wife who is "a cripple and weak-minded" and a daughter who is "a cripple and a hunchback,"[37] not to mention the other children. The image of the "rotting family in the rotting house"[38] and even that of the mother clinging to a mirage of the past occurs, even more pitifully, in *Crime and Punishment* when Marmeladov confesses to the hero.[39] Except for the cult of tradition and the nostalgia of a defunct prosperity, nothing distinguishes the former leaders now on the garbage heap from the "poor folk." There are many estranged, alienated, debauched or penniless noblemen in Dostoevsky: Valkovsky in *The Insulted and the Injured*, Svidrigailov in *Crime and Punishment*, Stavrogin in *The Possessed*, Versilov in *A Raw Youth*, and finally old Karamazov. Myshkin is the only exception, but he is an "idiot" and cut off from his class by his virtues as much as the others are by their vices. No one is capable of fulfilling the role assigned by Versilov to the nobility, except Dmitri and Alyosha in the last novel. But for these two successes, how many failures. In Petersburg and Jefferson twilight falls on the masters of yester-year; the rabble pushes against the gates of the estates where degenerates and criminals vegetate. . . . A few still resist; many are already vanquished. Dmitri and Alyosha, Chick Mallison and Gavin Stevens offer little more than a belated note of consolation.

Dostoevsky the thinker condemns the doctrinal aspect of the nascent industrialism of his time: the scientific and materialistic spirit, the utilitarianism, etc., while Faulkner underscores its gaudy cheapness and its ugliness: the rape of nature by the auto-mobile, the railroad and the factory chimneys. They are, none-theless, of one mind about its social corollaries. Both denounce parasites of science and technology like the Verhovenskys and the Snopes who scorn ethics and seek to wrench power from its traditional guardians. Faulkner and Dostoevsky make the critical moment when an outmoded code of conduct can no longer solve all of the problems resulting from historical development one of the pivots of their work. They both live this moment with the same intensity and wish to fill the moral vacuum in the same way. To the rational amorality of Raskolnikov, the agitator Verho-vensky, and Ivan Karamazov, who believes that everything is permitted, corresponds the instinctive amorality of Senator Clarence Snopes (*Sanctuary*), of Jason Compson, the renegade of *The Sound and the Fury*, and of Flem Snopes: "who had begun life as a nihilist and then softened into a mere anarchist and now was not only a conservative but a tory too: a pillar, rock-fixed, of things as they are."[40] In both Dostoevsky and Faulkner, the epoch's confusion is explored in detail:

And the fire of corruption is spreading visibly, hourly, working up from above downwards. The spirit of isolation is coming upon the people too. Money-lenders and devourers of the commune are rising up. Already the merchant grows more and more eager for rank, and strives to show himself cultured though he has not a trace of culture, and to this end meanly despises his old traditions, and is even ashamed of the faith of his fathers. He visits princes, though he is only a peasant corrupted. The peasants are rotting in drunkenness and cannot shake off the habit. And what cruelty to their wives, to their children even! All from drunkenness! I've seen in the factories children of nine years old, frail, rickety, bent and already depraved. The stuffy workshop, the din of machinery, work all day long, the vile language and the drink, the drink is what a little child's heart needs? He needs sunshine, childish play, good examples all about him, and at least a little love. There must be no more of this.[41]

the new man . . . may lightheartedly overstep all the barriers of the old morality of the old slave-man, if necessary.[42]

What are the causes of our indifference, our lukewarm attitude to such deeds, to such signs of the times, ominous of an unenviable future? Is it our cynicism, is it the premature exhaustion of intellect and imagination in a society that is sinking into decay, in spite of its youth? Is it that our moral principles are shattered to their foundations, or is it, perhaps, a complete lack of such principles among us? . . . the majority of our national crimes of violence bear witness to a widespread evil, now so general among us that it is difficult to contend against it.[43]

the inhuman type which Flem is a manifestation of. I think that Jason Compson in another book of mine is completely inhuman.[44]

our economy, which is an economy based on success rather than on any quality of the human spirit.[45]

I feel sorry for the Compsons. That was blood which was good and brave once, but has thinned and faded all the way out. Of the Snopes, I'm terrified.[46]

He (Clarence Snopes) was unprincipled and without morals . . . all he had was his blind instinct for sadism and overreaching, and was himself really dangerous only to someone he would have the moral and intellectual ascendency of, which out of the entire world's population couldn't possibly be anybody except another Snopes.[47]

Mosquitoes (1927) already contains a sketch of the social theme of Faulkner's *Comédie humaine*: the class struggle that developed and continued to develop in the South, whose haunting image is reflected in *The Brothers Karamazov*: "Well, imagine for yourself a situation like that: a tradition of ease unassailable and unshakable gone to pieces right under you, and out of the wreckage rising a man who once held your stirrup while you mounted."[48] At stake are power, fame and wealth; the adversaries are two ways of behaving: the great families, exhausted, helpless or ruined—the Benbows, the Sartorises, the Compsons—and the Snopeses, intruders, swindlers. The triumph of this robust and cynical tribe is surely an inglorious one! The Snopeses give no quarter, but their success is due as much to the weakness of their victims as to their own vigor and skill. The usurpation of power achieved in Faulkner is already anticipated in Dostoevsky. While Flem momentarily supplants the patricians, in *The Possessed* the latter escape narrowly, and the scepter eludes the rabble's grasp; the crisis has not yet reached its peak. In addition, the two camps present different images according to their situation in the rural American milieu or the urban and intellectual spheres dear to the Russian. In Dostoevsky it is the thinkers who dominate. His "Snopeses" are minds on fire, the young liberals and radicals poisoned by the West: Raskolnikov, Terentiev, Verhovensky, Rakitin, whose amorality, that is, whose inhumanity, he hates as much as Faulkner. Philosopher or horse trader, revolutionary or banker, the *Streber* always sacrifices the angel to the animal. And whether it be by the artifices of reason or greed, he succeeds in rallying to his cause some of his enemies: Ivan Karamazov and Jason Compson both strike the colors that their brothers Dmitri and Quentin still defend, for better or for worse. One has only to compare Dmitri's courage and Alyosha's activism to Quentin's suicide in order to estimate the decline of the ruling class from 1870 to 1910 and to realize what separates Dostoevsky's nobility from Faulkner's moribund gentry. All of the Compsons destroy themselves or go to seed; two of the Karamazovs still manage to act effectively. One might object that *The Sound and the Fury* describes an exceptional case.[49] In general, Dostoevsky's families show much greater weaknesses than do those of Faulkner, who remained close to the rural community: see *As I Lay Dying*. If Dmitri's role falls to Nancy Mannigoe, a servant, a negress and, in addition, a prostitute, the young patrician of *Intruder in the Dust* shows that he can play Alyosha's role. In conclusion, the children of industrialism—capitalists, *nouveaux riches* like Luzhin and Flem Snopes and their brother enemies, the progressivists of every stripe—prefer utility to the good, success to virtue, cold and pragmatic logic to love.[50] This is what is objected to. The old order seems better than "the tragic topsy-turvydom of today,"[51] for as perverted as it is, it at least allows a man the latitude of calling himself such, of asserting himself as a human being. Science and technology enclose us in a dungeon, like the small children that Zossima saw at the factory, far from the sun and space of the pastoral paradise.[52]

It should be further stated that both writers, following local custom,[53] put woman—certain women—on a pedestal, and that they are unanimous in regretting the passing of a way of life which formerly united blacks and whites,[54] the elite and the people.[55] But we will pass over these details and retain the essential. Dostoevsky does not propose to paint a fresco of society, a task to which Faulkner, a student of Balzac, directed a great deal of care. Despite this fact and the schematizations of the one and the nuances of the other, and despite their different historical perspectives, the analyses are alike: the same dislocation of the ruling class under the pressure of the abolitionist laws, the same substitution of mechanization for the agrarian economy.

Everything denotes an acute sense of the mutability of things, the consciousness of living amidst the disorder characteristic of a period of "transition." Faulkner and Dostoevsky are torn beings, in the image of their age. The Russian is, for his part, particularly sensitive to the contemporary malaise:

I have already hinted that some low fellows of different sorts had made their appearance amongst us. In turbulent times of upheaval or transition low characters always come to the front everywhere. I am not speaking now of the so-called "advanced" people who are always in a hurry to be

in advance of everyone else (their absorbing anxiety) and who always have some more or less definite, though often very stupid, aim. No, I am speaking only of the riff-raff. In every period of transition this riff-raff, which exists in every society, rises to the surface, and is not only without any aim but has not even a symptom of an idea, and merely does its utmost to give expression to uneasiness and impatience. . . .
What constituted the turbulence of our time and what transition it was we were passing through I don't know, nor I think does anyone, unless it were some of those visitors of ours.[56]

a multitude of unquestionably aristocratic Russian families are with irresistible force passing in masses into exceptional families, and mingling with them in the general lawlessness and chaos. A typical example of such an exceptional family is sketched by you in your manuscript. Yes, Arkady Makarovitch, you are *a member of an exceptional family*, in distinction to the aristocratic types who have had such a very different childhood and adolescence from yours. . . .

But such an autobiography as yours might serve as material for a future work of art, for a future picture of a lawless epoch already passed. Oh, when the angry strife of the day has passed and the future has come, then a future artist will discover beautiful forms for depicting past lawlessness and chaos![57]

It is probably in the delineation of Ivan Karamazov that Dostoevsky best portrayed the contemporary malaise that he diagnosed throughout his *Diary*:[58] the antinomy of science and faith, the duel of barbarism and morality, the annihilation of public values and the anguished search for a reason for living, the disintegration of society, scepticism and confusion. The rhythm of history accelerated during this period. Dostoevsky already unmasks the "riff-raff" and is aware of the advent of a bourgeoisie[59] that he detested because he identified it with modern materialism and the West. For that matter, it is to the intrusion of capitalism within a relatively stable society that Bakhtin attributes the polyphonic form of his novels.[60]
Faulkner suffers in the same way from seeing the world going to rack and ruin. The old negro Simon, speaking to the shade of Colonel Sartoris, complains that his descendants have lost all sense of decorum and, like the rabble, ride in an automobile:

You jes' got ter lay down de law ter 'um, Marse John; wid all dese foreign wars en sich de young folks is growed away fum de correck behavior; dey don't know how ter conduck dyselfs in de gent'mum way. Whut you reckon folks gwine think when dey sees yo'own folks ridin in de same kine o' rig trash rides in? . . . Ain't Sartorises sot de quality in dis country since befo' de War? And now jes' look at 'um.[61]

Simon attacks only the machine; others, more perceptive—notably the author—denounce the pullulation of the parasites.[62] The motor supplants the horse, a symbol of sovereignty, and the knights are driven to the wall by villains come from God knows where: an inevitable transformation that *Sartoris* presents as a calamity. The past will lose its aura with the years; it will even be stigmatized, but Faulkner will never offer the present more than half-hearted acceptance. The old novelist straightforwardly admits to the students at Virginia that he misses the old days:

> That that's to me is a sad and tragic thing for the old days, the old times, to go, providing you have the sort of background which a country boy like me had when that was a part of my life. That I don't want it to change, but then that's true of everyone as he grows old. He thinks that the old times were the best times, and he don't want it to change.[63]

Beneath the mask of Flem Snopes, stuffed with dollars and swollen with respectability, Verhovensky reigns in Jefferson. The social climber has reached the top; he has even become a complacent bourgeois. And yet Faulkner does not have Dostoevsky's scorn for the third estate. He even deplores their effacement.[64] On this point they seem to contradict one another. In fact their views are identical, for what Dostoevsky castigates in the bourgeois, what Faulkner cannot pardon in the Snopeses, is their baseness.

For Dostoevsky there is only the nobility and the people—and the gulf that separates them. The one is corrupt, but how can one deny the debauchery of the other? This does not prevent each class from incarnating a principle capable of regenerating society. Versilov in *A Raw Youth*, Zossima in *The Brothers Karamazov*, each defines in his turn the ideal nobleman and the ideal peasant, all the more similar because they reflect the essence of the Russian nation: the ability to suffer for the world and thus to save it.[65] At bottom, Dostoevsky is doubly torn. Historically he was between the aristocratic order that was and the liberal

151

order which appeared, in all likelihood, to be in the process of creation; so he withdrew from them both, but in different degrees: let us say rather that he transcended them and attempted to reconcile them by raising himself to the level of ideas. This new perspective, however, permitted nothing more than a theoretical synthesis: it alienated the intellectual from action, condemned him to utopia, fiction and the solitude of art. From the forties until the address on Pushkin (1880), Dostoevsky constantly aimed at political action. But his evolution after the exile in Siberia excluded precisely this. And the more he attempted to influence politics by his writing, the more he lost himself in dreams.

Faulkner lived in a time and place where social compartments were much less tightly sealed. There remained in the South only two more or less stable poles in the immense moving mass of those going up and those declining: the gentleman, often impoverished but attentive to the exigencies of his *ethos*, on the one hand, and on the other the black—a victim of well-known prejudices. Faulkner, like Dostoevsky, was not blind to their shortcomings, and yet it is on these remnants of the past that he relies, glorifying simultaneously the "masters" and the "slaves", in contradiction to Raskolnikov.[66] He also anticipates the saving grace of a rapprochement of human ideals from opposite extremes of the social scale. And if they are not always identified, they are at least presented as complementary, as indispensable components of the Southern nation. The division observed in Dostoevsky is expressed in Faulkner only on the historical level, in the political and moral opposition of yesterday and tomorrow. Once more the two orders are simultaneously repudiated and spiritualized. However, the construction of this visionary city does not isolate this writer from action: Faulkner was not a politician despite his addresses to students and learned societies in his later years. An artist from the beginning, he never renounces this vocation, even when he crams his novels with preachings, in contrast with Dostoevsky who goes to jail, starts periodicals, stores up articles and speeches throughout his life, but imprisons himself in literature by his vain social speculations. Faulkner never knew this conflict any more than he did the Dostoevskian passion which seeks to enter reality and yet remains irremediably the slave of itself.

Neither is descended from an aristocratic family. Although the son of a modest doctor and despite a rather "bourgeois" education in the western sense, Dostoevsky always claimed, rightly or wrongly, membership in the nobility. But one is surely a long way from the brilliant circles of Turgenev and Count Tolstoy: several rungs lower, at that undefinable level which is distinguished from the commoners less by its income, often meager, than by its sense of dignity and mission. Despite spending his life in financial troubles, Dostoevsky detested the third estate and clung tenaciously to his noble rank. He wrote from Siberia to his brother Michael on February 22, 1854:

> Their [the convicts'] hatred for the nobility is boundless; they regard all of us who belong to it with hostility and enmity. They would have devoured us if they could. Judge then for yourself in what danger we stood, having to cohabit with these people for some years, eat with them, sleep by them, and with no possibility of complaining of the affronts which were constantly put upon us.
> "You nobles have iron beaks, you have torn us to pieces. When you were masters, you injured the people, and now, when it is evil days with you, you want to be brothers."
> This theme was developed during four years. A hundred and fifty foes never wearied of persecuting us—it was their joy, their diversion, their pastime; our sole shield was our indifference and our moral superiority, which they were forced to recognize and respect; they were also impressed by our never yielding to their will. They were for ever conscious that we stood above them.[67]

In *The House of the Dead* the chapter entitled "The Complaint" goes even further on this point.

> Nothing is more terrible than living out of one's natural surroundings. . . . They [the gentlemen] are divided from the peasants by an impassable gulf, and this only becomes fully apparent when the *gentleman* is by force of external circumstances completely deprived of his former privileges, and is transformed into a peasant. You may have to do with peasants all your life, you may associate with them every day for forty years, officially for instance, in the regulation administrative forms, or even simply in a friendly way, as a benefactor or, in a certain sense, a father—you will never know them really. It will all be an optical illusion and nothing more.[68]

This avowal casts a strange light on the transfiguration of the peasant. Seen close up he is nothing more than a country bumpkin. Dostoevsky, in "going to the people," does not abdicate his privileges of birth and education. The writer, like the patronesses of the fashionable charities, does not tarry among these "good people." His gifts distributed—a halo, not civil rights—he returns to his books. In fact, Dostoevsky's love of the people differed little from the philanthropy of the liberals. He loved the peasant at a distance and less for himself than as a kind of instrument. Dostoevsky installed himself at a crossroads in the system of classes and opinions. Of noble stock, he is, nonetheless, preeminently an artist and in particular a painter—even a spokesman—of the city's classless:[69] aristocrats, seminarians *raznotchintsy* who form the intelligentsia. Very attached to his origins, he is equally so to the earth, the basis of the old order from which, however, he felt cut off. He would be a conservative and a "Russian". But he was also a rootless lord, a landowner without land and an urban man of letters, a philosopher in search of a new world, and that is why he occasionally flirted with the radicals.

This, in general outline, is very nearly the situation of Faulkner. Mississippi, one remembers, remained a land of pioneers for a long time. But on the frontier, the good wine is drunk young. The age of lineages was measured in years, not centuries. Although it went back no further than to the novelist's great-grandfather, Colonel William C. Falkner (died 1889) planter, Civil War hero, writer, politician, and railroad builder, the celebrity of the Faulkner family was well established. Without having the same rank as a Virginia gentleman, Faulkner could pride himself on his patrician origins. His brother John evokes in his memoirs the ease and unity of the family,[70] the sense of responsibility that it inculcated, a childhood passed in the country[71]—"Every home was a long way toward being self-supporting"[72]—a rural atmosphere that reminds us a good deal of the Russia of the well-born. It is far from being the milieu in which Dostoevsky was raised and which he describes in his novels, but it corresponds to the facts that he knew and also attests to Faulkner's social rank. However, titles of nobility no longer bring in any income. The American had also to work for his living and did so in the same way as the Russian. It is by the expedient of literature that he manages to tie himself more closely to the soil by acquiring, despite his hostility to private property, a house and land. Let us not be deceived: Faulkner could only pretend to be a "farmer" because he wrote books. Attached to the land, he, like the Agrarians,[73] criticizes urban, industrial and Yankee progressivism; with them, he deplores abstraction and expatiates on the homogeneity of the South. On the other hand, his allegiance to the local, agrarian, and traditional order is far from implying unconditional approval. Indeed, he also censures it and, by ricochet, the ultraconservatives who dream of an American Middle Ages. To correct their extravagances, Faulkner even goes so far as to make an appeal to their adversaries.

In conclusion, Faulkner and Dostoevsky, confronted with foreign materialism, take sides with traditional and local values. However, the problem is complicated by the fact that they are able neither to identify with the rulers whom they regard—sometimes—as decadent or corrupt, nor to commit themselves fully to a cause they regard as defective. So they raise themselves above the melee, playing the arbitrator by virtue of the distance that separates them from both camps and, notably, from their own. Socially neither are princes, and as intellectuals they have the tendency to stand back from their milieu. In addition, they owe their prestige much more to their talent than to their birth. The ties that join them to the established order are not so loose as to allow them to be unconcerned, but they are loose enough to permit them to judge it and urge reforms. To revitalize the aristocracy by reminding them of their moral obligations to those whom they oppress; to underline the personal interdependence of blacks and whites, of peasants and landowners; to atone by an organic evolution for the sins of the past and to rehabilitate suffering as expiation; to dematerialize progress: it is, in sum, to return to some feudal principles or, rather, to move towards an ideal feudalism, founded on the suzerainty of God, and eventually to transcend political forms in aspiring beyond the ties of obedience and protection to the love of one creature for another: a spiritual equality, available, as Saint Paul tells us, to all the children of God who are led by the Spirit (Rom. 8: 12-17).[74] It is to wish by conversion to save everyone, one's own, others and oneself—and to save no one. It is also to oppose all

155

parties "by being present yet detached, committed and attainted neither by Citizen's Council nor NAACP; by being in the middle" to use Faulkner's terms from his "Letter to a Northern Editor" (1956).[75] It is finally and above all to impress the seal of the spirit on the material, the writer's specific task. Their artistic profession, their capacity as critics and individualists, explains better than any other reason their sliding from the right toward the center and "higher" spheres of ideas . . .

After allowing for the irreducible uniqueness of the men, unquestionable analogies remain: the tensions resulting from the historic evolution and from the sometimes uncertain, sometimes hostile, relations with existing opinions and social groups. These tensions are reflected in feelings and ideas and produce the same shocks, motivate similarly eclectic choices, and lead to comparable syntheses.

NOTES TO CHAPTER V

1. See *Letters of Fyodor Dostoevsky* trans. Ethel Colburn Mayne (New York: Horizon Press, 1961), pp. 156-59 (Letter to Appollon Nikolayevitch Maikov dated December 11, 1868), pp. 165-68 (Letter to Nikolay Nikolayevitch Strachov dated February 26, 1869).
2. Johannes van der Eng, *Dostoevskij romancier* ('s-Gravenhage: Mouton, 1957), p. 14.
3. *Ibid.*, p. 15.
4. *The Brothers Karamazov*, p. xix.
5. See Donald Fanger, *Dostoevsky and Romantic Realism* (Cambridge, Mass.: Harvard Univ. Press, 1965), p. 264.
6. See Reinhard Lauth, *Die Philosophie Dostojewskis* (München: R. Piper Verlag, 1950), pp. 359-60; *Faulkner in the University*, p. 19.
7. See Roger Dow "Seichas: A Comparison of Pre-Reform Russia and the Ante-Bellum South," *The Russian Review*, VII, 1 (Autumn, 1947), pp. 3-15; Clement Eaton, *The Growth of Southern Civilization 1790-1860*, pp. 22-23.
8. Irving Howe, *William Faulkner* (New York: Vintage Books, 1962), p. 23.
9. Cited by C. Bouglé, *Essais sur le régime des castes* (Paris: Félix Alcan, 1935), p. 9. See Anatole Leroy-Beaulieu, *L'Empire des Tsars et les Russes I* (Paris: Hachette, 1881), p. 368; T. Harry Williams, Richard Current, Frank Freidel, *A History of the United States* (New York: Alfred A. Knopf, 1959), p. 475.
10. See Armand Cuvillier, *Manuel de Sociologie II* (Paris: Presses Universitaire, 1962), p. 621; Joseph Calmette, *Le monde féodal* (Paris: Presses Universitaire, 1951), p. 158ff; Marc Bloch, *La société féodale. La formations des liens de dépendance et Les classes et le gouvernement des hommes* (Paris: Albin Michel, 1939), passim.
11. See Pierre Klossowski, *Sade mon prochain* (Paris: Editions du Seuil,

1947), pp. 22-24; Alexandre Eck, "L'asservissement du paysan russe" in *Le Servage* (Bruxelles: Editions de la Librairie Encyclopédique, 1959), pp. 262-63.

12. See Anatole Leroy-Beaulieu *op. cit.*, p. 266; Clement Eaton *op. cit.*, pp. 21, 23, 151, 309; William R. Taylor *Cavalier and Yankee* (Garden City, N. Y.: Doubleday, 1963), pp. 49, 104.

13. See Clement Eaton *op. cit.*, p. 23; Clement Eaton, "Class Differences in the Old South," *The Virginia Quarterly Review* XXXIII, 3 (Summer, 1957), p. 370.

14. See Clement Eaton, *The Growth of Southern Civilization*, p. 24.

15. See *ibid.*, p. 151; Dr. J. W. Schulte Nordholt, *Het volk dat in duisternis wandelt* (Arnhem, Van Loghum Slaterus, 1957), p. 50.

16. See T. Harry Williams et al. *op. cit.*, pp. 479-80.

17. Roger Portal, *Les Slaves* (Paris: Armand Colen, 1965), p. 193.

18. See E. Lampert, *Sons Against Fathers* (Oxford: The Clarendon Press, 1965), p. 55.

19. Anatole Leroy-Beaulieu, *op. cit.*, p. 422.

20. *Ibid.*, p. 443.

21. Pierre Belperron: *La guerre de Sécession (1861-1865)*, p. 577: "Even if the planter was able to hang on to his lands, he was no longer the lord in his fiefdom. Where paternalism, on the one hand, and fidelity, on the other, continued between the master and the freed slave it was an anachronism." (Translated by D.McW.)

22. See *ibid.*, p. 735: "these planters had conceived a ideal of life which, by virtue of the emphasis placed on the individual, seemed particularly attractive at a time when the concentration of economic powers in the hands of the State tended to impose on man a labor determined by wills other than his own, restricting his choice in life and its related responsibilities, transforming him into a machine capable of being transplanted according to his master's needs, depriving him of his essential freedoms in exchange for a standardized well-being, that is to say, making him a tool without thoughts or reactions, such as were the field slaves before the Civil War.

23. See Armand Cuvillier *op. cit.*, p. 584.

24. See William R. Taylor, *op. cit.*, pp. 271, 303, 315. See also Clement Eaton, *The Growth of Southern Civilization 1790-1860*, ch. 10.

25. See Johannes van der Eng, *op. cit.*, p. 13.

26. See Reinhard Lauth, *op. cit.*, p. 79.

27. *Crime and Punishment*, p. 251.

28. *The Notebooks of Crime and Punishment*, p. 221.

29. *The Possessed*, p. 290.

30. See *ibid.*, p. 301.

31. *The Diary of a Writer*, p. 995.

32. See *ibid.*, p. 703.

33. See *Absalom, Absalom!*, p. 155.

34. *The Sound and the Fury and As I Lay Dying*, p. 17. See also *The Mansion*, pp. 323-24.

35. *The Sound and the Fury and As I Lay Dying*, p. 8.

36. *The Brothers Karamazov*, p. 127.

37. *Ibid.*, p. 211.

38. *The Sound and the Fury and As I Lay Dying*, p. 17.

39. *Crime and Punishment*, pp. 13-14.

40. *The Mansion*, p. 222.

41. *The Brothers Karamazov*, p. 330.

42. *Ibid.*, p. 688.

43. *Ibid.*, pp. 735-36.

44. *Faulkner in the University*, p. 132.

45. *Ibid.*, p. 154. See also p. 164.

46. *Ibid.*, p. 197, See also p. 201.
47. *The Mansion*, pp. 297-98.
48. *Mosquitoes*, p. 374.
49. See Cleanth Brooks, *William Faulkner: The Yoknapatawpha Country* (New Haven, Conn.: Yale Univ. Press, 1963), p. 334.
50. See Frederick J. Hoffman, *William Faulkner* (New York: Twayne Publishers, Inc., 1961), p. 334.
51. *The Brothers Karamazov*, p. 737.
52. See *Faulkner in the University*, pp. 218-19:
"Q. . . . Do you think . . . that the advent of industry in the South, the industrialization of the South, and the possible eventual destruction of the remaining—of agrarian society will have any effect upon this problem?
A. It will in that I think the agrarian culture was the only culture the white man went to much trouble to train the Negro in. As that vanishes the Negro becomes more and more of a problem, when that's completely gone he'll be still more of a problem, and for that reason the white man will have to do something to substitute that agrarian economy which took care of the Negro. I mean by "took care" which assimilated the Negro. The Negro had a definite place in that economy. Now the only contact the Negro has with the white man's culture is the time-payment ice box and the automobile that he owns some day if he doesn't tear it up before he finishes paying for it. There's no other contact with the white man's culture that the Negro has since he was—since he left the agrarian economy of slavery."
53. See Roger Portal, *Les Slaves* (Paris: Armand Colin, 1965), p. 288; William R. Taylor, *op. cit.*, pp. 119, 126, 150, 153.
54. See *Absalom, Absalom!*, pp. 97-98: "the six or seven of them, of an age and background, only in the surface matter of food and clothing and daily occupation any different from the Negro slaves who supported them— the same sweat, the only difference being that on the one hand it went for labor in the fields where on the other it went as the price of the spartan and meager pleasures which were available to them because they did not have to sweat in the fields . . . ; the same pleasures."
55. See *The Diary of a Writer*, pp. 702-03.
56. *The Possessed*, pp. 469-70.
57. *A Raw Youth*, pp. 614-15.
58. See *The Diary of a Writer*, pp. 142-43, 188-89, 704-5, 759-62, 959.
59. See *ibid.*, p. 417.
60. See Donald Fanger *op. cit.*, p. 210.
61. *Sartoris*, p. 114.
62. *Ibid.*, pp. 172-74. This passage prefigures the Snopes trilogy: *The Hamlet, The Town* and *The Mansion*.
63. *Faulkner in the University*, p. 68. See also p. 98.
64. See *ibid.*, pp. 188-89.
65. *A Raw Youth*, p. 510; *The Brothers Karamazov*, pp. 330-31.
66. See Philip Blair Rice, "Faulkner's Crucifixion" in Frederick J. Hoffman and Olga Vickery (eds.), *William Faulkner: Three Decades of Criticism* (East Lansing, Mich.: Michigan State Univ. Press, 1960), pp. 380-81.
67. *Letters of Fyodor Michailovitch Dostoevsky* (trans.) Ethel Colburn Mayne, pp. 59-60.
68. *The House of the Dead*, p. 242.
69. See Donald Fanger, *op. cit.*, pp. 133-34, 210; E. Lampert, *op. cit.*, p. 63.
70. See John Faulkner, *My Brother Bill* (London: Victor Gollancz Ltd., 1964), pp. 80, 82, 219.
71. *Ibid.*, p. 81.
72. *Ibid.*, p. 44.
73. See John M. Bradbury, *Renaissance in the South* (Chapel Hill, N. C.:

AN ATTEMPT AT HISTORICAL EXPLANATION

Univ. of North Carolina Press, 1960), p. 54; Alexander Karanikas, *Tillers of a Myth* (Madison, Wisc.: University of Wisconsin Press, 1966), passim.
74. See *The Brothers Karamazov*, p. 379: "Equality is to be found only in the spiritual dignity of man, and that will only be understood among us."
75. *Essays, Speeches and Public Letters*, p. 87. See also p. 95 and Dostoevsky's reactions to the abolition of the serfs: see C. Kastler "L'Intelligentsia et la Réforme," in *Le Statut des paysans libérés du servage 1861-1961* (Paris-La Haye: Mouton, 1963), p. 211.

159

PART TWO

Since we would like to separate simple kinships from influences, perhaps it is appropriate, before tracing the history of Faulkner's relationship with Dostoevsky, to recall briefly the pitfalls that await an enterprise of this kind. Without a formal admission by the author or obvious evidence of a pastiche or plagiarism, there is no certitude about borrowings. The word "borrowing" is, admittedly, rather ambiguous, for it applies sometimes to the means of expression, sometimes to the things expressed, or at other times to both. In addition, in some cases it means a conscious line of action, elsewhere an involuntary reminiscence. On the factual level, the borrowing is indistinguishable from both the fortuitous analogy and the activity exercised on congenial temperaments by a common source, and yet it is worthy of the name only in virtue of a more or less direct relationship which is sometimes difficult to reconstruct.

As we have said, although Faulkner more than once acknowledged having read and reread Dostoevsky, and although he was even aware of having been influenced by him, as he affirmed on March 13, 1957, at the University of Virginia, we have no other precise testimony on this subject: neither letters, diaries nor critical studies, at least none that have been published. Thus we are without the external proofs which would enable us to determine a borrowing in a specific case. As for references to Dostoevsky's name in the novels, they are virtually non-existent. In general, it will then be impossible to differentiate influences from affinities with certitude.

Moreover, it goes without saying that from *Soldiers' Pay* (1926) to *The Reivers* (1962) the effects of these contacts are not uniformly felt. The attraction operates, according to the period, with greater or lesser force and in different areas; if in exceptional cases it leads to near plagiarism, it is also, at other times, interrupted. In addition, in many cases the authentic artist uses another only in order to be guided in paths which he has already decided to explore: as soon as he is able to take off on his own, he fires his teacher. To what degree did Dostoevsky aid Faulkner to define himself? What did he provide him: situations, characters, ideas, techniques? Was Faulkner aware of this or not? These are some of the questions which we intend to answer here, without claiming to lead invariably to uncontested certitude.

VI

FIRST CONTACTS (1926-29)

It is rather strange that, although Faulkner's first three novels bristle with literary references and quotations, none deal with Dostoevsky, the reading of whom seems to have left few traces. What is more, no text proves that Faulkner read him before writing *The Sound and the Fury*. But this first masterwork dates from the same period as *Sartoris* (1929), and the novelist later cited Dostoevsky—in 1957!—among the authors that he preferred at eighteen or nineteen years of age. To believe him—but how seriously are these rambling remarks to be taken—the first contact goes back to 1915-16. However that may be, Dostoevsky does not seem to have contributed to the writer's formation and neither *Soldiers' Pay* (1926), nor *Mosquitoes* (1927), nor even *Sartoris* clearly bear his imprint. It would seem that that influence acted belatedly or following new (?) readings around 1929.

While *The Sound and the Fury* frequently and unequivocally evokes *Crime and Punishment* as well as, to a lesser degree, *The Brothers Karamazov*, it is impossible to infer anything certain from *Sartoris*, written at nearly the same time. One can barely detect, here and there, echoes, parallels and resemblances. And if we could not draw on *The Sound and the Fury*, *Sartoris* would tend to weaken the legitimacy of our study rather than to strengthen it. In short, only the author's declarations, the chronology of his works, and the obvious borrowings to which the latter bear witness, beginning in 1929, permit us to set Faulkner next to Dostoevsky and assume an influence during this period.

A hypothetical influence, then, defying all rigorous control, whose probability is fortified only by comparison with the future.

Within these narrow limits what conclusions are to be dared? As the following chapter will confirm, eventual borrowings are much less concerned with themes and ideas than with situations. In addition, the clearest correspondences concern *Crime and Punishment* and *The Brothers Karamazov*, two works to which we will return repeatedly: Raskolnikov's comings and goings before his crime (I,5) and his confession to Sonia (V, 4); the "Rebellion" episode in which Ivan Karamazov expatiates on suffering (V, 4) and perhaps also his "poem," "The Grand Inquisitor" (V, 5). These analogies are sketched in *Sartoris*. As for Faulkner's first novel, *Soldiers' Pay*, it immediately poses one of the questions that will fascinate us throughout our inquiry: had Faulkner read *The Idiot*?

To summarize, an influence at this stage is only a possibility, and the most precise date that can be offered is that of *The Sound and the Fury*. One can, nonetheless, wonder why, of two works written almost simultaneously, one so resembles Dostoevsky and the other hardly at all and why did the impress of the Russian novelist affirm itself so suddenly when Faulkner, according to his own statement, had known him for nearly fifteen years. It should be pointed out that it was not until 1929 that he discovered the subject that he was to exploit for the rest of his life. *The Sound and the Fury* is the first panel in his *Comédie humaine*; *Sartoris*, which is its overture and which sketches its outline, is more closely related to the autobiographical vein of his earlier narratives, especially to *Soldiers' Pay*, where the former flyer sums up the meaning of the war for his generation. A transitional volume, *Sartoris* recounts, among other things, the soldier's return. But, as we shall see, it is when he is inspired directly by observed facts, in his war stories, for instance, when his art turns to confession or "reportage," that Faulkner is most remote from Dostoevsky. On the other hand, he is closest when he erects the fictional world of Yoknapatawpha. This can explain both the sudden multiplication of echoes in *Sartoris*, in comparison with *Mosquitoes*, and their invasion of *The Sound and the Fury*. The more Faulkner leaves the field of observation and reality and plunges into the imaginary, the more he leans on Dostoevsky, in whom he saw above all an inventor of novelistic forms and an instrument to be used in the construction of his own forms.

In *Soldiers' Pay* (1926) Mrs. Powers embodies self-sacrifice accomplished more for the beauty of the act and in view of moral redemption than for its practical efficacy. Confronted with two men, Faulkner's first heroine marries the one she pities (Donald Mahon, a disabled war veteran) and whom she knows is irremediably lost, not the one whom she probably would have loved (Joe Gilligan). Sex has nothing to do with her choice: the war has mutilated her feelings as it maimed Donald's body.[1] It is very nearly the same triangle that Myshkin, Nastasya Filippovna and Aglaia constitute in *The Idiot*. The prince, equally innocent of carnal desires, also prefers the woman who needs protection and compassion[2] (Nastasya) to the one he loves. In addition, in both cases, one of the rivals is doomed to a fatal end: Donald is condemned from the beginning, while Myshkin reads Nastasya's later troubles in her portrait. Finally, these same characters each have two suitors: Donald has Emmy, who was his mistress, and Cecily, his fiancee; Nastasya has Totsky, her ex-suitor, and Rogozhin, who also courts her. Let us add that Donald and the prince are sick and recover temporarily only to die or to fall into idiocy. The correspondences end there. It is, however, necessary to underline their superficial character and point out that the relations between the heroes are different in the two novels. These seem to be only coincidences of situation, and nothing proves that Faulkner had read *The Idiot* at this time.

The most striking analogy turns out to be the decision of Mrs. Powers and the prince. To be sure, their conduct is not based on the same values: for Myshkin's Christ-like *caritas*, Faulkner substitutes a stoic courage, less gratuitous than it seems, for in marrying Donald, Mrs. Powers expiates a sin she committed against her first husband who fell at the front at the moment that she sent him a letter breaking off their relationship.[3] It is above all her disinterested helpfulness that recalls *The Idiot*, this love through compassion tied to suffering, spiritualized, detached from the senses: the love which in *Crime and Punishment* is borne for Raskolnikov by Sonia, who has also "destroyed and betrayed"[4] herself for the sake of her family. But the victory of spiritual discipline over the anarchy of the instincts and the desire for redemption also characterize the sacrifice accepted by Dmitri Karamazov. The heroine's act, despite its stoic nuance— *Per ardua ad astra*—unquestionably evokes a fundamental theme of the major Dostoevskian novels, without being explicitly based on any one of them. The idea finds further development in Emmy and a contrast in the selfish amoralism of Jones and Cecily, a coquette, who appears in this situation as a "manifest Serpent."

There is nothing worthy of note in *Mosquitoes* (1927), the relations between the wealthy Mrs. Maurier and Mr. Talliaferro no more call to mind the couple formed by Stavrogin's mother and Stepan Trofimovitch in *The Possessed* than a similar situation in a film like *Duck Soup*. There is nothing more here than the identical dependence of a middle-aged man of modest means on an older and wealthier woman: a subject too banal to detain us. Only two short sentences defining freedom as an insupportable burden—"No one needs freedom. We cannot bear it."[5]—seem to allude to the Grand Inquisitor.

The harvest will be richer in *Sartoris* (1929), a novel about war or the aftermath of war, like *Soldiers' Pay*, and a prologue to the Yoknapatawpha saga with several surprising details. Let us pass over the fact that young Bayard Sartoris returns home unexpectedly like Ivan Karamazov whose visit the narrator thinks "rather mysterious;"[6] that Narcissa Benbow receives anonymous letters from the Snopeses like those with which "some low creatures," "some rascals"[7] keep bombarding Praskovya Ivanovna and Varvara Petrovna in *The Possessed*; that Bayard suffers, like Kirillov, from the death of his brother[8] and wishes to die in his turn. These are only trifles. There is, however, a passage in *Crime and Punishment* (I,5) that could very well have awakened the attention of the author of *Sartoris*: Raskolnikov's dream on the eve of the murder and in particular the cruelty inflicted on the little horse. The dream is related to the crime planned by the hero: it provides a safety valve for the revolt of the subconscious against the schemes constructed by the intellect. But the function assigned to the episode in the criminal's psychology matters little; the essential, in relation to Faulkner, rests in all that refers to the mute and resigned courage of the animal beneath the blows. We are told at the beginning that Raskolnikov "always liked looking at these great cart-horses, with their long manes, thick legs, and slow even pace, drawing along a perfect mountain with no appearance of effort, as though it were easier going with a load than without it."[9] This is followed by the description of a "thin little sorrel beast"[10] pulling a heavy cart which is soon filled by a "number of big and very drunken peasants."[11] Whipped by a sadistic brute, the animal collapses before the child (the dream is retrospective). Here is how Dostoevsky sees the animal:

> the mare tugged with all her might, but far from galloping, could scarcely move forward; she struggled with her legs, gasping and shrinking from the blows of the three whips which were showered on her like hail.[12]
>
> She sank back on her haunches, but lurched forward and tugged first on one side and then on the other, trying to move the cart. But the six whips were attacking her in all directions . . .
> "She's a tough one," was shouted in the crowd.[13]
>
> With all his might he dealt a stunning blow at the poor mare. The blow fell; the mare staggered, sank back, tried to pull, but the bar fell again with a swinging blow on her back and she fell on the ground like a log.[14]
>
> The mare stretched out her head, drew a long breath and died.[15]

The anecdote, elaborated in *Crime and Punishment*, makes a brief reappearance in *The Brothers Karamazov* (V, 4), when Ivan, speaking of Russian sadism, summarizes a poem by Nekrassov:

> There are lines in Nekrassov describing how a peasant lashes a horse on the eyes, 'on its meek eyes,' every one must have seen it. It's peculiarly Russian. He describes how a feeble little nag had foundered under too heavy a load and cannot move. The peasant beats it, beats it savagely, beats it at last not knowing what he is doing in the intoxication of cruelty, thrashes it mercilessly over and over again. 'However weak you are, you must pull, if you die for it.' The nag strains, and then he begins lashing the poor defenceless creature on its weeping, on its 'meek eyes.' The frantic beast tugs and draws the load, trembling all over, gasping for breath, moving sideways, with a sort of unnatural spasmodic action.[16]

Dostoevsky, in fact, has here taken up—indirectly, to be sure— one of Faulkner's pet topics: the theme of the mule, a symbol of endurance, patience and perseverance. It appears in *Sartoris*

as a kind of digression, and the author immediately associates it
with the Dostoevskian dualism of pride and humility:

> Some Homer of the cotton fields should sing the saga of the mule and of
> his place in the South. He it was, more than any other one creature or
> thing, who, steadfast to the land when all else faltered before the hope-
> less juggernaut of circumstances, impervious to conditions that broke
> men's hearts because of his venomous and patient preoccupation with the
> immediate present, won the prone South from beneath the iron heel of
> Reconstruction and taught it pride again through humility, and courage
> through adversity overcome; who accomplished the well-nigh impossible
> despite hopeless odds, by sheer and vindictive patience. . . . Misunder-
> stood even by that creature, the nigger who drives him, whose impulses
> and mental processes most closely resemble his.[17]

Is there a relationship between Dostoevsky and this passage from
Sartoris? And if so, by which of Dostoevsky's novels was Faulkner
inspired? From *Crime and Punishment*, which he had read once
according to his own statement,[18] and we may suppose that he
did so during this period, one finds at first glance little of importance—neither the dream, its psychological function nor the hero
himself—but a simple image which is, moreover, stripped of its
exotic trimmings and adapted to the Southern milieu. The little
horse is changed into a mule, the muzhik into a negro, the Russian
country into a plantation. The significance of the animal, however,
remains exactly the same, with the slight difference of being
pushed into the limelight. Where Dostoevsky only sketches the
theme, amplified later by Sonia, of tenacity in suffering, and while
he links it to the animal only in passing, Faulkner develops it
fully and openly. The glorification of the mule, the paradoxically
victorious victim, echoes through his entire work; it rests undoubtedly on observable phenomena which will help him to bolster
his faith in the perenniality of life. But it is not excluded that
the reading of *Crime and Punishment* confirmed his experience
and contributed to its expression. The conjecture appears all the
more admissible in that the animal is linked in *Sartoris*, as—implicitly—in the Dostoevsky passage, to humility and pride. The fact
that Faulkner stresses this union while Raskolnikov is torn between the two emphasizes the margin separating the two novelists. On the other hand, the allusion to the Homer of the South

170

and the fact that the mule survives suffering corresponds rather to Ivan's comments on Nekrassov's lines. Although one leans in favor of *The Brothers Karamazov*, the similarities remain too vague for anything to be inferred. We must wait until *Light in August* to find in Faulkner a passage which flows more clearly from those we have just cited.

In another area Bayard's confession to Narcissa (III, 7) repeats almost detail for detail, in its circumstances, Raskolnikov's to Sonia, only on a less emotional level. In both cases, the thing announced—the death of a brother, the avowal of a crime—is of such importance that it explains the derangement of the hero. Bayard and Raskolnikov, traumatized and physically ill, confide in a woman whom they expect to give them peace; instead of blurting it out immediately they temporize—so that Raskolnikov must bring the matter up twice—and their tongues are loosened only at the price of a struggle against pride.

> [Raskolnikov] felt at that very time not only that he could not help telling her, but also that he could not put off the telling. He did not yet know why it must be so, he only *felt* it, and the agonising sense of his impotence before the inevitable almost crushed him.[19]

> And beneath it all, the bitter struggling of his [Bayard's] false and stubborn pride.[20]

Finally, while Dostoevsky constantly punctuates the dialogue with the same dumb show—Sonia stupefied, Raskolnikov seated on the bed, the two young people joining hands,

> With the same helplessness and the same terror, she looked at him.[21]

> She got up, moved quickly to him, seized both his hands and, gripping them tight in her thin fingers, began looking into his face again with the same intent stare.[22]

> She jumped up seeming not to know what she was doing, and, wringing her hands, walked into the middle of the room; but quickly went back and sat down again beside him, her shoulder almost touching his.[23]

> She squeezed his hand.[24]

> He turned to her, looked sadly at her and took her hands.[25]

> snatching his two hands, squeezing them in hers and gazing at him with eyes full of fire.[26]

171

Bayard and Narcissa are seen in an analogous attitude: he in the bed she at his bedside:

> he had to grasp her hand to hold the flame steady, and still holding her wrist, he drew deeply several times. She tried to free her wrist, but his fingers were like steel, and her trembling body betrayed her and she sank into her chair again, staring at him with terror and dread . . . still holding her wrist he began to talk of his dead brother . . . she sitting with her arm taut in his grasp and her other hand pressed against her mouth, watching him with terrified fascination.[27]

> He talked on and her hand came way from her mouth and slid down her other arm and tugged at his fingers . . . his fingers shifted, and just as she thought she was free they clamped again, and now both of her wrists were prisoners. She struggled, staring at him dreadfully.[28]

Such is the most precise concordance that can be established between *Sartoris* and Dostoevsky's work. Let us admit: it is not very much,[29] but this presumption will not be long in being justified.

NOTES TO CHAPTER VI

1. See *Soldiers' Pay*, p. 152: "Can nothing at all move me again? Nothing to desire? Nothing to stir me, to move me, save pity?" See also p. 162-63.
2. *The Idiot*, p. 332.
3. *Soldiers' Pay*, p. 164.
4. *Crime and Punishment*, p. 285.
5. *Mosquitoes*, p. 243.
6. *The Brothers Karamazov*, p. 14.
7. *The Possessed*, pp. 166, 169.
8. *Ibid.*, p. 116.
9. *Crime and Punishment*, p. 50.
10. *Ibid.*, pp. 50-51.
11. *Ibid.*
12. *Ibid.*, pp. 51-52.
13. *Ibid.*, p. 53.
14. *Ibid.*
15. *Ibid.*
16. *The Brothers Karamazov*, p. 249. In *The Idiot* (p. 51) Myshkin admits that he is "awfully fond of asses . . . a useful creature . . . industrious, strong, patient, cheap, long-suffering."
17. *Sartoris*, pp. 278-79.
18. See Frederick L. Gwynn, "Faulkner's Raskolnikov," *Modern Fiction Studies*, IV, 2 (Summer, 1958), p. 170: "of *Crime and Punishment* he (Faulkner) has said, 'I have never re-read it.' (Conversation September 15, 1956). Yet this statement of course implies one reading, and the reading would come at a time to affect the writing of *The Sound and the Fury*."

19. *Crime and Punishment*, p. 357.
20. *Sartoris*, p. 251.
21. *Crime and Punishment*, p. 361.
22. *Ibid.*, p. 362.
23. *Ibid.*
24. *Ibid.*, p. 364.
25. *Ibid.*, p. 366.
26. *Ibid.*, p. 370.
27. *Sartoris*, p. 251.
28. *Ibid.*, pp. 252-53.
29. It is unnecessary to insist here on a theme such as the benevolent influence of the earth (p. 203), nor on certain techniques of composition analyzed earlier: the alternation of the different groups (the Sartorises, the Benbows, the MacCallums) and the relation of events from several points of view (pp. 154-57).

VII

EVIL AND FATE: RASKOLNIKOV (1929-1934)

The year 1929 marks the beginning of an extremely fertile period for Faulkner, a period which is also that of his dark novels. It is at this time that the influence of Dostoevsky suddenly and forcefully asserts itself. Three phenomena coincide: the quality and quantity of the works, the restriction of the novelistic world to Yoknapatawpha county, and the spell of the Russian novelist. According to all available evidence, we cannot subordinate the first two to the third, for Faulkner never considered Dostoevsky as a model to *imitate*. Moreover, for a talent of this class, influence remains a secondary factor, an auxiliary to a will operating in complete independence. Between Dostoevsky on the one hand and *The Sound and the Fury*, *Sanctuary* and *Light in August* on the other, there is no cause and effect relationship but rather an instrumental relationship. In *The Sound and the Fury*, for instance, the affinities between Quentin Compson and Raskolnikov finally count less than their differences, the area where the genius of the creator is sovereign, and the comparison will aim as much at evaluating the number and the nature of the modifications added to the source as at interpreting the work written in terms of the work read.

Quentin is more decadent, more demented and unfortunate than Raskolnikov. The young Faulkner, insofar as he builds his world on the pattern of *Crime and Punishment* and *The Brothers Karamazov*, sees in these books only the phantoms of his personal obsessions: death and crime, the gulf that separates the tragic hero from the community, the fatality which directs the course of events. The redemptive side of Dostoevsky still escapes him. If he read others of the Russian's novels around 1930, very little of them entered his own work. As a general rule it is a matter of accidental resemblances, possible but very doubtful borrowings, a question we will not be able to settle definitively. Thus we have no proof for *The Idiot*, and the indications are scarcely stronger for *The Possessed*, although the passages evoked are virtually all from Part Three (ch. III, V, VI, VII and VIII), and two copies of this novel dating from 1936 were found in Faulkner's library.

The key work in this period is surely *Crime and Punishment*, and the precedence it enjoys is easily explained. In *Sartoris*, even in *Soldiers' Pay*, Faulkner asserts himself as a novelist of fate and violence, themes that cannot reasonably be said to depend on Dostoevsky, since their appearance precedes his influence. These themes have their origins either in other literary sources or, more likely, in the shock produced by the war, the Southern lifestyle, the atmosphere of the twenties, and even the temperament of the writer. It would be naive to maintain that Faulkner began to believe in fatality while reading the adventures of Raskolnikov. It is rather the reverse that happened: it is because he already thought, like Raskolnikov, that man is a prisoner of a hostile power that Faulkner shows such a predilection for *Crime and Punishment*. Nothing is more foreign to Dostoevsky than this belief of his character, and we can once again infer from this the disagreement of our authors on the doctrinal level. This does not prevent the American from discovering the confirmation of his most intimate convictions in the student's vagaries. Other motifs prove as fascinating: the central theme of the novel—violence, a murder whose preparations and consequences we follow step by step—and the murderer himself, a maniac more inclined to perseverance in evil than to its expiation, if Sonia did not set him on the right track.

The contribution of *Crime and Punishment*, preponderant in *The Sound and the Fury*, subsequently diminishes until it is counterbalanced by that of *The Brothers Karamazov*. Beginning with *Sanctuary* (1931), the latter grows almost in inverse proportion to the former, although the evolution does not display the regularity suggested by this mathematical expression. *As I Lay Dying*, for instance, represents a clear step backward and a rupture of the influences seen in the works which precede and follow it: it is a kind of "anti-Dostoevsky" novel that Faulkner published in 1930, a novel about farmers in which violence, weary of killing after Quentin's suicide, exhausts itself by unleashing nature against man. The novelist seems to stop for a while before beginning to paint his gallery of criminals: he braces himself amidst the untiring energy of these rednecks, admirable and comic at the same time, between the degeneracy of the Compsons and the tragedy of Joe Christmas. Physical force does not destroy the heroes in *As I Lay Dying*; but the aspect of *Crime and Punishment* that seems to draw Faulkner's preference above any other is the ins and outs of the act by means of which one attempts to take a life, one's own or that of another. The choice of subject matter thus temporarily sets him at a distance from Dostoevsky, but not so much as to cut all bridges. Then came *Sanctuary* and *Light in August*, both of which surely owe something to *Crime and Punishment*, but also perhaps as much or more to *The Brothers Karamazov*. The priority acquired little by little by the latter bears a close relationship to the substitution of the criminal (Popeye, Joe Christmas) for the suicide victim (Quentin Compson and, to a certain degree, Bayard Sartoris) as the central character. Although there is a suicide in both of the Dostoevsky novels, that of *Crime and Punishment* is described in much greater detail than the hanging of Smerdyakov. On the other hand, while there can be no doubt about Raskolnikov's guilt, *The Brothers Karamazov* makes a subtle distinction between legal and moral crime. Such is precisely the question which Faulkner pondered in 1931-32 after having considered the motives of suicide in depth: why does the individual turn his destructive instincts against another and to what degree is he responsible? Of course, we need not turn to Smerdyakov and Ivan Karamazov to account for these new preoccupations. It is possible that the reading of *The Brothers Karamazov* engendered them by ricochet, but such reflections occur sooner or later to every attentive observer of society, particularly in those latitudes where bootleggers, gangsters and lynchers flourish. In Faulkner they are, moreover, associated with a determinism that Dostoevsky repudiated. . . . In any case, the problems of *The Brothers Karamazov* are related to those about which Faulkner was curious during this period. He is not, however, interested in posing them explicitly and theoretically or *a fortiori* in resolving them in the same spirit as Dostoevsky, although in *Light in August* he attempted timidly to repeat his major ideas on sin and suffering.

But can one be sure of this influence? This time the answer is categorically affirmative. *Sanctuary* contains three unquestionable echoes from the same chapter of *Crime and Punishment* (VI, 6), *Light in August* has very probable borrowings from Book VIII of *The Brothers Karamazov*, and in *The Sound and the Fury* our thesis is supported by frequent and precise parallels.

The borrowed elements are for the most part novelistic materials, components of psychology and plot: images, ways of acting, motives, relationships between characters, episodes, etc., to which one can perhaps add several technical procedures: the soliloquy, the leitmotif, the reverse schema, the accentuated opposition of the heroes. We will also notice the persistent attraction exercised by Raskolnikov, probably by virtue of his double quality as a criminal and a "victim of Fate." There is nothing surprising, on the other hand, in the fact that the doctrine of the Russian philosopher is not adopted. Faulkner would need a veritable rebirth to subscribe to its essential tenets, and it is not until *Light in August* that he will show himself more receptive on this point. The author of *As I Lay Dying*, in cutting in half certain Dostoevskian theses, turns squarely toward heresy, or even blasphemy. From another perspective, the themes developed get closer and closer to those of *The Brothers Karamazov*. In *Sanctuary* and *Light in August*, Faulkner passes from the suicide and honor exploited in *The Sound and the Fury* "in the manner of" *Crime and Punishment* to the suffering of children, the antagonism between law and truth, the denunciation of fanaticism and the revolt against the father of which Dostoevsky's last novel offers some striking examples.

An examination of his favorite passages shows unequivocally that young Faulkner saw a novelist and not an intellectual mentor

177

in Dostoevsky. Of *Crime and Punishment* he seems to recall above all the first part (I, 3, 4, 5, and 6) and the sixth (VI, 4, 5, and 6), in addition to fragments of the second (II, 1, 6, and 7) and of the third, (III, 6). That is to say, in the order indicated above: all that precedes Raskolnikov's crime (I); Svidrigailov's confession to him, his dramatic meeting with Dounia and his activities just before his suicide (VI); then Raskolnikov's strange behavior after the murder, and the death of Marmeladov (II); finally the dream in which the assassin repeats his act (III). There is apparently no reference to the scene of the murder itself (I, 7) and very few to Raskolnikov's theories (III, 5) or to the two "Christian cult of suffering" tableaux in which the murderer pours out his soul on the prostitute's generous bosom (IV, 4 and V, 4). It is less violence itself than what leads to it and what flows from it that interests our reader of *Crime and Punishment*—but that was after all the effect Dostoevsky wished to achieve—and he cares very little for its philosophical message. The relations between the two writers still develop almost exclusively on the level of the sensuous and concrete image. In addition, the images taken spring from what is most Dostoevskian in the novel, namely the tragic, the unusual, the grotesque and the melodramatic: the alienation born of an obsession which is linked with the desire to kill, the demon of lechery and the suicide of its slave, the accident that befalls the drunkard and his scandalous funeral, the nightmare of the murderer, etc. Basically—and it is his essential contribution around 1929—Dostoevsky aided in creating the pattern of extravagance and excess which shaped the wrathful and the melancholy, the heretics, the violent, the cheats and the traitors, in short the damned of the Faulknerian hell. This hypervoltage of passions and acts, the very nature of the imagination, remains in the final analysis the primordial affinity of these two temperaments, that which explains practically all of the others, and the influence of the elder on the younger.

We come to identical conclusions with *The Brothers Karamazov*. Here the favorite episodes are situated in Book V, where chapter 4, "Rebellion", and its anecdotes on suffering have greater importance than the theses of "The Grand Inquisitor" (5); in Book VIII (4 and 8), where the father dies a violent death; and finally in Book XI, devoted to Ivan who is morally guilty of parricide. Once again the accent falls on what happened before and after the crime, and the most discursive passage, the famous Book VI centered on the edifying biography and teachings of Father Zossima, does not seem to have drawn Faulkner's attention. Zossima will be the great discovery of the next period.

The Sound and the Fury (1929)

It is *Crime and Punishment* which the most "Dostoevskian" fragments of *Sartoris* suggest; it is once more *Crime and Punishment* which the first of Faulkner's great novels insistently recalls.

Raskolnikov and Sonia, Dounia and Luzhin: these are the ghosts that haunt the dilapidated home of the Compsons. The analogies, as manifest as they are numerous, have considerable critical interest. The subject has been skillfully approached by Frederick L. Gwynn in *Modern Fiction Studies* in 1958,[1] but his treatment is too summary not to need supplementary material and distinctions.

Gwynn directs his attention principally to the character of Quentin and Raskolnikov and is content to point out other correspondences. He does not tell us how the study of sources, although useful in clarifying the work's genesis, can help to define its meaning. As regards sources, we should not overlook the impact of a local literary type, the "Southern Hamlet,"[2] nor the contribution—extremely difficult to measure—of direct observation.[3] We will limit ourselves in this section to drawing from the skein of sources the single thread of Dostoevskian inspiration.

Quentin Compson resembles Raskolnikov in several essential traits which, far from clashing with the American setting, are perfectly adapted to it.

They are both young intellectuals—educated at the cost of a family sacrifice of which they are all too aware—dreamers fond of foolish theories, who push the taste for abstraction until it leads to death. Raskolnikov kills to prove an idea and considers killing himself but fails to do so; Quentin actually commits suicide because reality does not square with his theory of the world. In both cases the hero revolts against the community's moral standards, subordinates the concrete to an abstraction of his own in-

179

vention, and realizes his failure: Raskolnikov after a foul crime that was to raise him to the level of the lords of the earth, but which instead only makes him want to throw himself into the Neva,[4] Quentin after hoping to save the Compson honor by accusing himself of illicit relations with his sister and just before his death by drowning. Their drama is not so much that of intellectual impotence as that of the mind incapable of remodeling reality to suit its dreams; it is above all the tragedy of a sick, degenerate mind operating where it has no business and thus going mad. Death is only the corollary of the obsession to which they are prey: the Russian takes himself for a Napoleon, the American, a Presbyterian Don Quixote, for a paladin of honor.

A redeemer of mankind or of foolish virgins, a dominator or a redressor of wrongs, the heroes' capital sin is pride. It is unnecessary to expatiate on Raskolnikov's: it is glaringly obvious. Although hidden, it is no less present in Quentin: if the latter loves death above all, as Faulkner says,[5] it is because life—read: reality —constantly frustrates the schemes to which he would bend it. The pallor of theories of which Mephisto speaks is very much that of the corpse. At least as introverted as Raskolnikov, Quentin is, however, no more satisfied to exist on the fringe: he also wants to be lord and master, to impose on others, even if it is only his sister, his own code of conduct. The spirit of conquest is exercised here at the expense of a single person—Caddy—and in a restricted area,[6] but must not Raskolnikov, in order to rule the world, begin by felling an old woman? His main motive, his *hubris*, is also found in Quentin, in whom it is joined to an even more acute awareness of his own weakness. In an identical fashion, pride takes the form of an obsession—the emulation of Napoleon or Don Quixote—which detaches the individual from the community and leads him straight to suicide. More alienated than Raskolnikov,[7] Quentin will not meet his Sonia: he cannot be saved.

Left to themselves, these near madmen cannot solve the problems which they pose so clearly. What would have happened to Raskolnikov without Sonia? Very likely he would have followed the path of Svidrigailov and Quentin. Dostoevsky, on the contrary, permits him to choose his salvation and even allows him to execute some of his plans, while Faulkner confronts Quentin with total failure and entangles him in a situation which only suicide can remedy. Nothingness is the price of freedom for these maniacs; for Quentin, however, it means the killing not of another but of himself. Dostoevskian freedom is thus opposed by the tyranny of fate. This is why Faulkner spotlights elements which play a minor part in *Crime and Punishment*. In presenting Quentin's suicide as an ineluctable consequence, he conceives time as Fate and directs its course by death. In the hundred pages or so of the second section of *The Sound and the Fury*, the events are viewed retrospectively at the very instant when on the evening of June 2, 1910, Quentin puts an end to his life. The die is cast; the hero declares bankruptcy and finds himself, in a certain sense, suspended between life and death. His interior monologue which flows out during his last seconds, the continual use of the flashback, all accentuate the irreversible, irrevocable side of things. This is also indicated by numerous allusions to time: the clocks which tick off the hours, the metamorphosis of Quentin's shadow on the ground and, above all, the story of his watch. The watch in *Crime and Punishment* is just a detail and serves only to tie the murder of the pawnbroker more closely to the family problems of Raskolnikov: their poverty, his sister's honor, etc. The two objects pawned by the murderer with his victim are "his father's old silver watch and a little gold ring with three red stones, a present from his sister at parting."[8] In the first pages the watch also enables Raskolnikov to scout the location of his projected crime.[9] Quentin's soliloquy begins with a closeup of the same object,[10] which formerly belonged to his grandfather and which his father has given to him. He first attempts—rather clumsily—to destroy it,[11] then it becomes a pretext to visit a jeweler.[12] But the watch, almost insignificant in the Russian novel, acquires a capital importance, for it reflects the very meaning of Quentin's character. Quentin can envision no other future than death, that is to say, the abolition of time, in view of the fact that his sister has scorned the concept of honor he wished to impose on her and, in marrying, will escape him forever. Deprived of his reason for being, the only test case for his theories and his pride and without a future, he annihilates first of all

181

the instrument which measures the time that is passing, then the time he is: his very person. Cleanth Brooks has seen very clearly[13] that the destruction of the watch foreshadows that of the hero. As with Raskolnikov, sinful pride leads to death: not that of another person which would have asserted it, but Quentin's very own which confirms its irremediable defeat. Raskolnikov, as we know, also dreamed of suicide after his heinous crime: even in *Crime and Punishment* the victory of pride coincides with its derision. In short, it is possible that Faulkner borrowed from Dostoevsky a means for expressing his obsession with time, that disgust for the present and the future from which Quentin suffers, as well as the fatality to which he submits him: the detail of the watch, removed from its primitive context, moves to the foreground and is simultaneously charged with new meaning.

The same is true of the character of the sister whose role grows in passing from *Crime and Punishment* to *The Sound and the Fury*. Dounia contributes indirectly, it seems, to the rather muddle-headed motives of Raskolnikov's crime. Among these there is more than the will to power as he explains to Sonia: opposed to selfish pride in this "double" is the altruistic desire to make the stolen money serve "humanity and the good of all"[14] and, above all, the well-being of his family: to satisfy the needs of his mother and to prevent "the insults inflicted on (his) sister."[15] Let us not forget that Dounia is on the verge of making a marriage of convenience with Luzhin, a man she does not love and whom her brother detests; in addition, she is the object of the advances of the infamous Svidrigailov. Her virtue triumphs and, unsoiled, she marries the good Razumihin. This is unquestionably a subplot and a minor theme in comparison with Raskolnikov's satanic designs. In *The Sound and the Fury* Faulkner, on the contrary, accentuates the incompatibility of the ties of brotherhood and marriage, and Quentin's death results from motives whose hierarchy is exactly the reverse of those indicated by Dostoevsky. While Raskolnikov kills much more from pride than from a concern for family honor or fraternal love, Faulkner assigns primacy to the latter two motives and attenuates and dissimulates the first. The reason is obvious. *The Sound and the Fury* does not relate an intellectual and moral adventure; it is an investigation

of the decadence of old families, of the disintegration of the concepts and sentiments that formerly united Southern society, at
which the defeat of 1865 had aimed a fatal blow. The gentleman
is transformed into a maniac bent on honor, the loving brother
into an incestuous brother, the wise virgin into a foolish virgin,
the arrogance of the Cavalier into despair. One has only to correct
Faulkner's point of view, all the while remembering that it is
this that confers on the work its originality and meaning, to discover a number of correspondences. In Raskolnikov, pride takes
precedence over everything: it can justify most of his acts, independent of his affection for Dounia and his legitimate concern
for her virtue. Faulkner obtains a curious alliance by fusing the
Dostoevskian motives. In Quentin pride is joined to affection
transformed into incestuous love and obliges the sister to respect
an honor not only outmoded but against nature: these are the
limits of its function. The sovereignty of egoism becomes blurred
by its combination with factors either social or altruistic, but it
defiles these in its turn with the morbidity attached to it in *Crime
and Punishment*. In short, pride declines, and fraternal love and
honor grow while being tainted by the contact with pride.

After making these reservations, we can state that Quentin and
Raskolnikov react identically before a sister's suitors. Luzhin, who
proposes to marry Dounia and take on her brother as a secre-
tary,[16] corresponds to Sidney Herbert Head, who marries Caddy,
gives Quentin a handout, and offers Jason a job in his bank. Luzhin and Head are upstarts, vulgar materialists, very strict about
"appearances"; they are loved neither by the sister nor by the
brother with whom they argue[17] and in whose eyes this marriage,
rather this arrangement, is an "infamy."[18] Even Svidrigailov, Dounia's rejected seducer, finds his counterpart in Dalton Ames, Caddy's lover, who succeeds easily in his purposes; in addition, in
both novels this character gets the best of the brother.[19] In Faulkner, however, it is not the sister, all too willing this time, who
must do battle with this man to preserve her virginity, as in the
unforgettable scene between Dounia and Svidrigailov. Here we
find Quentin substituted for her,[20] too late moreover. Once more
the difference in situation results from the fact that Faulkner
shifts the accent to another motive. What he wanted to show

was not Svidrigailov's amorality but Quentin's vain opposition to human nature. Finally one other passage inevitably calls *Crime and Punishment* to mind: the one in which Quentin refuses to kill Dalton Ames with the revolver the latter presents to him, just as Dounia throws away the gun of Svidrigailov—after missing him.[21]

Similarity of motives, affinity of designs, concordance of circumstances—there is more. Before his suicide, through this long hot day of June 2, 1910, Quentin does nothing but move from one place to another, and his wanderings bear a striking resemblance to those of Raskolnikov before and after his crime. In both cases we watch the hero explore the area, although his peregrinations have more than a merely utilitarian purpose, for they also serve to translate his inner struggle. Raskolnikov has scarcely received the letter in which his mother announces his sister's marriage when he leaves his room to head towards Vassilyevsky Ostrov outside of town; similarly, at the beginning of Quentin's monologue, the brother, having received the wedding announcement and tormented by this news, leaves Cambridge to go into the countryside.[23] On their way, they show an interest in others which contrasts with their egocentricity and which momentarily frees them from their obsession with death. Although their encounters in the course of their walks do not follow each other in the same order, they are nonetheless much the same. Thus the young girl who is bothered by the well-dressed man and whose protector Rodion becomes because of her resemblance to Dounia in the clutches of Svidrigailov and Luzhin can be bracketted with the child that Quentin constantly calls "sister" and to whom he gives money, a roll, and ice cream.[24] Granted the nature of the affection Quentin bears Caddy, there is no possibility of a third person in *The Sound and the Fury*: thus it is the young man himself who finds himself accused of suspicious intentions. In addition, during this entire scene, Quentin and Raskolnikov leave their shells and forget their plans: alienation is temporarily abolished. The episode is ended in Faulkner by Quentin's arrest and by a parody of interrogation, at the end of which the justice of the peace releases him—a comic interlude which evokes Raskolnikov's visit to the police station and the intervention of the lieutenant.[25]

Moreover, Gwynn notes that the two men laugh in the face of the police and several times show themselves generous: Raskolnikov towards the Marmeladovs, the policeman, the street singer, the beggar; Quentin when he meets the shoe shine man, the Virginia negro, the little girl, etc.[26] Finally, they each receive, directly or indirectly, an invitation from a fellow student: Rodion from Razumihin, Quentin from Gerald Bland's mother.[27] But the most obvious resemblances reside in their interminable wanderings, accompanied by a profound revery from which they emerge from time to time to accomplish similar gestures or to occupy themselves with the same people, whom they associate with their preoccupations.

One notices that they think of doing away with themselves in the same manner. Quentin's comings and goings constantly bring him alongside the water, and it is also there that they end. As for Raskolnikov, he is seen several times on a bridge leaning on the parapet.[28] He will change his mind and live, unlike Svidrigailov who will shoot himself, but not before he has also considered drowning.[29] Throughout the sixth part of *Crime and Punishment* the references to water foreshadow Faulkner's use of similar imagery in Quentin's monologue: it is sometimes Raskolnikov, sometimes Svidrigailov who leans over the Neva; the night before the death of the latter there is a torrential downpour,[30] etc. In short, we find here a combination of the leitmotif technique, the image of water, and the theme of suicide which will dominate the second chapter of *The Sound and the Fury*. Faulkner had to do little more than systematize their use.

There remain only a few details to complete our comparison. For instance, when Nikolay, because of his thirst for suffering and expiation, takes upon himself a crime he has not committed—that of Raskolnikov—he prefigures Quentin's astonishing confession to his father,[31] with the difference that if Compson accuses himself of incestuous relations with his sister and wishes to be damned, it is to be with her and her alone.[32] The theme of incest here eclipses that of disinterested redemption. On this point it should perhaps be pointed out that the feelings of Svidrigailov's wife for Dounia are not without a certain erotic element: "[she] simply fell in love herself—literally fell in love—with your sister."[33] It is precisely this degeneracy of passion that Faulkner illuminated in the portrayal of Quentin.[34] Let us further mention that the two heroes suffer from choking fits[35] and hallucinations, those of Compson repeating the general outline of the nightmare in which Dostoevsky's murderer sees himself in the act of repeating his crime:

> A huge, round, copper-red moon looked in at the windows. "It's the moon that makes it so still, weaving some mystery," thought Raskolnikov. . . . he noticed in the corner between the window and the little cupboard something like a cloak hanging on the wall. "Why is that cloak here?" he thought, "it wasn't there before. . . ." He went up to it quietly and felt that there was some one hiding behind it. He cautiously moved the cloak and saw, sitting on a chair in the corner, the old woman bent double so that he couldn't see her face; but it was she. He stood over her. "She is afraid," he thought. He steathily took the axe from the noose and struck her one blow, then another on the skull. . . . he began hitting the old woman on the head with all his force, but at every blow of the axe the laughter and whispering from the bedroom grew louder and the old woman was simply shaking with mirth. He was rushing away, but the passage was full of people, the doors of the flats stood open and on the landing, on the stairs and everywhere below there were people, rows of heads all looking but huddled together in silence and expectation.[36]

> I . . . seemed to be lying neither asleep nor awake looking down a long corridor of grey halflight where all stable things had become shadowy paradoxical all I had done shadows all I had felt suffered taking visible form antic and perverse mocking without relevance inherent themselves with the denial of the significance they should have affirmed.[37]

In conclusion, in addition to the origin of some materials and techniques and to certain essential mainsprings and situations of the plot, the comparison with *Crime and Punishment* elucidates an aspect of the Faulknerian hero too often neglected: his pride, a sin the author himself underlines in the Appendix to *The Sound and the Fury*. This pride establishes a direct kinship between Quentin and Raskolnikov—"away from God," and "given . . . over to the devil"[38] as Sonia says—and, to take an extreme case, Kirillov, rival of the Creator:

> [Quentin] Who loved not the idea of the incest which he would not commit, but some presbyterian concept of its eternal punishment: *he, not God*, could by that means cast himself and his sister both into hell, where

he could guard her forever and keep her forevermore intact amid the eternal fires.[39]

Dostoevsky seems also to have marked, to a lesser degree, the character of Benjy. He has traced unforgettable portraits of the idiot and the halfwit: Myshkin in particular; the sister of Lebyadkin in *The Possessed*; and Lizaveta, Smerdyakov's mother. But rather than Benjy's unconsciousness, it is his meaning, indicated at the end of the novel, which interests us:

> Then Ben wailed again, hopeless and prolonged. It was nothing. Just sound. It might have been all time and injustice and sorrow become vocal for an instant by a conjunction of planets.[40]

> he bellowed slowly, abjectly, without tears; the grave hopeless sound of all voiceless misery under the sun.[41]

The two passages echo almost word for word the symbolic definition given Sonia by Raskolnikov when he kisses her feet: "I did not bow down to you, I bowed down to all the suffering of humanity."[42] Although he is a kind of synopsis of the world's misery, there is no odor of the cult of suffering about Benjy. Barely capable of expressing itself, his sorrow conceals no redemptive virtue: the idiot plays the role of a witness or, at best, a proof of the Compsons' fall. He attests to the curse placed by the author on the entire family, a fatal sentence that Raskolnikov also reads—but he is alone in doing so—in Sonia's tribulations.[43]

Benjy is unable to find or aid in finding in his trials the germ of a rebirth: Faulkner assigns the role to Dilsey, the old black servant whose moral health and whose unobtrusive but most efficacious acts contrast strikingly with the degradation of her masters. Dilsey represents the tenacity, the robustness of the race, qualities that are spiritual as well as physical, for they are on a par with self-sacrifice[44] and even, one might say, with a kind of disincarnation.[45] Basically, the character of Sonia was split: Benjy inherits the passivity and the symbolic function of the Christ-like victim, while Dilsey, a fervent believer and also a Christian according to the Gospels, takes on her spiritual nature and her redemptive power. But Dilsey, although she accepts suffering and, by that very act, conquers it, is far from exercising

187

as decisive an influence as Sonia. Faulkner obviously admires her courage and surreptitiously prescribes it for us. The epilogue, however, shows the idiot on the way to the cemetery bawling beneath the marble gaze of the Confederate soldier, and, in the final analysis, the negress' faith, her abnegation, her endurance remain isolated and undeveloped suggestions to which Quentin's suicide, Jason's treachery and Caddy's misconduct give the lie. Even the parents of Quentin and Sonia share common traits. Gwynn has already observed that their fathers like to philosophize while drinking and that they watch over their progeny very poorly. We can further state that they have both known better days and that, whether lawyer or titular counsellor, these alcoholics prefer windy discourse to work. It is hardly necessary to insist on the kinship of Mrs. Compson and Marmeladov's wife: they take a ridiculous pride in their family, lament their decline, have an exaggerated respect for etiquette, wish to hang on to their rank,[46] are ill or pretend to be[47] and announce their coming end in pathetic terms.[48] Faulkner has, however, renounced the eccentricities and the violence of Katerina Ivanovna: his Mrs. Compson is less crazy, more selfish and plaintive, but just as incompetent in practical matters.

As for Caddy, we have seen that the position she occupies between Dalton Ames and Head and in relation to Quentin is comparable to that of Raskolnikov's sister who is courted by a seducer (Svidrigailov) and a husband (Luzhin), both equally hated by the brother. In her case we will focus only on the dream she recounts to Quentin—the grinning faces could very well have come from Raskolnikov's nightmare cited earlier: *"There was something terrible in me sometimes at night I could see it grinning at me I could see it through them grinning at me through their faces it's gone now and I'm sick."*[49]

Jason's character poses a problem: seen from a certain perspective he seems to belong as much to *The Brothers Karamazov* as to *Crime and Punishment*. One remembers, in fact, that Dounia has only one brother and Caddy three: Benjy, Quentin and Jason. This single accident would not justify a comparison with Dostoevsky's last novel were it not that Jason seems to owe several of his peculiarities to Ivan Karamazov and his disciple Smerdyakov.

EVIL AND FATE: RASKOLNIKOV (1929-1934)

First of all, his narrow rationalism: "Logical rational contained and even a philosopher in the old stoic tradition: thinking nothing whatever of God one way or the other and simply considering the police."[50] Smerdyakov, a caricature of Ivan, takes literally and in an oversimplified fashion the ideas he has heard explained to him. While Ivan doubts, searches and speculates, Smerdyakov, sure of himself, acts coldly and basely. He is, like Jason, a philosopher at the lowest level: he has "a certain incoherence in his mind" and betrays "a boundless vanity, and a wounded vanity too."[51] Painted in the darkest colors, he provokes in Ivan the same antipathy experienced by Faulkner's character.[52] Again like Jason, he is a "mean soul"[53] and steals[54] out of greed. In addition, neither believes in God[55] and both believe anything is permitted. Here we recognize the motto of Ivan, a character to whom Jason is related by his reluctance to love, pushed to spiritual impotence. The Russian is not without passion, and his alienation is more metaphysical than social;[56] Jason, on the other hand, is as cold-blooded as a reptile. Incapable of imitating Ivan's philosophical flights, immured in a monstrous inhumanity, he finds value in money alone. If Dostoevsky and Faulkner agree in making the intellect the cause of isolation, of the negation—theoretical or actual—of *caritas*, and finally of evil itself, Ivan and Jason differ in that one is a noble soul on the way to hell and the other is an out-and-out blackguard. Ivan has none of the low meanness that permeates Smerdyakov or, to take another example, Luzhin, a business man, sordid and calculating, who takes a wife as one might buy a kitchen table. In *Crime and Punishment* Dostoevsky has already sketched a full length portrait of Jason:

Luzhin	Jason
a thoroughly estimable man[57]	I've got a position in this town[58]
a practical man[59]	Logical rational contained[60]
he seems a little conceited[61]	letting your own uncle be laughed at by a man that would wear a red tie[62]
rather abrupt[63]	Once a bitch always a bitch, what I say.[64]

189

a man ought not to be indebted to his wife, but that it is better for a wife to look upon her husband as her benefactor.[65]

Lorraine is always after me to write to her but I says anything I forgot to tell you will save till I get to Memphis again but I says I don't mind you writing me now and then in a plain envelope, but if you ever try to call me up on the telephone, Memphis won't hold you I says. I says when I'm up there I'm one of the boys, but I'm not going to have any woman calling me on the telephone. Here I says, giving her the forty dollars. If you ever get drunk and take a notion to call me on the phone, just remember this and count ten before you do it.[66]

For these disciples of the Snopeses, converted to the new ideas—one to a utilitarian morality, the other to the "get rich quick" mentality—everything is for sale, everything has a price.[67] In short, the superficial pedant, the gross materialist, of *Crime and Punishment* appears to be much closer to Quentin's brother than does Ivan Karamazov, although Jason would seem to have inherited his incapacity to love from the latter. Moreover, Razumihin specifically reproaches Raskolnikov[68] for this fault, although the murderer, surrounded by his mother, sister, Sonia and his friends, does not know the glacial wasteland in which Faulkner's cheap sharpster—and his suicidal brother—are lost.[69] Quite frankly, some extraordinary metamorphoses take place during the transition from Petersburg to Jefferson. While the character of Sonia splits in two, it is the opposite process that occurs here. Jason assumes the traits of three of Dostoevsky's characters. The ghosts of Ivan and Smerdyakov can undoubtedly be seen throughout that day of April 6, 1928, but finally it is *Crime and Punishment* that wins out over *The Brothers Karamazov*. For proof one need look no further than the crucial passage which deals with the struggle between Jason's will and his fate. Jason, a theoretician after his own fashion, rationalizes existence and, like Quentin, tries to force it to conform to his plans, but reality resists his pathetic schemes. On paper, everything is arranged: he will have his niece, who has stolen his nest egg, and her lover where he wants them;

he will see them before being seen; he will have no trouble recognizing them, the girl or the man with her, providing he wears the same necktie, etc. In any case, he cannot afford to make a mistake. But when he attempts to set them in motion, his strategies fail: the pursuer comes home empty-handed, a victim of a strange power that is hostile to his plans and which governs the entire novel.

> He could see the opposed forces of his destiny and his will drawing swiftly together now, toward a junction that would be irrevocable; he became cunning. I can make a blunder, he told himself. There would be just one right thing, without alternatives: he must do that. He believed that both of them would know him on sight, while he'd have to trust to seeing her first, unless the man still wore the red tie. And the fact that he must depend on that red tie seemed to be the sum of the impending disaster; he could almost smell it, feel it above the throbbing of his head.[70]

> It never occurred to him that they might not be there, in the car. That they should not be there, that the whole result should not hinge on whether he saw them first or they saw him first, would be opposed to all nature and contrary to the whole rhythm of events.[71]

The outrageous gap between the best laid plans and life's accidents, between the will and the intellect on one hand and, on the other, that unfathomable contingency which the frustrated individual calls fate—this is one of the major themes of the first part of *Crime and Punishment*, where nothing happens according to the plans that have been prepared: "when the hour struck, it all came to pass quite differently, as it were accidentally and unexpectedly."[72] In both cases the will is conquered in the test and the reasoning shown to be false. The error, feared from the beginning,[73] actually takes place, but in an unexpected manner. Much more than simply a halting of the tactical deployment of the operation, it is inherent in the strategy itself: Jason cannot imagine that he will not even see his niece, Raskolnikov cannot conceive that he will also have to kill the moneylender's sister. In addition, Raskolnikov believes in fate[74] insofar as he senses that reality is beyond his control: a subjective opinion that surely did not fail to arouse the interest of young Faulkner, who makes fate one of the mainsprings of the plot. It is, in fact, the novelist himself who speaks of fate in regard to Jason in the last chapter of *The Sound and the Fury*, while Dostoevsky is always careful to present fate as an illusion of the hero. This conviction could explain, nonetheless, Faulkner's preference for *Crime and Punishment* during this period.

What is to be concluded from all of this? First of all there are too many correspondences, and they are too marked to allow us to reject an influence. Among the sources of *The Sound and the Fury* we must reserve a high place for *Crime and Punishment* and an honorable mention for *The Brothers Karamazov*. The borrowings, as we have seen, are never literal:[75] it is a matter neither of quotations nor of plagiarism but of resemblances in the situations, motives, themes and procedures. The works read constitute a reservoir of material from which the creator can draw freely and sovereignly: they remain entirely subordinate to the new work. Here it is the relations between the motives and the characters that are changed; there a detail is thrust suddenly into the limelight; elsewhere Dostoevsky's heroes are disassembled or welded together to give birth to Benjy, Dilsey or Jason. Sometimes intensified, at other times muffled, the Russian elements are perfectly integrated into the Faulknerian vision. Even the soliloquy technique, systematically used throughout the first three parts, can be linked to *Crime and Punishment* where the narration often gives way to the "indirect" interior monologue. In any case, it seems certain that Faulkner read *Crime and Punishment* very attentively before writing his first masterpiece.

As I Lay Dying (1930)

The next volume seems to have been conceived in reaction against Dostoevsky's thought, which still situates it within his orbit.

Perhaps the relations between Darl and Dewey Dell are still a residue of *The Sound and the Fury*. Here the brother also manifests an exaggerated concern for the actions of his sister; however, Darl's madness and the clairvoyance with which he uncovers the thoughts of others[1] recall Myshkin rather than Quentin Compson or Raskolnikov.

But it is, above all, with the central character that we must deal, for Addie Bundren, the driving force of the novel and the axis in relation to which the other heroes are defined, can herself be described by ideas defended or combatted by Dostoevsky. Addie, completely attached to the concrete and physical, scorns words which, in her opinion, do not stick to things.

> That was when I learned that words are no good; that words don't fit even what they are trying to say at.[2]

> the . . . words that are not deeds, that are just the gaps in peoples' lacks.[3]

The same incompatibility between language and action that Raskolnikov underlines at the beginning of *Crime and Punishment*: "But I am talking too much. It's because I chatter that I do nothing. Or perhaps it is that I chatter because I do nothing."[4] Simple coincidence? There is more. The concrete, in which Addie wishes to participate but from which she is isolated by words, is identified with the instinct, the blood, with the earth itself of which she is a daughter and to which her body returns after a long exile and a strictly material redemption, as Cleanth Brooks indicates.[5] Addie Bundren, a character worthy of D. H. Lawrence, has, in fact, a thirst for that Life—"the duty to the alive"[6]—so highly praised by Dostoevsky, but she excludes any spiritualistic nuance: "me . . . . the wild blood boiling along the earth."[7] While extending this notion, she mutilates it and, therefore, reverses its meaning. Raskolnikov also speaks of "only to live, to live and live! Life, whatever it may be!"[8], Razumihin sees in the evolution of humanity a "living process"[9] while Dmitri Karamazov relates existence to suffering,[10] but none of them reject the intervention of a transcendent mystery. The exaltation of life in Faulkner results in a kind of pantheism that reduces God to the level of a Magna Mater.[11] And although one can find similar traits in Marya Timopheievna's ideas—"God and nature are just the same thing . . . the mother of God is the great mother—the damp earth"[12]—the idiot girl of *The Possessed* does not, for all that, elevate what is commonly called a sin into divine creation.[13] For Addie secularizes Christianity.[14] Her God is not that of the Churches; he belongs to her alone in the world of the novel, and one could even say that he was created expressly for her—a projection of her incoercible life force, her implacable will to affirm herself. Her revolt against the Christian God and the condition he has imposed on man calls to mind, in a very different context, Ivan Karamazov, or better still, Kirillov or Terentiev of *The Idiot* who, knowing himself condemned, intends to put an end to his life because "perhaps suicide is the only action [he] still [has] time to begin and end by [his] own will."[15] Unlike Dostoevsky, Faulkner does not set Addie's rebellion in direct opposition to the faith of an Alyosha or a Myshkin. Nonetheless, Cora Tull quite rightly accuses her of sacrilege,[16] and Cash Bundren remarks that his brother Jewel, the fruit of Addie's sin, rebels against God when he saves his mother's coffin from the water,[17] an act which is done, moreover, to fulfill his mother's wish. Salvation then consists in wrenching the flesh from the water and fire of the Earth; the good Life necessarily involves sin. Like Quentin Compson, whose puritan rigorism and impotence she contradicts, Addie believes in her own way that only sin can give a sense to existence. She goes even further still, for she appropriates the Dostoevskian ideas on the saving power of evil. Speaking of Jewel, her bastard son, she predicts: "He is my cross and he will be my salvation. He will save me from the water and the fire. Even though I have laid down my life, he will save me."[18] This is, at bottom, a parody of *The Brothers Karamazov*, all the more so in that Addie is, according to Cora, conscious of her sin and accepts the punishment for it.[19] A double parody, because the redemption does not concern the soul and because the expiation which should bridge the gap between sin and salvation is here linked not with the adulteress' remorse but with her resignation to the isolation from which she momentarily escaped thanks to her sin. After a single moment of communion with life, Addie makes the best of solitude, the prelude to death.[20] The pious Cora is quite right to tell her that, for her, sin has a unique meaning.[21] Nothing is more hostile to the Christian tradition than this vitalistic reversal of spiritual values: virtue seen as sorrow and alienation, sin regarded as an offering to God, the spirit of the Earth. To tell the truth, it would be difficult to find a creature less faithful to the teachings of Dmitri and Alyosha Karamazov than Addie Bundren. In the—very doubtful—hypothesis that the Russian writer left his imprint on this rural novel, whose plot, atmosphere and setting contrast strikingly with his work, his influence could scarcely have responded to his hopes. Except for the "polyphonic" structure, what one finds in *As I Lay Dying* is not what Dostoevsky preached, but just the contrary.[22]

Sanctuary (1931)

Less than a week after its appearance, John Chamberlain compared Faulkner's new novel to *The Brothers Karamazov*[1] without developing the idea further. The idea was to be taken up again in 1959 by Edward Wasiolek, but the latter, far from believing in a profound influence, limits Dostoevsky's contribution to three passages by Faulkner.[2] It appears, nonetheless, that a detailed examination of *Sanctuary* can bear more appreciable results.

The plot, or at least its most crucial moments, takes place indoors as is so often the case in Dostoevsky. The wind-and-rain-swept country crossed by the Bundrens is left in order to penetrate into a bootlegger's hideout, dilapidated rooms, a barn, a bordello, a bar, or a court room. The setting suffocates the characters by its tightness, ugliness, filth: everthing here, like Raskolnikov's garret, indicates a separation from nature.

Sanctuary, in its general outline, recounts the same story as *Crime and Punishment* and *The Brothers Karamazov*: a serious infraction of the law (a murder accompanied by rape or theft) followed by an investigation and a trial. In the cases of Popeye and Raskolnikov, the reader is informed of the crime from the outset while he watches Goodwin's lawyer, Horace Benbow, and Porfiry, the examiner, attempt with great difficulty to reconstruct the facts. On the other hand, the role assigned to the trial in *Sanctuary* squares rather well with the episode described in Book XII of *The Brothers Karamazov*, "A Judicial Error." We shall see later that Faulkner was inspired by both novels at the same time.

Three scenes in *Sanctuary* are, in fact, more or less directly related to these novels. They are in ascending order of importance: the second part of chapter 24, the beginning of the next chapter and chapters 27 and 28, passages which are all located near the end of the book. The first, the most distant from the supposed model, recounts the conversation of Popeye, Red and

Temple at the dancehall: a banal situation of two rivals circling a woman disgusted by one of them and in love with the other. The circumstance recalls, in a general way, the scene at the inn in *The Brothers Karamazov* (VIII, 8) during which the Pole and Dmitri give themselves over to "almost an orgy, a feast to which all were welcomed"[3] in the company of Grushenka: the gaming table, the lascivious music,[4] the woman's drunkenness[5] and the awakening of desire,[6] all of this is also noted by Faulkner. In chapter 25, we witness the consequences of the preceding scene, Red's funeral, a grotesque and macabre tableau showing a "disorderly and drunken crowd"[7] and ending in a general uproar, like the long funeral banquet in *Crime and Punishment* (V, 2 and 3). But it is well known that naturalism thrived on such drinking bouts and, all things considered, nothing proves Dostoevsky's influence here.

Such is not the case with the trial of Goodwin (chapters 27 and 28) the development of which follows Book XII of *The Brothers Karamazov* rather closely in its general outline. The situations, in fact, are in no way different. The guilty parties, Popeye and Smerdyakov, both portrayed as abnormal, do not even appear, and escape legal punishment, although the author repairs this injustice by disposing of them himself, while an innocent person, Goodwin or Dmitri, expiates in their place based on the dubious testimony of a woman (Temple, Katerina Ivanovna). The two writers thus demonstrate the incompatibility of morality and law, to which Dostoevsky adds the theme of redemption through suffering; in Faulkner evil and error triumph, without being able to transform themselves into good. In addition, there are some details which correspond. Just as Goodwin begins by concealing Popeye's presence at the scene of the murder from Horace, his lawyer, so also does Dmitri initially refuse to furnish the prosecutor with explanations that might clear him; their motives, although different, lead to an analogous conduct.[8] The trial itself, which occupies all of the last book of *The Brothers Karamazov* (around a hundred pages) is in *Sanctuary* reduced to a short chapter (chapter 28) and to two fragments of the preceding one: in all about ten pages. In addition to the indictment and the defense which he recounts in detail, Dostoevsky speaks in Book

XI of Grushenka and Alyosha's visits to Dmitri in prison awaiting the judgement. If, in *Sanctuary*, Temple's accusation and testimony are brief, the visit takes on greater importance. We watch the accused, his mistress (Ruby) and his lawyer reunited in the cell, but because he wishes to underline Horace's weakness and not to regenerate Goodwin, Faulkner plunges the latter in a deep sleep while Horace rehearses Ruby in her role for the fatal day, an effort which proves fruitless. The visit cuts the trial scene in two, dividing the two days over which it is spread; in Dostoevsky the trial develops in a single, unbroken movement. With the exception of this difference, the ceremonial is identical: the introduction of evidence,[9] the description of the room,[10] the appearance of witnesses, the duel of the defense and prosecution, the decisive role of the jury, and the rapidity of deliberations: "exactly an hour, neither more nor less" for the Russian, a mere eight minutes for the American.[11] The essential similarity is obviously the sudden change produced by defense witnesses, Temple and Katerina Ivanovna, who quite unexpectedly crush the accused by consciously lying. In both cases the material proofs which support their statements and reflect two social taboos, that is, a young girl's virginity and a father's life, are isolated from the circumstances to which they originally belonged. The corn cob, the instrument of rape, was not used by Goodwin, whose virility precludes such artifices, but by Popeye, an impotent voyeur. As for Dmitri's letter announcing that he is going to kill his father, which is introduced by Katerina, it was written while in an inebriated state.[12] Finally, as if to accentuate the irony of the judgement, Popeye is executed for a murder he did not commit and Smerdyakov hangs himself. True justice takes its revenge in the end, thanks to the novelist's good will and not by means of the tribunal whose blindness and futility is denounced. It is, moreover, a pyrrhic victory: the innocent are punished along with the guilty, and the instigator gets off free. Morally, in any case, Ivan and Temple bear a good portion of the responsibility: Smerdyakov does no more than put into practice ill-digested theories, and Popeye succumbs, like so many others, to the blandishments of an eighteen-year-old Eve. Once more, the value and the relations of the characters are modified in passing from one book to another. It is, for example, impossible to confuse Katerina Ivanovna, Dmitri's former fiancee, and Temple Drake, who scarcely knows Goodwin: the two women have nothing in common except their perjury. But in *Sanctuary* the role of traitor falls not only to Temple: she shares it with Narcissa, the lawyer's sister, who—following Katerina's example—sells the accused to save the being dearest to her. Narcissa aids the prosecution out of love for her brother (or his respectability), Katerina to cover Ivan. Thus the Dostoevskian heroine is dismembered, Temple and Narcissa together fulfilling the function assigned to Katerina Ivanovna alone.

In addition to the trial, one discovers a host of even more precise analogies in the situations and reactions of the characters.

Temple, hunted down and raped at gunpoint by Popeye (chapter 13), surpasses Dounia of *Crime and Punishment*, whose virtue barely triumphs over Svidrigailov's importunities (VI, 5). The latter, as we know, courts a young maiden: "a girl who'll be sixteen in another month" who sometimes "steals a look at [him] that positively scorches [him]";[13] Temple—"her eyes blankly right and left looking, cool, predatory and discreet"[14]—is not much older, although infinitely more dangerous. Her long confession to Horace (chapter 23) could have developed from those loved by Dostoevsky; in any case, it contains a direct borrowing from *Crime and Punishment*. She explains that during the night while Popeye handled her, she believed herself dead:

> I could see myself in the coffin. I looked sweet—you know: all in white. I had on a veil like a bride, and I was crying because I was dead or looked sweet or something. No: it was because they had put shucks in the coffin.[15]

Minus the details, it is precisely the dream that Svidrigailov had before his suicide:

> on a table covered with a white satin shroud, stood a coffin. The coffin was covered with white silk and edged with a thick white frill; wreaths of flowers surrounded it on all sides. Among the flowers lay a girl in a white muslin dress, with her arms crossed and pressed on her bosom, as though carved out of marble. But her loose fair hair was wet; there was a wreath of roses on her head. The stern and already rigid profile of her face looked as though chiselled of marble too, and the smile on her pale lips was full of an immense unchildish misery and sorrowful appeal.[16]

To be sure the meanings diverge: that which in the Russian novel is meant to express the criminal's remorse, in *Sanctuary* takes on the victim's anguish. Nonetheless, the image of the dead young girl, although seen from opposite angles, remains linked to the theme of rape.

All of this chapter (VI, 6) seems to have made a vivid impression on Faulkner, for one finds its traces in two other places in *Sanctuary*, already pointed out by Wasiolek. Just after his first dream, Svidrigailov encounters in a "long narrow corridor . . . a little girl, not more than five years old"[17] whom he cares for like a mother. Leaning over her once she is asleep, he sees her pure features twist into a lewd grimace:

> He suddenly fancied that her long black eyelashes were quivering, as though the lids were opening and a sly crafty eye peeped out with an unchildlike wink, as though the little girl were not asleep, but pretending. Yes, it was so. Her lips parted in a smile. The corners of her mouth quivered, as though she were trying to control them. But now she quite gave up all effort, now it was a grin, a broad grin; there was something shameless, provocative in that quite unchildish face; it was depravity, it was the face of a harlot, the shameless face of a French harlot. Now both eyes opened wide; they turned a glowing, shameless glance upon him; they laughed, invited him. . . . There was something infinitely hideous and shocking in that laugh, in those eyes, in such nastiness in the face of a child. "What, at five years old?" Svidrigailov muttered in genuine horror. "What does it mean?" And now she turned to him, her little face all aglow, holding out her arms . . . "Accursed child!" Svidrigailov cried, raising his hand to strike her, but at that moment he woke up.[18]

Horace assists at the same metamorphosis while he contemplates the photograph of Little Belle, the daughter born of his wife's first marriage. The first time in chapter 19:

> He moved, suddenly. As of its own accord the photograph had shifted, slipping a little from its precarious balancing against the book. The image blurred into the highlight, like something familiar seen beneath disturbed though clear water: he looked at the familiar image with a kind of quiet horror and despair, at a face suddenly older in sin than he would ever be, a face more blurred than sweet, at eyes more secret than soft.[19]

A second time at the end of chapter 23, the chapter in which Temple has already just taken an image from Svidrigailov's nightmare:

The photograph sat on the dresser. He took it up, holding it in his hands. Enclosed by the narrow imprint of the missing frame Little Belle's face dreamed with that quality of sweet chiaroscuro. Communicated to the cardboard by some quality of the light or perhaps by some infinitesimal movement of his hands, his own breathing, the face appeared to breathe in his palms in a shallow bath of highlight, beneath the slow, smoke-like tongues of invisible honeysuckle. Almost palpable enough to be seen, the scent filled the room and the small face seemed to swoon in a voluptuous languor, blurring still more, fading, leaving upon his eye a soft and fading aftermath of invitation and voluptuous promise and secret affirmation like a scent itself.[20]

Wasiolek shows very clearly that the heroes experience an identical disgust before the transformation of innocence into lasciviousness, an imaginary "fall" that is accomplished either in a dream or by an optical illusion caused by the lighting. In his view, the passage indicates a moment of awareness: Svidrigailov, after reading his own lewdness on the child's face, puts a bullet in his brain; Horace, for his part, could conclude with the apostle that all of the world is under the power of evil. Such is, moreover, the central idea of the book, in which Temple applies the reflections of Lise and Alyosha in *The Brothers Karamazov* literally: "I want to do evil . . . there are moments when people love crime."[21]

Little Belle is not the only child about which Horace is concerned. The image of Ruby's sickly nurseling, glimpsed at the beginning,[22] accompanies him like a reproach,[23] similar to the obsession from which Ivan Karamazov suffered. The arguments the latter develops for the benefit of Alyosha (V, 4 "Rebellion") are well known: how does one understand, justify, accept the suffering of these young innocents who have not eaten of the forbidden fruit and yet "must suffer for their fathers' sins."[24] In Faulkner, despite the absence of any religious nuance, the child is nonetheless defined similarly as condemned to suffer in a way that is absurd, irremediable and, therefore, revolting. Horace, without posing as a philosopher reacts like Ivan (chapter 16), but the menacing presence that crushes innocence, far from resulting from the imponderable decrees of God, is here materialized in the person of Popeye, the instrument of Evil.

[Horace] looking down at the child, at its bluish eyelids showing a faint crescent of bluish white against its lead-colored cheeks, the moist shadow

of hair capping its skull, its hands uplifted, curl-palmed, sweating too, thinking Good God. Good God.
He was thinking of the first time he had seen it, lying in a wooden box behind the stove in that ruined house twelve miles from town; of Popeye's black presence lying upon the house like a shadow of something no larger than a match falling monstrous and portentous upon something else otherwise familiar and everyday and twenty times its size; of the two of them —himself and the woman—in the kitchen lighted by a cracked and smutty lamp on a table of clean, spartan dishes and Goodwin and Popeye somewhere in the outer darkness peaceful with insects and frogs yet filled too with Popeye's presence in black and nameless threat.[25]

And it is again the same passage from *The Brothers Karamazov* whose echo one perceives in a dialogue between Horace and Miss Jenny. Horace delivers himself of a violent diatribe against society and the Church which, stigmatizing murder and adultery—crimes of which Goodwin is guilty in their eyes—would put the parents to death and take charge of their illegitimate child in order to raise him in the terror of sin.

Then they all jumped on him [Goodwin]. The good customers, that had been buying whiskey from him and drinking all that he would give them free and maybe trying to make love to his wife behind his back. You should hear them down town. This morning the Baptist minister took him for a text. Not only as a murderer, but as an adulterer; a polluter of the free Democratico-Protestant atmosphere of Yoknapatawpha county. I gathered that his idea was that Goodwin and the woman should both be burned as a sole example to that child; the child to be reared and taught the English language for the sole end of being taught that it was begot in sin by two people who suffered by fire for having begot it. God God, can a man, a civilised man, seriously. . . .[26]

Horace thus tears away the Christian garments in which his fellow citizens have dressed themselves. In Jefferson, the concern for respectability and the desire for vengeance have smothered love for one's neighbor. Brothers have become tormentors; charity, indifferent to misery, is used only to judge and torture. This is precisely what Ivan explained to Alyosha when he told him about the execution in Geneva:

Five years ago, a murderer, Richard, was executed—a young man, I believe, of three and twenty, who repented and was converted to the Christian faith at the very scaffold. This Richard was an illegitimate child who

was given as a child of six by his parents to some shepherds on the Swiss
mountains. They brought him up to work for them. . . . Richard had been
given to them as a chattel, and they did not even see the necessity of
feeding him. . . . he lived like a brute and finished by killing and robbing
an old man. He was caught, tried, and condemned to death. They are not
sentimentalists there. And in prison he was immediately surrounded by
pastors, members of Christian brotherhoods, philanthropic ladies and the
like. They taught him to read and write in prison, and expounded the
Gospel to him. They exhorted him, worked upon him, drummed at him
incessantly, till at last he solemnly confessed his crime. He was converted.
He wrote to the court himself that he was a monster, but that in the end
God had vouchsafed him light and shown grace. All Geneva was in ex-
citement about him—all philanthropic and religious Geneva. All the aristocratic and well-bred society of the town rushed to the prison, kissed Richard and embraced him; "You are our brother, you have found grace. . . ."
And so, covered with his brothers' kisses, Richard is dragged to the scaffold and led to the guillotine. And they chopped off his head in brotherly
fashion because he had found grace.[27]

Faulkner condenses the story and tones down the irony. However,
if Horace does not "admit" the world any more than Ivan, his
attack is directed less against the Creator than against the creatures: Yoknapatawpha, its laws, morality, churches. It is appropriate to add to Wasiolek's pertinent commentary that the story
of Richard immediately precedes that of the "little horse" which
Faulkner reworked (?) in *Sartoris*. Of all of the episodes in *The
Brothers Karamazov*, "Rebellion" takes on a major significance
around 1930: stripped of its metaphysical implications, it could
serve as an epigraph for the denunciations of Southern society
and its violence that are to be found in *Sanctuary* and *Light
in August*.

In addition to these, the most convincing of the analogies, other
details also strike the reader. Miss Reba, the madam of the bordello in which Popeye, Temple and Red amuse themselves, seems
to borrow several traits from the madam of *Crime and Punishment*—her "very stout, buxom" figure, her "glittering jewels"[28]
("the other hand ringed with yellow diamonds as large as gravel,
lost among the lush billows of her breast."[29]) her sense of bourgeois propriety,[30] and finally her comic appearance. But nothing
can be inferred from the traditional attributes of this literary type;
none of this denotes a direct filiation. The same remark can be

made about Ruby, Goodwin's mistress and devoted servant—one need not be influenced by *Crime and Punishment* and Sonia Marmeladov, in particular, to sacrifice everything for someone one loves.[31] It is not so much the resemblances, in themselves imprecise and perhaps accidental, which bestow a Dostoevskian stamp on *Sanctuary* as their accumulation. And then they are not limited to such futile details. The splitting of the personality which afflicts successively Horace[32] and Temple,[33] the use of a leitmotif such as the rouged lips and cheeks of Temple,[34] the opposition established between the Christian facade and true charity:[35] does one not recognize here, more or less confusedly, Ivan Karamazov's hallucinations, Svidrigailov's careful appearance and one of the themes of "Rebellion"? *Sanctuary's* dependence on Dostoevsky is probably less extensive than that of *The Sound and the Fury*. But the links, although fewer, are also tighter.

Light in August (1932)

In *Light in August* Faulkner begins *Sanctuary* over again, but in so doing opens entirely new perspectives on evil. Thus it is not surprising that in 1933 F. R. Leavis posed the question "Dostoevsky or Dickens?"[1], while contenting himself with declaring Faulkner much closer to the latter than to the former. With the exception of a remark by Frederick L. Gwynn we have had up to the present no indications on the subject.[2] And yet the story of Joe Christmas recalls *Crime and Punishment* much more than does that of Popeye. If the three novels have a murderer for a hero, Christmas and Raskolnikov are portrayed without any antipathy, while Faulkner visibly execrates Popeye. Pure evil, of which he is the symbol, is revolting; the others are only unfortunates, and their crimes are at least understandable. There is nothing tragic about a robot: Popeye has only the appearance of a man; *Light in August* and *Crime and Punishment*, on the other hand, give a detailed account of how an individual worthy of pity comes to violate the precepts of morality and society. In both cases, the plot develops backwards and against the chronological succession of events. As in certain detective novels, the crime and the criminal are uncovered at the beginning, then the motives are reconstructed by means of flashbacks. The act itself counts less than the motives—Raskolnikov's theories, Christmas' milieu—and the effects: the regeneration of one and the death of the other. It matters little that causes and consequences are, in many respects, diametrically opposed; the important thing for us is the identical manner of telling the story and looking at the hero. The construction "against the grain" already adopted in *Sanctuary* for Horace Benbow's investigation, draws less from *The Brothers Karamazov*, whose plot is more respectful of chronology, than from the modern murder stories and their ancestor, *Crime and Punishment*.[3] For that matter, the trial scene, whose importance for the innocents—Dmitri Karamazov and Goodwin— we well know, disappears in both *Light in August* and *Crime and Punishment*: this time the die is cast, the suspects *are* guilty.

In the matter of violence, Faulkner concedes nothing to Dostoevsky. In this regard, the period from *Sanctuary* to *Light in August* (1931-36) even appears to be the most Dostoevskian: the fanatics, murderers, and madmen of Yoknapatawpha and the Russia of *The Brothers Karamazov* are viewed through remarkably similar prisms. We have just seen the fascination exercised on Faulkner by the "Rebellion" chapter (V, 4), devoted entirely to cruelty, innocent suffering and its theological legitimization. The fate of Joe Christmas and that of Richard resemble each other to such a degree that one could very well flow from the other. The hero of *Light in August*, just as in the anecdote reported by Ivan, is a natural child given at the age of five[4] to farmers who raise him according to their own ideas; although the views of the foster parents on education do not concur, they treat the child as a thing, which is to say they mistreat him; "till he grew up and was strong enough to go away and be a thief"[5] and then "He was caught, tried, and condemned to death."[6] In their general outline the plot and the theme are the same. Society, which Ivan shows has done everything to prepare the crime and to lead its victim to it, throws itself on him when he actually commits it: society thirsts after blood. The echo, scarcely discernible in *Sanctuary*, grows in force, while undergoing, as usual, numerous manipulations. Richard and Christmas are cursed because their very existence challenges the sacred laws of the community; both expiate a fault for which they cannot reasonably be held responsible. The ostracism which they suffer is obviously a result of their irregular birth: the natural child is, by definition, set outside the law; he transgresses the customs of the State and the Church. *Light in August* is the first of Faulkner's novels to attach a predominant importance to religion or, to be more exact, to its social implications.

We find here the germ of one of the guiding ideas of *Absalom, Absalom!*: the likening of slavery to sin and—in the American context—to original sin, since the white race must expiate it as a collective, hereditary guilt, inherent in existence.[7] To be sure, this is still only an opinion expressed in passing by one of the characters—all of the passages referring to it are to be found in Joanna Burden's autobiographical narrative—but the idea of solidarity in sin, seen first from the specific angle of racial relations, reappears on the universal level at the end of the novel when Hightower glimpses the faces of those he has met in the course of his life, all jumbled and resembling one another. It is a crucial moment in which Faulkner suggests that all human actions mutually imply one another and a moment in which Hightower, after having tried in vain to keep aloof, senses, with less acuity, however than Dmitri Karamazov or Zossima, that "we are all responsible for all."[8] In short, we assist here at the outlining of a fundamental principle, the erection of one of the pillars of Faulknerian thought, whose Dostoevskian origins are all the more likely since the Russian impregnated the American's imagination during this period. It is, indeed, the foundation of the doctrine propounded later in *Go Down, Moses* and *Requiem for a Nun*. Moreover, the idea that the individual ought to atone for a sin which stains the whole community but which he has not personally committed constitutes, at bottom, the central lesson of the drama of Joe Christmas, the crucified Christ of Yoknapatawpha. It is probably in *The Brothers Karamazov* that Faulkner found the moral and political solution to the South's problem: redemption through suffering.

Basing himself, through the intermediary of Dostoevsky, on Christian concepts, he, at the same time, launches in *Light in August* a regular offensive against the Church and, above all, against the fanaticism of the faithful. Puritanism plays a primary role among the forces which destroyed Christmas, so much so that the novel in places almost becomes a pamphlet. Hightower, meditating on the tyranny of the priests and the evil power of a Protestantism hostile to love and life,

> seems to see them, endless, without order, empty, symbolical, bleak, sky-pointed not with ecstasy or passion but in adjuration, threat, and doom. He seems to see the churches of the world like a rampart, like one of those barricades of the middleages planted with dead and sharpened stakes, against truth and against that peace in which to sin and be forgiven which is the life of a man.[9]

Hightower imitates in his fashion the diatribes against Rome in "The Grand Inquisitor" and notably the famous denunciation of authority. And yet it is not Hightower, defrocked despite himself, who incarnates the perversity of the illuminated and fanatical, but Hines and McEachern, the grandfather and foster father of Christmas. Both find a counterpart in the ridiculous Father Ferapont and Grigory, the servant of the head of the family.

Hines and the Father are ignorant fools who preach the Gospel without ever having been ordained[10] and imagine themselves the elect of God. They even pretend to speak with him.

> And old Doc Hines said to God . . . and God said, 'You wait and you watch. . . .'[11]

> There was a strange belief . . . that Father Ferapont had communication with heavenly spirits and would only converse with them, and so was silent with men.[12]

> "Holy and blessed Father . . . is it true, as they noise abroad even to distant lands about you, that you are in continual communication with the Holy Ghost?"
> "He does fly down at times."[13]

In their pride they set themselves up, one more so than the other, for instruments of divine will:

> I (it is allegedly God speaking through Hines) have set you there to watch and guard My will. It will be yours to tend to it and oversee.[14]

> he hadn't begun then to take God's name in vain and in pride to justify and excuse the devil that was in him.[15]

206

"Casting out I cast out," he roared again. He was wearing his coarse gown girt with a rope. His bare chest, covered with grey hair, could be seen under his hempen shirt. His feet were bare. As soon as he began waving his arms, the cruel irons he wore under his gown could be heard clanking.

. . . .

"You cast out the evil spirit, but perhaps you are serving him yourself," Father Paissy went on fearlessly. "And who can say of himself, 'I am holy.' Can you, Father?"[16]

The Lord of Hines and Ferapont has nothing in common with Christ: it is the wrathful God of the Old Testament.[17] Faulkner's fanatic has, however, the peculiarity of railing against women. The Father, to be sure, reproaches Zossima for adoring sweets—"ladies brought them to him in their pockets"[18]—but the subject is beyond his experience. Hines, for one, is married and the father of a daughter who has gone wrong: he knows what he is talking about. His misogyny calls to mind rather Grigory according to whom "every woman is dishonest."[19] But this trait, the sign of a Miltonic Protestantism intensified out of all proportion, is surely the product of the American milieu and, also, of the creative vision.

In any case, McEachern seems to descend more directly from Grigory than Hines from Father Ferapont. While the last two can be ranked among the visionaries and the maniacs, the others are simply righteous to the point of inhumanity. Here are their parallel portraits.

McEachern	Grigory
His voice was deliberate, infrequent, ponderous; the voice of a man who demanded that he be listened to not so much with attention but in silence.[20]	It was remarkable how little they spoke to one another in the course of their lives, and only of the most necessary daily affairs. The grave and dignified Grigory thought over all his cares and duties alone, so that Marfa Ignatyevna had long grown used to knowing that he did not need her advice. She felt that her husband respected her silence.[21]

Upon the table, facing him and open, lay a Presbyterian cate-chism.[22]	He was fond of the book of Job, and had somehow got hold of the copy of the sayings and sermons of "the God-fearing Father Issac the Syrian," which he read persistently for years together.[23]
His voice was not unkind. It was not human, personal, at all. It was just cold, implacable, like written or printed words.[24]	He was firm and determined and went blindly and obstinately for his object, if once he had been brought by any reasons . . . to believe that it was immutably right. He was honest and incorruptible.[25]

They reign as despots in their homes, ruling their wives with a rod of iron. They detest the pleasures of the world and, child-less, they adopt an orphan whose mother died in childbirth and whose father has disappeared. One has the impression that Faulkner has this time amplified the meager elements furnished by the short chapter of *The Brothers Karamazov* entitled "In the Servants' Quarters" (III, 1) to make it into one of the key episodes of his novel. Similarly, note this detail which occurs a little later (III, 6):

> Grigory taught him to read and write, and when he was twelve years old, began teaching him the Scriptures. But this teaching came to nothing. At the second or third lesson the boy suddenly grinned.
> "What's that for?" asked Grigory, looking at him threateningly from under his spectacles.
> "Oh, nothing. God created light on the first day, and the sun, moon, and stars on the fourth day. Were did the light come from the first day?"
> Grigory was thunderstruck . . . Grigory could not restrain himself. "I'll show you where!" he cried and gave the boy a slap on the cheek. The boy took the slap without a word, but withdrew into his corner again for some days.[26]

In *Light in August* it occupies no less than half of chapter 7 (nine pages). Of course, the distance between Grigory and Mc-Eachern is as great as that between a preliminary sketch and a finished portrait, but despite the enlargement and retouching resulting from the new setting, it is very much the profile of Karamazov's servant that we glimpse behind the Presbyterian farmer.

In both novels the adopted son turns against the father: Smerdyakov kills the old Fyodor Pavlovitch of whom he is very likely the illegitimate son, while Christmas attacks McEachern. The revolt against the father is, in fact, one of their common pivots: in addition to Smerdyakov, Ivan and Dmitri are potential parricides; as for Christmas' act, it echoes the quarrel between Calvin and Nathaniel Burden (chapter 11). Freud, taking the Oedipus complex as a starting point, shows how the father of the primitive tribe, the object of the hostility of his sons, was replaced by the idea of the Divine Creator—a Father murdered but nonetheless all-powerful. His theory has the advantage of establishing a link between atheism and parricide, two problems dealt with in *The Brothers Karamazov*. Not only does Ivan rise up against Christ, but Smerdyakov can justly accuse him of having killed—morally, of course—Fyodor. In Faulkner, it is unnecessary to have recourse to psychoanalysis to link Christmas' crime to the hatred of religion. The author of *Light in August* willingly expatiates on the question. But, while Ivan undermines the very foundations of Christianity, Christmas rebels only against the Church and its servants who, with the Bible in their pocket and a sword in their hand, slake their thirst for violence with the blood of their neighbor. Faulkner is little concerned with the essence of faith: he limits his diagnosis to its social excrescences and, rather than the ideas of "The Grand Inquisitor," it is the image of fanaticism, notably Father Ferapont, that he remembers, relieved of its comic overtones. In *Light in August* the revolt against the father does not culminate in metaphysics: it is developed exclusively on the level of the collectivity. Behind McEachern it is not Christ that one glimpses, but America, the South and Yoknapatawpha county.

Before passing on from the themes to the hero that expresses them, let us further point out that Miss Burden's family presents certain analogies with the Karamazovs. The father—Nathaniel or Fyodor—is married twice; Joanna is, like Alyosha, a child born of a second marriage; both are led to the cemetery wherein rest, respectively, Joanna's half-brother and Alyosha's mother.[27] It is while recounting this visit, made at the age of four, that Joanna mixes a Dostoevskian allusion to the suffering of children with the racial question:

after that I seemed to see them (the blacks) for the first time not as people, but as a thing, a shadow in which I lived, we lived, all white people, all other people. I thought of all the children coming forever and ever into the world, white, with the black shadow already falling upon them before they drew breath . . . I saw all the little babies that would ever be in the world, the ones not yet even born—a long line of them with their arms spread, on the black crosses.[28]

Joe Christmas is closely related not only to Richard of "Rebellion," but, even more strikingly, to Raskolnikov, Smerdyakov, and Dmitri.

In *As I Lay Dying* Faulkner had already depicted the search for identity. Such is again the problem that haunts Christmas, but it is here treated in the tragic mode. The hero of *Light in August*, an abandoned illegitimate child, does not know whether he is white or black. He hesitates between two extremes which correspond to the terms of Raskolnikov's dilemma, transplanted in the Southern soil. For the differences in skin overlay differences in social status: Christmas succeeds in identifying neither with the clan of the masters nor with that of their former slaves. His fate is, nonetheless, infinitely more tragic than that of his Russian counterpart. First of all, because his solitude is carried to the breaking point and, secondly, because his freedom is virtually non-existent and he goes directly to his fatal end without the slightest chance of salvation being offered, finally, because the fate in which Faulkner locks him is posited as an objective component of his universe and not an individual belief. Christmas has neither friends, nor relatives, nor a loving wife and, if in both cases the hero's crime concretizes his isolation from nature and society, there is an enormous abyss between Raskolnikov's theoretical calculations and Christmas' existential bewilderment. Where in *Crime and Punishment* alienation proceeds from the sin of pride and deliberately cultivated speculations, the worker of *Light in August* feels himself smothered by forces beyond his control. Raskolnikov can think and act differently, can choose to be or not to be an assassin, and in fact considers it;[29] master of his fate, he himself in complete independence poses a dilemma which has not been forced on him by circumstances. But how is Christmas, who has no parents and is doubtful about his race, to oppose the constraints of public opinion which wishes everyone to have a home and family and to conduct himself according to the color of his skin? All the more so since, raised in the Puritan tradition, he remains its prisoner even in revolt.[30] Determined within and without, he has very little room for maneuver. On the one hand, he finds himself rejected by the community insofar as it does not know how to label him; on the other, he shares all of its prejudices. There is for him no freedom except in crime, no redemption but death (we are reminded of Quentin Compson, but Quentin does not even have a choice). His murder, in addition to actualizing the split latent in his being and causing him to be officially banned by society, permits him to recover his dignity as a man. Both Raskolnikov and Christmas kill to attain freedom, but one understands that to mean the will to power and the other the legitimate claims of any individual. Assuming that freedom is something good in itself, the Russian misconstrues it and, like Christmas, uses reprehensible means to acquire it. With the difference that the latter is unable to find any other means. Not to kill Joanna, the Yankee nymphomaniac and religious fanatic who is his lover, would be equivalent to abdicating his quality as a man, to be chained forever to the Southern heritage; the reverse solution amounts to proclaiming his autonomy from that which binds him, to perishing, but without admitting defeat. In other words, Christmas has only the preposterous freedom of choosing his own defeat, a particle of freedom bent by the environment toward evil and death: "It was not alone all those thirty years which she did not know, but all those successions of thirty years before that which had put that stain either on his white blood or his black blood, whichever you will, and which killed him."[31] Stuck between the grave of tomorrow and the wall of yesterday, Christmas does not choose his choice: he lacks the initial freedom that allows Raskolnikov to formulate an alternative. He is obliged either to kill and die physically, or to submit and die spiritually: this is the sum of his freedom and it gives access only to death or servitude, that is to say, its own negation. His crime is, at bottom, nothing more than a desperate means of winning, through evil, the initial freedom stolen from him by the environment. Christmas, in spilling blood, breaks out of his pris-

on; Raskolnikov, for his part, simply indulges in a gratuitous
dream. The situation of the former is thus revealed as particularly
pitiful, because the act by which he asserts himself is also the
act by which he kills himself. In comparison with Raskolnikov,
the weight of fatality attenuates his responsibility; while the Russian student imagines himself hounded by Fate and spontaneously renounces his own freedom, Joe Christmas is literally crushed
by the narrator. From *Crime and Punishment*, Faulkner retains
only the lesson he wished to read there: the idea of fatalism which
he dissociates from the private nightmares of the alienated hero.
As a matter of fact, he had already illustrated these vain imagin-
ings in Quentin Compson and they had probably become less
interesting in his eyes than the social pressures. Strangely enough,
Christmas at times thinks he has *chosen* his path;[32] but it is
an illusion, as Faulkner points out: "he believed with calm paradox that he was the volitionless servant of the fatality in which
he believed that he did not believe."[33] As in *The Sound and the
Fury*, the novelist himself introduces destiny into the plot,[34] a
destiny in which moreover, other heroes believe.[35]

In this way, despite fundamental divergences of opinions and
intentions, it is possible to explain individual resemblences in behavior and situation. Whether destiny is or is not a part of the
world in which the heroes move matters little since, in any case,
they act as if it existed. Both Christmas and Raskolnikov sometimes feel at the moment before acting that they are prisoners
of a force beyond them:

> He [Christmas] took that coin and went straight to the restaurant. He did
> not even put the coin into his pocket. He did it without plan or design,
> almost without volition, as if his feet ordered the action and not his
> head.[36]

> But in the last resort he [Raskolnikov] simply ceased to believe in him-
> self, and doggedly, slavishly sought arguments in all directions, fumbling
> for them, as though some one were forcing and drawing him to it.[37]

Before they are arrested they lose, as if by common consent, the
sense of chronology, for fate entangles the conventions and pre-
visions of the mind:

> Time, the spaces of light and dark, had long since lost orderliness. It
> would be either one now, seemingly at an instant, between two move-

ments of the eyelids, without warning. He could never know when he would pass from one to the other, when he would find that he had been asleep without remembering having lain down, or find himself walking without remembering having waked.[38]

A strange period began for Raskolnikov: it was as though a fog had fallen upon him and wrapped him in a dreary solitude from which there was no escape. Recalling that period long after, he believed that his mind had been clouded at times, and that it had continued so, with intervals, till the final catastrophe. He was convinced that he had been mistaken about many things at that time, for instance as to the date of certain events. Anyway, when he tried later on to piece his recollections together, he learnt a great deal about himself from what other people told him.[39]

As in *Crime and Punishment*, where Raskolnikov explores the premises before he murders the moneylender, Christmas, in fact indulges in a veritable rehearsal of the drama when, before strangling his mistress, he exhibits himself stark-naked to a woman in a passing automobile.[40] Several minor traits render the parallel even more convincing: the relations of the murderer and the prostitute, the peregrinations before the crime, the hole in the wall from which Christmas steals the money and where Raskolnikov hides that which he has stolen,[41] and above all—once again—the blows inflicted on the horse.[42]

This episode, in truth, could as easily come from *The Brothers Karamazov* as from *Crime and Punishment*. To the numerous affinities between *Light in August* and Dostoevsky's last novel that we have already brought to light, certain scenes from the life of Christmas must be added, notably the one in which he breaks with McEachern and expresses his rebellion against the father, the Church, and the South, all at the same time (chapter 9). Christmas and Smerdyakov are bastards, born of an unknown or scarcely known father, aggressive toward the heads of the family that received them—the first knocks McEachern out, the second kills Fyodor Karamazov—and they are rather undecided about religion which they reject and submit to at the same time.[43] However, chapter 9 clearly shows that Joe Christmas often patterns his conduct on that of Dmitri Karamazov and that his character is a result of the combination of several Dostoevskian actors. If Smerdyakov assassinates old Fyodor, Dmitri strikes Grigory who "was like a father" to him.[44] And the events told by Faulkner in chapter 9, in effect, reproduce in their general outline those of Book VIII of *The Brothers Karamazov*, dominated by "Mitya" (chapter 4 and following). The scene takes place at night. The "parricide" goes to meet the one he loves—and whom he loves despite her past and against his father's will—in a dance hall or an inn, either before or after coming to blows, for McEachern literally disrupts the festivities, while Dmitri has already knocked out Grigory, who had surprised him beneath Fyodor's windows. Christmas brandishes a chair, Dmitri a brass pestle to rid themselves of the intruders. It is this precise moment that the two novelists choose to recall that their heroes have already threatened their fathers with death.

> "Stand back! I said I would kill him some day! I told him so!"[45]

> A horrible fury of hatred suddenly surged up in Mitya's heart, "There he was, his rival, the man who had tormented him, had ruined his life!" It was a rush of that sudden, furious, revengeful anger of which he had spoken, as though forseeing it, to Alyosha, four days ago in the arbour, when, in answer to Alyosha's question, "How can you say you'll kill your father?"[46]

In Dostoevsky, Dmitri menaces Fyodor whom he spares and wounds Grigory who formerly looked after him; in *Light in August* these two figures are blended in the traits of McEachern, Christmas' adopted father. Once he has struck, the rebel finds himself strangely exalted[47] and goes in search of his beloved in a scene which takes place against a background of disputes or brawls.[48] In both passages mention is made of a nocturnal disturbance.[49] Let us further note that after killing Miss Burden, Christmas exposes himself to arrest just as futilely as Dmitri when he has Grigory's blood on him, that he no more behaves as is expected of a guilty person[50] than Dmitri does, and that he accepts his punishment, although one cannot speak of moral regeneration in his context.[51]

The hero of *Light in August* very likely borrowed his fatalistic vision of the world, the existential dilemma he poses for himself and the solution he chooses, from Raskolnikov, the rebellion against paternal authority and certain forms of behavior from Smerdyakov and Dmitri, and finally his inveterate hatred of ecclesiastical authority from Ivan.

214

EVIL AND FATE: RASKOLNIKOV (1929-1934)

Lena Grove opposes him in the same way that Sonia contradicts Raskolnikov's pride, with the exception that Faulkner accentuates the contrast, for Lena and Christmas have nothing in common, in contrast with their Dostoevskian correspondents. From Marmeladov's daughter, Lena might be said to inherit patience in adversity, the unbreakable faith in Providence, but her attitude springs less from the passivity of the slave than from the serene robustness of Life, Woman, and the fertile Earth.[52] Her existence operates on the level of pure animality, on this side of the consciousness which tortures Quentin, Horace Benbow, and Hightower; Lena would have had a hard time reading the Bible, as Sonia did so efficaciously, and it is not she who does her utmost to aid Byron Bunch nor who walks in his wake; here the roles are reversed. The two women, nonetheless, represent the same haven of peace, the same source of happiness amidst torments, the same beneficent force for the man they meet. Lena fundamentally confirms the ideas from *The Possessed* which could serve as an inscription for the heart-breaking story of Christmas: "the man who loses connection with his country [and the earth] loses his gods, that is, all his aims."[53]

Lena leaves Jefferson in search of the father of her child in the company of his replacement, Byron Bunch, whose acts here and there evoke Dostoevsky without one's being able to identify a precise model. This time it is not, in fact, *Crime and Punishment* or *The Brothers Karamazov* that *Light in August* reflects but other of Dostoevsky's narratives which we are not sure Faulkner ever read. As in *White Nights* and in *The Insulted and the Injured*, Byron, although in love with Lena, tries to unite her with his rival.[54] Actually, the sacrifice made for the benefit of the loved one and indirectly in favor of a third party is also found in *Poor People* which Faulkner possessed in translation as early as April 1, 1932, (*Light in August* appeared in October)[55] and even, in an attenuated form, in *The Brothers Karamazov*, in which Katerina Ivanovna announces, rather rashly, her intention of making Dmitri happy despite his betrayal.[56] Such a situation ought to have been fascinating to Dostoevsky, for it immolates selfishness to love. Thus, in the same, or nearly the same, line of thinking Mavriky of *The Possessed* defies all conventions, refuses to judge

215

Liza and erases her "sin," so great is his passion;[57] the same work also shows a husband displaying extraordinary concern for the woman who has cheated on him and who is in transports of joy when, upon her return home, she gives birth to a son which is not his.[58] Despite the fact that the relations between Byron and Lena reproduce on certain points the situation of *Poor People*, there remains this troubling thematic analogy with *The Possessed*. Influence? affinity? It would be foolhardy to attempt a decision.

The same uncertainty hangs over the "doubles" which, occasionally, Miss Burden,[59] Christmas,[60] Lena[61] and Hines[62] show themselves to be. The case of Miss Burden is all the more disconcerting in that, according to her lover, she acts like two heroines in *The Gambler* or *The Idiot*. Joanna is a virgin on the decline. Every time that she gives herself to Christmas she acts as if she had been despoiled of her virtue for the first time[63] and even as though she hates him for having deflowered her.

> She did not resist at all. It was almost as though she were helping him, with small changes of position of limbs when the ultimate need for help arose. But beneath his hands the body might have been the body of a dead woman not yet stiffened. But he did not desist; though his hands were hard and urgent it was with rage alone. 'At least I have made a woman of her at last,' he thought. 'Now she hates me. I have taught her that, at least.'[64]

Abandon and resistance, love and hatred are interlaced and succeed one another in *The Gambler*, where Polina repulses her lover as soon as the night is over. Similarly, the capricious Nastasya Filippovna (*The Idiot*) makes Totsky dance over a volcano.

> it was a new and surprising creature who laughed in his face and stung him with venomous sarcasms, openly declaring that she had never had any feeling in her heart for him except contempt—contempt and loathing which had come upon her immediately after her first surprise.[65]

These proud women cannot forgive themselves for having succumbed and therefore execrate the seducer who conquered them: wondering about the causes of his break with Polina, the suitor of *The Gambler* speaks, among other things, of Polina's "despair at having brought herself to come to me."[66] Faulkner does not project such an implacable light on the mysteries of the feminine heart, but it is very much a characteristic of this kind that he sketches in *Light in August*. The passages which recall, closely or more distantly, Dostoevsky are virtually innumerable. The first chapter, for instance, in which we see Lena seated on a cart talking with the driver while the house of the crime burns on the horizon could be compared to "Stepan Trophimovitch's Last Wandering" in *The Possessed* (III, 7). When the dietician declares that children have an intuition superior to that of adults[67] she seems to provide a commentary on the opinions of Myshkin.[68] Hightower lives the life of a recluse, as do Raskolnikov and Kirillov. Fanatic leaders such as Percy Grimm and Verhovensky are animated by the same destructive spirit, the same desire to reign by terror, etc., etc. But are these anything more than coincidences?

In the composition, the initial juxtaposition of large independent panels, the introduction of correspondences and contrasts by means of which the isolated elements are insensibly welded together, the fact that the hero is flanked by antithetical figures such as Hightower and Lena Grove: there is nothing in all this that is not already found in *Crime and Punishment* and *The Brothers Karamazov*.

These 13 (1931) and Doctor Martino and Other Stories (1934)

To conclude with this period, we must still review two collections of short stories. In this genre, concentrated and allusive by its very essence, the points of contact will be rare—indeed, nonexistent.

Of all the stories in *These 13*, only "Ad Astra" (1931) sometimes reflects the philosophical preoccupations of the Russian. It is rather strange the way this war story exalts, through the intermediary of an Indian prince and a German intellectual, love of one's neighbor, self-mastery which is above all mastery of the senses, effort, the values of the heart, and the fraternity of men in opposition to nationalism. But these ideas are born as much from the views of the characters who express them or the author's own stoicism as from, for example, the doctrine of Zossima. However that may be, Faulkner has, with the exception of *A Fable*, written nothing on the First World War which is closer to the teachings of Dostoevsky. As for the rest, there are no important analogies, although one notes, here and there, a "double" ("That Evening Sun," 1931; "Red Leaves," 1930); an isolated idea—Earth regarded as the mother of man;[1] some situations and psychological traits: Nancy's sensing the presence of an armed man ("That Evening Sun"), a presentiment that one encounters—linked with the razor—in *The Idiot* and *The Eternal Husband*;[2] or better yet the definition of the born bachelor ("Hair," 1931) that one will find again later, this time more consistent with the opinions of Velchaninov, in *The Town*.[3]

With the exception of "Smoke" (1932), which reappears later in *Knight's Gambit*,[4] and "Beyond" (1933), the original edition of *Doctor Martino and Other Stories* yields very little in the way of fodder for comparatists. There are examples of anonymous letters as in *Sartoris* ("There Was a Queen," 1933), a ritual ablution (*ibid.*), the support a man furnishes his rival as in *Light in August*, and a situation in which honor does not exclude forgiveness ("Honor," 1930), but we will not insist on these trifles. "Beyond," nonetheless, is worth a stop because the novelist here attempts, in a very different spirit, the big question which obsesses Ivan Karamazov: the search for God. It is this also that puzzles Faulkner's agnostic hero. Mothershed, his atheistic friend, maintains opinions which Kirillov of *The Possessed* would not disavow: both, in fact, consider suicide to be a victory of human freedom over the Christian God:

[Mothershed] glared at the Judge. "God damn it, I remember raising the pistol; I remember the little cold ring it made against my ear; I remember when I told my finger on the trigger . . ." He glared at the Judge. "I thought that that would be one way I could escape the preachers, since by the church's own token . . ."[5]

Every one who wants the supreme freedom must dare to kill himself. He who dares to kill himself has found out the secret of the deception. There is no freedom beyond; that is all, and there is nothing beyond. He who dares kill himself is God. Now everyone can do so that there shall be no God and shall be nothing.[6]

I am killing myself to prove my independence and my terrible new freedom.[7]

218

Just like Kirillov, Mothershed remains more religious than he thinks, for his atheism, far from rejecting any notion of God or of resolving itself into rational doubt, very much constitutes a form of faith. Bishop Tihon explains himself on this point in "Stavrogin's Confession": "the complete atheist . . . stands on the next to top step to the most perfect faith (he may step over or he may not), but the indifferent man has no faith whatever except a bad fear."[8] and Mothershed shares his opinion:

> "Agnosticism." He snarled it. "Won't say 'Yes' and won't say 'No' until you see which way the cat will jump. Ready to sell out to the highest bidder. By God, I'd rather have given up and died in sanctity, with every heaven-yelping fool in ten miles around."[9]

In addition, his friend treats him metaphorically as a nihilist,[10] and in *The Possessed* Kirillov lends himself to the machinations of a terrorist movement. The story's epilogue, however, in no way agrees with the Christian concept of a future life. Taken as a whole, the doctrinal analogies, more frequent in this volume than in the preceding volume, announce the turning point of 1935-36: the glorification of life, the supreme value, attested by the anguish and suffering that it contains—"In thousands of agonies— I exist"[11]—("Doctor Martino," 1931; "Mountain Victory," 1932; "Beyond"); the burden of freedom ("Mountain Victory"); and above all the possibility offered to man to exercise his free will, even if it is only in sad choices (*ibid.*) "living consists in choosing wrongly between two alternatives."[12] Here is a new accent. To exist is no longer to submit to one's fate, it is to choose it.

NOTES TO CHAPTER VII

The Sound and the Fury

1. See Frederick L. Gwynn, "Faulkner's Raskolnikov," *Modern Fiction Studies*, IV, 2 (Summer, 1938), p. 170.
2. William R. Taylor, *Cavalier and Yankee* (New York: Doubleday and Co., 1963), pp. 137-40 (on Quentin and the other heroes of the same family).
3. See John Faulkner, *My Brother Bill* (London: Victor Gollancz Ltd., 1964), pp. 271-73 (on Benjy Compson).
4. *Crime and Punishment*, pp. 429, 459.
5. *The Sound and the Fury and As I Lay Dying*, p. 9.
6. See the dialogue between Quentin and Caddy (*ibid.*, p. 181):

"she tried to break her wrists free
let me go
stop it I'm stronger than you." See Lawrence Bowling, "Faulkner: The Theme of Pride in *The Sound and the Fury,*" *Modern Fiction Studies* XI, 2 (Summer, 1965), pp. 129-39.

7. See *The Sound and the Fury and As I Lay Dying,* p. 99: "It's not when you realise that nothing can help you—religion, pride, anything—it's when you realise that you dont need any aid."

8. *Crime and Punishment,* p. 58.

9. *Ibid.,* pp. 4-7. See also p. 215.

10. *The Sound and the Fury and As I Lay Dying,* p. 95.

11. *Ibid.,* p. 99.

12. *Ibid.,* pp. 102-04.

13. See Cleanth Brooks. *William Faulkner: The Yoknapatawpha Country* (New Haven: Yale Univ. Press, 1963), pp. 329-30.

14. *Crime and Punishment,* p. 60.

15. *Ibid.,* p. 366. See also pp. 28, 175, 412.

16. *Ibid.,* p. 33.

17. *The Sound and the Fury and As I Lay Dying,* pp. 126-29, and *Crime and Punishment* II v, and p. 194.

18. *Crime and Punishment,* p. 175. Thus we have the choice posed by Raskolnikov to his sister "It is me or Luzhin" (p. 206).

19. The brother resents all seducers. See the "fat dandy" who pursues the drunken girl (*Crime and Punishment,* I, iv) and Quentin in relation to Gerald Bland (*The Sound and the Fury,* pp. 184-85).

20. See *The Sound and the Fury and As I Lay Dying,* p. 179, and *Crime and Punishment* VI, 5.

21. See *The Sound and the Fury and As I Lay Dying,* p. 179-80, and *Crime and Punishment,* p. 438.

22. See also the beginning of *Crime and Punishment,* p. 1: "On an exceptionally hot evening early in july. . . ."

23. See *Crime and Punishment,* pp. 36, 49, and *The Sound and the Fury and As I Lay Dying,* pp. 96, 112, 131. Rastignac in *Le père Goriot* also receives a letter from his mother discussing family affairs. See Balzac, *La comédie humaine II* (Paris: Editions de la Nouvelle Revue Française, 1935), pp. 922-24.

24. See *Crime and Punishment,* pp. 42-46, and *The Sound and the Fury and As I Lay Dying,* pp. 144-47.

25. See *Crime and Punishment,* pp. 86-93, and *The Sound and the Fury and As I Lay Dying,* pp. 161-64.

26. See *Crime and Punishment,* pp. 24, 166, 44, 139, 141, 463, and *The Sound and the Fury and As I Lay Dying,* pp. 102, 106.

27. See *Crime and Punishment,* pp. 150, 169, and *The Sound and the Fury and As I Lay Dying,* p. 165.

28. See *Crime and Punishment,* pp. 151, 429, 456, 459, 477, and *The Sound and the Fury and As I Lay Dying,* pp. 109, 111, 134-35.

29. See *Crime and Punishment,* pp. 443, 445. Lucien, in *Illusions perdues,* considers the same kind of suicide. See Balzac, *La comédie humaine IV* (Paris: Editions de la Nouvelle Revue Française, 1935), pp. 1013-14. And Bloom in *Ulysses*; see Richard P. Adams, "The Apprenticeship of William Faulkner," *Tulane Studies in English* XII (1962), 140.

30. See *ibid.,* pp. 440, 441, 443, 447, and *The Sound and the Fury and As I Lay Dying,* second part, *passim.*

31. See *Crime and Punishment,* p. 401, and *The Sound and the Fury and As I Lay Dying,* pp. 98-99.

32. See *The Sound and the Fury and As I Lay Dying,* pp. 167, 195.

33. *Crime and Punishment,* p. 417.

34. We note in passing that one of the characters of *The Possessed* (p. 546) describes virginity as a "prejudice." Marmeladov's wife is little concerned for that of Sonia (*Crime and Punishment*, p. 15) This is also Mr. Compson's attitude (*The Sound and the Fury and As I Lay Dying*, p. 135).

35. See *Crime and Punishment*, pp. 86, 245, 246, and *The Sound and the Fury and As I Lay Dying*, p. 192.

36. *Crime and Punishment*, pp. 245-46.

37. *The Sound and the Fury and As I Lay Dying*, p. 188.

38. *Crime and Punishment*, p. 368.

39. *The Sound and the Fury and As I Lay Dying*, p. 9. Our underlining.

40. *Ibid.*, pp. 303-4.

41. *Ibid.*, p. 332.

42. *Crime and Punishment*, p. 285.

43. See *ibid.*, p. 291, and *The Sound and the Fury and As I Lay Dying*, p. 3.

44. *The Sound and the Fury and As I Lay Dying*, p. 311.

45. *Ibid.*, p. 282.

46. See *Crime and Punishment*, pp. 13, 159, 161, 212, 232, and *The Sound and the Fury and As I Lay Dying*, pp. 122, 315.

47. See *Crime and Punishment*, pp. 159, 165, 379, and *The Sound and the Fury and As I Lay Dying*, p. 295.

48. See *Crime and Punishment*, pp. 382, 383, and *The Sound and the Fury and As I Lay Dying*, pp. 79, 81.

49. *The Sound and the Fury and As I Lay Dying*, p. 131.

50. *Ibid.*, p. 16.

51. *The Brothers Karamazov*, p. 276.

52. *Ibid.*, pp. 276-77.

53. *Ibid.*, p. 652.

54. See *ibid.*, pp. 662-70, and *The Sound and the Fury and As I Lay Dying*, pp. 234, 246.

55. See *The Brothers Karamazov*, p. 670, and *The Sound and the Fury and As I Lay Dying*, pp. 16, 212.

56. See *The Brothers Karamazov*, pp. 245, 272-73, and *The Sound and the Fury and As I Lay Dying*, pp. 226, 245, 264.

57. *Crime and Punishment*, p. 32.

58. *The Sound and the Fury and As I Lay Dying*, p. 207. See also p. 250.

59. *Crime and Punishment*, p. 34.

60. *The Sound and the Fury and As I Lay Dying*, p. 16.

61. *Crime and Punishment*, p. 32.

62. *The Sound and the Fury and As I Lay Dying*, p. 260.

63. *Crime and Punishment*, p. 32.

64. *The Sound and the Fury and As I Lay Dying*, p. 198.

65. *Crime and Punishment*, p. 33.

66. *The Sound and the Fury and As I Lay Dying*, pp. 211-12.

67. See *Crime and Punishment*, pp. 37-38, 133, 194, and *The Sound and the Fury and As I Lay Dying*, p. 221.

68. *Crime and Punishment*, p. 191.

69. *Ibid.*, p. 459.

70. *The Sound and the Fury and As I Lay Dying*, p. 323.

71. *Ibid.*, p. 234.

72. *Crime and Punishment*, p. 65.

73. *Ibid.*

74. See *Ibid.*, pp. 55, 57, 57-58, 60-61, 64, 465, 476.

75. Even in parallel passages such as these: "any live man is better than any dead man" (*The Sound and the Fury*, p. 121) and "Only to live, to live and live! Life, whatever it may be" (*Crime and Punishment*, p. 142).

As I Lay Dying

1. See *The Sound and the Fury and As I Lay Dying*, p. 426.
2. *Ibid.*, p. 463.
3. *Ibid.*, p. 466.
4. *Crime and Punishment*, p. 1.
5. See Cleanth Brooks, *William Faulkner: The Yoknapatawpha Country* (New Haven, Conn.: Yale University Press, 1963), p. 153.
6. *The Sound and the Fury and As I Lay Dying*, p. 466.
7. *Ibid.*, p. 467.
8. *Crime and Punishment*, p. 142.
9. *Ibid.*, p. 227.
10. *The Brothers Karamazov*, pp. 627-28.
11. *The Sound and the Fury and As I Lay Dying*, p. 466.
12. *The Possessed*, p. 144.
13. *The Sound and the Fury and As I Lay Dying*, p. 466.
14. See Cleanth Brooks, *op. cit.*, p. 153.
15. *The Idiot*, p. 395.
16. *The Sound and the Fury and As I Lay Dying*, pp. 460-61.
17. See *ibid.*, p. 510.
18. *Ibid.*, p. 460.
19. See *ibid.*, p. 459.
20. See *ibid.*, p. 467: "My father said that the reason for living is getting ready to stay dead. I knew at last what he meant and that he could not have known what he meant himself, because a man cannot know anything about cleaning up the house afterward. And so I have cleaned my house. With Jewel—I lay by the lamp, holding up my own head, watching him cap and suture it before he breathed—the wild blood boiled away and the sound of it ceased. Then there was only the milk, warm and calm, and I lying calm in the slow silence, getting ready to clean my house."
21. *Ibid.*, p. 459.
22. On Addie see Robert W. Weber's article, "Raskol'nikov, Addie Bundren, Meursault. Sur la continuité d'un mythe," *Archiv fur das Studium der neueren Sprachen*, 202. Band, 117 Jahrgang, 2. Heft, pp. 81-92.

Sanctuary

1. See John Chamberlain, "Dostoevsky's Shadow in the Deep South," *The New York Times Book Review*, February 15, 1931, p. 9.
2. Edward Wasiolek, "Dostoevsky and *Sanctuary*," *Modern Language Notes* LXXIV (February 2, 1959), 114-17.
3. *The Brothers Karamazov*, p. 457.
4. See *ibid.*, p. 460, and *Sanctuary*, p. 281.
5. See *The Brothers Karamazov*, p. 465, and *Sanctuary*, p. 286.
6. See *The Brothers Karamazov*, p. 467, and *Sanctuary*, *ibid.*
7. *Crime and Punishment*, p. 356. See *Sanctuary*, pp. 297-98.
8. See *Sanctuary*, pp. 136, 155-56, and *The Brothers Karamazov*, p. 508.
9. See *Sanctuary*, p. 323, and *The Brothers Karamazov*, p. 700.
10. See *Sanctuary*, pp. 337-38, and *The Brothers Karamazov*, pp. 697-99.
11. See *Sanctuary*, p. 349, and *The Brothers Karamazov*, p. 796.
12. *The Brothers Karamazov*, pp. 655, 729-30.
13. *Crime and Punishment*, p. 423.
14. *Sanctuary*, p. 32.
15. *Ibid.*, p. 263.
16. *Crime and Punishment*, p. 447.
17. *Ibid.*, p. 448. One finds an echo in *Sanctuary*, p. 265: "the long corridors of sleep."

18. *Crime and Punishment*, p. 449.
19. *Sanctuary*, p. 200.
20. *Ibid.*, pp. 267-68.
21. *The Brothers Karamazov*, p. 617.
22. *Sanctuary*, pp. 19-20.
23. *Ibid.*, pp. 142-43, 192.
24. *The Brothers Karamazov*, p. 246.
25. *Sanctuary*, pp. 142-43.
26. *Ibid.*, pp. 150-51.
27. *The Brothers Karamazov*, pp. 248-49.
28. *Crime and Punishment*, p. 86.
29. *Sanctuary*, p. 171.
30. See *ibid.*, p. 252, and *Crime and Punishment*, p. 90.
31. See *Sanctuary*, pp. 130, 194.
32. *Ibid.*, p. 19.
33. *Ibid.*, pp. 109, 111. See Part One, Chapter IV.
34. *Ibid.*, pp. 32, 42, 256, 281, etc. See Part One, Chapter IV.
35. *Ibid.*, pp. 216-17.

Light in August

1. F. R. Leavis, "Dostoevsky or Dickens" *Scrutiny* II, 1 (June, 1933), 91-93.
2. Frederick L. Gwynn, "Faulkner's Raskolnikov," *Modern Fiction Studies* IV, 2 (Summer, 1958), p. 172, n.8. Let us note, however, that John L. Longley, Jr., speaks of a scene in Chapter 20 (pp. 465-67) which "might have come straight out of Dostoevsky." See John L. Longley, Jr., "Joe Christmas: The Hero in the Modern World," *William Faulkner: Three Decades of Criticism* (East Lansing, Mich.: Michigan State University Press, 1960), p. 276.
3. It is interesting to note that Faulkner also considered *The Brothers Karamazov* to be in this vein. See Cynthia Gremer, "The Art of Fiction: An Interview with William Faulkner," *Accent*, XVI, 3 (Summer, 1956), 169.
4. *Light in August*, p. 133. Richard has six. See *The Brothers Karamazov*, p. 248.
5. *The Brothers Karamazov*, p. 248.
6. *Ibid.*
7. *Light in August*, pp. 234, 238, 239, 240.
8. *The Brothers Karamazov*, p. 627. See *Light In August*, pp. 465-67, 345.
9. *Light in August*, p. 461. See also p. 347.
10. *The Brothers Karamazov*, p. 173.
11. *Light in August*, p. 351. See also p. 362.
12 *The Brothers Karamazov*, p. 173.
13. *Ibid.*, p. 175. See also pp. 175-76.
14. *Light in August*, p. 351. See also pp. 360, 365.
15. *Ibid.*, p. 352.
16. *The Brothers Karamazov*, p. 351.
17. See *ibid.*, p. 176, and *Light in August*, p. 362.
18. *The Brothers Karamazov*, p. 352.
19. *Ibid.*, p. 95, and *Light in August*, pp. 120, 124, 353, etc.
20. *Light in August*, p. 133.
21. *The Brothers Karamazov*, p. 97.
22. *Light in August*, p. 137.
23. *The Brothers Karamazov*, p. 99.
24. *Light in August*, p. 139.
25. *The Brothers Karamazov*, p. 95.
26. *Ibid.*, p. 129.

27. See *ibid.*, p. 19, and *Light in August*, pp. 238-39.
28. *Ibid.*, p. 239.
29. *Crime and Punishment*, p. 48.
30. *Light in August*, p. 264.
31. *Ibid.*, p. 424.
32. *Ibid.*, pp. 244, 251.
33. *Ibid.*, p. 264.
34. *Ibid.*, pp. 321, 437.
35. *Ibid.*, pp. 414, 423, 424.
36. *Ibid.*, p. 166.
37. *Crime and Punishment*, p. 64.
38. *Light in August*, p. 315.
39. *Crime and Punishment*, p. 386.
40. *Light in August*, pp. 100-101, 104.
41. See *ibid.*, pp. 157-58, 179, and *Crime and Punishment*, p. 81.
42. See *Light in August*, p. 197; *Crime and Punishment*, pp. 50-54; *The Brothers Karamazov*, p. 249. The detail has already been noted by Frederick L. Gwynn, *loc. cit.*.
43. See *Light in August*, p. 115, and *The Brothers Karamazov*, p. 663.
44. *The Brothers Karamazov*, p. 487. See also p. 6.
45. *Light in August*, p. 193. See also p. 194.
46. *The Brothers Karamazov*, pp. 415-16.
47. See *ibid.*, p. 421, and *Light in August*, p. 194.
48. See *The Brothers Karamazov* VIII, 7, and *Light in August*, pp. 199-206.
49. See *The Brothers Karamazov*, p. 433, and *Light in August*, p. 199.
50. *Light in August*, p. 331.
51. *Ibid.*, pp. 419, 425.
52. *Ibid.*, p. 23.
53. *The Possessed*, p. 686.
54. *Light in August*, pp. 394, 398.
55. See *William Faulkner's Library—A Catalogue*, compiled by Joseph Blotner (Charlottesville: University Press of Virginia, 1964), p. 82.
56. *The Brothers Karamazov*, pp. 195-96.
57. *The Possessed*, p. 547.
58. *Ibid.*, pp. 576-78, 602-3.
59. *Light in August*, pp. 221, 246, 248.
60. *Ibid.*, p. 224.
61. *Ibid.*, p. 285.
62. *Ibid.*, p. 353.
63. *Ibid.*, p. 221.
64. *Ibid.*, p. 223.
65. *The Idiot*, p. 38. See also p. 40.
66. *The Gambler and Other Stories*, p. 109.
67. *Light in August*, p. 125.
68. *The Idiot*, p. 62.

These 13 and Doctor Martino and Other Stories

1. *Collected Stories*, p. 900 ("Carcassone"), and *The Possessed*, p. 144.
2. *Collected Stories*, pp. 295, 297 ("That Evening Sun"); *The Idiot*, pp. 211-223 (II, 5); *The Eternal Husband and Other Stories*, pp. 119-22.
3. *Collected Stories*, p. 137 ("Hair"), and *The Eternal Husband and Other Stories*, p. 29.
4. See *Knight's Gambit*, p. 3.
5. *Collected Stories*, p. 787.
6. *The Possessed*, p. 115.

7. *Ibid.*, p. 630.
8. *Ibid.*, p. 698. See also pp. 628, 633.
9. *Collected Stories*, p. 787.
10. *Ibid.*, p. 786.
11. *The Brothers Karamazov*, p. 628. See in particular *Collected Stories*, p. 796 ("Beyond").
12. *Collected Stories*, p. 774.

VIII

GOOD, EVIL AND FREEDOM (1935-1936)

The decisive turning point in the Faulknerian oeuvre, the first step toward a less tragic vision of existence and toward the novel of ideas, does not coincide with *The Unvanquished* (1938), as had formerly been thought. The confrontation with Dostoevsky shows that it is, in fact, situated in the period of *Pylon* and *Absalom, Absalom!*, which were conceived at the same time. The movement, almost imperceptible in *Light in August*, is accentuated: the wall of Fate is veined with cracks through which one already glimpses the vistas of salvation. Faulkner begins to question the slavery of man; still enclosed within the world of violence and death, with *Pylon* he leaves the zone of crime and he grafts a number of constructive ideas onto Sutpen's distressing story. Obviously these potentially hopeful ideas which he continues to elaborate from 1938 to 1954 seem to be extracted from Dostoevsky and *The Brothers Karamazov* in particular.

Let us attempt to isolate them from the hesitations and contradictions with which they are accompanied during these transitional years. For the first time, the author of *Pylon* makes his main character an apostle of good: while Dilsey (*The Sound and the Fury*) and Horace Benbow (*Sanctuary*) play only accessory roles, his reporter, the younger brother of Myshkin and Alyosha Karamazov, occupies center stage. Although his virtues miss their mark and sow nothing but unhappiness, *Pylon* is a patch of blue admidst the gallery of the dark novels. "Riposte in Tertio", published in 1936, then in *The Unvanquished*, changes evil into good, reversing the idea expressed in *Pylon,* according to the dialectics of antithesis. The optimistic note penetrates even the horror of *Absalom, Absalom!,* for the demoniacal Sutpen could perhaps have been saved: at least, that is what one of the witnesses of the drama believed. Never again will Faulknerian evil indulge itself in such orgies: *Absalom, Absalom!* marks its zenith and the beginning of its decline. Another novelty: free will. The reporter of *Pylon* exercises it in vain, but without incurring large losses and in the unique purpose of trying to comfort others. *Absalom, Absalom!* is the last novel in which fatality is omnipotent, and yet it already finds itself confronted there by a formidable adversary. There are, finally, other themes which constitute Christian principles: the conviction that the individual can assume the sin and suffering of others, the notion of solidarity in guilt and redemption, the link established between redemption and suffering. In addition, we might also note again certain affirmations on the nature of faith and landed property.

Faulkner's tone and manner recall the Dostoevskian masterpieces just as the philosophic infrastructure does. The meditations on history are multiplied in *Absalom, Absalom!* well before *Intruder in the Dust* and *Requiem for a Nun;* the painting of situations gives rise to many reflections, indeed, prophecies, but without degenerating into unadulterated exposition.

It remains to estimate the role played by Dostoevsky in this evolution. In our opinion, it could have assumed a capital importance. In joining to the picture of the world an explicit analysis of the forces which govern it, in drawing a lesson from events that he had until then restricted himself to rendering in images, Faulkner obviously approaches the Russian novelist, who has a particular yen for speculation. What is more, his commentary is, in many respects, patterned on that of Dostoevsky. But must the origin and the direction of its development really be attributed to this single influence? Let us not exaggerate. Other factors are involved. The same themes cannot be repeated indefinitely, even violence and crime exhaust themselves and eventually become as tiresome as peaceful virtue: hell, even a fictional one, causes in one who stays there a desire to escape. The high voltage, the excesses of the earlier works, are sufficient to justify a gradual estrangement. Is there anything more logical than to replace the observation of a phenomenon with an interpretation, the diagnosis of an illness with its treatment? Dostoevsky does not seem to have given the initial impulse; but once again, he furnished the means of solving the problems Faulkner confronted at the time. Problems, we hasten to point out, which concern less the art of the novelist than the aspirations of the moralist. How to escape evil and Fate? How to jump the wall between hell and purgatory? Faulkner had detailed the situation over a period of four or five years, often with the aid of Dostoevskian images. One can assume that the redemptive ideas with which they are associated did not escape him and, as a result of playing with the images, he little by little became receptive to the teachings. In any case, it is an established fact that he read *Crime and Punishment* and *The Brothers Karamazov* before formulating his new doctrine. It is equally certain that this doctrine, from the instant in which it takes shape, agrees on its essential points with Dostoevsky's system, and the more it develops after 1938, the closer it comes to it. The catalog of Faulkner's library indicates a growing interest in the Russian author between 1931 and 1936. Two copies of *The Brothers Karamazov* bear, written in Faulkner's own hand, his name and a date: 1931 and 1932, signs of a marked preference; *Poor People* is dated in the same way (1932), and one of the copies of *Crime and Punishment* is an edition from the same year; as for those of *The Possessed*, they were both published in 1936. Let us not exaggerate the importance of these facts, less revealing than one might believe: neither the date of the publication nor the autographs in themselves indicate the first contact. Only the multiplicity of analogies enables us to appreciate the favor that Dostoevsky enjoyed during this period. Faulkner's spiritual metamorphoses, a veritable black to white reversal, took place over a period of years. In the meantime, there is a strong temptation to tie the paths explored during 1935-36 to the Dostoevskian magnetism.

One could go even further and assert that the failure of *Pylon* is a result of the difficulty in shifting directions, of an inability to bestow a convincing fictional life on ideas that were too new, too poorly assimilated, in short, too foreign and yet ardently wished for—as well as of the desire to leave behind the familiar haunts of Yoknapatawpha. And does not this same desire denote a nostalgia for larger horizons, a flight from the masks of evil and fate beneath which the face of Raskolnikov is so often discovered? Faulkner's first optimistic novel, if we dare use the term, takes place far from the town of Jefferson; in addition, it was written as a sort of an antidote at a time when Faulkner caused this town to still resound with the baleful exploits of Sutpen. Faulkner apparently could not bring himself to imagine the good acting freely in an environment he had crushed so long under the weight of evil. He would have been hard put, it seems, to reconcile Dostoevsky's "New Testament" teachings with the images of violence related to *Crime and Punishment* and *The Brothers Karamazov* and linked with Yoknapatawpha. He still dissociates the novelist from the thinker in Dostoevsky. *Pylon*, after all, recalls the latter rather than the former, and, in another connection, the lessons of Myshkin rather than those of Sonia or Zossima. Does not Faulkner, in leaving Yoknapatawpha, abandon the novels he knew best and enter—perhaps without knowing it—the orbit of *The Idiot*? Setting aside the question of influences, the movement of his thought authorizes a comparison with this other aspect of Dostoevsky, a parallel from which we will draw some fruitful conclusions.

Conversely, the most explicit ideas of *Absalom, Absalom!* permit only a faint glimmer of hope: salvation is vaguely depicted at the end of a lengthy expiation which is still to be accepted. We are still very much beneath the evil spell of *Sanctuary* and *Light in August*, for the new elements are distributed most parsimoniously. While *Pylon* marks a virtual about-face, *Absalom, Absalom!* exhausts in one fell swoop the reserves of evil: it pushes it all the way to the end. With the termination of this book, the writer abandons his panting demon, exhausted by his own excesses. This novel constitutes the climax of the period inaugurated seven years earlier by *The Sound and the Fury*; it serves at the same time as a transition between the portrayal of situations and the exposition of ideas. But to say that Faulkner remains faithful to the images of the past is to say that he sticks to his old conception of Dostoevsky. To all appearances, he was not yet ready either to completely assimilate nor, therefore, to handle skillfully the other Dostoevsky that he was beginning to explore: the philosopher of redemption, the advocate of the good and freedom. And, who knows, was it not perhaps because he was too close to this in *Pylon* and sufficiently removed from it in *Absalom, Absalom!* that he failed with one and succeeded with the other?

Absalom, Absalom! is the last novel in which the influence of *Crime and Punishment*, already absent from *Pylon*, reveals itself so intensely. The lion's share henceforth will go to *The Brothers Karamazov*, whose philosophy better responds to Faulkner's need to explicate and save the universe. Curiously, the single indisputable borrowing deals precisely with the Christian legitimization of suffering (*The Brothers Karamazov* V, 4). To be sure, it is always by means of the characters and situations that Faulkner is drawn to Dostoevsky, but he nonetheless requires ideas as well.

It is possible that around 1935 he read other of Dostoevsky's works in addition to his two special favorites. There is no material proof except the analogies with *The Idiot* present in *Pylon* and with *A Raw Youth* in *Absalom, Absalom!*, resemblances as clear as the majority of those which concern *The Brothers Karamazov* and *Crime and Punishment*. As for *The Idiot*, let us resign ourselves to the conclusion that the influence, although possible, remains purely conjectural. It is perhaps permissible even to discard the hypothesis of a direct reading: the character of Myshkin is so distinctive that it would have been enough to have learned of him through a good plot summary, a critical study, or general hearsay to have been inspired. One hardly needs to immerse oneself in *The Iliad* to construct a portrait of Achilles. The case of a less known work like *A Raw Youth* is different, although a resumé would have been enough here. This time, however, there are more arguments in favor of an attentive reading: similarity of psychological traits, family relations, episodes and themes; the same manner of splitting and regrouping the Dostoevskian characters as in *The Sound and the Fury*; the possible persistence of analogies in *The Unvanquished*; finally, the repetition and concentration of presumed models: the chapters in question all come from the first (chapter I, 7; V, 1, 2, and 3; VI, 4) and the third part (chapter III, 2 and IX, 4) of *A Raw Youth*. Did the curiosity stimulated by *Crime and Punishment* and *The Brothers Karamazov* lead Faulkner to search other contacts with Dostoevsky? Unfortunately the texts do not enable us to settle the question.

Pylon (1935)

The birth of *Pylon* is explained by the dynamism proper to the Faulknerian oeuvre: its pendulum movement, the oscillation between contradictory propositions. *Sanctuary* retraced the lightning invasion of the native land by evil. In *Light in August* the double malediction of Puritanism and racial prejudices drove the individual to crime. *Pylon* provides, in comparison, a comforting note. Faulkner installed himself at "New Valois" far from the places soiled by so much blood, mused on the chances of good, and created the reporter of *Pylon*, an odd character without a name and practically without a body, the antipode of Popeye and Joe Christmas. Dostoevsky, one remembers, followed parallel paths. *Crime and Punishment* (1866), the novel of a vainglorious murderer, was succeeded by *The Idiot* (1868) in which the humility of a "perfect" man takes a resounding revenge. To jump from one pole to another is a common practice in literature as in life. What is less common is the mutation of evil into good. In both cases, there is the same manner of thinking, an identical concern to correct either the disorders of a poorly understood freedom or the cruel blows of destiny.

Pylon is a mediocre book. Not because of the failure of the hero—the campaign of goodness launched by Myshkin scarcely proves more successful—but rather because the reporter embodies an idea in which the author only half believes and which is, by his own admission,[1] particularly difficult to translate into novelistic form. The portrayal of good, as we shall see, poses problems which few writers have been able to resolve.

There is no analogy here with *Crime and Punishment*; as for *The Brothers Karamazov* it provides fewer clarifications than usual. We do not know if Faulkner had read *The Idiot* and, yet, *Pylon* approaches it very closely. Borrowing or coincidence, it matters little, after all, since even according to the second hypothesis, the comparison only confirms the kinship of the authors, the central idea of this work. In addition, through the mediation of Myshkin we will meet other heroes, Dostoevskian or not, that Faulkner knew well.

Physically the reporter and Myshkin have nothing in common except their debilitated, sickly, almost disincarnate appearance. The Idiot's portrait goes back to the iconography of Christ, while Faulkner's insists on the spectral thinness of his protagonist.[2] These are pure spirits, accidentally inhabiting flesh, and as such they clash with their milieu: the sinners, the worldly and rapacious, the young people with whom Myshkin debates; the machine and money, the aviators and businessmen faced by the reporter. The idea they embody stands in isolated opposition to the omnipotence and malignity of the material—isolated, and so to speak inoperative, although they cause a scandal and succeed in changing, if even only to the slightest degree, those whom they shock.

If the hero is seen as an original, it is very much because of his moral force. To complete the paradox, this fragile shadow, lonely and conspicuous, profoundly deranges the materialistic society, for it introduces something unheard of: generosity, devotion, pardon, love of one's neighbor pushed even to self-sacrifice. The Idiot and the reporter "pay" for others. One has only to think of the marriage of compassion planned by the first with Nastasya Filippovna, of the attitude of the second at the moment when the policeman grabs Jiggs: "He's just drunk. I'll be responsible."[3] The strangest of all is that their milieu recognizes their spiritual superiority and is so fascinated by it that their behavior is affected. The catalytic power exercised by Myshkin over others is also possessed by the reporter. Thus the passage in which Keller confides his indiscretions to the prince approximately prefigures the confession of the theft committed by the airmen.[4] And the thought which comes to Myshkin while listening to Keller— "whether anything could be made of the man by any good influence"[5]—is literally put into practice by the reporter who humanizes Jiggs, Laverne and her two "husbands" by inculcating the sense of good and evil in them by his own example:[6] "it seems I am bound to offer her the chance to tell me that they stole . . . not the money. It's not the money. It's not that."[7]

The appearance of a body so puny and a mind so strong among

the servants of materialism results in a series of misunderstandings, blunders and catastrophes. Just as the Idiot brings unhappiness to almost everyone whose path he crosses (Nastasya Filippovna, Rogozhin, Aglaia), similarly the reporter provokes evil in willing good. While forcing others to become aware of moral values, he causes the death of Shuman by ricochet. To be sure, Faulkner seems to have learned since *Sanctuary* that idealism does not always fail in its objectives, for, contrary to Horace Benbow, *Pylon* opens a window onto hope. But the balance shows, in the final analysis, more losses than gains. The advance of good is minuscule in comparison with the ravages accomplished in its name. Far from being ripe for its triumph, the Faulknerian universe grudgingly half-opens its door to this intruder and puts it on short allowance.

The Idiot also reaps nothing but disappointment. The incarnation of good, the prince's virtues, his face, such and such episode of his life: it is this that makes Myshkin a modern copy of Christ. It is, in fact, of the Gospel that Dostoevsky was thinking in writing his novel;[8] even the hero's defeat on the earthly level echoes the tortures inflicted by men on the Crucified. According to the *Diary of a Writer* (1873), Belinsky once remarked that, if Jesus were born in the nineteenth century, he would be effaced "in the presence of contemporary science and contemporary propellors of mankind."[9] Such is, in the final analysis, the fate of Myshkin and the reporter, both equally associated with the unfortunate Redeemer:

Does the race committee think he is Jesus too, the same as the rest of you do?[10]

patron (even if no guardian) saint of all waifs, all the homeless, the desperate and the starved.[11]

Protector, guardian angel, or savior: the idea is the same and the analogy of the heroes is beyond dispute. Since we cannot establish a material link between Faulkner and *The Idiot*, we ought to let matters be at this point. But are we not justified in risking some speculations? For this is not the first reference to *The Idiot* in these pages. We have already mentioned it in regard to *Soldiers' Pay*, and in support of this thesis one can invoke, if necessary, the sketch entitled "Out of Nazareth"[12] published April 12, 1925, in the New Orleans *Times-Picayune*. If we set aside the role of chance and temperamental affinities, we have to ascribe the resemblances of the prince and the reporter either to a common origin or to another work by Dostoevsky in which the Idiot reappears in a form different from Myshkin and more similar to that of the reporter.

It goes without saying that the source from which *Pylon* and *The Idiot* both flow is the Gospel. The hero of the New Testament presents all of the particularities that have been enumerated; Christ is, in a direct or indirect filiation, the literary prototype of both Myshkin and the reporter. Dostoevsky declares this expressly; Faulkner implies it covertly when he says of the airmen who are set in contrast to his character: "they were outside the range of God, not only of respectability, of love, but of God too."[13] Don Quixote, father of all idealists, offers another possibility. The Russian was inspired by him as his "Notebooks"[14] and Aglaia's allusions to "the poor knight" (II, 6 and 7)[15] testify. Faulkner, for one, insisted many times that he loved Cervantes as much as the Bible, Shakespeare, Dickens, Conrad, Balzac, Flaubert and Dostoevsky.[16] In certain respects his reporter is even closer than Myshkin to the Knight of the Sorrowful Countenance. Faulkner compares them explicitly,[17] and while the prince is in no way a comic figure,[18] the redresser of wrongs in *Pylon* is frankly ridiculed.

Let us not insist. In all fairness, we must recognize that the heroes of *The Idiot* and *Pylon* differ on several points. If they both have premonitions of catastrophe[19] and a passion for the truth,[20] the American, contrary to the Idiot, spends himself in aiding his protégés and shows no propensity to speechifying. He is, above all, a man of action, a pragmatic moralist, not a glib drawing room philosopher. Less intellectual than Myshkin, he is more efficacious. The easiest explanation would be to turn to Taine and the determinism of race, milieu and moment. Unfortunately, these commonplaces are generally contradicted by the facts: Alyosha Karamazov, a Russian, a monk and, in addition, more than half a century earlier than the citizen of "New Valois," is there to prove it. He does not like theories either, and he is

234

incessantly scurrying around trying to help others.[21] It is not just this dynamism that the reporter could have inherited; Alyosha is also in love: a youthful and timid suitor, but sensual like his father and brothers.[22] Without wallowing in the debauchery of old Fyodor or Dmitri, he repudiates the sexless sanctity that radiates from Sonia Marmeladov and, in particular, from the Idiot. The reporter, for his part, has a soul that is less pure than it might seem: throughout the novel he dreams of sleeping with Laverne. Love here takes a more concrete, more active form than with Myshkin. Finally, the protective quality with which Faulkner endows him is found, almost literally, in Dmitri's apostrophe to Alyosha: "you are an angel on earth."[23]

The young Karamazov and the reporter are unquestionably more down to earth and less ethereal characters than the prince. In wishing to portray the good, Faulkner came up against the same artistic problems as Dostoevsky who, obsessed with the guiding idea of *The Idiot*, but dissatisfied with his treatment of it, took it up once more in *The Brothers Karamazov*. It is pointless to discuss the literary merits of Myshkin and Alyosha, but it is glaringly obvious from a strictly realistic point of view that the latter is superior to the former. Already in *The Idiot* Dostoevsky attenuates the perfections of his character by endowing him with minor defects intended to make him more truthful and convincing. Virtue in a pure state easily turns into a sanctimonious piety: the prince acts as a saint, but he has his feet firmly on the ground. In Alyosha, the saint is effaced at the expense of the man, and the same is true of the journalist who gets drunk, desires Laverne, etc.

It is not surprising that the prince, the monk, and the reporter, all born of an aspiration toward the good, have traits in common: for instance, they all three love children. However, the correspondences pointed out between *Pylon* and *The Idiot*—and secondarily *The Brothers Karamazov*—leave us unsatisfied. And yet the comparison with Dostoevsky, in addition to leading to a new interpretation of *Pylon*, defines this period, which is also the period of *Absalom, Absalom!*,[24] as a turning point in the Faulknerian evolution. The novel, published in 1935, betrays a desire to escape evil and fate, opening new horizons of good and freedom. It is not impossible that Dostoevsky and *The Idiot* in particular contributed to this transformation.

Absalom, Absalom! (1936)

There is at least one, and perhaps two, unimpeachable allusions to Dostoevsky in this book. The first deals with the hackneyed topic of the suffering of children and has Quentin Compson's grandfather repeat Ivan Karamazov's arguments against God:

> (and your grandfather said, 'Suffer little children to come unto Me': and what did He mean by that? how, if He meant that little children should need to *be* suffered to approach Him, what sort of earth had He created; that if they had to *suffer* in order to approach Him, what sort of Heaven did He have?)[1]

The second, more hypothetical and situated at the end of the novel, could be an adaptation of one of old Fyodor's outbursts:

> "Now I want you to tell me just one thing more. Why do you hate the South?"
> "I don't hate it," Quentin said, quickly, at once, immediately; "I don't hate it," he said. *I don't hate it* he thought, panting in the cold air, the iron New England dark; *I don't. I don't! I don't hate it. I don't hate it.*[2]
> My dear, if you only knew how I hate Russia. . . . That is, not Russia, but all this vice! But maybe I mean Russia.[3]

A rather meager harvest, to be sure,[4] but all the more significant in that these two parallel passages concern two of Faulkner's major themes: religion and the South.

Before beginning our study of them, we will note that the development of the plot—the testimony on the facts, followed by a conjectural reconstruction of their motives—corresponds generally with that of *Sanctuary* and *Light in August*, with the exception that the author there presents his account as true and unequivocal, while in *Absalom, Absalom!* characters and reader are lost in a labyrinth of suppositions. On one side, the plot "in reverse" and the departures from chronology are derived in part from the detective novel and *Crime and Punishment*. On the other, the accumulation of hypotheses evokes the trial of Dmitri Kara-mazov (Book XII) in which opinions on the events—prosecution and defense—are set in opposition without the author commenting on their value. One does not know whom to believe; the points of view alternate, complete and contradict one another: one wanders in an ambiguous netherland. As we have already seen, Dosto-evsky had recourse to second and third hand narratives in *The Brothers Karamazov* and *A Raw Youth*.

The link between *Absalom, Absalom!* and the dark novels which precede it is not just architectural. Two of Dostoevsky's philosophical ideas, welded together and associated with the history of the United States, were already to be found in *Light in August*, i.e., solidarity in guilt and atonement through suffering. But these views, formulated in 1932 by the Burdens, are this time sanctioned by the author himself and the majority of his characters.[5] Obviously, the accent falls much more heavily on the curse inherent in the guilt than on the hope of redemption, but in the Christian world and for a fervent reader of Dostoevsky, the distance from sin to salvation is only a step. In short, Faulkner describes the creation of the Southern economy on racial and social injustice as a crime and the Civil War and the ensuing decadence as its punishment. Dostoevsky also passes effortlessly from morals to politics, applying the same formulas to the state and society as to the problems of good and evil. Both Ivan Karamazov and Zossima do so (II, 5; VI, 3): but the prophetic tone in which Shreve speaks at the end of *Absalom, Absalom!* of the conquest of the Western hemisphere by the mulatto, the taste for trenchant generalizations on History, these suggest rather the brilliant tirades of Myshkin and Shatov. The theoretician of American history, the thinker of *Go Down, Moses, Intruder in the Dust*, and *Requiem for a Nun*, made his debut as early as 1936. He found his principles in *Crime and Punishment*: in Raskolnikov's ideas on masters and slaves,[6] in the example of stoic resignation given by Sonia, in the conduct of Dmitri. And if he had not read the dissertations on the future victories of the Russian Christ in *The Idiot*, perhaps he already knew those in *The Possessed*. In any case, he was able—unconsciously perhaps, although one sometimes doubts it—to find the same accent.

These ideas developed apparently in inverse ratio to the hatred
of fanaticism, whose Dostoevskian associations we have already
indicated. Only one of the Puritans who populate *Light in August*
survives here: Mr. Coldfield, Sutpen's father-in-law. But the
theme once again is amplified, rising well above the individual
level to be placed within a national and cultural context. Corresponding to Roman Catholicism which Dostoevsky made the
western religion par excellence is the Puritan mysticism whose
baleful influence on the Anglo-Saxon countries Faulkner inflates
and caricatures: "I can imagine him, with his puritan heritage—
that heritage peculiarly Anglo-Saxon—of fierce proud mysticism."[7]
Taken together, we find in both cases the same black and white
views, the same gross antithesis of native and foreigner, the same
identification of the church with the country, the same diatribes
against the zealots of a perverted faith: Western or Mississippian.

The third theme of *Light in August*, the parricidal revolt so
brilliantly illuminated in *The Brothers Karamazov*, is also extended into *Absalom, Absalom!* and even assumes a preponderant
role. The rebellion, however, does not result in open warfare:
it aborts, and the father triumphs, while the sons are destroyed.
Rosa Coldfield's relations with her father are strained,[8] but, as
regards Dostoevsky, the most interesting relations are those maintained by Sutpen with his sons: Charles Bon, the issue of his
first marriage with a woman whom he repudiated because of her
mixed blood, and Henry, his child by Ellen Coldfield. *Absalom,
Absalom!*, however, diverges on many points from *The Brothers
Karamazov*, not only by reason of Sutpen's ironic victory, but
also because neither Ivan nor Alyosha is forced to choose between
his father and his oldest brother (Dmitri), an alternative with
which Faulkner confronts Henry; moreover, the latter kills Charles, not Sutpen. Nothing remains here except the antagonism between generations: "the father who is the natural enemy of any
son."[9] On the other hand, Bon, who is related to Christmas in
that we do not know exactly how much he knows of his own
origins, desires to make his presumed father recognize him, a
father who, because of his racial prejudices, continues to turn
a deaf ear to these entreaties and causes a chain reaction that
results in his own death. Here the son is only the remote, indirect,

and accessory cause of the father's death. Dostoevsky did not deal in his last novel with the problem of the *Vatersuche*, the individual's identity in relation to the family, and particularly, to the father. To summarize, the analogies with the situations of *The Brothers Karamazov* are severely limited: the hostility between father and son, and perhaps the genealogical tree of the Sutpens.

Thomas Sutpen, like Fyodor Pavlovitch Karamazov, has been married twice. The son of the first bed, Dmitri or Charles Bon, is, in both cases, an innocent victim: one purges a legally unjustified punishment, the other is murdered. In both cases, two children are born of the father's second marriage: Ivan and Alyosha, Henry and Judith. In addition, Karamazov and Sutpen, both vigorous males, engender bastards, Smerdyakov or Clytemnestra, who occupy the position of a subaltern in the home: they are domestics. It is, however, impossible to pursue the parallel further: Charles does not resemble Dmitri any more than Ivan does Henry, or Alyosha, Judith. In Dostoevsky the struggle takes place, above all, between the father and the children united against him, with the exception of Alyosha; in *Absalom, Absalom!* the all powerful Sutpen withdraws into the wings, while keeping control of the strings and leaving his children to tear one another apart. If Charles and Henry oppose their father like Dmitri and Ivan, the substitution of Judith for Alyosha and the mystery surrounding the repudiation of Eulalia Bon radically modify the relations between the children: Judith, unaware that he is her half-brother, falls in love with Charles. Alyosha also loves Dmitri, but with the purest of intentions. In addition, even the fraternal love which unites Judith and Henry (who according to the above genealogy correspond to Alyosha and Ivan) starts to look rather suspicious[10] and, finally, Henry's friendship for Charles could quite justifiably be described as a bit unusual.[11] As in *The Sound and the Fury*, family affection, still healthy in Dostoevsky, turns into amorous passion: it borders on incest and homosexuality. Henry, in fact, identifies simultaneously with Charles and Judith, that is, with both of the fiancés;[12] he links both poles, playing a role fundamentally similar to that of Dmitri, placed half-way between the perversity of Ivan and the sanctity of Alyosha. One could argue further that Ivan is related to Charles, the family "philosopher," and at the same time to Henry, as a "murderer." But let us leave aside these subtleties. In the final analysis, among the Dostoevskian families, the Sutpens are related to the Karamazovs less than to that heterogeneous menage, the Versilovs (a legitimate son and daughter, an illegitimate son and daughter) in *A Raw Youth*, where the relations between father and son, Versilov and Dolgoruky, are complicated by the irregular birth of the latter. We shall return to this question.

Sutpen is, like so many Faulknerian characters, the prisoner of an obsession. He appears here alongside of Quentin Compson, his biographer and portraitist, a narrator-confidant who is stunned by the horror he discovers or supposes and is the prey of a mania. We have seen what the hero of *The Sound and the Fury* owed to Raskolnikov, a theoretician frustrated by reality to whom Sutpen is also akin. In Sutpen, the notion of honor defended by Quentin in defiance of reality gives way to a "plan" which is equally unreasonable and which is closer on several points to the projects of Raskolnikov. For Sutpen's design which, at first glance, comes down to "get rich quick," concretizes his will to dominate and to endure, his *hubris*. A supremely logical man, he reduces behavior to mathematics: it is a matter, as Jason Compson also thinks, of not making a mistake.[13] Sutpen repudiates morality and, for good measure, also throws out common sense, or rather, the sense of what is. Eventually, the schemes of the intellect, by attempting to substitute for life, automatically draw their own failure after them. Sutpen's dream, according to Rosa Coldfield, is that of a fool, but a curable fool, for she even thinks it possible—momentarily—to save him, following the example of Sonia.[14] Despite his inhumanity, Sutpen is not cast into hell like Quentin on the eve of suicide, he is not beyond redemption: despite his perseverance in evil and the failure of his race against the clock, this possibility contradicts the curse of an earlier time and directly recalls *Crime and Punishment*. Another coincidence with Raskolnikov: the plan initially conceived in a spirit of social freedom to shake the yoke of inequality—a minor motive in Raskolnikov—soon departs from this purpose and degenerates into a desire to rival and be accepted by the lords of the land.

Although Sutpen wishes to combat the propertied class,[15] he passes from the camp of the oppressed to the oppressors. But just as Raskolnikov will never be a Napoleon, Sutpen will not be able to keep his goods nor succeed in founding a dynasty. The failure is total, as much on the level of social freedom, mixed much less with altruism than in *Crime and Punishment*, as on that of the "will to power." There is a final detail which ties Sutpen to *Crime and Punishment*, although it differentiates him from Raskolnikov: his absolute lack of scruples, his fundamental immorality which inspires him to *buy* his independence from his first wife. There is in this a baseness worthy of Luzhin but not of Luzhin's future brother-in-law.

In sum, Sutpen does not know Raskolnikov's moral anguish. Less intelligent and more satanic, he never hesitates, and as a good Puritan he charges across obstacles of which he, in his disarming "innocence," is ignorant. The spirit of evil acts mechanically: the "everything is permitted" caressed by Ivan Karamazov becomes a tangible reality in *Absalom, Absalom!*. Sutpen, whom the narrators are right in calling a demon, becomes a star in the gallery of the possessed alongside the inexorable Verhovensky.

The interest our novelists display in monomania springs from their warning against the falsification of the intellect, against the cramped dogmatism in which rationalists, radicals, and Puritans take such pleasure. One discovers, in leafing through the album assembled by Dostoevsky, a portrait which prefigures in almost every detail the character of Sutpen. Dolgoruky, the hero of *A Raw Youth*, also has his plan, his "idea": "My 'idea' is to become a Rothschild, to become as rich as Rothschild. Not simply rich, but as rich as Rothschild. . . . First I will simply show that the attainment of my object is a mathematical certainty."[16] This is, in essence, a definition of Sutpen's methods. But let us attend for a moment to chapter V of Part One, in which Dolgoruky expatiates on his projects and compare them with those of Faulkner's hero.

Dolgoruky	*Sutpen*
The whole secret lies in two words: *obstinacy* and *perseverance*[17]	his fifty years of effort and striving to establish a posterity[18]

I was allowed five rubles a month for pocket money. I resolved to spend only half. This was a very great trial. . . . The result of these two experiments was of vast importance to me. I had learned that I could so will a thing as to attain my objects[19]

Speaking generally, I proposed beginning my enterprise alone, that was a *sine qua non*.[21]

As for clothes, I resolved to have two suits, one for every day and one for best.[23]

My first principle will be to risk nothing.[25]

I have will and character, and the science of the streets is a science like any other: persistence, attention, and capacity can conquer it . . . What need is there of the wisdom of Solomon so long as one has character? Efficiency, skill, and knowledge come of themselves. If only one does not leave off "willing"[27]

That besides isolation, I want power . . . . money is the one means by which the humblest nonentity may rise to the *foremost place* . . . . at the same time it is the greatest leveller[29]

He did not drink at all, he told them . . . . it was years later before even Quentin's grandfather . . . learned that the reason Sutpen did not drink was that he did not have the money with which to pay his share or return the courtesy[20]

so had vanity conceived that house and, built it in a strange place and with little else but his bare hands. . . . And then he live in it, alone[22]

these spectators did not realize that the garments which Sutpen had worn when he first rode into Jefferson were the only ones in which they had ever seen him[24]

that unsleeping care which must have known that it could permit itself but one mistake[26]

the West Indies to which poor men went in ships and became rich, it didn't matter how, so long as that man was clever and courageous: the latter of which I believed that I possessed; the former of which I believed that, if it were to be learned by energy and will in the school of endeavor and experience, I should learn.[28]

He thought. 'If you were fixing to combat them that had the fine rifles, the first thing you would do would be to get yourself the nearest thing to a fine rifle you could borrow or steal or make, wouldn't it?' and he said Yes. 'But this ain't a question of rifles. So to combat them you have got to have what they have. . . . You got to have land and niggers and a fine house to combat them with. You see?' and he said Yes again,[30]

Perseverance, ascetic discipline, solitude pushed to alienation, spartan thrift, calculated ambition, self-confidence and, finally, the will to power: Dolgoruky and Sutpen share all of this equally. The only change is the perspective according to which vices and virtues are put into practice. The "raw youth" pursues a gratuitous dream which he refuses to explain by the determinism of birth and his "sorrowful childhood:"[31] he has a natural thirst for freedom, that is to say, "the calm and solitary consciousness of strength."[32] Sutpen, on the other hand, initially protests against the caste that oppresses him.

Slaves to their idea or plan, they bestow a sovereign scorn on those around them and reduce them to the level of an object, an instrument, or a toy. In addition, their project, whatever its origin or ultimate objective, is realized through ambition, that is to say, by an immoderate desire for social prestige and, therefore, for money. The comparison can be extended even further. Both are, in the beginning, poor and homeless children, the outcasts of fortune. Dolgoruky, a natural child, was placed with strangers.[33] Sutpen, born among the starvelings of the frontier, leaves his family to seek his fortune. His plan dates from exactly this period: he is approximately fourteen years old.[34] The bastard's idea goes back to nearly the same age: between twelve and seventeen years of age;[35] "in the sixth form of the grammar school"[36] it took its definitive form. In Faulkner it results from the boy's brutal initiation to social inequality. One day young Sutpen presents himself at the door of a rich planter for whom his father works and is rejected by a Negro servant before he has even had a chance to deliver his message.

He was a boy either thirteen or fourteen, he didn't know which, in garments his father had got from the plantation commissary and had worn out and which one of the sisters had patched and cut down to fit him, and he was no more conscious of his appearance in them or of the possibility that anyone else would be than he was of his skin, following the road and turning into the gate and following the drive up past where still more niggers with nothing to do all day but plant flowers and trim grass were working, and so to the house, the portico, the front door. . . .[37]

And now he stood there before that white door with the monkey nigger barring it and looking down at him in his patched made-over jeans clothes and no shoes . . . and he never even remembered what the nigger said, how it was the nigger told him, even before he had had time to say what he came for, never to come to that front door again but to go around to the back.[38]

In *A Raw Youth* Dolgoruky has a similar experience, except that it only strengthens him in his resolve. Just before going from Moscow to Petersburg, he receives some money from his father through the mediation of his half-brother, "Andrei Petrovitch's [legitimate] son, the *Kammerjunker* Versilov."[39] And this is how the scene develops (III, chapter IX, 4):

The next day, at exactly eleven o'clock, I turned up at Prince V.'s flat, which, as I was able to judge, was splendidly furnished, though it was a bachelor's establishment. I was kept waiting in the hall, where there were several lackeys in livery. And from the next room came sounds of loud talk and laughter. Prince V. had other visitors besides the *Kammerjunker*. I told the footman to announce me, and I fancy in rather haughty terms. Anyway, he looked at me strangely, and as I fancied not so respectfully as he should have done. . . .

I waited standing, knowing that it would be impossible and unseemly for me, "just as much a gentleman," to sit down in a hall where there were footmen. My pride would have prevented me under any circumstances from entering the drawing room without a special invitation. Overfastidious pride perhaps it was, but that was only fitting. To my amazement, the two lackeys who were left in the hall had the impertinence to sit down. I turned away to avoid noticing it, and yet I could not help quivering all over. . . .

suddenly the lackey who had taken my name returned. Between his fingers he held fluttering four red notes—forty rubles!

"Here, sir, will you please take forty rubles!"

I boiled over. This was such an insult! . . . .

I shouted so violently at the lackey that he started and stepped back. I told him he must go back at once and "his master must bring the money himself." . . .

I took the money and walked to the door, I took it simply because I was confused, I ought not to have taken it, but the lackey, no doubt wanting to mortify me further, ventured upon a regular flunky's impertinence. He flung the door extra wide-open before me, and pronounced with exaggerated emphasis and dignity, as I went out:

"This way, if you please!"

"You blackguard," I roared at him, and I raised my hand, but I did not bring it down. "And your master's a blackguard too! Tell him so directly," I added, and went down the stairs. . . .

244

I went down the stairs. It was a grand open staircase, and above I could be watched as I went down the red-carpeted steps. All three lackeys came out and stood looking over the banisters.[40]

Dostoevsky emphasizes this episode for the unique purpose of clarifying the relationship between the bastard and his father, but the victim says of it that it has left "a wound that has not healed to this day;"[41] Faulkner makes it into the initial outrage from which the hero's entire career develops. As with *The Idiot*, we have no external evidence which permits us to infer an influence. Let us use the *reductio ad absurdum* and provisionally set aside this possibility. Two solutions remain: simple coincidence or recourse to the same model.

It is impossible and useless to survey the innumerable books used by the two novelists. The chronological distance which separates them, their acknowledged preferences, the very nature of the scene fortunately simplify our task. All things considered, only Dickens and Balzac seem worthy of attention, unless there is a third figure, Walter Scott for instance, pulling the strings—a hypothesis that deprives our argument of any certainty. Having made these reservations, we recall Dostoevsky's fidelity to Dickens—who is cited in *A Raw Youth*[42]—and to Balzac, whose *Louis Lambert* probably furnished the name of Dolgoruky's friend.[43] The Russian's debt to Balzac has been the object of excellent studies dating back to 1924 and 1927.[44] As for Faulkner, he cites the two authors frequently together among those to whom he often returned,[45] and his library attests to the truth of this statement.

Great Expectations (1860-61), notably contains a scene which rather resembles the ones we have just compared. In chapter eight, young Pip penetrates into the once-sumptuous home of Miss Havisham—whose "case" prefigures "A Rose for Emily"—by a side door, and he becomes aware, through the contrast, of his poverty and poor manners. "That was a memorable day to me, for it made great changes in me:"[46] it was on that very day, in fact, that was born the desire to shine: to become a gentleman. Pip, to be sure, is humiliated by Estella, but the major annoyance is that he is neither expelled nor ridiculed by a servant; on the contrary, he is invited to come back.

Le père Goriot, as is well known, made a strong impression

245

on Dostoevsky. He read Raskolnikov's theories on the superior man in the dialogue between Bianchon and Rastignac in the Luxembourg Gardens,[47] in Vautrin's discourses to the latter—or to Rubempré[48] in *Illusions perdues.*[49] The hero of *Crime and Punishment* is a Rastignac with a greater gift for metaphysics, and the hero of *A Raw Youth* is equally his kin. It should be noted that Vautrin in *Le père Goriot* also summarizes Faulkner's subject:

> You see, I have an idea. My idea is to go to live the life of a patriarch amidst a great estate, a hundred thousand acres (Sutpen's Hundred!) for instance, in the United States, in the South. I want to become a planter, to have slaves, and make a few nice millions out of selling my cattle and my tobacco and my timber. I shall live like a king, and do exactly everything I want: a life unthinkable in the plaster foxhole we are all huddled in here. I'm a great poet. I don't put my poems on paper: they consist of actions and feelings. I have at this moment fifty thousand francs. That will buy me only about forty Negroes. I need two hundred thousand francs because I shall want two hundred Negroes if I'm really going to satisfy my taste for the patriarchal life. You see, Negroes are just grownup children; you do as you like with them with no inquisitive public prosecutor coming to investigate. With this black capital, in two years I shall have three or four millions. If I succeed, no one is going to ask me: "Who are you?" I shall be Mr. Four-Million, American citizen. I shall be fifty. I shan't be worn out, I shall enjoy myself exactly as I choose.[50]

Have we put our finger on the common source of *Crime and and Punishment* and *Absalom, Absalom!*? It is very possible. Sutpen, however, owes many more traits to Raskolnikov—or to Melville's Captain Ahab[51]—than to Balzac's social climber and his mentor.[52] To return to our initiation scene, Rastignac is seen in *Le père Goriot* at the moment in which this ambitious but penniless student visits the Countess de Restaud. Upon his entry he is the object of the scornful glance of the people who saw him crossing the courtyard on foot, and he understands his inferiority. Madame has the valet tell him that she is very busy. Rastignac commits numerous mistakes but is finally received, although the countess gives him a look which suggests that he is unwelcome.[53] A little later, upon his arrival at the hotel de Beauséant, the domestics mock his appearance,[54] but here also he does gain admittance.

In conclusion, in the situation with which we are concerned, it is *Absalom, Absalom!* and *A Raw Youth* which are in greatest agreement, and while keeping in mind the always possible intrusion of chance—or a third author—we feel entitled to admit the hypothesis of Dostoevskian influence. For, in addition to the social gulf, the crushing insult of riches, the sudden revelation of the hero's poverty and weakness, there is in both Dostoevsky and Faulkner what is missing elsewhere, that is the impossibility of the visitor's establishing a dialogue with the "master."

A Raw Youth, written in 1874-75, precedes by several years *The Brothers Karamazov* and introduces one of its major themes: the stormy relations between father and son that Faulkner was to take up in *Light in August* and *Absalom, Absalom!*. The humiliation suffered at the planter's door, Sutpen in turn inflicts upon Charles Bon, when, swimming in riches, he refuses to treat him as a son. This time it is no longer Sutpen who must be compared with Dolgoruky, but Charles, who is also a bastard. The short passage (I, chapter I, 7) in which the memorialist of *A Raw Youth* defines his father's attitude summarizes precisely Sutpen's attitude toward Charles: "This cold, proud man, careless and disdainful of me after bringing me into the world and packing me off to strangers, knew nothing of me at all and had never even regretted his conduct. Who knows, perhaps he had only a vague and confused idea of my existence."[55] Unlike Sutpen, Versilov, however, has no reason to turn his back on his son. He invites him to Petersburg where he lives; he finds him a job and even makes him his confidant. Sutpen, however, is as cold as marble. Faced with a father who is unmindful of his duty and whom he seeks with love and hate in his breast,[56] Dostoevsky's bastard succeeds easily where Faulkner's fails. In addition, the situations are diametrically opposite in the roles of the mother and the legitimate children. To summarize, the character of Dolgoruky fills a double role in *Absalom, Absalom!*, for we find him sometimes behind Sutpen, sometimes beneath the mask of Charles Bon. Here is a phenomenon that can account for the divergence of situations, provided, of course, Faulkner read *A Raw Youth* and was inspired by it. The splitting of the Dostoevskian hero only confirms our hypothesis. After all, these transmutations, observed more than

247

once in relation to the Russian works, here take place at the very heart of the novelistic world.[57]

It is, in any case, certain that *Absalom, Absalom!* reflects the Dostoevskian tradition in its ideas, themes, and plot—a conviction reinforced again by a number of details: the marriage of pride and humility,[58] the propensity of the characters to become doubles,[59] the primacy of life,[60] the victory gained by stoic suffering,[61] above all in women, and finally the prestige enjoyed by blind faith in defiance of facts.[62]

NOTES TO CHAPTER VIII

Pylon

1. See *Faulkner in the University*, p. 5.
2. See *The Idiot*, p. 4, and *Pylon*, pp. 23, 27-28, 41, etc.
3. *Pylon*, p. 157. See also pp. 179-80.
4. *The Idiot*, pp. 291-92, and *Pylon*, p. 162.
5. *The Idiot*, p. 292.
6. See *Pylon*, pp. 103, 115, 122.
7. *Ibid.*, p. 142. See also p. 141.
8. As *The Notebooks of The Idiot* prove. See "Prince Christ" (p. 191).
9. *The Diary of a Writer*, p. 7.
10. *Pylon*, p. 188.
11. *Ibid.*, p. 183.
12. See *New Orleans Sketches*, pp. 99-110.
13. *Faulkner in the University*, p. 36.
14. *The Notebooks of The Idiot*, p. 191.
15. *The Idiot*, pp. 236, 238.
16. *Faulkner in the University*, pp. 50, 145, 150.
17. *Pylon*, p. 49.
18. See *The Idiot*, p. 236. See also *The Notebooks of The Idiot*, p. 191.
19. *Pylon*, p. 42.
20. *Ibid.*, p. 228. See also p. 214.
21. *The Brothers Karamazov*, pp. 193-94.
22. *Ibid.*, pp. 79-80.
23. *Ibid.*, p. 108.
24. See *Faulkner in the University*, p. 36.

Absalom, Absalom!

1. *Absalom, Absalom!*, p. 198. See also *Essays, Speeches and Public Letters*, p. 111, where Faulkner expresses the same attitude as Ivan.
2. *Absalom, Absalom!*, p. 378.
3. *The Brothers Karamazov*, p. 138.
4. Others might prefer to ignore these parallels and see an allusion to "Notes from the Underground" (*White Nights and Other Stories*, p. 75) in the following passage: "You give me two and two and you tell me it makes five and it does make five" (*Absalom, Absalom!*, p. 118). Similarly, Rosa Coldfield cannot be likened to the hero of this novel merely because she

speaks of "this cellar earth of mine" (p. 146) or because of her alienation, her bitterness, and her predilection for dark and confined places.

5. *Absalom, Absalom!*, pp. 11, 12, 21, 221, 260, 261.
6. See *ibid.*, p. 235.
7. *Ibid.*, p. 108. See also pp. 56, 109, 116.
8. *Ibid.*, p. 83.
9. *Ibid.*, p. 104. See also p. 79.
10. *Ibid.*, p. 99.
11. *Ibid.*, pp. 91-92.
12. *Ibid.*, p. 96.
13. *Ibid.*, pp. 263, 267, 268, 273. Note the similarity with Part Four of *The Sound and the Fury*.
14. *Ibid.*, pp. 166-68.
15. *Ibid.*, p. 238. See also *Faulkner in the University*.
16. *A Raw Youth*, pp. 81-82.
17. *Ibid.*, p. 82.
18. *Absalom, Absalom!*, p. 275.
19. *A Raw Youth*, p. 84.
20. *Absalom, Absalom!*, pp. 33-34.
21. *A Raw Youth*, p. 85.
22. *Absalom, Absalom!*, p. 51.
23. *A Raw Youth*, p. 86.
24. *Absalom, Absalom!*, p. 37.
25. *A Raw Youth*, p. 87.
26. *Ibid.*, p. 53.
27. *A Raw Youth*, pp. 87-88.
28. *Absalom, Absalom!*, p. 242.
29. *A Raw Youth*, pp. 90-93.
30. *Absalom, Absalom!*, p. 238.
31. *A Raw Youth*, p. 90.
32. *Ibid.*, p. 93.
33. *Ibid.*, p. 14.
34. *Absalom, Absalom!*, pp. 53, 229.
35. *A Raw Youth*, pp. 90, 94, 96.
36. *Ibid.*, p. 14. See *The Diary of a Writer*, p. 160: "I took an innocent soul, but one already polluted with the dreadful possibility of depravity, early hate, because of his nothingness and 'accidentalness,' and that breadth with which a still chaste soul already admits vice to his thought, fondles it in his bashful but already daring and tempestuous visions."
37. *Absalom, Absalom!*, p. 229.
38. *Ibid.*, p. 232.
39. *A Raw Youth*, 539.
40. *Ibid.*, pp. 539-42.
41. *Ibid.*, p. 542. See the earlier humiliation of Dolgoruky, *ibid.*, pp. 125-26.
42. *Ibid.*, pp. 477-78.
43. *Ibid.*, p. 32.
44. See J. W. Bienstock, "Dostoevsky et Balzac," *Mercure de France* CLXXVI, 635 (December 1, 1924), 418-25; and André Levinson, "Dostoevsky et le roman occidental. Cours fait à la Sorbonne (1926-27), *Revue des Cours et Conférences*, XXVIII, 5 (February, 1927), 425-33; 7 (March 15, 1972), 590-601; 8 (March 30, 1927) 686-697; 10 (April 30, 1927), 169-79. See also the more recent study by Marthe Blinoff, "Dostoievski et Balzac," *Comparative Literature*, III, 4 (Fall, 1951), 342-55.
45. *Faulkner in the University*, pp. 50, 61, 231-32.
46. Charles Dickens, *Great Expectations* (Harmondsworth, Penguin Books Ltd.), p. 68.

47. Balzac, *La comédie humaine*, II (Paris: Editions de la Nouvelle Revue Française, 1935), pp. 960-61.

48. *Ibid.*, pp. 932-42.

49. Balzac, *La comédie humaine*, IV (Paris: Editions de la Nouvelle Revue Française, 1935), pp. 1020 ff.

50. *La comédie humaine*, II, pp. 937-38. (Translated by D.McW.)

51. See the letter in the *Chicago Tribune* dated July 16, 1927, (*Essays, Speeches and Public Letters*, p. 197) in which, in the context of a discussion of *Moby Dick*, he sketches the subject of *Absalom, Absalom!*. See also Richard P. Adams, "The Apprenticeship of William Faulkner," *Tulane Studies in English* XII (1962), 146.

52. A curious parallel to the asceticism which Sutpen and Dolgoruky use in pursuit of their plans can be found in *La peau de chagrin*. See Balzac, *La comédie humaine* IX (Paris: Editions de la Nouvelle Revue Française, 1937), pp. 87-88.

53. Balzac, *La comédie humaine* II, pp. 891-95.

54. *Ibid.*, p. 901.

55. *A Raw Youth*, p. 14.

56. See *ibid.*, pp. 16-17 and 128-129 and *Absalom, Absalom!*, pp. 319, 341.

57. See *Absalom, Absalom!*, p. 351.

58. *Ibid.*, pp. 317, 320 and 328.

59. *Ibid.*, pp. 254, 351, etc.

60. *Ibid.*, pp. 207, 349.

61. *Ibid.*, p. 144.

62. *Ibid.*, pp. 90, 111.

IX

THE PATHS TO FREEDOM, GOODNESS AND SALVATION
THE BROTHERS KARAMAZOV (1938-54)

This long period, which was one of glory and official honors, is characterized by a slowing down and decline of the creative powers. The works are, proportionally, fewer and Faulkner never again managed to repeat such masterpieces as *The Sound and the Fury* and *Absalom, Absalom!*

The years 1938 to 1954 do not constitute a homogeneous block. From 1938 to 1940 in *The Unvanquished, The Wild Palms,* and *The Hamlet,* Faulkner still hesitated between the unhappy criminal and the virtuous benefactor, between the tragic solution and the happy ending, between the narrative and discursive modes. This is very clear in the two stories juxtaposed in *The Wild Palms.* Nonetheless, he has already begun his study of freedom and choice, occasionally falls in to symbolism, and has been inspired as early as 1938 by the exemplary life of Father Zossima.

With these preparations out of the way, in the period 1942 to 1954 he takes up the novel of ideas. *Go Down, Moses, Intruder in the Dust,* and especially *Requiem for a Nun* and *A Fable,* teem with doctrinal borrowings from Dostoevsky. Here fiction sometimes borders on exposition, sometimes on parable, as in the passages of *The Brothers Karamazov* from which Faulkner takes some of his ideas: the conversations of Zossima (VI, 3) and the legend of "The Grand Inquisitor" (V, 5). Faulkner always loved to expatiate: note the dialogues in the Huxlean manner of *Soldiers' Pay* and *Mosquitoes,* Quentin Compson's ruminations before his death, etc. The new element is the will to teach, to put the idea in the service of the good, to communicate the acquired wisdom with an educational purpose. Quentin thought only in terms of his character, to define his concrete situation in the world; this time it is quite the contrary that takes place: the hero exists only for the sake of the idea he incarnates. During the time that he is making his entrance into public life, writing letters to the newspapers, haranguing the intellectuals, Faulkner so overloads the narrative with ideas that the novelistic elements at certain points completely vanish or are so reduced that they become clumsy and lead a separate existence. By his own admission,[1] at certain moments it is less the treatise than the action in which it is inserted, which becomes a kind of an extraneous accessory. A similar divorce is rarely seen in Dostoevsky, who had the supreme gift of feeling and thinking, of imagining and philosophizing simultaneously, by means of the same forms. Faulkner has nothing of the system-building intelligence: if he excels at welding the abstract and the concrete and at sprinkling his portraits with semi-impressionistic commentaries which have sprung from the nerve center of experience, the philosophical method is not his strength. His wish to practice it at any cost and with a growing zeal, beginning in 1942, was entirely mistaken: *A Fable*, the most audacious of his meditations on the human condition, is also probably his most resounding failure. How was it possible for him to be so mistaken about himself? The gap between desire and ability, between intention and talent, is too common a phenomenon to require attention: it accounted, notably, for Gogol's downfall. The movement against the stream, against the grain of his artistic dispositions, is well explained by the desire to escape evil and to impose a spiritual order on it; as might be expected, the evolution accelerates with the war. But, as it asserts itself at the novelist's expense, the moralist relies more and more heavily on Dostoevsky's thought. The latter, above all, shapes the features of the later Faulkner. A mediocre philosopher in search of a philosophy of salvation, the author of *Requiem for a Nun* and *A Fable* listens to the speeches of Zossima and the Grand Inquisitor much more attentively than he had formerly watched the actions of Raskolnikov. The Dostoevskian influence reaches its culmination in these two books but, in the reverse of his earlier development, Faulkner now prefers the dialectician to the story teller. And it is no longer the image of the criminal but the antithetical archetypes of *The Brothers Karamazov* that haunt him. Let us outline his position: he has just completed a despairing fresco of his native land and wishes to liberate himself—as well as his creatures—from chaos, he seeks an exit and finds it where he had formerly seen nothing but excess and violence. Everything confirms what we hesitated to certify about the years 1935-36, that is, that not only was the doctrine of Dostoevsky the port toward which he set sail and that he reached in *Requiem for a Nun*, but also that he was seduced by Dostoevsky's ideas as early as *Pylon* and those ideas, in the long run, led him astray. Although beneficient during 1929-36, the influence, in intensifying after his reorientation, led him to inauthenticity. The gain on the level of doctrinal solutions is accompanied by a corresponding literary deficit.

The progressive assimilation of Dostoevskian ideas, a veritable centrifugal movement, inspired between 1938 to 1954 six works on free will, incarnated finally (in *A Fable*) by the same figure as in Ivan's poem: that of Christ. Similarly, the views on atonement through suffering, first applied to history, no longer exceed the limits of the individual soul within which Dostoevsky kept them. Even the Faulknerian nation is now linked to the concepts of *The Idiot, The Possessed, The Brothers Karamazov*. In short, the resemblances are accentuated and concentrated, the borrowings occasionally become outright liftings. While the model furnishes fewer and fewer situations, its "redemptive" and spiritualistic aspect is fully exploited. What the American seeks in the Russian is, above all, the key to hope and serenity, the means of understanding and accepting the terrible gift of existence. Necessarily, their views are never perfectly identical. The road is too long and arduous between the hell of Fate and the Kingdom of Christ. Faulkner has only a presentiment of the latter. Although his thirst for redemption pushes him into enterprises for which he is poorly equipped, they do not cause him to disavow his earlier self.

For once the influence is established by means of a cluster

of unassailable proofs, but all of them, with one possible exception from *Crime and Punishment,* concern *The Brothers Karamazov,* and the majority are located in *Requiem for a Nun* and *A Fable.* Here certitude is much stronger than probability.

It is not, therefore, surprising that Faulkner refers above all to the discursive and didactic passages of *The Brothers Karamazov.* Those chosen are in decreasing order of preference: from Books V and VI, "The Grand Inquisitor" (V, 5) and the "Conversations and Exhortations of Father Zossima" (VI, 3), that is to say the philosophical chapters of the work, two corresponding panels; then "Rebellion" (V, 4) and "The Mysterious Visitor" (VI, 2, d). Next come IV, 7 ("And In the Open Air"); XI, 4 ("A Hymn and a Secret"); XI, 9 ("The Devil: Ivan's Nightmare") and other fragments of Books V and VI (V, 1 and 3; VI, 2, a, b and c) as well as extracts of Books II and III. The comparison with the years 1929-34 shows unequivocally that the accent has shifted from the anecdotes to the philosophical system. "Rebellion" gives way to "The Grand Inquisitor"; Book VIII, devoted to crime, yields priority to Book VI; chapters 4 and 9 of Book XI, on sacrifice and evil, acquire an entirely new importance, but Book XII ("A Judicial Error"), on the other hand, fades out of the picture. It is no longer in the anguish of action, violence, and despair that Faulkner extends his hand to Dostoevsky but from the heights of the chair of a thinker, sage and apostle.

The parallel examination of *Crime and Punishment* is equally interesting. After having marked Faulkner for so long, Raskolnikov's infamous crime is nearly forgotten. Only the image of the maniac survives: a vestige of earlier readings, the residue of former contacts, which have become part and parcel of the novelist's imagination. The echoes are amplified only when, in 1951 and 1954, he starts to repeat, sometimes word for word, the teachings of the Master. At this stage the savior's face eclipses, or is superimposed upon, that of the assassin: penance, purification of the soul, and the happy ending that Faulkner sought so doggedly are accepted by Raskolnikov less enthusiastically, and also less gratuitously and less generously, than by Dmitri Karamazov, who took upon himself the sins of others. *Crime and Punishment* does not yet proclaim that "we are all responsible for all"; it is precisely this notion, the very foundation of *The Brothers Karamazov*, that Faulkner needed in order to interpret and exorcise the curse inherent in the South. As for *Crime and Punishment*, he seems interested henceforth in its social and moral message—Raskolnikov's theories on humanity (III, 5), the two scenes in which he explains his problems to Sonia (IV, 4 and V, 4), the public confession of his crime (VI, 8)—rather than in the plot. In comparison with the years 1929-34, the roles are reversed: no further traces of the first part nor, virtually, of the second; as for the others, they exercised infinitely less influence and by different ways.

During the period when Faulkner so resembles Dostoevsky that he becomes one of his disciples, that is in *Requiem for a Nun*, the borrowings undergo only minor transformations. The liberties taken with the model are kept to a minimum. If, in adapting ideas, Faulkner does not depart from the method that he applies to situations, images, and portraits, he does not manipulate them as freely and as happily. It is, obviously, an area in which he feels less at ease, at the mercy of an inclination more willed than spontaneous. But let us not be mistaken by the fidelity of the echoes. In reality, the true, the authentic Faulkner remains at a distance from Dostoevsky even when he seems closest. He must draw closer if he is to receive the thing he most covets, but he cannot accept this gift as it is, without forcing himself. The effort explains, perhaps, among other things, the assurance—mingled with restrictions—which surrounds the problem of God in *Requiem for a Nun*. *A Fable* shows a greater prudence in this regard.

If *The Possessed* had repercussions between 1938 and 1954, Faulkner remembered only a few details—ideas or episodes—of the first part (chapter IV, 5; V, 3, 7 and 8) and the second (chapter I, 7) much more than the third. But in view of the paucity of evidence at our disposal, the influence remains questionable. The same remark applies to *The Idiot* of which the passages most worthy of attention are dispersed throughout the plot. Analogies, although obvious, prove nothing: impregnated with *The Brothers Karamazov*, Faulkner could easily have stumbled by accident on an idea of Myshkin's. Moreover, they disappear when in 1951 he follows in Dostoevsky's wake. In short, the contact is possible but even more doubtful than in the preceding case. While one can exclude *A Raw Youth* from the range of hypotheses after *Absalom, Absalom!* and *The Unvanquished, The Eternal Husband* seems to have marked the psychology of *The Wild Palms.* Of the numerous similarities that one discovers with Dostoevsky's minor works—*Poor People, The Insulted and the Injured, White Nights, The Diary of a Writer*—the portraits of Charlotte and her husband in *The Wild Palms* are those which argue in favor of an influence. Thus the question remains open for *The Possessed, The Idiot,* and *The Eternal Husband.* We will be more circumspect as regards *The House of the Dead,* whose echoes barely cross the threshold of audibility. In any case, a simple kinship intensifies the directing idea of our study. To try to distinguish at each step influences from the affinities of temperaments so close to one another is to attempt the squaring of the circle. The evidence furnished by the texts is wantonly distorted; moreover, we lack external proofs. *Poor People,* for instance, in Faulkner's possession since 1932, has apparently left infinitely fewer marks than *The Idiot,* which we do not know if Faulkner ever saw.

1938-40
The Unvanquished (1938)

There is little to be gleaned from the seven stories collected under this title. The passages that can be compared to Dostoevsky, rare though they be, nonetheless reinforce our thesis. First of all, because the resemblance is, in general, very clear; in addition, because most of them relate to themes or ideas: they constitute the philosophical framework of the book and in at least one case ("An Odor of Verbena") correspond to a crucial situation.

The idea, advanced by Uncle Buck and Uncle Buddy,[1] that the land does not belong to men, is outlined already in *Absalom, Absalom!* when Quentin, recounting Sutpen's childhood, alludes to the freedom of the Frontier.[2] It passes into the foreground in *Go Down, Moses* to culminate in the repudiation of private property, defined as early as *Soldiers' Pay* as "the curse of our civilization."[3] In addition, Buck and Buddy put into operation a kind of collective use of the soil, a cooperative or an anticipation of the kolkhoz—"which Father said people didn't have a name for yet."[4] It is unnecessary to resume the analogies, probably fortuitous, that this agrarian "communism" presents with the theories set forth in *A Raw Youth* and *The Diary of A Writer*.[5] Elsewhere in "Riposte in Tertio" (1936) it is a change from evil to good, in sum, a reversal of moral values that is in question: the sins of the individual—lying, fraud, theft—are enrolled in the service of social justice and charity.[6] On this point, *The Unvanquished* confirms the optimistic note of *Pylon*. Unquestionably, around 1935-36, evil lost its omnipotence and the fatally harmful character that Faulkner attributed to it in *Sanctuary*: it can even become useful, a quality it also displays in *The Brothers Karamazov*.[7]

But the story that best reflects Dostoevsky is the one that ends the volume, "An Odor of Verbena." After *Light in August* and *Absalom, Absalom!*, Faulkner anathematizes the traditional Southern code, in particular the cult of honor which coincides with the Mosaic law of talion, that blood thirst for which Bayard Sartoris substitutes a more humane, more Christian and more Dostoevskian attitude. Although public opinion expects him, according to custom, to kill the murderer of his father, Bayard renounces the heritage of violence imposed by blood, education, the milieu, and the land itself.[8] Against all of that he opposes a principle, the "thou shalt not kill" that he had himself violated earlier[9]—not wishing, probably, to fall again into error. "An Odor of Verbena" shows a hero confronted with the difficulties of choice. On one side, there is all the weight of local tradi... and instincts; on the other, a rational morality,[10] individual, but founded on an idea of general application. In refusing to fight while braving his adversary's bullets (he goes to him alone and unarmed), Bayard succeeds in making his convictions victorious without alienating his fellow citizens. He saves, at the same time, his conscience and his reputation.[11] Far from posing as a rebel and attacking conventions head on, he sacrifices to them as far as it is possible. The conservatism is flagrant, although the respect for custom survives only as a facade, for the courage with which Bayard does his duty purifies violence and is spiritualized.[12] The episode seems copied in its entirety from a paragraph of the "Recollections of Father Zossima's Youth" (VI, 2, c; "The Duel") which illustrates marvelously the contrast between the spirit of vendetta and Christian honor.

> By the time we left the school as officers, we were ready to lay down our lives for the honour of the regiment, but no one of us had any knowledge of the real meaning of honour, and if any one had known it, he would have been the first to ridicule it.[13]

The young girl whom he loved having preferred another, Zossima feels a "sudden irrepressible fury."[14] What follows is a challenge which the husband, jealous of Zossima, willingly accepts, Zossima's ignoble drubbing of his orderly and finally the abrupt illumi.·ation on the morning of the encounter:

> And all at once the whole truth in its full light appeared to me: what was I going to do? I was going to kill a good, clever, noble man, who had done me no wrong, and by depriving his wife of happiness for the rest of her life, I should be torturing and killing her too.[15]

The officer throws himself at the soldier's feet, then presents his excuses to his rival, not without waiting for him to fire, but disdaining to use his gun himself. Like Bayard, Zossima braves his adversary's fire and proves that to pardon is not necessarily a sign of cowardice. He also obeys tradition, for his courage is recognized by some of his friends. To be sure, the Russian officer pushes abnegation to the point of asking forgiveness of one he has offended. Bayard does not go so far: he is content to lay down his arms before chasing off the murderer. The theme—the refusal of the duel—is nonetheless identical, as well as the idea of replacing the barbarism of the clan with an ethic that is unique in the setting but basically of a universal implication. It is not new in Faulkner, for this sublimation of aggression operates successively in *As I Lay Dying*,[16] *Light in August*,[17] and *Absalom, Absalom!*,[18] but the motives are very different and are very much less explicit than in *The Unvanquished*.

Other elements which can be derived directly from *The Brothers Karamazov* or *Crime and Punishment* are crystallized around the character of Drusilla, Bayard's step-mother, "the woman of thirty, the symbol of the ancient and eternal Snake,"[19] a Southern

Phaedra in whom the insane pride and devouring passion of a Katerina Ivanovna[20] is reborn. By her love for Bayard, she introduces into the work the theme, dear to Dostoevsky, of a father and son in love with the same woman.[21] Like Katerina Ivanovna and also like Raskolnikov, Drusilla is a "double" who humiliates herself out of pride. Believing that Bayard is preparing to avenge the death of his father, she has an authentically Dostoevskian reaction: she kisses his hand.

> she had taken my right hand which still held one of the pistols before I knew what she was about to do; she had bent and kissed it before I comprehended why she took it. Then she stopped dead still, still stooping in that attitude of fierce exultant humility, her hot lips and her hot hands still touching my flesh, light on my flesh as dead leaves yet communicating to it that battery charge, dark, passionate and damned forever of all peace.[22]

One thinks of the proud Katerina prostrating herself before Dmitri "with her forehead to the floor"[23] when he loans her the five thousand rubles that will save her father from dishonor, or again of Raskolnikov at the feet of Sonia, although Drusilla's kiss pays homage, above all, to violence. In addition, the heroine repeats in reverse order—a sure sign that she wishes to substitute herself for God's justice—Captain Snegiryov's objections to duelling:

> she stood holding out to me, one in either hand, the two duelling pistols . . . "Take them. I have kept them for you. I give them to you. Oh you will thank me, you will remember me who put into your hands what they say is an attribute only of God's, who took what belongs to heaven and gave it to you. . . . How beautiful: young, to be permitted to kill, to be permitted vengeance, to take into your bare hands the fire of heaven that cast down Lucifer."[24]
>
> "It's a sin to kill," I said, "even in a duel."[25]

And, except for a few details, Ilusha's response to the captain announces Bayard's behavior as much as Zossima's "when I grow up, I'll knock him down, knock the sword out of his hand, I'll fall on him, wave my sword over him and say: 'I could kill you, but I forgive you, so there!' "[26] "An Odor of Verbena" furnishes material for one of the most convincing parallels we have thus far attempted.[27]

The Wild Palms (1939)

We have already noted[1] the allusion to "The Grand Inquisitor" contained in Harry Wilbourne's long speech to McCord in *The Wild Palms*: "If Jesus returned today we would have to crucify him quick in our own defense, to justify and preserve the civilization we have worked and suffered and died shrieking and cursing in rage and impotence and terror for two thousand years to create and perfect in man's own image."[2] Here also the coming of Christ would "disturb" a purely human order where it would be as out of place, Wilbourne specifies, outdoing Zossima, as love.[3] The association is interesting, for it shows the way in which Dostoevskian thought is exploited by Faulkner: in the direction of a secularization, in the form of an application to the concrete, particular and terrestrial. It is perhaps also within the context of Ivan's poem that the rather doubtful reference to the temptation of Jesus in the desert is situated.

> *There are rules! Limits! To fornication, adultery, to abortion, crime* and what he meant was *To that of love and passion and tragedy which is allowed to anyone lest he become as God Who was suffered likewise all that Satan can have known.*[4]

The quotation could, up to a point, reflect Matthew (4: 1-11) and Luke (4: 1-13) amplified by Dostoevsky in the famous chapter of *The Brothers Karamazov*.

During this period, Faulkner makes two of Dostoevsky's essential problems, freedom and suffering, his own, although he treats them in a different spirit.

It has often been remarked that man's submission to fate in Faulkner's novels tends to relax after *Light in August*. In 1939, after having considered the chances of good (*Pylon*) and choice free of environmental determinism (*The Unvanquished*), Faulkner deals once more with freedom as opposed to imprisonment, marriage and the moral order. *The Wild Palms* is a contrapuntal novel in which the episodes of two plots alternate with, or answer, each other. Just as in *The Brothers Karamazov* "The Russian Monk" contrasts with "Pro and Contra," *The Wild Palms* sets the story of two couples in ironic contrast. Considered primarily from a masculine point of view and narrated by a particularly "virile" author, it poses the question of whether freedom can be reconciled with love, or even woman's presence.[5] Confronting freedom with the laws, customs and the code of the community, Faulkner simultaneously examines it from several angles: legal, social, psychological and ethical. While the lovers, Harry and Charlotte, arrogate an illusory freedom to themselves and suffer a cruel expiation for their rebellion, the convict renounces the freedom he could continue to enjoy with impunity and willingly returns to a condition of order—the order that governs society and its morality: Faulkner cares little for the metaphysical depths of Kirillov, and his freedom is without any religious nuance. Moreover, he is less interested in it for itself than for the "psychological" problems it poses for the individual.[6]

We have affirmed that the transcendence of despair, Faulkner's long march toward a less tragic outlook on life, was accomplished thanks to Dostoevsky. The proof is that Faulkner sets about to reevaluate and sublimate suffering. Between *Light in August* and *Absalom, Absalom!* sorrow already becomes charged with meaning, becomes a test, an expiation, a possibility for redemption. In *The Wild Palms* Faulkner pushes the idea even further. The value of love, Charlotte declares, is measured by the sacrifices that it requires; this is what she learned in books, very probably in *The Brothers Karamazov*: "You will see great sorrow, and in that sorrow you will be happy. This is my last message to you: in sorrow seek happiness."[7] and is what she now experiences on the level of passion: "that love and suffering are the same thing and that the value of love is the sum of what you have to pay for it and any time you get it cheap you have cheated yourself."[8] Elsewhere, Charlotte describes suffering as something deserving praise—"*to be worthy to love or suffer*"[9] a dignity which creates a link between all those who share it. To judge by the fate of her husband, it comes without one's desiring it, whether one is innocent or guilty.[10] Suffering displays another virtue—a cardinal one: it testifies to existence. Harry incites Charlotte, almost dying, to cling to physical suffering: "You've got to hurt. That's what you've got to hold on to,"[11] thus evoking Dmitri Karamazov's profession of faith: "I'm tormented on the rack—but I exist! Though

I sit alone in a pillar—I exist. I see the sun, and if I don't see the sun, I know it's there. And there's a whole life in that, in knowing that the sun is there."¹² But we must emphasize the fact that it is not in a Christian perspective that suffering is glorified by the lovers. The life in question is not that which springs from God nor which overflows with His "joy."¹³ In any event, Faulkner does not enlarge on this point: the life to which Harry awakens, thanks to Charlotte, is based exclusively on worldly, sensual and, so to speak, "biological" attractions:

> the wisdom to concentrate on fleshly pleasures—eating and evacuating and fornication and sitting in the sun—than which there is nothing better, nothing to match, nothing else in all this world but to live for the short time you are loaned breath, to be alive and know it—oh, yes she taught me that.¹⁴

It is specified at the end of the book that memory cannot survive outside the flesh; this is the reason why Wilbourne prefers suffering to death:

> *Because if memory exists outside of the flesh it wont be memory because it wont know what it remembers so when she became not then half of memory became not and if I become not then all of remembering will cease to be.—Yes, he thought, between grief and nothing I will take grief.*¹⁵

We are far from the punishment that Dmitri accepts to achieve his salvation. The idea, although formally identical with Dostoevsky's, is grafted onto the vitalism of *As I Lay Dying*; it does not overflow into the beyond, and the sublimation operates only on earth. While making overtures to the Russian, Faulkner remodels him to suit his own tastes.

In addition to these two problems which relate directly to Dostoevsky, *The Wild Palms* includes some accessory scenes and ideas that should be cataloged in passing. Thus Harry could maintain with Myshkin that he has seemed somehow "to understand the extraordinary saying that *there shall be no more time*,"¹⁶ but their experiences in the matter are not quite the same. The epilogue of "Old Man," like that of *The Brothers Karamazov*, sets in relief the opposition between living reality and abstract, anonymous law. In the same way, Faulkner does not spare us the inevitable trial scene, and his tableau of humanity reborn after the Flood is, in its mythical context, somewhat akin to that of the golden age detailed by Versilov in *A Raw Youth*.[17]

But a truce to vagaries. "Old Man," the convict's story, gives rise to more interesting comparisons with a work by Dostoevsky that we have so far neglected. Did Faulkner know *The House of the Dead*? We cannot say. However, the fact of devoting more than a hundred pages to the odyssey of a prisoner, and secondarily to a prison, already constitutes a coincidence. It is scarcely their guiding idea that causes these stories to resemble each other: the American convict wants none of the freedom of which his Russian counterparts dream, and he is happy only where the others are clamoring to escape. Note the contradictory testimony on this point:

> He wouldn't have nowhere to go if he was out. None of them do. Turn one loose and be damned if he aint right back here by Christmas like it was a reunion or something, for doing the very same thing they caught him at before.[18]

> Every convict feels that he is, so to speak, *not at home*, but on a visit.[19]

And yet, the two novelists set similar details in relief: the proximity of the river, the isolation of the prison within society, the columns of fettered convicts surrounded by armed men,[20] and, above all, their spiritual qualities. Dostoevsky underlines the latter several times:

> Sometimes one would know a man for years in prison and despise him and think that he was not a human being but a brute. And suddenly a moment will come by chance when his soul will suddenly reveal itself in an involuntary outburst, and you will see it in such wealth, such feeling, such heart, such a vivid understanding of its own suffering, and of the suffering of others that your eyes are open and for the first moment you can't believe what you have seen and heard yourself.[21]

As for the convict of "Old Man," Faulkner makes him almost a model of virtue: "his good name, his responsibility not only towards those who were responsible towards him but to himself, his own honor in the doing of what was asked of him, his pride in being able to do it, no matter what it was."[22] To such a degree that the remarks on "the strong characters" in *The House of the Dead* (I, 1) could, with some slight alterations at the end, serve as the synopsis of this entire panel in the diptych: "these men . . . behaved with exceptional dignity, were reasonable and almost always obeyed the authorities—not from any principle of obedience, nor from a sense of duty, but as though it were a sort of contract with the authorities for the mutual advantage of both."[23] Let us also point out that the description of the mine in "Wild Palms"—"something out of an Eisenstein Dante"[24]—is even better suited to the Dostoevskian episode of "The Baths" (X, 9).

The analogies are, however, too uncertain to permit any conclusions: the milieu of "Old Man" evokes Dostoevsky only very distantly. On the other hand, behind the hero, a theoretician whose criminal plans are upset by the facts,[25] one glimpses once again the image of Raskolnikov and the idea that always and everywhere life wins out over the intellect, if one may so put it, since the convict of *The Wild Palms* is in no way a thinker. On this lower level he behaves, however, like the intellectual of *Crime and Punishment*: he plans his crime, fails when he attempts to put it into action, then shows his desire to expiate and his conversion, less out of a craving to recover the peace of prison than out of his untiring devotion toward the woman whom he feels he must save. Faulkner, in commenting on this book twenty years later, has implicitly spotlighted its "Raskolnikovian" quality:

> He knew as long as he was in that penitentiary and he was expiating the crime—he did something wrong, he knew that—and he was expiating his crime, he was doing the best he could to lead a decent life while he was there, to expiate his crime against society. He had a standard of morals, and that was, I think, his strength.[26]

The characters of *The Wild Palms*, the triangle formed by Charlotte, the husband and the lover, are also affected by the epidemic which during this period touches all areas of Faulkner's work.

Like Drusilla of *The Unvanquished*, Charlotte is one of those women-vampires who love with rage and hatred. We are reminded of Katerina Ivanovna and Grushenka in *The Brothers Karamazov*.[27] Like them, like Nastasya Filippovna, the heroine of *The Idiot*, like so many of Dostoevsky's lovers, Charlotte suffers and makes the object of her affections suffer.[28] In love, they are all extremists.[29] Oddly enough, Charlotte gives a definition of passion that overlaps Zossima's views on *caritas*. Love, she asserts, does not know half measures and should be earned: it is a grace which demands that the being put its self totally at its disposal.

> Listen: it's got to be all honeymoon, always. Forever and ever, until one of us dies. It cant be anything else. Either heaven, or hell: no comfortable safe peaceful purgatory between for you and me to wait in until good behavior or forbearance or shame or repentance overtakes us. . . . They say love dies between two people. That's wrong. It doesn't die. It just leaves you, goes away, if you are not good enough, worthy enough. It doesn't die; you're the one that dies.[30]

And Zossima: "Brothers, love is a teacher; but one must know how to acquire it, for it is hard to acquire, it is dearly bought, it is won slowly by long labour. For we must love one not only occasionally, for a moment, but forever."[31] At this point, the resemblances are accentuated, for Harry's mistress and the austere preacher stumble on the same image, rather common in this context, to express their absolute desire:

> It's (love) like the ocean: if you're no good, if you begin to make a bad smell in it, it just spews you up somewhere to die. You die anyway, but I had rather drown in the ocean than be urped up on to a strip of dead beach and be dried away by the sun into a little foul smear with no name to it.[32]

> My brother asked the birds to forgive him; that sounds senseless, but it is right; for all is like an ocean, all is flowing and blending; a touch in one place sets up movement at the other end of the earth.[33]

But of all of the women portrayed by Dostoevsky, the one who most closely approximates Charlotte, both physically and morally, is Natalya Vassilyevna in *The Eternal Husband* (IV, "The Wife, the Husband and the Lover"):

Natalya	*Charlotte*
She was twenty-eight[34]	a woman of under twenty-five[35]
she was not exactly pretty[36]	a face which laid no claim even to prettiness[37]
her eyes were not pretty: there was something like an excess of determination in them[38]	her eyes were not hazel but yellow, like a cat's, staring at him with a speculative sobriety like a man might, intent beyond mere boldness, speculative beyond any staring.[39]

And here is how the description continues in *The Eternal Husband*:

> so there must have been in that woman something exceptional—a power of attracting, of enslaving, of dominating. . . . her keen intelligence was unmistakable, though she was one-sided in her ideas. . . . In character she was resolute and domineering; she could never make up her mind to compromise in anything: it was all, or nothing. In difficult positions her firmness and stoicism were amazing. She was capable of generosity and at the same time would be utterly unjust. To argue with the lady was impossible: "twice two makes four" meant nothing to her. . . . She was fond of tormenting her lover, but she liked making up for it too. She was of a passionate, cruel and sensual type.[40]

Although one hesitates to liken Charlotte Rittenmeyer to a precise prototype, her Dostoevskian affinities leave no doubt.

The Eternal Husband has been cited on purpose. Rittenmeyer has inherited from Byron Bunch, the man enamoured of Lena Grove in *Light in August*, a spirit of sacrifice that borders on the thirst for self-immolation and even masochism.[41] His behavior imitates models with which we are familiar: like Byron and the lovers of *Poor People, White Nights,* or *The Insulted and the Injured,* he effaces himself before the will of the loved one, going so far as to aid in reuniting her with his rival. Against all prejudice and ready to take her back despite her "sin," he installs his inconstant spouse on the train and entrusts her to Harry.[42] There are analogous cases of magnanimity in *The Possessed*. But the close relations which are established after Charlotte's death between Rittenmeyer and Harry on, so to speak, the altar of her memory reflect rather *The Eternal Husband*, although the two plots are entirely different, since one of them, Dostoevsky's, begins where the other ends. What Faulkner wanted to stress was above all the husband's respect for the wishes of the deceased, his unconditional fidelity to his unfaithful spouse.[43] Finally, once in prison, Harry refuses to flee or commit suicide, two solutions proposed by Rittenmeyer.[44] To choose death would be equivalent to destroying the memory of his love that his flesh preserves; to flee would be to avoid, to soften the suffering linked to their love.[45] Although the motives which cause him to pay his penalty do not agree with those of Dmitri Karamazov, Harry escapes suffering even less than he, since he discards immediately any hope of escape.

It is obvious that, if we are often unable to localize the origin of the ideas, situations, settings and psychology of *The Wild Palms*, the correspondences are no less striking. The screen of creative genius always stands between the presumed source and the work, and at the end of our investigation the elements that seem to be borrowed are recognizable only by a vaguely Dostoevskian flavor. And yet, during this period, even the basic conception of the Faulknerian novel is patterned on Dostoevsky's dissertations, as Wilbourne's long speech to McCord testifies.[46] "We don't talk, we moralize at each other like two circuit riding parsons travelling the same country lane."[47] There is a certain piquancy in the fact that it is precisely this passage which contains the least contravertible reminiscence of *The Brothers Karamazov* and perhaps also a reminiscence of *The Idiot*. The novel of ideas is going to exercise a growing attraction on Faulkner beginning in 1942 with varying results.

The Hamlet (1940)

The overture to the Snopes trilogy, which *The Town* (1957) and *The Mansion* (1959) will complete, presumably goes back to 1925.[1] Despite the mythic dimensions which foreshadow *Go Down, Moses*, *The Hamlet* is a narrative with what is, on the whole, a traditional treatment and a rather loose construction. In it Faulkner, faithful to his method, little by little links disparate panels together. A family chronicle, *The Hamlet*, as its name implies, sinks its roots deep into the annals of the land: the regionalist materials are grounded on a definite moral and metaphysical position but this does not result in a novel of ideas. Analogies with Dostoevsky are extremely rare in the "rural life" genre. The concern for concrete and typical details, the reduction of a portrait to the close-up of a detail, the painting of the soul through outward appearances and behavior, the narrative method which uses circumstantial expositions, the alternation of the tragic and the comic: all of this rather reminds one of Western realism, of Balzac and Dickens, from whom Faulkner, nonetheless, deviates rather notably.

However, we do discover here several traces of *Crime and Punishment* and *The Brothers Karamazov.* Thus in Book II ("Eula") Labove, obsessed by the feminine archetype incarnated by Eula Varner, blindly obeys his *idée fixe*, just as Quentin Compson, Thomas Sutpen, and Dostoevsky's little Napoleon do.[2] A poor student who, on the one hand, proudly scorns mediocrity and ambitiously pursues his plans, ready even to kill in the service of his mania;[3] and on the other hand, madly in love with a young girl who is already too much of a woman, Labove joins within himself Raskolnikov's *hubris* and Svidrigailov's eroticism. He, like that other lover of Lolitas, would destroy the object of his love, and his fight with Eula in the empty class room evokes the one from which Dounia also escapes in *Crime and Punishment.*[4] Finally, in *The Hamlet* it is once more a question of a brother jealous of his sister's virtue,[5] and we also find a frustrated seducer who, rejected as a lover, commits suicide. There is in all of this only the skeleton of the Dostoevskian situations.

Labove is not the only maniac in the book. Henry Armstid, ("The Peasants") who obstinately digs up imaginary treasures, is another.[6] But it is not just the *idée fixe* which isolates man from his peers: crime has the same effect. In *Crime and Punishment*, murder is only a consequence of private obsessions. Mink Snopes ("The Long Summer") is, for his part, both a monomaniac and a murderer; he is by this fact doubly "alienated," like Raskolnikov.[7] After killing Houston, he draws the same conclusions from his acts as Dostoevsky's hero:

> I thought that when you killed a man, that finished it, he told himself. But it don't. It just starts then.[8]

"Surely it isn't beginning already! Surely it isn't my punishment coming upon me? It is!"[9]

Another small detail: it is with an axe, Raskolnikov's weapon, that Mink strikes his victim's dog.[10] In addition, this episode contains, like a blurred memory, the theme of the good prostitute—"loyal, discreet, undemanding, and thrifty with his money"[11]—although Houston's concubine does not possess the redemptive power of Sonia Marmeladov.

The correspondences between *The Hamlet* and *The Brothers Karamazov* are both more accentuated and more limited. They are reduced to three pages in italics at the end of Book II ("Eula") —a Faustian apologue whose solemnity Faulkner deliberately attenuates by using the vernacular to better incorporate it into the rural setting. In substance, the story shows Flem Snopes in conflict with the Prince of Darkness and tricking him. It is basically a symbolic narrative, springing from the same genre as "The Grand Inquisitor," and practically a "satanic" counterpart of Ivan's poem and the Gospel verses that inspired it (Matthew 4: 1-11 and Luke 4: 1-13). As regards the biblical sources, *The Hamlet* builds a bridge between *The Wild Palms* and *A Fable*. Dostoevsky's interlocutors (Christ and the Inquisitor) and those of the Bible (Jesus and the Devil) are replaced by Flem and the Demon, or rather the son of the Demon, since the action develops after the Biblical times, as in *The Brothers Karamazov*. At one point, one of the Prince's old courtiers alludes to Jesus' temptation in the desert: *"Your father made, unreproved, a greater failure. Though maybe a greater man tempted a greater man."*[12] It is the Prince's attempt to suborn Flem that could be derived from the New Testament; the anachronism, on the other hand, is along the lines of the Russian novelist. In addition, vis-a-vis the Gospels, Flem appears as the replica and the opposite of the Lord. He scorns the offers of the Son of the Devil just as the Son of God rejected those of Satan, but he wins only through perversity. Faulkner's social climber is, no less than the Russian Christ, an intruder who would upset the established order. Purer, one in goodness, the other in evil, than their adversaries, they run up against the half-hearted who have bastardized a principle that they embody in its completely orthodox form, and who pose the same question to them: *"Who are you?"*[13] "Is it Thou? Thou?"[14] In *The Hamlet* as in *The Brothers Karamazov*, evil (Flem or the Inquisitor) triumphs, while the Gods (the Prince or Christ) are expelled by their faithful who renounce them.[15] Faulkner's epilogue achieves, very clearly, the crossing of the folk tale, the Bible, and *The Brothers Karamazov*.

We shall pass over the trial scenes (IV, 1, 2) and Eula's split personality.[16] Let us turn rather to the passage in which Ratliff makes Flem burn a note of debt,[17] after the example of Nastasya Filippovna who in *The Idiot* throws one hundred thousand rubles into the fire.[18] Here also the gesture is essentially an act defying greed. Finally, *The Hamlet*, like *The Brothers Karamazov*, compares several concepts of honor.[19] After all is said and done, this work, conceived in the same period as *Soldiers' Pay*, bears Dostoevsky's mark less than those that preceded and followed it.

1942-54
Go Down, Moses (1942)

The stories assembled here reflect much better the preoccupations which will dominate the years to come. And they do so less by their symbolism or the multiplication of ritual acts and mythical references, characteristics which can already be glimpsed in *The Hamlet*, than by their optimism and their discursive manner. *Go Down, Moses* strikes an optimistic note on the racial theme, but it is mitigated by the conviction that these problems will not soon find their solution: the victory of the half-breed, predicted by Shreve at the end of *Absalom, Absalom!* can occur only after one or two millennia ("Delta Autumn," 1942). And yet it is with *Go Down, Moses* that Lucas Beauchamp, a more estimable character than many of his white relatives whom he is capable of outwitting, makes his entry into Yoknapatawpha county. While Joe Christmas anxiously questions his origins, the two races, rather than warring with one another, are wedded in the person of Lucas.[1] At the same time, the recently discovered free will consolidates its position. In addition, the taste for general ideas recalls, at least in "The Bear" (IV) and here and there in "Delta Autumn," the most confused and windy sermonizing of *The Brothers Karamazov*, the long "Conversations and Exhortations of Father Zossima" (VI, 3) which inspired Faulkner more than once. From a technical point of view, he imitates Dostoevsky in having recourse to the Bible to support the dialogue and plot. In "The Bear" (IV) McCaslin and Isaac cite *Genesis* (25:5[2] and 9:18-27[3]), following the example of Raskolnikov, who has the resurrection of Lazarus read to him,[4] or the Grand Inquisitor, or even Zossima when he persuades "the mysterious visitor" to denounce himself on the strength of two New Testament verses. In this respect, Faulkner seems to have retained one of the "visitor's" objections to Zossima, for he both amplifies it and meets it. Compare Zossima:

> I had just been reading that verse when he came in. He read it.
> "That's true," he said, but he smiled bitterly. "It's terrible the things you find in those books," he said, after a pause. "It's easy enough to thrust them upon one. And who wrote them? Can they have been written by men?"
> "The Holy Spirit wrote them," said I.
> "It's easy for you to prate," he smiled again, this time almost with hatred.[5]

and Issac:

> 'So these men who transcribed His Book for Him were sometime liars.'
> and he
> 'Yes. Because they were human men. They were trying to write down the heart's truth out of the heart's driving complexity, for all the complex and troubled hearts which would beat after them. What they were trying to tell, what He wanted said, was too simple. Those for whom they transcribed His words could not have believed them. It had to be expounded in the everyday terms which they were familiar with and could comprehend, not only those who listened but those who told it too.[6]

The question of free will assumes an essential importance in "The Bear" (1935-42): Isaac freely repudiates the heritage that is rightfully his. *The Unvanquished* and *The Wild Palms* had already suggested that the individual has the power to oppose his will to circumstances.[7] And we have seen earlier[8] that choice depends on the irrational stirrings of the heart and defines itself irrespective of knowledge,[9] that man does not use his freedom wittingly.[10] Perhaps it is appropriate to note once more the kinship of views on the matter of the "fearful burden"[11] of freedom. Between Faulkner's idea: "no man is ever free and probably could not bear it if he were"[12] and that of the Grand Inquisitor: "Nothing is more seductive for man than his freedom of conscience, but nothing is a greater cause of suffering. . . . Instead of taking possession of men's freedom, Thou didst increase it, and burdened the spiritual kingdom of man with suffering forever."[13] there is both opposition and perfect accord. Note the conditional used by the first, still surprised, one might almost say, to have been able to outstrip Fate—but already certain that freedom can bring only torments. And when one reads a little later in "The Bear" that Hell also came from the hands of the Creator, it is as though one were listening to the Inquisitor proclaim that "men . . . are . . . rebellious by nature."[14] By endowing man with free will, God obviously permitted him to choose evil.

Go Down, Moses constitutes the synthesis and the crowning of the ideas which have become more and more vigorous since *Absalom, Absalom!*. We assist, in fact, at the simultaneous reinforcement and fusion of such elements as the philosophy of American history—based on the pattern of sin/expiation—and the denunciation of private property.

In a post-feudal society like that of the South, wealth rests above all in the soil, in the landed estates: the heritage that Isaac renounces is the plantation of his fathers. Industrialism was already anathematized in *Pylon*, and "Delta Autumn" gives us to understand pretty much the same thing.[15] For those who, like Faulkner, are attached to the land, technical progress ordinarily represents an offense against nature, the created order and the secular traditions which flow from it: the industrial revolution is in their eyes, at the very least, an object of suspicion. In Faulkner, agrarian conservatism, hostile to the machine—itself linked with the North—goes hand-in-hand with a communism of Biblical origins, a desire to go back to a golden age or an Edenic freedom, an intention which nonetheless remains conscious of its own impotence. For the South cannot boast of all virtues in comparison with the North: it also is corrupt and for the same reasons as technology. Like the industrial cities, it was built by violating

272

nature: by stripping the great virgin wilderness, cutting it up into parcels, buying and selling it without any right to do so, since the earth belongs only to itself and offers itself to everyone.[16] In addition, the crime against nature was accompanied by a second infamy against that other creature of God: the black. Each time, the sin is the same: it amounts to abolishing original freedom and monopolizing the earth and man, both reduced to slavery.[17] We see how concerned Faulkner was with the problem of freedom during this period. Isaac bases his condemnation of property explicitly on *Genesis* (2:15):

> He told in the Book how He created the earth, made it and looked at it and said it was all right, and then He made man. He made the earth first and peopled it with dumb creatures, and then He created man to be His overseer on the earth and to hold suzerainty over the earth and the animals on it in His name, not to hold for himself and his descendants inviolable title forever, generation after generation, to the oblongs and squares of the earth, but to hold the earth mutual and intact in the communal anonymity of brotherhood, and all the fee He asked was pity and humility and sufferance and endurance and the sweat of his face for bread.[18]

The rejection of mine and thine in favor of the collective enjoyment of the soil is an idea that Dostoevsky also caressed in *The Diary of a Writer*. Read, for instance, "The Dream of a Strange Man" (April, 1877)[19] or better still, certain extracts—suppressed by the censor—of "The Land and the Children."[20] The fact of dividing the land unequally, we have said,[21] is compared to alienation, consequence of the Fall: to possess is humanity's great sin. The parallel goes back, to be sure, to an analogous interpretation of the Bible. But *The Brothers Karamazov* and, in particular, Book VI to which Faulkner incessantly refers in *Go Down, Moses*, evinces opinions which, although more general, are rather similar to Faulkner's on "isolation" and the cupidity which is one of its manifestations:

> Until you have become really, in actual fact, a brother to every one, brotherhood will not come to pass. No sort of scientific teaching, no kind of common interest, will ever teach men to share property and privileges with equal consideration for all. Everyone will think his share too small and they will be always envying, complaining and attacking one another.
> . . .

273

All mankind in our age have split up into units, they all keep apart, each in his own groove; each one holds aloof, hides himself and hides what he has, from the rest, and he ends by being repelled by others and repelling them. He heaps up riches by himself and thinks, 'how strong I am and how secure' and in his madness he does not understand that the more he heaps up, the more he sinks into self-destructive impotence. For he is accustomed to rely upon himself alone and to cut himself off from the whole: he has trained himself not to believe in the help of others, in men and in humanity, and only trembles for fear he should lose his money and the privileges he has won for himself. Everywhere in these days men have, in their mockery, ceased to understand that the true security is to be found in social solidarity rather than in isolated individual effort. But this terrible individualism must inevitably have an end, and all will suddenly understand how unnaturally they are separated from one another. It will be the spirit of the time, and people will marvel that they have sat so long in darkness without seeing the light.[22]

The influence is possible, but divergences in the contexts make it uncertain, all the more so in that the fraternity—Faulkner uses the same word: "brotherhood"—presented in the novel and in the *Diary* as a primordial state to which man will one day return remains irremediably lost for the American.

"The Bear" offers, in addition, an ethico-theological exegesis of the history of the United States and the South which has already been analyzed.[23] The spiritualization of political, economic, and social problems strangely recalls, even in its failure to give an immediate and practical solution and its opposition to humanitarian liberalism, the attitude which supports the views of *The Idiot* (IV, 7); *The Possessed* (II,I, 7); *The Diary* and *The Brothers Karamazov* (II, 5 "So Be It!"; V, 5 "The Grand Inquisitor"; VI, 2, d "The Mysterious Visitor"). Similarly, the Faulknerian dialectic which opposes Europe to America, North to South, black to white, is also found in the antithesis between Russia and the West which Dostoevsky, like many of his compatriots, enjoyed underlining. The American and the Russian, in fact, occupy similar positions which permit them to condemn Europe. One remembers the virulent attacks of Myshkin and Shatov against Rome, socialism and atheism, so many products of Western Europe, which Isaac in turn accuses of contaminating pre-Columbian America simply by its presence, even before conquering the land.[24] What these writers thus suggest is that evil came from

Europe and soiled the primitive innocence of the fatherland. The expiation of this evil, Faulkner adds, thus falls to the white, the bringer of evil: "He (God) used the blood which had brought in the evil to destroy the evil as doctors use fever to burn up fever, poison to slay poison."[25] At this point we leave the area of mental attitudes, for which it is difficult to establish agreement by means of precise texts, to approach the realm of ideas. The ordeals of the South, the Civil War and the ensuing defeat, only prove, according to Isaac, God's love for his creatures, a love which subjects them to suffering in order to save them.

> So He turned once more to this land which He still intended to save because He had done so much for it—' and McCaslin
> 'What?' and he
> . . .He said and not in grief either Who had made them and so could know no more of grief than He could of pride or hope: *Apparently they can learn nothing save through suffering, remember nothing save when underlined in blood—'*[26]

We are here at the very heart of the Dostoevskian cult of suffering, beneath the immense shadow of the Cross. Basing himself on the Scriptures, Dostoevsky teaches that the criminal—and we all are criminals, sometimes because of our acts, always in virtue of our human condition—will be redeemed through suffering,[27] a fundamentally Christian theme whose originality in Faulkner is limited to its being applied to the history of a people and not simply to individual cases. *Absalom, Absalom!* had already extended the central idea and the title of *Crime and Punishment* to the Southern past, but it accentuated the guilt in so doing; *Go Down, Moses*, on the other hand, allows us a glimpse of the distant moment of a redemption obtained through perseverance.[28] Faulkner, in the meantime, places his confidence in the virtues of the black—or those of mulatto. Those which Isaac discerns in Sam Fathers are so close to the qualities attributed to the "people" by Zossima that they come very close to plagiarism:

> In the boy's eyes at least it was Sam Fathers, the negro, who bore himself not only toward his cousin McCaslin and Major de Spain but toward all white men, with gravity and dignity and without servility . . . , bearing himself toward his cousin McCaslin not only as one man to another but as an older man to a younger.[29]

I've been struck all my life in our great people by their dignity, their true and seemly dignity. I've seen it myself, I can testify to it. . . . They are not servile, and even after two centuries of serfdom, they are free in manner and bearing, yet without insolence, and not revengeful and not envious.[30]

America, like Russia in *The Idiot* and *The Possessed*, finds itself charged with a historic mission; both serve as a second chance, offered to humanity after the Old World's fiasco:

until He used a simple egg to discover to them a new world where a nation of people could be founded in humility and pity and sufferance and pride of one to another.[31]

Reveal to the yearning and feverish companions of Columbus the 'New World,' reveal to the Russian the 'world' of Russia, let him find the gold, the treasure hidden from him in the earth! Show him the whole of humanity, rising again, and renewed by Russian thought alone, perhaps by the Russian God and Christ.[32]

Erected as a citadel of political freedom,[33] just as the homeland of the Russian Christ was transformed into a bastion of spiritual freedom, America, or at least the South, will thus become the racial melting pot: "This Delta. *This land . . . where . . . Chinese and African and Aryan and Jew, all breed and spawn together until no man has time to say which one is which nor cares.*"[34] A passage worth comparing to the *Diary* where the same notion is expressed in identical terms:

Europe is our second fatherland, and I am the first ardently to profess this; I have always professed this. To us *all* Europe is *almost* as dear as Russia; in Europe resides the entire tribe of Japheth, and our idea is the unification of all nations descending from that tribe; even much farther—down to Shem and Ham.[35]

The repudiation of the heritage, discussed in "The Bear" (IV), also lends itself to some interesting comparisons. It is the decision of a free agent who, like Ivan Karamazov, gives back his "entrance ticket,"[36] but who, in his revolt against an ungodly order, intends, on the contrary, to replace it with a Christian order. However, by throwing in his cards and leaving the game, Issac withdraws himself from collective atonement. He rejects not just his grandfather's incest and the right to possess, oppress and exploit: he also discards the suffering which purifies, eludes his responsibilities, and isolates himself from others. His desertion, despite his praiseworthy intentions, is not as far from Ivan's as it might at first seem. The author, moreover, considers it skeptically[37] and in retrospect describes it as inefficacious.[38] On the question of preferring action to abstention, there is between Faulkner and Dostoevsky the gulf which separates the pragmatist of the Protestant New World from an orthodox raised in the veneration of the saints—stylites among others—and hermits and wanderers. This does not prevent Father Ferapont, the ascetic of *The Brothers Karamazov*, from being crushed beneath Dostoevsky's satirical pen—nor alter the fact that neither Zossima nor Alyosha, the latter in particular, refuse to offer practical help to their neighbors. Isaac, for his part, has nothing of the anchorite about him; he lives in the world as a carpenter, like the Nazarene,[39] and, while he opposes Alyosha in his refusal to become involved and suffer, he resembles him on other points. With Sam Fathers he forms a duo very like that of Zossima and his disciple: in "The Bear" the young man is also initiated by his spiritual father—less by his words this time, than by his acts—to the ideal life which is located on a more secular level than in *The Brothers Karamazov*. At the moment of their masters' death, their education completed, Alyosha and Isaac are ready to confront the world, and the fact that the holy man sends his disciple away by ordering him to leave the monastery accentuates the coincidence with *Go Down, Moses*, in which the virgin forest plays, with regard to Isaac, the same role of Alma Mater. In addition their symbolic names prefigure basically the same "life line": Alyosha is not simply one who gives assistance (*alexis*), he is also "the man of God;"[40] just as it is said in *Genesis* (17:19) that God will establish his covenant with Isaac, McCaslin does, in fact, concede that his cousin has been chosen by the Lord.[41] Isaac, by stripping himself of his patrimony, in effect takes a vow of poverty, like Dostoevsky's novice.[42] Both thus follow the counsel of Christ (Matthew 19:21), but Isaac's expiatory gesture, the sacrifice of his earthly goods that he makes to atone a sin committed earlier and whose stigma all people bear, also suggests the punishment

—legally undeserved—which Dmitri accepts. The Faulknerian hero thus unites in himself the traits proper to each of the brothers: Ivan's revolt, Dmitri's desire for expiation and, above all, Alyosha's spiritual purity. Their combination is, nonetheless, original. Faulkner rarely preserves his borrowings just as they are: he modifies their value, mixes them and recombines them according to his needs. But we must admit that the influences barely exceed the limits of conjecture. Moreover, it is not in *The Brothers Karamazov* that Dostoevsky treats Isaac's problem most explicitly. The culpability engendered by property is a question that he presents at length in *The Diary of a Writer* (February, 1877) in relation to *Anna Karenina* (VI, 11). He imagines, in commenting on the conversations of Tolstoy's two characters, that one of them, Levin, tormented by remorse, distributes his goods, after the example of Nekrassov's Vlass.[43] The subject interested Tolstoy very deeply; he expatiates on it in *Anna Karenina*, which Faulkner cites among his favorite books. All things considered, the hero of "The Bear" is inspired by as much as, if not more than, by *The Brothers Karamazov*: so far as property is concerned, Isaac does nothing more than put into practice the dreams of Levin.

Faulkner intones, in *Go Down, Moses,* the canticle of the great verities of the heart, the litany of moral conquests that will earn him the Nobel Prize. The most striking thing here is the affective, irrational, intuitive character of the virtues thus enumerated and the insistence with which the novelist couples humility with a praiseworthy pride.[44] It is not the "wise men of the earth—rulers, chief priests, learned men, philosophers, poets"[45] whom the Grand Inquisitor cites, the Raskolnikovs and Ivan Karamazovs who truly know, but "the doomed and lowly of the earth who have nothing else to read with but the heart,"[46] such as Sonia Marmeladov.

Doctrinal correspondences are far more important than analogies of characters and situations. Among the former one must still include the aversion for the great humanitarian slogans,[47] as well as the idea, developed by Zossima and repeated by Issac, that domestics must be treated in the same way one treats one's relatives:

Why should not my servant be like my own kindred, so that I may take him into my family and rejoice in doing so?[48]

those who serve you even for pay are your kin.[49]

Among the others, let us recall: the sacrilegious mania which plagues Lucas Beauchamp ("The Fire and the Hearth," 1940), obsessed, like Henry Armstid in *The Hamlet* by a hidden treasure;[50] the scene in which he leans, razor in hand, over his sleeping adversary[51] and which recalls a passage from *The Eternal Husband* (XV); perhaps even the appearance of the bear, a symbol of virgin nature as it was made by the Creator and whose death coincides with that of Sam Fathers. Sam, the mentor of Isaac, lives as a hermit in the woods and, although a hunter, he does not kill Old Ben. Zossima—him again!—also speaks of the union that can be established between man and the wild beasts, expressing it in Christian terms.

"I know nothing better than to be in the forest," said he, "though all things are good."

"Truly," I answered him, "all things are good and fair, because all is truth. . . . Christ has been with them [the animals] before us."

"Why," asked the boy, "is Christ with them, too?"

"It cannot but be so," said I, "since the Word is for all. All creation and all creatures, every leaf is striving to the Word, singing glory to God, weeping to Christ, unconsciously accomplishing this by the mystery of their sinless life. Yonder," said I, "in the forest wanders the dreadful bear, fierce and menacing, and yet innocent in it." And I told him how once a bear came to a great saint who had taken refuge in a tiny cell in the wood. And the great saint pitied him, went up to him without fear and gave him a piece of bread. "Go along," said he, "Christ be with you," and the savage beast walked away meekly and obediently, doing no harm. And, the lad was delighted that the bear had walked away without hurting the saint, and that Christ was with him too.[52]

Without trying to compete with Saint Francis of Assisi, Isaac also meets Old Ben[53] armed only with his love of nature and extricates himself safe and sound. Do we have here one of the sources of "The Bear"? The hypothesis is, in any case, admissible, considering the profound influence *The Brothers Karamazov* seems to have exercised on the philosophy of *Go Down, Moses*.

Intruder in the Dust (1948)

When, after a long interval, Faulkner published *Intruder in the Dust*, he returned to the formula of the detective novel with which he had had such success in *Sanctuary, Light in August* and *Absalom, Absalom!*. Like the author of *Crime and Punishment*, although more clumsily, he joins the mystery story and the novel of ideas. The "reverse" pattern, the reconstruction of motives after the fact, recalls very strongly Raskolnikov and Porfiry, but the fact that the suspect shows himself innocent and that we do not know the identity of the guilty party, all this is linked rather to *The Brothers Karamazov* and, in general, to the "whodunit." Unlike the dark novels, however, *Intruder in the Dust* does not have a criminal for a hero: morality triumphs along with the law. Although he risks a lynching, for Lucas Beauchamp, and for his black and white defenders, all is well that ends well.

Intruder in the Dust is the fourth Faulknerian variation on free will. Young Chick Mallison's choice is, in its consequences, akin to that of Bayard Sartoris ("An Odor of Verbena"), inasmuch as he puts a brake on the violence of the community, an anonymous force which aimed in *The Unvanquished* at dictating the conduct of the individual.[1] But here the significance of choice exceeds the framework of private life: it is situated in a collective, racial and national context, since Chick, by acting as he does, saves a black from death. All the same, nothing distinguishes his decision from Isaac's, whose Dostoevskian affinities are known. Faulkner, who has more than once denounced the danger of theories, insists here that man is not primarily a rational animal, an idea that Shatov develops in *The Possessed*:

> [Chick] thought of man who apparently had to kill man not for motive or reason but simply for the sake the need the compulsion of having to kill man, inventing creating his motive and reason afterward so that he could still stand up among man as a rational creature. . . .[2]

> Science and reason have, from the beginning of time, played a secondary and subordinate part in the life of nations. . . . Nations are built up and moved by another force which sways and dominates them, the origin of which is unknown and inexplicable: . . . It is the force of the persistent assertion of one's own existence, a denial of death.[3]

When Chick engages himself in the service of Lucas, he has no rational certitude of his innocence. His choice is equivalent to a leap into darkness from a springboard which is no more than an undemonstrable belief, a shaky faith in the suspect's statements although, on the other hand, it does flow from conscience.[4] The exposition relates how Chick contracted a debt toward Lucas which he was unable to acquit, whatever he thinks of it. We recognize here, dechristianized, Zossima's "Credo, but I don't know in what."[5] As he had done in "An Odor of Verbena," Faulkner once again reveals the hero's tergiversations at the decisive moment. The choice, although intuitive, is accompanied by doubts, impulses to flee,[6] which call to mind, for instance, those of Dmitri Karamazov. Although Chick does not, at bottom, feel quite free in relation to Lucas and moves heaven and earth to save him, his freedom, far from being crushed under the pressure of destiny, has no reins save his conscience. The Faulknerian hero no longer moves at the mercy of events; without repudiating the determinism of the environment,[7] he henceforth asserts himself as a free agent. Dostoevsky's contribution to this reorientation is not measured uniquely by the analogies observed in the fundamental characteristics of choice which are, moreover, also found in Kierkegaard and numerous other modern thinkers. While criticizing contemporary America, Gavin Stevens also rails against the selfish materialism which has been baptized with the name of freedom but which is its very opposite:

> we are willing to sell liberty short at any tawdry price for the sake of what we call our own which is a constitutional statutory license to pursue each his private postulate of happiness and contentment regardless of grief and cost even to the crucifixion of someone whose nose or pigment we dont like.[8]

Such confusion is already denounced word for word in *The Brothers Karamazov*, more precisely in "Conversations and Exhortations of Father Zossima" (VI, 3,e):

> The world has proclaimed the reign of freedom, especially of late, but what do we see in this freedom of theirs? Nothing but slavery and self-destruction. For the world says: "You have desires and so satisfy them, for you have the same rights as the most rich and powerful. Don't be afraid

of satisfying them and even multiplying your desires." That is the modern doctrine of the world. In that they see freedom. And what follows from this right of multiplication of desires? In the rich, isolation and spiritual suicide; in the poor, envy and murder; for they have been given rights, but have not been shown means of satisfying their wants. . . . To have dinners, visits, carriages, rank and slaves to wait on one is looked upon as a necessity, for which life, honour and human feeling are sacrificed, and men even commit suicide if they are unable to satisfy it. . . . while the poor drown their unsatsified need and their envy in drunkenness. But soon they will drink blood instead of wine, they are being led on to it. I ask you is such a man free?[9]

The tone and the point of view are probably different, but the Jefferson lawyer and the Russian monk adopt very nearly the same attitude.

Dostoevsky and Faulkner, we have said,[10] rise up against abstraction which they replace by living, concrete, individual reality. Lucas refuses to obey the stereotyped reflexes that whites expect of blacks,[11] and Stevens maintains that it is absurd to wish to do violence to facts by the blows of decrees and regulations.[12] Our prudent evolutionists prefer the steep path of moral expiation, that is, suffering, to the statute books and slogans with which the liberals intend to cut the Gordian knot of politics. The negro Lucas already deals as an equal with his white protectors; exceptionally, racial and social cliches give way to personal relations. When Chick wishes to pay him for his hospitality, Lucas scorns the money offered, without going so far as to trample it as Snegiryov does with the two hundred rubles of Katerina Ivanovna: In fact, it is not a matter of charity in *Intruder in the Dust*, but of simple reimbursement. Later, in appealing to Chick, the proud Lucas means only to barter one service for another. Their disproportion is such, however, that he finds himself basically in the situation of one under obligation. But not in his eyes, apparently, since he would approve wholeheartedly and almost word for word Alyosha's commentaries on the captain: "he is on an equal footing with us, in spite of his taking money from us . . . and not only on an equal, but even on a higher footing."[13]

On the technical level, the love of individuals does not exclude that of ideas, and the hatred excited by such and such a doctrine goes hand in hand with the will to present another one. Dostoevsky is particularly fond of argumentation and exposition, and he usually succeeds in fusing ideas with the story. A cloudier thinker, Faulkner has neither the depth nor the dialectical gifts of the Russian. Beginning with *Absalom, Absalom!* Faulkner becomes progressively enmired in the swamp of argumentation, generalization and prophecy. *Intruder in the Dust* is a failure to the degree that, swollen with digressions, the narrative degenerates into a treatise.[14] Of all the aspects of Dostoevsky, it is perhaps the only one which Faulkner ought not to have taken as an example.

A spokesman for opinions that Faulkner refrains from offering in his own name, Gavin Stevens in many respects repeats the message of *Go Down, Moses* on the history of the United States. He extols the patience of the black, which is also that of the Dostoevskian "people"[15] or of Sonia Marmeladov; underlines the necessity to collectively atone the sin of slavery[16] and, an heir to a tenacious isolationism, expresses his mistrust of Europe. In this regard, Gavin even borrows the Grand Inquisitor's arguments against freedom, transferring them, as he must, from the spiritual to the political. Compare Gavin's remarks with three statements by the Inquisitor:

'Not all white people can endure slavery and apparently no man can stand freedom (Which incidentally—the premise that man really wants peace and freedom—is the trouble with our relations with Europe right now, whose people not only dont know what peace is but—except for Anglo Saxons—actively fear and distrust personal liberty . . .); with one mutual instantaneous accord he forces his liberty into the hand of the first demagogue who rises into view.[17]

some promise of freedom . . . which they fear and dread—for nothing has ever been more insupportable for a man and a human society than freedom.[18]

So long as man remains free he strives for nothing so incessantly and so painfully as to find some one to worship. But man seeks to worship what is established beyond dispute, so that all men would agree to worship it. For these pitiful creatures are concerned not only to find what one or the other can worship, but to find something that all would believe in and worship; what is essential is that all may be *together*. . . . I tell thee that man is tormented by no greater anxiety than to find some one quickly to whom he can hand over that gift of freedom with which the ill-fated creature is born.[19]

all that man seeks on earth—that is, some one to worship, some one to keep his conscience, and some means of uniting all in one unanimous and harmonious ant-heap.[20]

Between *Go Down, Moses* and *Intruder in the Dust,* Faulkner, nonetheless, adjusts his perspective, since Gavin poses as the advocate of a Southern nation whose foundations are hardly less immaterial than those of the Russian nation constructed by Myshkin, Shatov and Father Paissy.[21] While Dostoevsky tied the nation to the concept of God, Gavin founds it on individual freedom,[22] indirectly linking the South to Shatov's "God-bearing" Russia since it is Christ—see Ivan's poem—who has bestowed this cumbersome gift on man. A mental construct and an object of aspiration, this spiritual nation is set up in opposition to the existing materialist nation of the United States in the same way in which the Church of which Paissy dreams contrasts with the established order of the State. The religious nuance does not appear in Faulkner, but his South, although more political, is, nonetheless, above all, the ideal entity to which a sovereign and obscure force aspires—"the persistent assertion of one's existence"[23] as Shatov says —similar to that which dictates the choices of the individual.[24] It is from this vantage point, obviously, that Faulkner criticizes a soulless America—dynamic, ruthlessly seeking gain and its gross pleasures:[25] the tyrannical State[26] which the spiritual nation should eclipse. In Paissy's formula, it is enough to replace "Church" with "South" and add the epithet "federal" to the word "State" to touch the heart of Faulknerian politics during this period:

> But Russian hopes and conceptions demand not that the Church should pass as from a lower into a higher type into the State, but on the contrary, that the State should end by being worthy to become only the Church and nothing else.[27]

> We—he [the black] and us [the whites]—should confederate: swap him the rest of the economic and political and cultural privileges which are his right, for the reversion of his capacity to wait and endure and survive. Then we would prevail; together we would dominate the United States; we would present a front not only impregnable but not even to be threatened by a mass of people who no longer have anything in common save a frantic greed for money and a basic fear of a failure of national char-

acter which they hide from one another behind a loud lipservice to a flag.[28]

There seems to be little doubt that these theories on the Southern "soul" are of Dostoevskian inspiration. Let us specify, moreover, that this criticism of the native land is not, any more than with the Russian novelist, the product of animosity.

The other similarities are negligible. It is principally in their philosophy that *Go Down, Moses* and *Intruder in the Dust* copy Dostoevsky, while the thematic and psychological echoes, little by little, fade out. Among the latter are numbered only the inevitable alliance of pride and humility,[29] the solitude which surrounds crime,[30] the incompatibility between the plans of the intellect and the hazards of existence,[31] and perhaps also the character of Chick Mallison, a daring adolescent, too clever for his age, but generous and gifted with an innate sense of the good, like Kolya of *The Brothers Karamazov* (X). These elements, several of which could originally derive from Dostoevsky, in 1948 offer nothing more than an intangible resemblance to their supposed model. Once assimilated, the literary borrowing undergoes the same metamorphoses as all other acquisitions of experience.

Knight's Gambit (1949) and *Collected Stories* (1950)

Knight's Gambit is an interlude in the detective vein, grouping six stories which, in comparison with the novels, seem to have been written as a recreational interlude. Gavin Stevens appears beneath the features of a Poirot or a Maigret; the choice of genre is a result of Faulkner's interest in crime, its punishment and the "reverse" structure, that is to say, in the impact of the past on the present—a constant in his thought.

Few resemblances with Dostoevsky are to be found here. The principal ones are reduced to the situations in the first story, "Smoke," which dates from the period of *Light in August*. The hatred between the father, Holland, a widower like old Karamazov, and his two sons; the violence of Anselm, who leaves home and returns to claim his portion of the maternal inheritance;[1] the cold, calculating nature of Virginius: all this recalls the portraits and relations of Fyodor Pavlovitch, Dmitri and Ivan. Anselm, like Dmitri but for other reasons, wishes to expiate a crime he has not, in fact, committed; Gavin, however, in time uncovers the real guilty party. Anselm has only struck his father, whom another finishes off: one recalls the blow which Dmitri deals Fyodor (III, 9 "The Sensualists") and in particular the scene in which Smerdyakov profits from the quarrel between father and son to kill the former (VIII, 4; "In the Dark" and XI, 8; "The Third and Last Interview with Smerdyakov"). Faulkner's Smerdyakov is a cousin of Anselm and Virginius, a character a little less repugnant to be sure, but just as ignorant as the Russian and, like him, passionately interested in speculations. To summarize, "Smoke" confirms the influence of *Crime and Punishment* around 1932.

"Tomorrow" (1940), the story of a man enamoured of a married woman, abandoned and already in advanced pregnancy, is an extension of *Light in August* (Byron Bunch and Lena Grove) rather than *The Possessed* (Shatov and his wife). "Knight's Gambit" rests on the triangle of the suitor, the mother and the daughter, a situation symmetrical with that of Grushenka, Fyodor and Dmitri Karamazov and with another one in *A Raw Youth*,[2] a situation which is moreover found literally in the latter work;[3] even the fight between the women finds a counterpart in *The Brothers Karamazov* (III, 10 "Both Together").

The clearest echo is heard in "Monk," in which the cult of suffering of *Requiem for a Nun* is announced in muted tones: "I have sinned against God and man and now I have done paid it out with my suffering."[4] Let us note in passing that the first publication of this story about convicts dates from 1937, preceding *The Wild Palms* by two years: Monk, moreover, refuses freedom like the hero of "Old Man."[5]

There remain only a few isolated details to conclude: Gavin Stevens' double personality,[6] the divorce between truth and justice[7] and the idea that the earth belongs to all.[8] But there is nothing new in this.

There are even fewer reminiscences in *Collected Stories of William Faulkner*, a volume which includes, in addition to *These*

286

13 and *Doctor Martino and Other Stories* (except for two items), stories published in various magazines between 1932 and 1948, but of which the majority appeared after 1934. We know that this literary form is largely impervious to the influence of Dostoevsky; the same is true for the theme of war, topical after Pearl Harbor ("Two Soldiers," 1942; "Shall Not Perish," 1943) and the "redskin" vein—subjects foreign to the Russian novelist. The absence of analogies indicates that certain sectors of the Faulknerian oeuvre elude Dostoevsky's influence, although it controls other areas. If "Uncle Willy" (1935) evokes the story of Richard in *The Brothers Karamazov* (V, 4) by its attacks on the conspiracy of the self-righteous, it is just barely so. "Lo!" announces in 1934 the idea of the collective ownership of the soil.[9] "The Tall Men" (1941), applying the ideal of freedom to economics, attacks government controls and anonymous laws in the name of individual responsibility: elsewhere, in "Shall Not Perish" it is suffering which finds itself exalted. But, although all of this could come from Dostoevsky, we are far from the original text here.

Requiem for a Nun (1951)

The Dostoevskian domination reaches its apogee in Yoknapatawpha County. Not only does *Requiem for a Nun* contain an allusion to the apostle of suffering,[1] the only one in Faulkner's novelistic work, but the borrowings from *Crime and Punishment* and *The Brothers Karamazov* are legion here—to such an extent that one might wonder if Dostoevsky's ascendancy did not provoke even the book's conception. *Requiem for a Nun* serves as a continuation of *Sanctuary*, published twenty years earlier amidst the full flowering of the dark novels. In the meantime, Faulkner entered the Russian school: he now knows how to oppose destiny, evil, damnation. Did he later repent having allowed Popeye to triumph so easily over Horace Benbow and Goodwin, and corrupt Temple to the very marrow? Did he wish to atone for the pessimism of his earlier work[2] and save Temple, the sinning woman, by remedies that had already been proven? Who will say? In any case, even if the creative impulse did not come directly from Dostoevsky, *Requiem for a Nun*, nonetheless, surely exalts a philosophy that he aided in forging. Even the narrative technique, the exclusive use of dialogue in the passages that are precisely the most Dostoevskian, evokes the tightly-knit conversations of Raskolnikov and Sonia, of Ivan and Alyosha. Camus had little difficulty in adapting this novel for the stage and, curiously enough, he became interested in it at about the same time that he adapted *The Possessed.*

Requiem for a Nun is not a rose-tinted story, far from it. However, in comparison with the despair of *Sanctuary*, Popeye's incurable perversity, the debauchery in which Temple indulges, and her perjury, the contrast could not be clearer. The crime of 1931 is followed by a punishment that Temple inflicts on herself of her own free will—or nearly—like Raskolnikov. The tone simultaneously becomes more idealistic, more Christian; ideas replace the acts of an earlier time; murder, finally, is disguised as aspiration toward the good. This also means that ambiguity increases. Faulkner, meditating on God, more often poses question marks than solves problems. And, while innocent and guilty are divided into two camps in *Sanctuary*, the later tribulations of these characters are overwhelmed by paradoxes. Nancy, the infanticide, becomes a "nun"; Temple the outraged mother, presents herself as the accused. In another respect, the epilogue, although ambiguous, testifies to a less depressing conception of existence, closer to the promise of salvation glimpsed by Raskolnikov and Dmitri Karamazov: Temple's soul is purged of the evil committed earlier and, in any case, at her age sin has lost its initial attraction.

The dramatic episodes of *Requiem for a Nun* constitute a veritable play interspersed with long-winded stories about the past. One finds in these preambles the familiar views of Faulkner on history, but developed in a frankly federal light, more American and less "Southern" than *Intruder in the Dust.* Thus the native land that Faulkner once again makes the standard-bearer of political freedom becomes identified with the United States.[3] Nonetheless, the crucial questions of the book, for which the retrospective panoramas serve as a backdrop, are situated in the play proper. They are also concerned with freedom—in the moral sense—and reflect most of the great Dostoevskian theses: choice, culpability, suffering, faith, good and evil.

We know the situation. Eight years[4] after the events narrated in *Sanctuary*, the reader finds Temple Drake married to Gowan Stevens and the mother of two children. Evil has not yet given up, for Temple has not abjured her past any more than Gowan has forgotten it. What is more, she is ready to relapse into crime: it is at the moment when she is going to flee with the brother of Red, her former lover, that Nancy intervenes. To block her flight and preserve a home for the elder of the children, the house-maid decides to kill the other. Nancy's choice draws after it a second, since Temple finally confesses her sins and purifies herself morally.

If destiny still hangs over this book,[5] the heroes have, to a large degree, free play. Even if the past presses heavily on the present,[6] Temple succeeds in wiping out its menace according to the formulas applied by Raskolnikov to cleanse himself of his crime. *Requiem for a Nun* belongs to the novels of free will inaugurated by *The Unvanquished*. In this regard Nancy advances opinions that one might say were extracted from "The Grand Inquisitor," in which Christ appears as the champion of freedom:

> He dont tell you not to sin, He just asks you not to. And He dont tell you to suffer. But He gives you the chance.[7]
>
> man must hereafter with free heart decide for himself what is good and what is evil, having only Thy image before him as his guide.[8]

The first fruit of liberty, and the strangest, is Nancy's crime: an irrational decision, dictated by the heart and not the intellect,[9] made by her conscience alone before God. When she proclaims herself guilty, Nancy addresses herself explicitly to God, rather than to men,[10] and although she accepts unflinchingly the sentence of the court, she, in fact, commits herself to divine justice. Legal guilt evaporates before moral guilt. Temple, although she has the law in her favor, becomes the accused. A similar reversal of values is also observed in Dmitri Karamazov, who "accepts [his] punishment, not because [he] killed him [his father], but because [he] meant to kill him."[11]—with the exception that, in *Requiem for a Nun*, justice does indeed have a score to settle with Nancy. On the other hand, Nancy imagines human suffering as a kind of deposit held in common, from which everyone may, it seems, draw according to his needs,[12] and her crime is inconceivable without the typically Dostoevskian notion of universal solidarity in suffering and guilt. Nancy suffers and makes Temple suffer in order that she avoid evil; in addition, she does it in her stead, she takes responsibility by proxy. In killing Temple's child, Nancy effectuates an authentic transfer of guilt, as if it were a banker's draft transferable to anyone. It is clear that she assumes the guilt for the sin planned by Temple, following the example of Dmitri who will go to Siberia "for the babes": "It's for the babe I'm going. Because we are all responsible for all. For all the 'babes,' for there are big children as well as little children. All are 'babes.' I go for all, because some one must go for all."[13] or of Zossima who advises: "There is only one means of salvation, then take yourself and make yourself responsible for all men's sins. . . .If you can take upon yourself the crime of the criminal your heart is judging, take it at once, suffer for him yourself, and let him go without reproach."[14] It goes without saying that the archetype which inspires this transfer is the sacrifice of Christ. Although unmentioned, the Savior's example nonetheless sustains the conduct of the Faulknerian character. Dostoevsky clings to it quite as completely, but he expounds the Christian doctrine willingly and fully, and the comparison with *The Brothers Karamazov* without a doubt elucidates Nancy's act. One might, in fact, question its utility since Nancy only replaces one evil by another, an irremediable one. One might also denounce the danger of rejecting the legal and social order in the name of such a personal and irrational morality. But the principal concern for us is the ethical and theological level on which the crime is situated: seen in its paradoxical aspect, the murder of *Requiem for a Nun* is related to Kirillov's philosophical suicide in *The Possessed*. On the other hand, the comparison with Zossima and Dmitri ought not to make us forget that Nancy has indeed killed: as a criminal who recognizes her wrongs and accepts the punishment, she makes us think of Raskolnikov. But once more the parallel leads us astray, for her confession is not the culmination of a series of lacerating struggles: it springs immediately to her lips. Spontaneous in her decision, blindly submissive to the ordeal ordained by God:[15] we see here rather a replica of Sonia Marmeladov. Nancy bases her behavior on the principles of Dmitri and Zossima, flirts with a paradox like Kirillov, and like Raskolnikov causes her banishment from society, but by her character and social position she belongs to the Dostoevskian "slaves." She is, like Sonia, a prostitute, and to push her to what is, in effect, the bottom of the social scale in her time and place, Faulkner makes her, in addition, a drug addict and a negress. She is, in Jefferson, the lowest of the low, and yet this paragon of infamy conceals a treasure of abnegation and uncompromising faith from which the would-be Napoleon has already been able to profit. Taken as a whole, her portrait sketched by Faulkner in 1957 at the University of Virginia corresponds to the image of Sonia:

> that tragic life of a prostitute which she had to follow simply because she was compelled by her environment, her circumstances, to be it. Not for profit and any pleasure, she was just doomed and damned by circumstances to that life. And despite that, she was capable within her poor dim lights and reasons of an act which whether it was right or wrong was of complete almost religious abnegation of the world for the sake of an innocent child.[16]

It will be necessary for us to come back to these ideas that Nancy expresses rather awkwardly, but it is already obvious that her character imitates, while mixing them, several Russian prototypes, of which Dmitri and Sonia are the most important.

It is, so to speak, through the microscope that we see Temple's evolution and the origin of her choice. Temple passes from the legal position of accuser to the moral one of the accused, confesses after an inner struggle and achieves her salvation through suffering. Aside from the governor-witness and Gavin Stevens, Temple's catalyst, Faulkner knows no innocents. All are guilty toward everyone: Gowan, the husband, on account of his earlier cowardice, atoned for better or worse, by marrying Temple out of a sense of honor and by half forgiving her; Temple because she persists in loving evil; Nancy because she kills the child of the first two. But Faulkner, we repeat, reverses the hierarchy of guilt. Just as, in *The Brothers Karamazov*, the author of the murder (Smerdyakov) appears less punishable than his grey eminence (Ivan), in the same way, it is Temple whose moral responsibility is most engaged. The secret understanding which is established

291

between mistress and servant, their long discussions on evil: this somehow echoes the relations between Ivan and his pupil;[17] and in both cases, the master calls his servant a spy.[18] When she is seen in the presence of Temple we sometimes perceive the shadow of Smerdyakov behind Nancy: it is an additional component that completes our mosaic. Seen from this angle, Temple herself fulfills the function of an evil spirit, an involuntary instigator of a crime analogous to Ivan's. On the other hand, her moral conversion which forms the nexus of the book, the road she climbs before denouncing herself: this aspect of her role likens her to Raskolnikov. We witness, in both cases, the same delays, the same torments. The heroes never succeed in making the decisions toward which conscience pushes them[19] without the aid of another. The obstacles they must overcome before denouncing themselves —Raskolnikov: his pride; Temple: the attraction of evil and bourgeois conventions—are not the same, but both providentially find at their side the antidotes they need: Sonia's humility, the love of truth incarnated by Gavin Stevens. In *Requiem for a Nun*, as in *Crime and Punishment*, the confession is effectuated in two steps. The preparatory stage which develops behind closed doors between the criminal and his confidant (Raskolnikov and Sonia IV, 4 and V, 4; Temple and Gavin in Act One) is succeeded by the public avowal (VI, 8; Act Two), which Dostoevsky can skip over, his character having already explained his conduct at length, but which Faulkner makes into his central scene. It is worth pointing out that Sonia and Gavin demand the unvarnished truth from their interlocutor: they do not stop until they have been told everything and will accept no hedgings or evasions.[20] Raskolnikov and Temple would not, in fact, have been able to disclose their secret immediately, so heavy were their sins and so confused their motives; moreover, neither Dmitri nor Smerdyakov unveil their past at the outset. On the other hand, Temple, transported by her fervor, falls into the same depths of humility as her Russian counterpart.[21] To conclude, let us underscore the fact that these proceedings seem inspired by Sonia's words, "Suffer and expiate your sin by it, that's what you must do,"[22] an idea amplified later in *The Brothers Karamazov*. And yet the situations of Raskolnikov and Temple differ in many ways. While

292

the former violates both the law and the moral order only once,
Mrs. Stevens is responsible for two quite distinct crimes. If her
earlier perjury and complicity with Popeye relate her to the murderer, no tribunal can accuse her of the death of her child; her
adulterous cravings and her passion for evil do not, any more
than do Dmitri's intentions of parricide, fall beneath the gavel
of justice. This latter portion of her confession, of course, reflects
only an ethical obligation, Nancy and the elder Karamazov boy's
favorite domain. Curiously, Faulkner deliberately sacrifices the
legal aspect of the problem, for it is rather surprising that Temple's tardy avowals do not draw in their wake Goodwin's official
rehabilitation. The essential thing is that she saves her soul.[23]

By splitting a few hairs we can distinguish many other, more
or less striking, resemblances between *Requiem for a Nun* and
Dostoevsky. Temple and Ivan both act as defense witnesses without helping the accused; debauchery and crime are combined
in two pairs (Temple and Nancy, Sonia and Raskolnikov) and
then blended in the character of Nancy—and even of Temple
etc., etc. According to the point of view from which they are
considered, the heroes resemble certain characters from *Crime
and Punishment* or *The Brothers Karamazov*, but these similarities will not bear closer examination, Nancy, for example, compares sometimes with Dmitri, sometimes with Sonia, but also with
Zossima, Raskolnikov, Smerdyakov and even Kirillov; Temple in
turn wears the mask of Raskolnikov and—secondarily—Ivan and
Dmitri. The combination of borrowed characteristics, a principle
which often governs the existence of Faulkner's characters, here
attains its culmination. Nancy and Temple, although they did
not step prefabricated from the Russian novel, were surely conceived in a Dostoevskian matrix. They inherit all of the lineaments
from their multiple ancestors, but reapportioned, mixed and fused
in such a way that imitation results in creation.

Other details deserve further attention. Gowan, who listens to
Temple's confession without her being aware of it, recalls Svid-
rigailov standing behind the door while Raskolnikov speaks to
Sonia.[24] Temple's slapping of Nancy[25] finds an equivalent in *The
Idiot*,[26] *The Possessed*,[27] and *The Brothers Karamazov*[28] in which
Ganya, Shatov and Dmitri inflict the same treatment on Myshkin,

Stavrogin, Grigory and in which the insult remains equally unpunished. As in *The Brothers Karamazov*, the trial is accompanied by a visit to prison (Act Three): Temple enters there with Gavin Stevens, Nancy's moral defender who thus copies Horace Benbow in *Sanctuary*. The words with which the mother intends to salute the murderess of her child at the end, her "I forgive you, sister"[29] has a typically Dostoevsky flavor: Raskolnikov wonders why Sonia is "looking after (him) like (his) mother or Dounia"[30] (Dounia is his sister) and when Myshkin and Rogozhin exchange their crosses they treat one another literally as brothers;[31] the analogy with *The Idiot* is extended further by the fact that Rogozhin kills the prince's fiancee. We shall pass over the anonymous letters, a device that Faulkner uses more often than the Russian novelist,[32] but Temple's split personality[33] is too characteristic not to be remarked.

The structure and ideas remain. The alternation of narrative and dramatic-passages, of the historical preambles and the acts of a contemporary tragedy, finds its roots in the counterpoint of *The Wild Palms* and, in the final analysis, in the polyphony for which Dostoevsky gave an example. The arrangement of the play testifies, on the other hand, to Faulkner's fidelity to the "reverse" pattern. Chronologically the drama begins where *Crime and Punishment, The Brothers Karamazov*, and *Sanctuary* end: with the trial. And although the plot apparently develops in the interval between the trial and the execution, it is almost entirely oriented on the past, Temple's confession reconstructing the antecedents (1929-37) of the condemnation with which the book opens. Recounted for the most part by the heroine, the past is itself actualized by a kind of cinematographic flashback (II, 2) at the moment when Nancy chooses to kill. *Requiem for a Nun* gives us a backward glance in which Temple reveals all that she concealed at the time of *Sanctuary*. Judge and the guilty party are blended in one and the same person, it is herself that Temple prosecutes, accuses, and forces to confess: Raskolnikov and Porfiry unite in her. The interiorization of the detective plot corresponds very well with the spiritual perspective from which Faulkner regards guilt. If it seems absurd to connect the work's construction to *Crime and Punishment*, this variation on the well-worn theme of the detective novel nonetheless refers, indirectly at least, to one of the models of this genre. But the contact with the source is more or less broken, so that the successive manipulations prevent a certain identification. All things considered, on the technical level it is the abundance of symbols which recalls Dostoevsky rather than the organization of the plot.

At the very heart of the work one discovers welded to the problem of freedom that of suffering which Faulkner treats under two aspects. First of all, the suffering of children which legitimizes Nancy's crime; then, the redemptive cult of suffering, preached by her and put into practice by her mistress.

The first aspect springs from *The Brothers Karamazov* (V, 4 "Rebellion"); already evoked in *Sanctuary*, it serves as a hinge between the two panels of the story. It forces itself to the foreground in *Requiem for a Nun* and becomes a key idea. Nancy is a child-murderer: one of her paradoxes consists precisely in killing one child to save another one as well as the mother.[34] As in the examples cited by Ivan, it is an innocent child which serves as a victim. Faulkner even improves on Dostoevsky, for his victim is part of an expiatory sacrifice, conceived and consummated arbitrarily by Nancy at the expense of a nurseling, that is to say, of an unconscious and defenseless being. In this regard her act is modelled on Abraham's, but the age of miracles is long past: the angel of the Lord does not appear to prevent Isaac's holocaust. Fifteen years after grandfather Compson (*Absalom, Absalom!*), Gavin Stevens repeats, with only the slightest alteration, Ivan's opinion in "Rebellion":

> all her observation having shown her that God either would not or could not—anyway, did not—save innocence just because it was innocent; that when He said 'Suffer little children to come unto Me' He meant exactly that: He meant suffer; that the adults, the fathers, the old in and capable of sin, must be ready and willing—nay, eager—to suffer at any time, that the little children shall come unto Him unanguished, unterrified, unde-filed.[35]

> Are you fond of children, Alyosha? I know you are, and you will understand why I prefer to speak of them. If they, too, suffer horribly on earth, they must suffer for their fathers' sins, they must be punished for their fathers, who have eaten the apple; but that reasoning is of the other world

and is incomprehensible for the heart of man here on earth. The innocent must not suffer for another's sins, and especially such innocents![36]

I understand solidarity in sin among men. I understand solidarity in retribution, too; but there can be no such solidarity with children. And if it is really true that they must share responsibility for all their fathers' crimes, such a truth is not of this world and is beyond my comprehension.[37]

Actually, although Gavin, like Ivan, claims that children should not have to suffer, he seems to assert that they participate in the universal sin and atonement and he limits himself to demanding that adults suffer in their place, as Dmitri does. Rebellion changes into acceptance, which rests in its turn on the hypothesis, rendered practically necessary, of the existence of God. The suffering of children is again the reason that Nancy implacably opposes Temple at the time of her flight with Pete (II, 2). Zossima's exclamation: "Woe to him who offends a child!"[38] a leitmotif of "Rebellion" and of more than one page in the Diary of a Writer, provides the central idea for the entire play; it explains Nancy's reaction to Temple's unnatural indifference and both of their punishments: the execution of the one and the confession of the other.

Ivan claims to understand "solidarity in sin (and) . . . retribution" and later in his speech he speaks—hypothetically—of "the sum of sufferings which was necessary to pay for truth."[39] We have seen—the examples of Dmitri and Christ prove it—that suffering is transferable: Nancy suffers for Temple, for Gowan and their surviving child. The "truth" which is involved is obviously "eternal harmony"—"If all must suffer to pay for the eternal harmony"[40]—and for the sinning soul, salvation. Nancy makes the hypothesis offered by Ivan into a certitude:

NANCY
you got to trust Him. Maybe that's your pay for the suffering.
STEVENS
Whose suffering, and whose pay? Just each one's for his own?
NANCY
Everybody's. All suffering. All poor sinning man's.
STEVENS
The salvation of the world is in man's suffering. Is that it?
NANCY
Yes, sir.

STEVENS
How?
NANCY
I dont know.[41]

This is, stripped of trimmings, the fundamental idea of *Crime and Punishment*[42] and, above all, of *The Brothers Karamazov*.[43] Nancy sacrifices herself uniquely for the benefit of another and is, in this, closer to Dmitri than to Raskolnikov, who suffers for his own account. Faulkner has so far used the cult of suffering principally in the area of history in order to analyze the process of guilt, defeat, and future rebirth which in his eyes characterizes the development of the South; here this theme of atonement by suffering returns to its starting point: the individual case. *Requiem for a Nun* glorifies suffering, as does Dostoevsky, in the perspective of the individual. Here are its salient characteristics. It possesses healing and purifying properties on condition that it is sought for its own sake: "not suffering for or about anything, just suffering;"[44] it is, according to Nancy, even the best thing God has given to man;[45] a human being—Temple is a case in point—can achieve his or her salvation only by enduring all of the torments of which he or she is capable: from all appearances, man has no other means to this end; our novelists also require public suffering, for it is not sufficient to accuse oneself behind closed doors;[46] to the solitude of the confessional, they prefer an orgy of humility in the presence of witnesses, if not an entire crowd. The proverbial Anglo-Saxon reticence was already something quite foreign to Quentin Compson, Charles Bon and Red's mistress, but Faulkner never pushed lack of inhibitions further than in Mrs. Stevens' penance, which is worthy of the frankest of Dostoevsky's masochists.

In protesting against the unjust suffering of children, Ivan attacks the very center of the Christian edifice. He returns, as he says, his ticket to God. Hence the title "Rebellion." From a rationalist point of view, setting aside all mystery, his reasoning is faultless.

I don't want the mother to embrace the oppressor who threw her son to the dogs! She dare not forgive him! Let her forgive him for herself, if she will, let her forgive the torturer for the immeasurable suffering of her mother's heart. But the suffering of her tortured child she has no right to forgive; she dare not forgive the torturer, even if the child were to forgive him! And if that is so, if they dare not forgive, what becomes of harmony? Is there in the whole world a being who would have the right to forgive and could forgive?[47]

To which the pious Alyosha objects:

> You said just now, is there a being in the whole world who would have the right to forgive and could forgive? But there is a Being and He can forgive everything, all and for all, because He gave His innocent blood for all and everything. You have forgotten Him, and on Him is built the edifice.[48]

The Brothers Karamazov is a contrapuntal and dialectical novel. Ivan's problem is also discussed by Zossima, but from opposed points of view and with an extreme idealism that Alyosha cannot match.[49] In the course of the dialogue between Alyosha and Captain Snegiryov (IV, 7) they talk only about asking the offended's forgiveness and giving it to the offender;[50] Zossima goes farther: discarding any idea of reparation, he advises those whom "the evil doing of men moves to indignation" to "seek suffering" for themselves as though they were themselves "guilty of that wrong."[51] Temple, it must be said, shares neither the holy man's extremism nor Ivan's refusal. The mother ends by absolving the torturer of her child, the sinner by covertly imploring God's pardon and by confessing,[52] for such seems to be the interpretation required by the last words of the play. Their ordeal at an end, Gowan and his wife will succeed in loving each other "in (their) sin" as Zossima says, no matter how often the sin—and the pardon —is repeated.[53] Another echo of *The Brothers Karamazov* (V, 1) is to be found in the subtle analysis of the intolerable gratitude that goodness draws in its wake contained in Temple's statement:

> Only maybe it wasn't the forgiveness that was wrong, but the gratitude; and maybe the only thing worse than having to give gratitude constantly all the time, is having to accept it—[54]

> You know, Lise, it's awfully hard for a man who has been injured, when other people look at him as though they were his benefactors.[55]

Alyosha's remark provides a paraphrase of the first part of Temple's. But he adds immediately that when the fiery captain accepts his offering, he will say to him "Forgive us!"[56] In other words, Alyosha will reject the gratitude of the one obligated to him, preferring, like Temple, to give it rather than to accept it.

Let us come back, after this digression, to the matter of faith. For Gavin Stevens, the existence of God is only a conjecture—"God—if there was one. . ."[57]—which he nearly makes a certitude at the very last moment.[58] This is also the case with Temple, who admits that she is "damned" unless there is someone who cares for her soul;[59] the hypothesis here almost becomes a necessary condition "for the order of the universe" as young Kolya says.[60] Nancy, for her part, preaches a blind faith, since she recognizes herself incapable of defining its object:

TEMPLE
. . . Is there a heaven, Nancy?
NANCY
I don't know. I believes.
TEMPLE
Believe what?
NANCY
I don't know. But I believes.[61]

The passage, in which one of the major themes of Act Three appears,[62] is rather ambiguous. Despite the fact that Nancy, aided by Temple and Gavin, insists that faith repays the believer for his suffering, his own and that which he assumes for another,[63] she never defines that in which she believes. In substance, she is content to repeat what Faulkner read in The Brothers Karamazov. We remember the words attributed to Zossima: "Credo, but I don't know in what."[64] Rather than denoting incredulity, as old Karamazov maliciously asserts, they refer quite simply to a mystery inaccessible to knowledge, which only love, total self-surrender, can embrace. To Lise's mother, who confesses her doubts about the future life to him, Zossima answers:

"But there's no proving it, though you can be convinced of it."
"How?"
"By the experience of active love."[65]

A little later, Zossima speaks, in the context of the paradoxes of the Christian *Minnedienst*, of "the miraculous power of the Lord who has been all the time loving and mysteriously guiding you."[66] He also advises her to believe "to the end, even if all men went astray and you were left the only one faithful."[67] The controversial passage of *Requiem for a Nun*[68] immediately becomes clear when it is placed alongside of the Dostoevskian doctrine of choice or Shatov's objections to the intrusion of science and reason in ethics.[69] Nancy's faith, divorced from knowledge, has God, but God as the Unknowable, as its object. In short, there are few borrowings in this book as manifest as the gamut of religious convictions.

Requiem for a Nun, as a sequel to *Sanctuary*, necessarily refers to evil, and it is here that the distance covered in twenty years is most clearly seen. Popeye could kill and corrupt with no restraint but the author's displeasure. Nancy and Temple, on the contrary, abolish the very notion of evil—"good can come out of evil"[70]—for the murderess commits it in view of the good and the sinner cleanses herself by suffering. Let us recall that they illustrate, each in his own way, the jibes of Ivan's devil (XI, 9):

> Mephistopheles declared to Faust that he desired evil, but did only good. Well, he can say what he likes, it's quite the opposite with me.[71]
>
> "Then it's for the salvation of my soul you are workin, is it, you scoundrel?"
> "One must do a good work sometimes."[72]

In addition, Temple, following Shatov's example, situates the choice between good and evil outside the realm of knowledge, making it spring from intuition or instinct.[73]

In conclusion, we can say that Faulkner has drawn his moral and theological system from *The Brothers Karamazov* and even, in part, from *Crime and Punishment* and *The Possessed*. Among the secondary, but equally obvious, affinities let us cite also: the hostility to the thesis of irresponsibility in criminal matters,[74] the gap between legality and morality, the preference given to truth and love rather than to the law,[75] the belief in man's unlimited resistance,[76] and the sublimation of the instinct for vengeance.[77]

Requiem for a Nun is much more than a book influenced by

Dostoevsky. It is an authentically Dostoevskian work, written at a moment when the author's views practically overlap those of *The Brothers Karamazov*. Faulkner's personal contribution is reduced to mixing situations, intensifying paradoxes, inventing a new plot. Did the novelist realize that these borrowings, so comforting after so many horrors, could be harmful to him? Perhaps. It is clear, in any case, that he was soon to renounce them.

A Fable (1954)

Three years later Dostoevsky's contribution had already diminished, although it can still be easily identified. Concentrated in precise locations, it has marked them indelibly, and the critics were not long in pointing them out: Philip Blair Rice in 1954;[1] then in 1955 Delmore Schwartz,[2] followed by Heinrich Straumann[3] (the latter alluding to the problem only vaguely) in 1956, Irving Malin in 1957,[4] Fredrick J. Hoffman in 1960,[5] Irving Howe in 1962.[6] The majority limit themselves to the similarities and dissimilarities displayed by one or two passages (the conversations of the corporal and the Marshal, the corporal and the priest) and Ivan Karamazov's poem, "The Grand Inquisitor" (V, 5) of which we are going to speak in our turn.

Simply by virtue of its overall plan, *A Fable* belongs to the same literary genre as the chapter of *The Brothers Karamazov*: it is one of the innumerable stories about Christ's return to earth or his reincarnation. The similarity ends there, for this bulky novel, contrary to the Inquisitor's soliloquy, constitutes an allegory of the Passion as heavy as it is transparent. Never has Faulkner attempted to ascend so high into the philosophical empyrean, and never has there been a downfall more brutal. Behind the parable that he imagined, another unintentional one takes shape, that of Icarus. Ironically he falls into the trap of abstraction, against which he incessantly warned. The most "profound" of his books is also the most boring of them, for it overflows with hazy, poorly digested ideas draped in heavy rhetoric. *A Fable* is, among other things, a pacifist pamphlet which justifies, after the fact, the attribution of the Nobel Prize (1950). Faulkner's extramural escapades hardly ever succeed (see *Pylon*), and this voyage to France—the France of 1914-15—primarily will interest only the literary critic and historian. The significance of the novel, taken in the context of Faulkner's work, comes down, in the final analysis, to a return to the past, that is to the theme of *Soldiers' Pay* and *Sartoris*, and this abstruse book has no other interest except for the contrast it presents with his earlier works. A war novel, *A Fable*, contains despairing, indeed agonizing, pages, but the thought which animates it remains, nonetheless, based on hope.

It is unnecessary to explicate the plot structure and its over-simple symbolism. The plot departs from chronology to reveal the motives of the action, for in the initial episode the reader sees the mutinous regiment arrive at the place of its judgment and consequently knows how things have turned out; in addition Faulkner, as usual, juxtaposes descriptions of different milieus. Ritual gestures also abound in these Gospel exercises: Faulkner, always fond of symbols, has a field day. Only two passages, however, can be mentioned in relation to Dostoevsky: the one in which a locket is passed to the condemned man's neck, which vaguely suggests the cross offered by Sonia to Raskolnikov;[7] then, the image of the priest kneeling at the corporal's feet as in the often cited episode from *Crime and Punishment*.[8]

It is rather the dualism of the Faulknerian thought which deserves our attention, that marriage of contraries which Dostoevsky celebrated even in its most extravagant implications. This dualism, which admits of several interpretations, has been admirably illuminated in Straumann's interpretation of the plot and the characters,[9] but let us first look at how this is translated on the philosophical level.

There is, first of all, the opposition between destiny and freedom; in Faulkner, it is between an old conviction, still perceptible although attenuated, and a new idea. This antagonism is fundamental;[10] since the corporal, although an enemy of Authority, is guided by the consecrated schema of the Passion, there is no need to linger: except in *Crime and Punishment*, Dostoevsky has never tackled the subject. Free will keeps the rank accorded it in Faulkner's later work; on this point, Faulkner draws still closer to the Russian novelist to the degree that he gives it form in traits borrowed from the Christ of Ivan Karamazov. His corporal, a champion of spiritual freedom, runs up against Power, like the Son of God, and the runner does it as well:[11] both of them—and we must also include their "apostles"—wish to break man's bonds, to rebel against the slavery in which the Marshal holds them.[12]

The coexistence of good and evil, on the contrary, faithfully reproduces the Manicheism proper to *The Brothers Karamazov*. The ideas of the old negro: "Evil is a part of man, evil and sin and cowardice, the same as repentance and being brave. You got to believe in all of them, or believe in none of them. Believe that man is capable of all of them, or he aint capable of none"[13] echo the demonology of Ivan, who retorts to the devil: "You are my hallucination. You are the incarnation of myself, but only of one side of me."[14] and even Zossima's theology: "Brothers, have no fear of men's sin. Love a man even in his sin, for that is the semblance of Divine Love and is the highest love on earth. Love all God's creation, the whole and every grain of sand in it."[15] Satan, we are also told by both sides, could not conquer man.[16] Popeye's chances, in the world of *A Fable*, are reduced to nothing: Straumann observes, quite appropriately, that the Marshal has nothing of the traditional villain about him[17] and that, for Faulkner, there is no Christ without Judas, no God without Satan.[18] We rediscover here the precise dilemma upon which Ivan stumbles: either happiness without God and without freedom, or rather God and freedom but also the suffering of innocents—heaven necessarily implies hell.[19]

Other alliances also recall Dostoevsky, for example those of pride and humility[20] or of humility and of strength. Compare this statement with two by Dostoevsky:

the crowd had already underswept the military, irresistible in that passive and invincible humility.[21]

Loving humility is marvelously strong, the strongest of all things.[22]

It was always this, that the most degrading cross became a great glory and a great power, if only the act of humility was sincere.[23]

Even the ecstasies of pity[24] strike a Dostoevskian chord. But let us rather direct our attention to the hero of this new Gospel.

The corporal and the Marshal are not only antipodes as Christ and the Grand Inquisitor were: they resemble and complement each other. On the one hand, they both display qualities and deficiencies,[25] on the other hand, they represent principles that can coexist very well: the first, the ideal and hope; the second, reality and its preservation.[26] In addition, they must unite their efforts to repeat, with a few variations, Faulkner's credo, his faith in the future of humanity, as he expressed it in Stockholm.[27] More nuanced and diverse than Ivan's characters, they contradict one another only in certain aspects, and even those do not invariably suggest Dostoevsky and, *a fortiori*, the chapter of *The Brothers Karamazov*. The Marshal happens to be the father of the corporal: insofar as the latter identifies with Christ, he is transformed into God the Father. Seen from this angle, he is devoid of interest for the comparatist. The son's revolt against paternal authority does not, in fact, interest us on the level of the persons of the Trinity but from the point of view of the family, that is to say, as a theme of *Light in August* and *The Brothers Karamazov*. It is, moreover, the father who kills the son in *A Fable*.

The situation is, then, far from coinciding with those encountered in Dostoevsky. The corporal's death, seen as an instrument of man's salvation, obviously derives from the Bible. The victim's character in many respects reflects the person of Christ: such references are usual in Faulkner's work, from the tramp of "Out of Nazareth" (1925)[28] to the reporter of *Pylon* whom we have compared to the Idiot for that reason. The corporal, for his part, scarcely speaks—while Myshkin is an incorrigible chatterbox—and he acts even less. He remains exclusively passive, at least as long as his Passion lasts, and as such he comes very close to Sonia Marmeladov, whom he also recalls by his forbearance, poverty and aptitude for suffering. In addition, Faulkner marries him to a prostitute[29] who sells her body only in order to aid her family. Let us be quite frank: these are insignificant analogies. And it would be even more futile to compare the death chosen by the hero to the epilogue of the Russian "legend," in which Christ causes his expulsion by the Inquisitor.

If the Son can be linked to his prototype in the Gospels without any intermediary influence, the Marshal tends to suggest alternately Ivan Karamazov and the Inquisitor. From the latter he has inherited, above all, the incredulity:

> The slight grey man with a face wise, intelligent, and unbelieving, who no longer believed in anything but his disillusion and his intelligence and his limitless power.[30]
>
> Your inquisitor does not believe in God.[31]

However, let us be wary of such superficial resemblances. Does not the Marshal also play the role of, among others, the Father? Such that for him to believe in God comes down to believing in himself. Moreover, it is he who predicts that man will "prevail."[32] In the extract quoted, the element to be stressed is his faith in his intelligence, while pointing out that he is without the doubts of a rationalist like Ivan. It is incontestably the Inquisitor, the supreme earthly authority, who is his closest ally—and his principal creditor. It is specified, for instance, that the Marshal has taken on the anguish of men to save them:

> doomed—no: not doomed: potent—to bear the fearful burden of man's anguish and terror and at last his hope.[33]
>
> every child even in France knew your face because you would save us— you, to be supreme of all, not to command our armies and the armies of our allies because they did not need to be commanded, since the terror and the threat was their terror and threat too and all they needed was to be led, comforted, reassured and you were the one to do that because they had faith in you, believed in you.[34]

In sum, it is necessary for man to abdicate his free will, surrender himself blindly to the Leader, obey rather than think and choose his destiny. Faulkner's attacks against the Army, through which he aims at the political and moral Dictatorship, come directly from "The Grand Inquisitor":

> Yes, we shall set them to work, but in their leisure hours we shall make their life like a child's game, with children's songs and innocent dance. Oh, we shall allow them even sin, they are weak and helpless, and they will love us like children because we allow them to sin. We shall tell them that every sin will be expiated, if it is done with our permission, that we allow them to sin because we love them, and the punishment for these sins we take upon ourselves. And we shall take it upon ourselves, and they

will adore us as their saviours who have taken on themselves their sins before God. And they will have no secrets from us. We shall allow or forbid them to live with their wives and mistresses, to have or not to have children—according to whether they have been obedient or disobedient—and they will submit to us gladly and cheerfully. The most painful secrets of their conscience, all, all they will bring to us, and we shall have an answer for all. And they will be glad to believe our answer, for it will save them from the great anxiety and terrible agony they endure at present in making a free decision for themselves. And all will be happy, all the millions of creatures except the hundred thousand who rule over them. For only we, we who guard the mystery, shall be unhappy.[35]

Let it be said in passing that the Marshal also treats his men as "children." Where Dostoevsky covers Rome and its autocracy with opprobrium, Faulkner aims—with less virulence—at the General Staff. But whether one passes from black to red, priests and warriors embody the same evil: a secular totalitarianism, hostile to the freedom of the soul. The superman—it is indeed he with whom we are dealing here—makes an invulnerable force subservient to his plans.

the one out of all earth to be free of the compulsions of fear and weakness and doubt which render the rest of us incapable of what you were competent for[36]

They will become timid [the Inquisitor says] and will look to us and huddle close to us in fear, as chicks to the hen. They will marvel at us and will be awestricken before us, and will be proud at our being so powerful and clever, that we have been able to subdue such a turbulent flock of thousands of millions.[37]

His is an energy hardened by an authentic asceticism, either literally or figuratively.

So now he has gone to a Tibetian lamasery.[38]

And we who have taken their sins upon us for their happiness will stand before Thee and say: "Judge us if Thou canst and darest." Know that I fear Thee not. Know that I too have been in the wilderness, I too have lived on roots and locusts.[39]

It should also be remarked that the Marshal, by retiring into the desert, pursues the goal assigned by Ivan—and Zossima—to the monastic life, that is, self mastery:

306

to free yourself of flesh without having to die, without having to lose the
awareness that you were free of flesh . . . to be conscious always that you
were merely at armistice with it at the price of constant and unflagging
vigilance[40]

only suppose that there was one such man among all those who desire
nothing but filthy material gain—if there's only one like my old inquisitor,
who had himself eaten roots in the desert and made frenzied efforts to
subdue his flesh to make himself free and perfect.[41]

What an enigmatic character is this soldier, even more confusing
than Stavrogin of *The Possessed*! At the same time, the first person
of the Trinity, Caesar or Pontius Pilate and Satan, Faulkner's Marshal steps out of the Bible and *The Brothers Karamazov* to sacrifice the Son once again and predict to humanity its still distant
triumphs.

The liftings from the Gospels and Ivan's poem could give the
impression that the novel centers above all on theology and the
problems of the beyond. Nothing of the sort. The ideas of "The
Grand Inquisitor" are detached from any ecclesiastical context
and applied to the purely temporal level. *A Fable* deals exclusively with the terrestrial order, ethics, politics, existence here and
now. Christ, of course, inspires the hero from one end of his Passion to the other, but analytical minds cannot help but be teased
by the dim presence of a God which is always felt but never
stated. Religion, in *A Fable*, is limited to a flirtation with the
unknown. Salvation is unambiguously considered in a secular perspective, for it consists, for the individual, in bearing his cross
valiantly and, for the species, in enduring and prevailing. Immortality is accorded, not to the soul, but to the blood.[42] The author
sprinkles his narrative with stoic sayings whose Dostoevskian affinities we have already indicated:

man can bear anything[43]

between grief and nothing only the coward takes nothing.[44]

nothing . . . is as valuable as simply breathing.[45]

Basically, Faulkner uses the Christian "myth" to express an essentially secular faith in man. Insofar as one can find one's bearings
in these clouds, *A Fable* shows more reticence toward God than

307

does *Requiem for a Nun*. Nancy, in effect, voices Zossima's views when she declares herself incapable of *knowing* the divine. Their formula—"Credo, but I don't know in what"—is restated approximately in *A Fable*, but here it is divorced from the idea of God: "To believe. Not in anything: just to believe."⁴⁶ Let us concede that it is possible for one not to know if there is a heaven and still believe in it, but these words are here, as in *Intruder in the Dust*, without religious significance. On the contrary, the runner addresses them to the old negro who has just spoken to him of man, the good and evil he bears within himself, and who affirms: "You got to believe in all of them, or believe in none of them. Believe that man is capable of all of them, or he aint capable of none."⁴⁷ This is probably the novelist's last word on the subject. Despite appearances, *A Fable* represents a clear retreat from the Christian spirit of *Requiem for a Nun*.

There is another facet of this dualism: Faulkner's views on society and history. Among the contrasts in which the work abounds, Straumann quite rightly insists on that of the crowd and the stranger.⁴⁸ The corporal is an exceptional being, but this "slave" possesses the humility, endurance, and capacity for suffering of the crowd. The Marshal contrasts much more strongly with the masses: he is the extraordinary individual of whom Raskolnikov speaks to Porfiry,⁴⁹ one of the "rulers"—the greatest—mentioned by the Inquisitor.⁵⁰ It is only a short step from the doctrine of *Crime and Punishment* on masters and slaves and the right of the former "to commit any crime, to transgress the law in any way,"⁵¹ to the Roman Catholic autocracy: the distance separating theory from practice, ambition from the taking of power, the dream from its fulfilment. In both cases, humanity is divided into two camps: a herd living in submission and a handful of tyrants who run over them, if need be, to lead them towards happiness.

A Fable refers directly to Raskolnikov's system in at least one place as this comparison shows:

> Once to each period of his inglorious history, one of us appears with the stature of a giant, suddenly and without warning in the middle of a nation as a dairymaid enters a buttery, and with his sword for paddle he heaps and pounds and stiffens the malleable mass and even holds it cohered and purposeful for a time. But never for always, nor even for very

long: sometimes before he can even turn his back, it has relinquished, dis-cohered, faster and faster flowing and seeking back to its own base anonymity.[52]

for the most part they seek in very varied ways the destruction of the present for the sake of the better. But if such a one is forced for the sake of his idea to step over a corpse or wade through blood, he can . . . find within himself . . . a sanction for wading through blood . . . the masses will scarcely ever admit this right, they punish them or hang them (more or less), and in doing so fulfil quite justly their conservative vocation.[53]

We have already said several times that the Faulknerian image of the South—whether it opposes socially blacks and whites or morally the elite to the mob—presents unquestionable analogies with these speculations. We might cite, in addition, the enumerations of the "giants" and "heroes" which appear like a leitmotif throughout the book:

Caesar and Christ, Bonaparte and Peter and Mazarin and Alexander, Genghis and Talleyrand and Warwick, Marlborough and Bryan, Bill Sunday, General Booth and Prester John[54]

Michelangelo and Phidias and Newton and Ericsson and Archimedes and Krupp[55]

Caesar and the Barcas and the two Macedonians, our own Bonaparte and the great Russian.[56]

Raskolnikov's speech is also adorned by: "Kepler and Newton. . . . Lycurgus, Solon, Mahomet, Napoleon."[57]

The Grand Inquisitor, although he cites only Caesar, the "Timours and Genghis-Khan,"[58] furnishes more material than the murderer of the moneylender. First of all, the key notion—and the term—of Authority[59] designated by the pronoun "We,"[60] in opposition to "them," the crowd. In Dostoevsky, Authority is not split in two parts, as happens on the battlefield; nonetheless, Ivan, explaining his poem, prefigures textually the conspiracy of the enemy commanders against the rank and file for the sole purpose of continuing the War and safeguarding Power.

perhaps the spirit of that accursed old man who loves mankind so obstinately in his own way, is to be found even now in a whole multitude of such old men, existing not by chance but by agreement, as a secret

309

league formed long ago for the guarding of the mystery, to guard it from the weak and the unhappy, so as to make them happy.[61]

'We did it,' the Quartermaster General said. 'We. Not British and American and French we against German them nor German they against American and British and French us, but We against all because we no longer belong to us. A subterfuge not of ours to confuse and mislead the enemy nor of the enemy to mislead and confuse us, but of We to betray all, since all has had to repudiate us in simple defensive horror; no barrage by us or vice versa to prevent an enemy running over us with bayonets and hand grenades or vice versa, but a barrage by both of We to prevent naked and weaponless hand touching opposite naked and weaponless hand.[62]

The Brothers Karamazov thus includes, in embryo, the scene in which the German general concludes a pact with the allied commanders to put a halt to the mutiny and undo the pacifists' plans.[63] The German, a thoroughgoing militarist, proposes in the course of the reunion to his colleagues to submit the entire universe to the Army:[64] The leaders' desire is, pushed to its logical conclusion, to proclaim themselves "sole rulers of the earth" as the Inquisitor says.[65] The exercise of power is accompanied by an alienation that our novelists enjoy setting in relief: dehumanized, their leaders are doomed to a crushing solitude, cut off forever from their dependents. For such are the despot's intention and mission: to satisfy the herd-like need to obey, the need to surrender oneself completely to an Other[66] who abolishes "freedom . . . to make men happy."[67] In addition, each time he has a new quarrel with the established order, Christ appears before an infinitely more powerful and efficient organization than the tribunal of Caiaphas and the cohorts of Pilate. In Dostoevsky, it is the Church which wishes to burn him without even a trial: in Faulkner, the execution is probably less summary—the corporal has to overcome a number of temptations before dying—but the disproportion between the mutineer and the Army[68] remains just as startling, all the more so in that the latter are reinforced by the priests.[69] Finally, Faulkner indicates, in the same way, that man has distorted Christ's message. Christianity, he says, is built on the rapacity of the heroes and their accomplices "who after nineteen centuries have rescued the son of heaven from oblivion and translated him from mere meek heir to earth to chairman of its board of trade."[70] An almost literal echo of Alyosha's indignant correction which assigns the Inquisitor's aims to the Jesuits alone:

> We know the Jesuits, they are spoken ill of, but surely they are not what you describe? They are not that at all, not at all . . . They are simply the Romish army for the earthly sovereignty of the world in the future, with the Pontiff of Rome for Emperor . . . that's their ideal, but there's no sort of mystery or lofty melancholy about it . . . It's simple lust of power, of filthy earthly gain, of domination—something like a universal serfdom with them as masters—that's all they stand for.[71]

Let us specify finally that the Marshal, in maintaining that the masses aspire to suffering,[72] discards the opinion expressed by Ivan[73] and takes support from those of a Zossima or, better, Porfiry.[74]

Let us summarize. Despite the fact that Faulkner mixes the ideas of "The Grand Inquisitor" to suit his tastes, shifting them from the area of the Church to that of the Army, grafting them onto elements either extracted from other works, Dostoevskian or not, or taken from his own experience, complicating the antagonisms—his borrowings from the celebrated "legend" are nonetheless identifiable to the naked eye. Faulkner has seen him triumph several times in his lifetime, this demon of spiritual and political tyranny who tempts Raskolnikov, Shigalov and Verhovensky, whom Myshkin denounces and upon whom Ivan Karamazov confers an obsessive reality. He is hidden behind Mussolini, Hitler, Stalin and Franco, behind the marshals, generals and colonels, more or less rebellious, behind all Authority which, forgetful of service to man, reduces him to the level of a thing. Among Dostoevsky's numerous dictators, the Inquisitor seems to have marked A Fable most clearly, for, contrary to the others and quite like the Marshal, he actually is in power; he maintains and preserves the real much more than he heralds the future. By a curious reversal of Raskolnikov's theory, it is the corporal, the humble "slave" born of the people, who becomes the revolutionary and true hero. Faulkner is not as conservative as he seems. The politics of A Fable are situated within the limits of liberal democracy, and it is indeed paradoxical that the Dostoevskian influence fortified him in this conviction. The common element in this area resides, in the final analysis, less in what the two men embrace than in what they eliminate, less in their conception of the ideal regime than in their hatred of tyranny.

Faulkner, following in the wake of the Master, gives voice in his turn to reflections on the world of tomorrow,[75] but the chronological gap renders them without interest for our purposes.

From the point of view of situations, the chapter of *The Brothers Karamazov* already exploited in *The Hamlet* in the form of an epilogue has left its traces in two, perhaps three, scenes of *A Fable*. It concerns, successively, the conversations between Marthe and the Marshal (pp. 285-301), between the latter and the corporal (pp. 343-356), and between the corporal and the priest (pp. 362-367). Each time, the lines tighten: Faulkner progresses by stages, so to speak, in Dostoevsky's direction.

The first episode is least conformable to "The Grand Inquisitor." The resemblances are reduced to a very few things: two characters of which one, nearly mute, is content to listen to the reproaches of the other. And again these are integrated into a long narrative which summarizes the antecedents of the Marshal and the corporal, and which has, therefore, nothing in common with the philosophical ideas of *The Brothers Karamazov*. In addition, although the Marshal is presented as the accused, like Dostoevsky's Christ, he is not ennobled by the confrontation.

The two other scenes repeat the schema introduced above: an interlocutor who carries the burden of the conversation; another, taciturn,[76] who is exposed to his assaults. In both cases, the corporal is, in effect, put to the test, either by the Marshal or by the priest, and he resists them victoriously. Beyond "The Grand Inquisitor" we glimpse here, as in *The Hamlet*, the verses of Matthew (4:1-11) and Luke (4:1-13) that Dostoevsky restates in his own way. *A Fable* evokes the Biblical episode quite as much as the situation of Christ imprisoned in Seville fifteen centuries after the Passion. And perhaps even more. For, in contrast with Faulkner's characters and that of the Gospel, the Inquisitor does not tempt the Prisoner: he simply retells the story of the forty days spent in the desert when he outlasted the devil and he seeks neither to save him nor to ruin him. The Inquisitor compares with the Faulknerian temptors only by this recollection of the past, that is, insofar as he refers to the Bible. In short, he does not take the place of the devils of Scripture, while Faulkner's Marshal does. As we have seen in regard to *The Hamlet*, Faulkner probably combined the Bible with *The Brothers Karamazov*. For instance, the corporal, the reincarnation of Christ, has to be taken out of prison where Authority has relegated him in order to meet his temptors, a minor detail which reminds one of Ivan's text. But once in their presence, everything develops as in Luke and Matthew—and as in Dostoevsky's flash-back. We notice here how difficult it is to decide between possible influences.

All things considered, the lion's share must, nonetheless, be assigned to Dostoevsky. Not only does Faulkner amplify the meager plot furnished by the Gospels with the same eloquence, but he borrows several ideas from *The Brothers Karamazov* along the way. The Roman citadel, the eminence to which the Marshal leads his son,[77] obviously corresponds to the mountain of the Bible (and "The Grand Inquisitor"[78]) from which the devil shows Jesus "all the kingdoms of the world." The Marshal predicts that humanity will hate the one sacrificed for it:

> You caused them to fear and suffer, but tomorrow you will have discharged them of both and they will only hate you: once for the rage they owe you for giving them the terror, once for the gratitude they will owe you for taking it away, and once for the fact that you are beyond the range of either.[79]

The same idea is expressed by the Inquisitor although the motives he attributes are less explicit: "For Thou hast come to hinder us. . . .And the very people who have to-day kissed Thy feet, to-morrow at the faintest sign from me will rush to heap up the embers of Thy fire."[80] The temptations which the corporal must resist are, as in the sources, three in number; this does not, however, prevent their being very different in nature. Dostoevsky follows Matthew to the letter and mentions, in the same order, the miracle of the bread, the test of the divine promises, and the glory of the kingdoms. Faulkner inverts the last two temptations, as Luke does. In their succession, the Russian patterns himself on Matthew; the American, like Milton, on Luke. The corporal

313

is offered the following things in turn: the physical freedom to wander the earth (pp. 346-488; "Take the Earth"),[81] the empire of the world (pp. 348-350; "take the world"),[82] and life (pp. 350-352; "take life").[83] We must ignore the supernatural and stick to the secular if we want to compare Faulkner with the Bible, for the novelist remodels the temptations while desacralizing them. Under these conditions, the Marshal's propositions agree more or less with those of the Gospels, as Dostoevsky comments on them, or rather, as a reader as subjective as Faulkner could understand them through "The Grand Inquisitor." What of the Russian text is, in fact, retained? Nothing but the terrestrial corollaries of the questions posed by the devil, nothing but the Inquisitor's "human" comments; that is: to free oneself from material servitude ("feed us," "bread enough for all"),[84] to rule ("the sword of Caesar")[85] and exist, or better, to survive ("Thou . . . wouldst have been dashed to pieces against that earth").[86] The correspondence leaves a good deal to be desired for a reader concerned with the "legend" in its literal form. It is perfect only on the second point: Christ and the corporal's refusal of power and glory in the name of the spiritual. As for the first, it is limited to the discarding of a purely *physical* deliverance, either from hunger (Dostoevsky), or from war and prison (Faulkner). As for the third point, although one must take a roundabout course to perceive any real equivalence, it truly seems to be the biased and incomplete interpretation of "The Grand Inquisitor"—the desire to find only what one seeks to the exclusion of all that might be discovered in addition—which explains the disappearance of the divine. In the Gospels, the devil, referring to the Psalms, tells Jesus that, if he is the Son of God, he can throw himself into the abyss without fear, for "in their hands they [the angels] shall bear thee up, lest at any time thou dash thy foot against a stone." (Matthew 4:6; Luke 4:11). Paraphrasing the Bible, Dostoevsky points out that, by giving in, Christ would have tempted the Lord —which agrees with the Scriptures—but the Inquisitor adds that he would also have lost his faith and, at the same time, his life: he would have killed himself by throwing himself from the temple. This comment on the Scriptures regarding biological death is the only thing that struck Faulkner: his priest, moreover, calls this temptation "that third and most terrible temptation of immortality."[87] When he says no to the devil, Ivan's Christ rejects the illusory immortality with which the devil tempts him, that is to say, a death that is both spiritual and physical, in order to preserve the true immortality promised by God and, at the same time, earthly life. The corporal's problem is simpler, for there is no other immortality for Faulkner and his characters than that of the human race, the infinite chain of generations that the corporal willingly interrupts by accepting his death. The supernatural dimension of the Gospels is missing in *A Fable*: Faulkner preserves only the secular side of the exegesis provided by *The Brothers Karamazov*.

Let us insist on this point: only this exegesis allows us to bridge the gap between Faulkner and the Bible. And it is this too that very likely inspired the scene under discussion. For instance, in relation to the first temptation, the Marshal agrees with the Inquisitor when he speaks of the anguish with which freedom fills man, an opinion that Dostoevsky associates precisely with "the first question": the miracle of the bread:

> Why else have I offered to buy my—our—security with things which most men not only do not want but on the contrary do well to fear and flee from, like liberty and freedom?[88] (*A Fable*)

> Remember the first question; its meaning, in other words, was this: "Thou wouldst go into the world, and art going with empty hands, with some promise of freedom which men in their simplicity and their natural unruliness cannot even understand, which they fear and dread—for nothing has ever been more insupportable for a man and human society than freedom. But seest Thou these stones in this parched and barren wilderness? Turn them into bread."[89] (*The Brothers Karamazov*)

In the second temptation we also encounter some fundamental elements of Ivan's poem: the need man feels to allow himself to be led and tricked,[90] the power exercised by the leaders with the aim of assuring the "happiness" of their subjects[91]—"giving them . . . more and sweeter *bread*."[92] The third can be compared with other passages of *The Brothers Karamazov*. The Marshal's argument:

> Then you realize that nothing—nothing—not power nor glory nor wealth nor pleasure nor even freedom from pain, is as valuable as simple breath-

ing, simply being alive even with all the regret of having to remember and the anguish of an irreparable worn-out body; merely knowing that you are alive.[93]

could even have flowed from the dialogue between Alyosha and Ivan ("The Brothers Make Friends"; V, 3) which precedes "Rebellion" and "The Grand Inquisitor":

> "I understand too well, Ivan. One longs to love with one's inside, with one's stomach. You said that so well and I am awfully glad that you have such a longing for life," cried Alyosha. "I think every one should love life above everything in the world."
> "Love life more than the meaning of it?"
> "Certainly, love it regardless of logic, as you say."[94]

or better yet Dmitri's profession of faith ("A Hymn and a Secret"; XI, 4):

> And I seem to have such strength in me now, that I think I could stand anything, any suffering, only to be able to say and to repeat to myself every moment, 'I exist.' In thousands of agonies—I exist. I'm tormented on the rack—but I exist! Though I sit alone in a pillar—I exist! I see the sun, and if I don't see the sun, I know it's there. And there is a whole life in that.[95]

Finally, the father uses an expedient that Dostoevsky particularly favored to convince his son: the example, the illustration. This French officer begins without warning to tell a story, borrowed from the annals of Mississippi, of a murderer condemned to death who eventually confesses his crime to a priest who has come to aid him. The killer, reconciled with God, hears on the morning of his execution, a bird—a symbol of the perenniality of life—singing on a tree near by and immediately recants: "Then take that bird. Recant, confess, say you were wrong."[96] The confession after the judgment, the fervor with which the proselyte accepts his punishment and aspires to the beyond: one would think one was reading the story of Richard ("Rebellion"; V, 4).[97] The last part—the appearance of the bird and the ensuing retraction—contradicts it, however. But this bird fulfills a similar function in another exemplary story, told by Zossima, which deals with his older brother.[98] To be sure, the bird does not, in Dostoevsky, incite someone to recant, since it confirms the believer, also near death, in his faith; but, just as in *A Fable*, it represents a fragment of life. As a matter of fact, by life Dostoevsky means Creation, while the Marshal's example erects a barrier between earth and heaven, enclosing life within biological limits. It is sufficient, once more, to translate the Dostoevskian element into secular terms to see the link. All things considered, it is quite possible that the Marshal's story was born of the interpolation of two anecdotes from *The Brothers Karamazov*, once isolated from their context.

Although there are numerous divergences between "The Grand Inquisitor" and Faulkner's confrontation of the corporal and his father, it is now impossible to doubt the filiation of these passages. Even if we consider only the main elements, we watch the same conflict between a spiritual ideal and material reality, as well as the victory of the first.

Let us pass on to the corporal's conversation with the priest, closer to the model than the preceding ones, for the priest recapitulates, quite literally this time, the three temptations of the Gospel and *The Brothers Karamazov*. He violates the traditional order in speaking of power (p. 363), but he makes "immortality" follow the miracle of bread (pp. 365-66) as do Matthew and Dostoevsky. In addition he plagiarizes from the latter throughout his commentary.

A Fable	"The Grand Inquisitor"
I. p. 363: Him who died two thousand years ago in the affirmation that man shall never never never, need never never never, hold suzerainty over another's life and death—absolved you and the man you mean both of that terrible burden: you of the right to and he of the need for, suzerainty over your life; absolved poor mortal man forever of the fear of the oppression, and the anguish of the responsibility, which suzerainty over human fate and destiny would have entailed	p. 264: the fearful burden of free choice p. 269: The most painful secrets ot their conscience, all, all they will bring to us, and we shall have an answer for all. And they will be glad to believe our answer, for it will save them from the great anxiety and terrible agony they endure at present in making a free decision for themselves. And all will be happy, all the millions of creatures except the hundred thousand who rule over them. For only we, we who guard the mystery, shall be unhappy.

on him and cursed him with, when He refused in man's name the temptation of that mastery, refused the terrible temptation of that limitless and curbless power when He answered the Tempter: *Render unto cæsar the things which are cæsar's* . . .

There will be thousands of millions of happy babes, and a hundred thousand sufferers who have taken upon themselves the curse of the knowledge of good and evil.

p. 266-7: Hadst Thou accepted that last counsel of the mighty spirit, Thou wouldst have accomplished all that man seeks on earth—that is, someone to worship, some one to keep his conscience.

II. p. 363: It wasn't He with his humility and pity and sacrifice that converted the world; it was pagan and bloody Rome which did it . . . . only Rome could have done it . . .

pp. 266-7: We have corrected Thy work. . . . We took from him Rome and the sword of Cæsar, and proclaimed ourselves sole rulers of the earth, though hitherto we have not been able to complete our work . . . but we shall triumph and shall be Cæsars.

III. p. 365: Change these stones to bread *and all men will follow Thee*. And He answered, *Man cannot live by bread alone*. Because He knew that too . . . : that He was tempted to tempt and lead man not with the *bread*, but with the miracle of that bread, the deception, the illusion, the delusion of that bread; tempted to believe that man was not only capable and willing but even eager for that deception, that even when the illusion of that miracle had led him to the point where the bread would revert once more to stone in his very belly and destroy him, his own children would be panting for the opportunity to grasp into their hands in their turn the delusion of that miracle which would destroy them.

p. 262: Turn them into bread. . . . Thou didst reply that man lives not by bread alone.

p. 268: They will see that we do not change the stones to bread.

p. 263: Choosing "bread"

p. 265: Thou . . . didst crave faith given freely, not based on miracle.

p. 271: he sees that he must follow the counsel of the wise spirit, the dread spirit of death and destruction, and therefore accept lying and deception, and lead men consciously to death and destruction, and yet deceive them all the way so that they may not notice where they are being led, that the poor blind creatures may at least on the way think themselves happy. And note, the deception is in the name of Him in Whose ideal the old man had so fervently believed all his life long.

p. 268: For they will remember only

too well that in the old days, without our help, even the bread they made turned to stones in their hands, while since they have come back to us, the very stones have turned to bread in their hands.

p. 265: But Thou didst refuse and wouldst not cast Thyself down. . . . Thou didst know then that in taking one step, in making one movement to cast Thyself down, Thou wouldst be tempting God and have lost all Thy faith in Him, and wouldst have been dashed to pieces against the earth which Thou didst come to save. And the wise spirit that tempted Thee would have rejoiced.

IV. p. 365: that terrible power over the whole universe which that mastery over man's mortal fate and destiny would have given Him had He not cast back into the Tempter's very teeth that third and most terrible temptation of immortality: which if He had faltered or succumbed would have destroyed His Father's kingdom not only on the earth but in heaven too because that would have destroyed heaven . . .

pp. 365-66: man in his turn by no more warrant than one single precedent casting himself from the nearest precipice the moment he wearied of the burden of his free will and decision, the right to the one and the duty of the other, saying to, challenging his Creator: *Let me fall—if You dare?*

p. 265: And couldst Thou believe for one moment that men, too, could face such a temptation? Is the nature of men such, that they can reject miracle, and at the great moments of their life, the moments of their deepest, most agonising spiritual difficulties, cling only to the free verdict of the heart? Oh, Thou didst know that Thy deed would be recorded in books . . . and Thou didst hope that man, following Thee, would cling to God and not ask for a miracle.

Plagiarism? Let's not overstate the case: the word is a bit strong. First of all the literal borrowings, underscored above, are both rare and banal and they do not always refer to the same context, with the obvious exception of the biblical quotations. Then we notice some curious mixtures. The priest gives Christ the same intentions, or very nearly, as those already attributed to him by the Inquisitor (I), but he nonetheless reproves the ends and means of the latter. Elsewhere the priest paraphrases Ivan's ideas and those of his character (II and III) and, like the Inquisitor, reflects the Gospels (III), but the parallelism of

319

the transmutation of bread into stone, for instance, remains purely verbal, this change taking place in different areas. The only passage which, in an extreme interpretation, might seem to border on plagiarism concerns the temptation of immortality (IV), and we have seen to what extent we must alter the original text to come to this notion. In addition, the stakes of the temptation—General Gragnon's life and that of the corporal on the one hand; man's free will on the other—are completely different, although an identical opposition is drawn on both sides between the individual's dream and the earthly authority of the Church, an institution founded not by Christ but by his "heirs."[99] We would be wrong to believe that Faulkner wrote this scene with *The Brothers Karamazov* before his eyes. As usual, he takes only that which will serve as grist for his own mill, where and when he pleases, regardless of the doctrinal coherence of the work and scorning its situations and ideas. Indeed, having taken "The Grand Inquisitor" to pieces, he assembles from the fragments obtained a mosaic whose resemblance to the original is as indubitable as it is elusive. Sometimes, fascinated by a word, one thinks one has put one's finger on the source, and one is a thousand miles away; sometimes the divergence seems to grow but, upon examination, Dostoevsky shows through the disguise. These are, in sum, only the repercussions of consecutive readings that one feels here, filtered by the imagination, decomposed, then regrouped in terms of a new idea. *A Fable* already respects the spirit of Dostoevsky less than does *Requiem for a Nun*.

Several additional traits complete the comparison. The priest after vainly distorting Christ's message and placing the Church of Paul above the Word, commits suicide in circumstances that recall Svidrigailov's end (*Crime and Punishment*; VI, 6).[100] The soldiers' cadavers at Verdun give off an odor of corruption quite like that of Zossima (*The Brothers Karamazov*; VII, 1) and—to a lesser degree—the corporal.[101] As for the ideas, if suffering is underlined less often than in *Requiem for a Nun*, it is, nonetheless, the cornerstone of the Faulknerian Gospel, in which the mutinous regiment, the corporal and his apostles, above all play the role of Nancy and Dmitri Karamazov by sacrificing themselves for the benefit of others.[102] Secondarily, *A Fable* is a study

320

of honor and its military varieties[103] a theme exploited, as we know, in Dostoevsky's last novel. That the earth, soiled, violated by the shells, is likened to the mother of man[104] will not be surprising for the reader of *Crime and Punishment*,[105] *The Brothers Karamazov*,[106] and *The Possessed*.[107] Finally, again as in *The Possessed*, allusion is made to the non-value of virginity,[108] and the corporal's half-sister not only bears the same name—Marya, transliterated from "Russian"[109]—as Lebyadkin's sister, but she is also a simpleton and shows the same serene expression.[110]

NOTES TO CHAPTER IX

1. See *Faulkner in the University*, p. 27.

The Unvanquished

1. *The Unvanquished*, p. 54.
2. *Absalom, Absalom!*, p. 221.
3. *Soldiers' Pay*, p. 60.
4. *The Unvanquished*, p. 55.
5. See Part One, Chapter III, of this study.
6. *The Unvanquished*, p. 167.
7. See Part One, Chapter II, of this study.
8. *The Unvanquished*, p. 249.
9. See *ibid.*, "Vendée."
10. *Ibid.*, p. 284.
11. *Ibid.*, p. 280.
12. See *The Diary of a Writer*, p. 13: "Christianity which, fully recognizing the pressure of the milieu, and which, having proclaimed mercy for him who has sinned, nevertheless makes it a moral duty for man to strugg. against environment, and draws a line of demarcation between where environment ends and duty begins."
13. *The Brothers Karamazov*, p. 308.
14. *Ibid.*, p. 309.
15. *Ibid.*, p. 311.
16. See *The Sound and the Fury* and *As I Lay Dying*, pp. 507-8.
17. *Light in August*, p. 241.
18. *Absalom, Absalom!*, p. 357-58.
19. *The Unvanquished*, p. 262.
20. *Ibid.*, p. 269.
21. See *A Raw Youth* and *The Brothers Karamazov*.
22. *The Unvanquished*, p. 274.
23. *The Brothers Karamazov*, p. 118.
24. *The Unvanquished*, pp. 273-74.
25. *The Brothers Karamazov*, p. 213.
26. *Ibid.*
27. Let us point out that the marriage of Drusilla and Colonel Sartoris causes a veritable scandal, as in *The Idiot* (*The Unvanquished*, pp. 238-40).

The Wild Palms

1. See Frederick L. Gwynn, "Faulkner's Raskolnikov," *Modern Fiction Studies*, IV, 2 (Summer, 1958) p. 169 and *Faulkner in the University*, pp. 72-73.
2. *The Wild Palms*, p. 136. See *The Brothers Karamazov*, pp. 257-59 and 269-70.
3. See *The Wild Palms*, pp. 135-36 and *The Brothers Karamazov*, pp. 317-18.
4. *The Wild Palms*, p. 280.
5. See *ibid.*, pp. 130, 153, etc.
6. See Frederick J. Hoffman, *William Faulkner* (New York: Twayne Publishers, Inc., 1961), p. 84.
7. *The Brothers Karamazov*, p. 77.
8. *The Wild Palms*, p. 48.
9. *Ibid.*, pp. 225-26.
10. *Ibid.*, pp. 318-319.
11. *Ibid.*, p. 285.
12. *The Brothers Karamazov*, p. 628.
13. *Ibid.*
14. *The Wild Palms*, p. 133.
15. *Ibid.*, p. 324.
16. *The Idiot*, p. 214. See *The Wild Palms*, pp. 176-77.
17. See *A Raw Youth*, p. 508 and *The Wild Palms*, pp. 176-77.
18. *The Wild Palms*, p. 328.
19. *The House of the Dead*, p. 92.
20. *The Wild Palms*, p. 28 and *The House of the Dead*, p. 79.
21. *The House of the Dead*, pp. 240-41.
22. *The Wild Palms*, p. 166.
23. *The House of the Dead*, pp. 11-12.
24. *The Wild Palms*, p. 187.
25. See *ibid.*, p. 24.
26. *Faulkner in the University*, p. 183.
27. *The Brothers Karamazov*, pp. 369, 630.
28. *The Wild Palms*, p. 11.
29. *Ibid.*, p. 83.
30. *Ibid.*
31. *The Brothers Karamazov*, p. 335.
32. *The Wild Palms*, p. 83.
33. *The Brothers Karamazov*, p. 335.
34. *The Eternal Husband*, p. 28.
35. *The Wild Palms*, p. 38.
36. *The Eternal Husband*, p. 28.
37. *The Wild Palms*, p. 38.
38. *The Eternal Husband*, p. 28.
39. *The Wild Palms*, p. 39.
40. *The Eternal Husband*, p. 28.
41. *The Wild Palms*, p. 223.
42. *Ibid.*, pp. 53-54.
43. *Ibid.*, pp. 225-26.
44. *Ibid.*, pp. 311-12.
45. *Ibid.*, p. 312.
46. *Ibid.*, pp. 135-39.
47. *Ibid.*, p. 138.

The Hamlet

1. See *The Mansion*, unnumbered preface, and *Faulkner in the University*, pp. 14-15.

2. *The Hamlet*, pp. 113-14.
3. *Ibid.*, pp. 100-101.
4. *Ibid.*, pp. 114-15.
5. *Ibid.*, p. 115.
6. *Ibid.*, p. 363.
7. *Ibid.*, pp. 220-22.
8. *Ibid.*, p. 247.
9. *Crime and Punishment*, p. 82.
10. *The Hamlet*, p. 258.
11. *Ibid.*, p. 215.
12. *Ibid.*, p. 152.
13. Flem ends up sitting on the devil's throne. See *ibid.*, p. 155.
14. *The Brothers Karamazov*, p. 259.
15. *Ibid.*, p. 272, and *The Hamlet*, p. 155.
16. *Ibid.*, p. 95.
17. *Ibid.*, pp. 73, 81.
18. *The Idiot*, pp. 162-64.
19. Cleanth Brooks, *William Faulkner: The Yoknapatawpha Country* (New Haven: Yale University Press, 1963), pp. 177, 183.

Go Down, Moses

1. *Go Down, Moses*, p. 97.
2. *Ibid.*, p. 257.
3. *Ibid.*, p. 260.
4. *Crime and Punishment*, pp. 287-91.
5. *The Brothers Karamazov*, pp. 323-24.
6. *Go Down, Moses*, p. 260.
7. *Ibid.*, p. 290.
8. See Part One, Chapter Two.
9. *Go Down, Moses*, pp. 288-89. See also p. 260.
10. *Ibid.*, p. 289.
11. *The Brothers Karamazov*, p. 264.
12. *Go Down, Moses*, p. 281.
13. *The Brothers Karamazov*, p. 264.
14. *Ibid.*, p. 265.
15. *Go Down, Moses*, pp. 340-41.
16. *Ibid.*, pp. 254-55, 353-54, etc.
17. *Ibid.*, pp. 255, 298, etc.
18. *Ibid.*, p. 257.
19. *The Diary of a Writer*, p. 686.
20. *Ibid.*, pp. 417-18, 420.
21. See Part One, Chapter Three.
22. *The Brothers Karamazov*, pp. 317-18.
23. See Part One, Chapter Three.
24. *Go Down, Moses*, p. 259.
25. *Ibid.*, p. 259. Faulkner thus repeats the idea, expressed earlier, that suffering is better than nothing. See p. 186.
26. *Ibid.*, pp. 285-86.
27. *The Brothers Karamazov*, p. 540.
28. *Go Down, Moses*, pp. 278-79.
29. *Ibid.*, p. 170. See also p. 118.
30. *The Brothers Karamazov*, pp. 330-31.
31. *Go Down, Moses*, p. 258.
32. *The Idiot*, p. 520. See also *The Possessed*, p. 255.
33. *Go Down, Moses*, p. 283.
34. *Ibid.*, p. 364.

35. *The Diary of a Writer* (January, 1877), p. 581. See also pp. 979-80 (August, 1880).
36. *The Brothers Karamazov*, p. 254.
37. *Go Down, Moses*, pp. 294, 351.
38. *Faulkner in the University*, p. 246.
39. *Go Down, Moses*, p. 309.
40. *The Brothers Karamazov*, p. 49.
41. *Go Down, Moses*, p. 299.
42. *The Brothers Karamazov*, p. 23, and *Go Down, Moses*, p. 309.
43. *The Diary of a Writer*, pp. 614-18.
44. See *The Brothers Karamazov*, pp. 303-31.
45. *Ibid.*, p. 261.
46. *Go Down, Moses*, p. 260.
47. *Ibid.*, p. 279, and *The Brothers Karamazov*, p. 82.
48. *The Brothers Karamazov*, p. 332.
49. *Go Down, Moses*, p. 311.
50. *Ibid.*, pp. 96-97.
51. *Ibid.*, p. 44.
52. *The Brothers Karamazov*, p. 307. The idea is also found in *The Notebooks of the Brothers Karamazov*, p. 106; "bear, harmony, nature."
53. *Go Down, Moses*, p. 208.

Intruder in the Dust

1. See the allusion to "Thou shalt not kill" and our discussion of *The Unvanquished* earlier in this chapter. See *Intruder in the Dust*, pp. 199-201.
2. *Ibid.*, p. 116-17.
3. *The Possessed*, p. 253.
4. *Intruder in the Dust*, pp. 72, 88, 94, 113, 126.
5. *The Brothers Karamazov*, p. 141.
6. *Intruder in the Dust*, pp. 41-52, 84-85.
7. *Ibid.*, pp. 12 and 151.
8. *Ibid.*, p. 243.
9. *The Brothers Karamazov*, pp. 328-29.
10. See Part One, Chapter Three.
11. *Intruder in the Dust*, pp. 22, 48-49, 137.
12. *Ibid.*, pp. 155, 203-4.
13. *The Brothers Karamazov*, p. 224. See *Intruder in the Dust*, p. 199.
14. See, for example, *ibid.*, pp. 238-39.
15. See *ibid.*, p. 96, 156, and *The Brothers Karamazov*, pp. 330-31.
16. *Intruder in the Dust*, pp. 204, 210.
17. *Ibid.*, p. 149. See also p. 243.
18. *The Brothers Karamazov*, p. 262.
19. *Ibid.*, pp. 263-64.
20. *Ibid.*, p. 267.
21. See Part One, Chapter Three.
22. *Intruder in the Dust*, p. 154.
23. *The Possessed*, p. 253.
24. See *Intruder in the Dust*, p. 152, where the North is defined as an "emotional idea." Dolgoruky speaks in another context of "an idea transformed into an emotion" (See *A Raw Youth*, p. 56).
25. *Intruder in the Dust*, pp. 155-56, 202, 238-39.
26. *Ibid.*, p. 153.
27. *The Brothers Karamazov*, p. 62.
28. *Intruder in the Dust*, p. 156.
29. *Ibid.*, p. 194.
30. *Ibid.*, p. 57.
31. *Ibid.*, p. 228.

PATHS TO FREEDOM, GOODNESS AND SALVATION

Knight's Gambit and Collected Stories

1. *Knight's Gambit*, p. 10, and *The Brothers Karamazov*, p. 8.
2. *A Raw Youth*, p. 533.
3. *Ibid.*, pp. 520-21.
4. *Knight's Gambit*, p. 49. See also p. 52.
5. *Ibid.*, p. 47.
6. *Ibid.*, p. 131.
7. *Ibid.*, p. 103.
8. *Ibid.*, p. 66.
9. *Collected Stories*, p. 401.

Requiem for a Nun

1. See *Requiem for a Nun*, p. 133: "you know: just anguish for the sake of anguish, like that Russian or somebody who wrote a whole book about suffering, not suffering for or about anything, just suffering. . . ." Temple probably means the author of *The Brothers Karamazov*. Let us add that it is also perhaps by association with Raskolnikov, Dmitri Karamazov, and the Russian novelist himself that Gowan Stevens speaks of the mines of Siberia (see p. 202).
2. See *Faulkner in the University*, p. 96.
3. *Requiem for a Nun*, p. 10.
4. On the imprecision of dates see Cleanth Brooks, *William Faulkner: The Yoknapatawpha Country* (New Haven: Yale University Press, 1963), pp. 394-95.
5. *Requiem for a Nun*, pp. 42, 100, etc.
6. *Ibid.*, pp. 71, 92.
7. *Ibid.*, p. 278.
8. *The Brothers Karamazov*, p. 264.
9. *Requiem for a Nun*, p. 189.
10. *Ibid.*, p. 200.
11. *The Brothers Karamazov*, p. 540.
12. *Requiem for a Nun*, p. 276.
13. *The Brothers Karamazov*, p. 627.
14. *Ibid.*, pp. 335-36.
15. *Requiem for a Nun*, pp. 275-76.
16. *Faulkner in the University*, p. 196.
17. See *Requiem for a Nun*, pp. 158-59, and *The Brothers Karamazov*, p. 670.
18. *Requiem for a Nun*, p. 179, and *The Brothers Karamazov*, p. 278.
19. *Requiem for a Nun*, pp. 62-63, and *Crime and Punishment*, p. 233.
20. *Requiem for a Nun*, pp. 87-88, and *Crime and Punishment*, p. 285.
21. *Requiem for a Nun*, p. 144, and *Crime and Punishment*, p. 285.
22. *Crime and Punishment*, p. 370.
23. *Requiem for a Nun*, p. 196.
24. *Crime and Punishment*, p. 293.
25. *Requiem for a Nun*, p. 182.
26. *The Idiot*, p. 109.
27. *The Possessed*, p. 205.
28. *The Brothers Karamazov*, p. 144.
29. *Requiem for a Nun*, p. 268.
30. *Crime and Punishment*, p. 461.
31. *The Idiot*, pp. 209, 515.
32. See, for instance, *The Possessed*, pp. 166, 169, and Dolgoruky's "document" in *A Raw Youth*, pp. 546-47.
33. *Requiem for a Nun*, pp. 85, 156.
34. *Ibid.*, p. 208.

35. *Ibid.*, p. 163.
36. *The Brothers Karamazov*, p. 246.
37. *Ibid.*, p. 253.
38. *Ibid.*, p. 334.
39. *Ibid.*, p. 254.
40. *Ibid.*, p. 253.
41. *Requiem for a Nun*, pp. 276-77.
42. *Crime and Punishment*, pp. 370, 406.
43. *The Brothers Karamazov*, pp. 540-41, 627-28.
44. *Requiem for a Nun*, p. 133.
45. *Ibid.*, p. 278.
46. *The Brothers Karamazov*, pp. 322, 325-27.
47. *Ibid.*, p. 254.
48. *Ibid.*, p. 255.
49. *Ibid.*, pp. 336-38.
50. *Ibid.*, pp. 211-13.
51. *Ibid.*, pp. 336-38.
52. *Requiem for a Nun*, pp. 268, 283.
53. *The Brothers Karamazov*, p. 334, and *Requiem for a Nun*, p. 206. See *Light in August*, p. 461: "that peace in which to sin and be forgiven which is the life of man."
54. *Requiem for a Nun*, p. 155.
55. *The Brothers Karamazov*, p. 223.
56. *Ibid.*
57. *Requiem for a Nun*, p. 163.
58. *Ibid.*, p. 286.
59. *Ibid.*
60. *The Brothers Karamazov*, p. 585.
61. *Requiem for a Nun*, p. 281.
62. *Ibid.*, pp. 277-78, 283.
63. *Ibid.*, p. 276.
64. *The Brothers Karamazov*, p. 141.
65. *Ibid.*, p. 55.
66. *Ibid.*, p. 57.
67. *Ibid.*, p. 337.
68. See, among others, Walter J. Slatoff, *Quest for Failure* (Ithaca, N. Y.: Cornell University Press, 1960), p. 209, and Frederick J. Hoffman, *William Faulkner* (New York: Twayne Publishers, Inc., 1961), p. 110.
69. *The Possessed*, pp. 253-54.
70. *Requiem for a Nun*, p. 208.
71. *The Brothers Karamazov*, p. 686.
72. *Ibid.*, p. 684.
73. *Requiem for a Nun*, pp. 134, 150-51.
74. *Ibid.*, pp. 85-88, and *The Brothers Karamazov*, p. 64.
75. *Requiem for a Nun*, pp. 88, 199-200, and *The Brothers Karamazov*, pp. 336-37, 698.
76. *Requiem for a Nun*, pp. 152, 162, and *The House of the Dead*, p. 7.
77. *Requiem for a Nun*, pp. 68-69, 149, and *The Brothers Karamazov*, p. 213.

A Fable

1. Philip Blair Rice, "Faulkner's Crucifixion" in Frederick J. Hoffman and Olga W Vickery, *William Faulkner: Three Decades of Criticism* (East Lansing, Mich.: Michigan State University, 1960), pp. 375, 379.
2. Delmore Schwartz, "*A Fable* by William Faulkner," *Perspectives USA*, 10 (Winter, 1955), 134-35.

3. Heinrich Straumann, "An American Interpretation of Existence: Faulkner's *A Fable*" in *William Faulkner: Three Decades of Criticism*, p. 354.
4. Irving Malin, *William Faulkner: An Interpretation* (Stanford, Calif.: Stanford University Press, 1957), p. 11.
5. Frederick J. Hoffman, "William Faulkner: An Introduction," in *William Faulkner: Three Decades of Criticism*, pp. 40-41.
6. Irving Howe, *William Faulkner: A Critical Study* (New York: Vintage Books, 1962), p. 271.
7. See *A Fable*, p. 267, and *Crime and Punishment*, p. 461.
8. See *A Fable*, p. 366, and *The Brothers Karamazov*, p. 285.
9. Straumann, *loc. cit.*.
10. On destiny see *A Fable*, pp. 291-92.
11. *Ibid.*, pp. 150-51, 311.
12. *Ibid.*, pp. 329-30.
13. *Ibid.*, p. 329.
14. *The Brothers Karamazov*, pp. 676, 681.
15. *Ibid.*, p. 334.
16. *A Fable*, p. 181, and *The Brothers Karamazov*, p. 684. See also Magda's excursus on evil, somewhat reminiscent of *Sanctuary* (*A Fable*, pp. 286-87).
17. Straumann, *op. cit.*, pp. 351-52.
18. *Ibid.*, p. 371.
19. See Eliseo Vivas, "The Two Dimensions of Reality," in René Wellek (ed.), *Dostoevsky* (Englewood Cliffs, N. J.: Prentice-Hall, 1962), pp. 85-86.
20. *A Fable*, p. 186.
21. *Ibid.*, p. 5.
22. *The Idiot*, p. 393. The idea is found in very nearly the same terms in *The Brothers Karamazov*, p. 334.
23. *The Possessed*, p. 726.
24. *A Fable*, p. 347.
25. See Straumann *op. cit.*, pp. 354-55.
26. *A Fable*, pp. 347-48.
27. See *A Fable*, p. 352, and *The Stockholm Address* in *William Faulkner: Three Decades of Criticism*, p. 348.
28. See *New Orleans Sketches*, pp. 101-110.
29. *A Fable*, pp. 285, 300.
30. *Ibid.*, p. 13. See also pp. 352-53.
31. *The Brothers Karamazov*, pp. 271, 269.
32. *A Fable*, p. 352.
33. *Ibid.*, p. 271.
34. *Ibid.*, p. 299.
35. *The Brothers Karamazov*, pp. 268-69.
36. *A Fable*, p. 328.
37. *The Brothers Karamazov*, p. 268.
38. *A Fable*, p. 270.
39. *The Brothers Karamazov*, pp. 268-69.
40. *A Fable*, pp. 258-59.
41. *The Brothers Karamazov*, pp. 270-71. See also p. 329.
42. See *A Fable*, pp. 42, 260-61.
43. *Ibid.*, p. 203.
44. *Ibid.*, p. 399.
45. *Ibid.*, p. 350.
46. *Ibid.*, p. 203.
47. *Ibid.*
48. Straumann *op. cit.*, pp. 358-60, 362, 370.
49. *Crime and Punishment*, pp. 229-30.
50. *The Brothers Karamazov*, pp. 268-69.

51. *Crime and Punishment*, pp. 229-30, and *The Brothers Karamazov*, p. 268.
52. *A Fable*, p. 30.
53. *Crime and Punishment*, p. 231.
54. *A Fable*, p. 181.
55. *Ibid.*, p. 260. See also p. 186.
56. *Ibid.*, p. 260.
57. *Crime and Punishment*, p. 230.
58. *The Brothers Karamazov*, p. 267.
59. *Ibid.*, p. 266, and *A Fable*, p. 68.
60. *The Brothers Karamazov*, p. 259 ff., and *A Fable*, p. 68.
61. *The Brothers Karamazov*, p. 271-72.
62. *A Fable*, p. 327.
63. *Ibid.*, pp. 302-9.
64. *Ibid.*, p. 304.
65. *The Brothers Karamazov*, p. 267.
66. *Ibid.*, p. 263, and *A Fable*, p. 349.
67. *The Brothers Karamazov*, p. 260, and *A Fable*, p. 349.
68. *A Fable*, pp. 205-6.
69. *Ibid.*, pp. 362-68.
70. *Ibid.*, p. 260.
71. *The Brothers Karamazov*, p. 270. See also p. 266: "We have corrected Thy work and have founded it upon *miracle, mystery* and *authority.*"
72. *A Fable*, p. 236.
73. *The Brothers Karamazov*, p. 265: "he (man) is weak and vile."
74. *Crime and Punishment*, p. 401.
75. *A Fable*, pp. 352-53.
76. *The Brothers Karamazov*, p. 272.
77. *A Fable*, p. 343.
78. *The Brothers Karamazov*, p. 267.
79. *A Fable*, p. 343.
80. *The Brothers Karamazov*, p. 259. See also p. 264.
81. *A Fable*, p. 348.
82. *Ibid.*, p. 348.
83. *Ibid.*, p. 350.
84. *The Brothers Karamazov*, p. 262.
85. *Ibid.*, p. 267.
86. *Ibid.*, p. 265.
87. *A Fable*, p. 365.
88. *Ibid.*, p. 347.
89. *The Brothers Karamazov*, p. 262. See also pp. 263-64.
90. *Ibid.*, p. 263.
91. *Ibid.*, p. 260.
92. *A Fable*, p. 349. Our underlining.
93. *Ibid.*, p. 350.
94. *The Brothers Karamazov*, p. 239.
95. *Ibid.*, p. 628. See also *Crime and Punishment*, p. 142.
96. *A Fable*, p. 351.
97. *The Brothers Karamazov*, pp. 248-49.
98. See *ibid.*, p. 301: "The windows of his room looked out into the garden and our garden was a shady one, with old trees in it which were coming into bud. The first birds of spring were flitting in the branches, chirruping and singing at the windows. And looking at them and admiring them, he began suddenly begging their forgiveness too, 'Birds of heaven, happy birds, forgive me, for I have sinned against you too.'" The bird plays a similar role in *The Sound and the Fury*. See Lawrence Bowling, "Faulkner: The Theme

of Pride in *The Sound and the Fury*," *Modern Fiction Studies*, XI, 2 (Summer, 1965), 135-36.
99. *The Brothers Karamazov*, p. 266, and *A Fable*, p. 365.
100. *A Fable*, pp. 369-70.
101. *Ibid.*, p. 416.
102. *Ibid.*, p. 126.
103. See Heinrich Straumann, *op. cit.*, p. 353.
104. *A Fable*, p. 400.
105. *Crime and Punishment*, pp. 370, 463.
106. *The Brothers Karamazov*, pp. 380-81.
107. *The Possessed*, p. 144.
108. *A Fable*, p. 252.
109. *The Possessed*, p. 141. Faulkner knew the name in its English spelling Marya Timofyevna. It is worth noting that Levine in *A Fable* (p. 89) bears a name very like that of one of the main characters of *Anna Karenina*.
110. *The Possessed*, p. 141, and *A Fable*, p. 213.

X

THE LEAVETAKING (1957-62)

After compromising himself with Dostoevsky to the point of making himself his propagandist, Faulkner begins a retreat which is as sudden as it is determined. *The Town*, a chronicle of rural Yoknapatawpha county, owes little to the Russian writer. Perhaps the genre must be taken into account. The rustic novels such as *As I Lay Dying* or *The Hamlet* have never been major figures in the pattern we have been tracing. In addition, *The Hamlet*, written in large part between November, 1955, and September, 1956, includes short stories published much earlier (1932-34), and the short story is a domain in which the influence is not decisive. It is nonetheless significant that, at the end of his career, Faulkner takes paths which have always deflected him from Dostoevsky. *The Reivers*, his last book, is a picaresque novel through which the breeze of humor blows as through the sleepy countryside on a May weekend. Only *The Mansion* restores the ties with the model, but during this last flirtation it is the old image which springs back, not the philosopher but the painter of crime, the inspiration of the dark novels.

It looks as though, distancing himself from the thinker, Faulkner wished to draw nearer to the story-teller he used to love so much. In 1954, he had received from Dostoevsky all of the precepts he could hope to obtain: the maximum and perhaps even more—in any case, more than he was capable of assimilating spontaneously, as *Requiem for a Nun* and *A Fable* seem to indicate. Finally freed from fatality, heading for salvation, knowing how to sublimate evil into good, he could renounce doing violence to his feelings, jettison the ballast which encumbered him, and become himself once more after temporarily wandering astray. The backward movement is abrupt and, all things considered, easily accomplished, although the benefits derived are not immediately felt. In *The Mansion*, however, the novelist abandons preaching and rediscovers his earlier manner and greatness. The Fate in which Mink Snopes believes seems to determine him as jealously as Joe Christmas; before his crime, the killer visits the same places, meets the same people—more or less—as Quentin Compson and Raskolnikov; Hines, the fanatic of *Light in August*, is reborn under the mask of another hero; Miss Reba, the madam of the bordello in *Sanctuary*, reappears in a starring role in *The Reivers*. Despite the fact that the Snopes trilogy was conceived in 1925, nothing obligated Faulkner to go back to his earlier manner when he actually wrote it. As for *The Reivers*, it exploits Dostoevskian ideas, accumulated during more than thirty years, but without falling into pomposity, generally expressing thoughts in terms of concrete acts. On the other hand, the analogies are blurred: the lesson of freedom, too well assimilated, turns against the Master, and Faulkner henceforth indulges in more and more audacious variations on Dostoevsky's teachings—to such a degree that the very idea of borrowing can be questioned. It is with the traces left by Dostoevsky, rather than with any of his texts, that Faulkner's last novel is apparently connected. The influence seems to act only indirectly, not under the pressure of an authority one has actually consulted, but through an earlier contact, an old friendship, the memory of which loses its clarity as it enriches the global context of experience. The spell is broken: the philosopher has fulfilled the task assigned to him by Faulkner; he has offered him Zossima's serenity and Alyosha's active optimism. The time has come to part and, for Faulkner, to recover all of his independence. This is one explanation, among others, of the break of continuity observed between *A Fable* and *The Town*. Once again, the curve of the Dostoevskian influence follows, if it does not determine, that of the work.

Faulkner's moving away from the philosopher does not mean that he wants to discard all of Dostoevsky. Once his spiritual evolution is accomplished, he simply wants to revert to the artistic tenets in which he believed in his youth. But history never repeats itself, and Faulkner's last three novels cannot be confused with *Sanctuary, Light in August,* or *Absalom, Absalom!*. The climate is less violent and the tone more peaceful, even in the portrayal of crime. The novelist does not repudiate his philosophical apprenticeship: he breaks with exposition and becomes absorbed once more in situations whose concrete rendering—he must be aware of the fact—suits him far better. In their general outlines, the divergent tendencies of the years 1929-34 and 1938-54 are seen to combine to such an extent that the picture appears rather confused. The admiration for Dostoevsky shown in Virginia, Japan, and elsewhere does not correspond to any clearly identifiable borrowing. In two of the three novels, the resemblances vanish; only in *The Mansion* does the influence flare up again, but it manifests itself rather on the level of novelistic material than in the area of ideas. Similarly, the parallelisms of episodes and psychological traits in *The Town* are more important than those of concepts. *The Reivers* is the sole exception in this regard, but even in this instance how far away we are from the intimate relationship of earlier times.

What confirms the movement away from speculation, the return to storytelling and the relaxing of the ties to Dostoevsky—which have become as supple as those at the time of *Absalom, Absalom!* —is the relative decline of *The Brothers Karamazov* at the profit of *Crime and Punishment*. This appears clearly in *The Mansion*. Here the portrait of the monomaniac once more eclipses the doctrine of Zossima and "The Grand Inquisitor." However, the balance of the years 1957-62 does not reveal a radical reversal of their respective contributions: although it diminishes, the influence of *The Brothers Karamazov* remains superior and even incontestably dominant in *The Town* and *The Reivers*. On the other hand, the image of Raskolnikov wins out in vividness over all other "borrowings." While the theories that blurred it fade away, it reappears intact in all of its fascination. For that matter, it is already recognizable in *Requiem for a Nun*. Since 1929, since Quentin Compson, it is one of the constants, one of the foundations of the Faulknerian universe. More precisely, its matrix, the

THE LEAVETAKING (1957-1962)

first part of *Crime and Punishment* (I, 4 and 5) which impregnated the dark novels, engenders thirty years later the last murderer depicted by the writer: Mink Snopes. We reread in *The Mansion* all the preparations for the crime, mixed perhaps with the memories of the conversations of Raskolnikov and Porfiry (III, 5 and IV, 5). As for *The Brothers Karamazov*, while little by little fading out in relation to *Crime and Punishment*, "The Grand Inquisitor" (V, 5) and the sermons of Book Six (VI, 3), which so recently were of obsessive importance, now must compete with passages whose action we have located between 1929 and 1934 (IV, 1; XI, 7 and 8). Most unfortunately, the inadequate evidence leads only to rather fuzzy conclusions.

Let us attempt to estimate for the last time the role the Russian's other novels might have played. Nothing new here. The inventory comes down, at the very most, to a timid question mark in regard to *The Eternal Husband, The House of the Dead,* and *The Idiot.* However, the analogies with *The Possessed* (second and third parts) multiply in *The Town* and *The Mansion* and even border on borrowing; but although probable, indeed more likely than ever, the influence could have acted only from a distance and intermittantly.

The Town (1957)

After his abortive incursion into parable and philosophy, Faulkner wisely falls back on more modest aims, while Dostoevsky's control is attenuated. With *The Town* (1957) and *The Mansion* (1959), the Snopes chronicle sketched in *The Hamlet* (1940) is completed. The theme of *The Town* does not lack power; ¹ ⁺ the ascension of Flem Snopes, an adventurer who undermines the community and its traditional values, is seen from a regional perspective and rather minimized, so that ambition and cupidity, deprived of their Balzacian exaggeration and sometimes portrayed with Dickensian humor, find themselves reduced to the scale of Trollope.

The plot resembles, in certain respects, that of *The Possessed,* and this is the most striking affinity that can be found. In the two novels, one or more chroniclers—three in *The Town*—attempt to describe the invasion of a small town by a rabble surging up from outside and guided by a leader. It matters little that the purpose is political in Dostoevsky and basely financial in Faulkner: their upstarts show the same cynicism, the same lack of honor and probity. It is enough to shift the basic materials of *The Possessed* the slightest bit to obtain those of *The Town*:

> I have already hinted that some low fellows of different sorts had made their appearance amongst us. . . . Yet the most worthless fellows suddenly gained predominant influence, began loudly criticising everything sacred, though till then they had not dared to open their mouths, while the leading people, who had till then so satisfactorily kept the upper hand, began listening to them and holding their peace, some even simpered approval in a most shameless way. . . . there was still among us a small group who held themselves aloof from the beginning and even locked themselves up.[1]

> Snopeses had to be watched constantly like an invasion of snakes or wildcats and . . . Uncle Gavin and Ratliff were doing it or trying to because nobody else in Jefferson seemed to recognize the danger.[2]

Corresponding to Faulkner's snakes and vermin are Luke's "swine" (8: 32-36) which Dostoevsky mentions in his epigraph.[3] Flem Snopes and Verhovensky thus both storm the town with their troops, but the similarity of their purposes, vices, and roles, too banal in itself, justifies no deductions unless we have clearer indications at our disposal. The extract quoted comes from the third part of *The Possessed*, more exactly from the beginning of the chapter entitled "The Fête." Let us sketch the situation in a few words. Verhovensky has ingratiated himself with the governor's wife by "the grossest flattery"[4]—he "ate, drunk, and almost slept in [her] house"[5] (gossiping tongues suggested: in her bed)[6]—and has done this exclusively to achieve his purposes. In addition, the charity fête organized by his protectress, thanks to his machinations, gives rise to a terrible scandal. The same elements figure in *The Town*. Flem owes his advancement to Eula's liaison with the mayor of the town: Faulkner's *Streber* goes well beyond Verhovensky, for he trades his wife for a career. The ball of the "Cotillion Club"—as the women's club calls itself—is accompanied by incidents comparable to those described in *The Possessed*. The scandal occurs when, after laborious preparations, Eula Snopes and her lover dance in one another's arms and Gavin Stevens attacks De Spain.[7] In Dostoevsky, the explosion

THE LEAVETAKING (1957-1962)

is of different kind: it results not from adultery and the jealousy of a rival, but the insolence of scoundrels;[8] in addition, the incident is detailed in more than ten pages, while, in *The Town*, it barely takes up three; finally Flem, contrary to Verhovensky, is in no way responsible for the affair. Although one can hardly maintain that "The Fête" and "The End of the Fête" (III, chapters I and II) are faithfully reproduced by Charles Mallison in the third chapter of *The Town*, the coincidence of the stories, taken as a whole, remains no less obvious.

This is not the only example. Other details reflect *The Possessed*; for instance, the obscene photographs which Montgomery Ward Snopes puts to such a lucrative use[9] and which Lyamshin already slid into the Gospel-woman's pack;[10] or better still, the illusory character of virginity, previously underscored in *The Sound and the Fury* and likened to a "prejudice" by Verhovensky.[11]

Like Raskolnikov, like so many Faulknerian heroes, Flem Snopes suffers from an obsession[12] which makes him forget everything and which consequently cuts him off from society:[13] the respectability he aims for serves only to provide a better setting for his fortune. In this rural social climber is incarnated a type which haunted both these novelists throughout their lives: the alienated monomaniac. Taciturn and impotent, a money-grubber and an embezzler, he has neither the persuasive eloquence of his Russian brothers, nor their universal ambition, nor above all, Valkovsky's sensuality; he preserves, nonetheless, the untiring commitment to doing evil, and solitude. Although rather simplified in comparison with the Russians—Flem is nearly a character from a morality play: Greed personified—he is their equal by the density of his malefic halo.

If circumstances cause Flem Snopes to play the role of the eternal cuckold and Gavin Stevens, who fails with both the mother and the daughter, that of the eternal suitor, Manfred de Spain is, according to the latter, the eternal bachelor, or better, the eternal lover: .

"I mean, like Uncle Gavin said: that there are some men who are incorrigibly and invincibly bachelor no matter how often they marry, just as some men are doomed and emasculate husbands if they never find a woman to take them."[14]

The definition seems to spring just as it is from *The Eternal Husband*, in particular from the passage (IV, "The Wife, the Husband and the Lover") that we have compared to the portrait of Charlotte in *The Wild Palms*:

> Velchaninov was convinced that there really was such a type of woman; but, on the other hand, he was also convinced that there was a type of husband corresponding to that woman, whose sole vocation was to correspond with that feminine type. To his mind, the essence of such a husband lay in his being, so to say, "the eternal husband," or rather of being all his life, a husband and nothing more. "Such a man is born and grows up only to be a husband, and, having married, is promptly transformed into a supplement of his wife, even when he happens to have an unmistakable character of his own.[15]

The work was not found in Faulkner's library but this, of course, does not prevent him from having read it. It is, in any case, difficult not to speculate when confronted with two such obvious parallels.

The platonic loves of Gavin remind us of *The Idiot* but, with this exception, this hero has little in common with Myshkin; however Gavin is, as Cleanth Brooks has said,[16] an emulator of Don Quixote, an archetype which the prince also imitates. Stevens' passions for Eula and Linda Snopes are tailored, rather freely, on another well known pattern, since they succeed one another rather than coexist as was the case in *Knight's Gambit*. It is unnecessary to stress, in this regard, the similarity with *The Brothers Karamazov* and, especially, *A Raw Youth*, in which Versilov falls in love in turn with Katerina Nikolaevna and her stepdaughter.[17]

There is nothing to be said about Eula, with the possible exception that this unfaithful wife provokes a discussion in Gavin's family. Is it proper to invite her to the ball? Should Stevens' sister visit her?[18] Obviously, if these bourgeois prejudices are shared by certain Dostoevskian characters,[19] it is because they were common during that period, and it would not be difficult to find other examples in nineteenth and twentieth century literature. Linda, Eula's natural daughter, is hardly more interesting for us. We will point out only her hatred of Flem, whom she believes to be her father, an extension of one of the Dostoevskian themes of *Light in August* and *Absalom, Absalom!*. In conformity with the Freudian prescription, Linda has a split personality in relation to Flem: sometimes loving and full of respect, sometimes in revolt.[20] Ratliff and Gavin also disintegrate on occasion.[21]

In contrast to the bountiful harvest yielded by *Requiem for a Nun, A Fable*, and even the dark novels, these are but a few scattered weeds. *The Town*, which has neither the grandeur of *The Sound and the Fury* nor the intellectual pretensions of *A Fable*, does not evoke Dostoevsky in either its atmosphere or its significance. Of the earlier infatuation, there is no trace or nearly so—except in the confidences of the lecturer! Barely a few situations and a few outworn ideas: the distinction between truth and justice,[22] the union of pride and abjection,[23] the rejection of nothingness,[24] the tyranny of the Church.[25] We are constrained to state that the withdrawal of the Russian writer does not coincide with a rewakening of inspiration. All things considered, if *The Town* is not a failure, neither would one rank it among Faulkner's successes.

The Mansion (1959)

In the last panel of the triptych, which contrasts with *The Town* only by its technical skill and vigorous colors, the Dostoevskian resemblances grow stronger but constitute, in the final analysis, little more than a thin scattering of details.

They are first of all, ideas or attitudes formulated randomly throughout the novel: the contradictions of the heart;[1] man's invincible resistance;[2] the mistrust of abstractions;[3] the certitude that the racial problem will be resolved only by a profound spiritual change;[4] the necessity of pardoning offenses[5] and of *doing* good, efficaciously, by acting in the world of practical affairs;[6] the terrible gift of freedom.[7] Centered on Mink Snopes, the avenger of his own honor and, quite despite himself, of Jefferson— Mink plots Flem's death during twenty-eight years in prison— *The Mansion* underlines the idea of fatality. But this seems less a conviction of the author than a belief of the hero[8] which, by permeating everything,[9] links this book to the first novels. On the other hand, evil is, as usual, minimized[10] or transformed into good, since Mink's crime signifies the elimination of Flem: the epilogue shows the city of Jefferson purged of a brood that had momentarily governed it.

It is superfluous to insist again on the psychological particularities, situations, or social groups studied earlier: the splitting of a character;[11] the inevitable trial scene, a repetition of that of *The Town*;[12] the views of prison life that one might say were borrowed from *The Wild Palms* or *The House of the Dead*;[13] the passion which Gavin Stevens bears for Linda and which is starting to affect his nephew Charles Mallison;[14] the image of a woman *quaerens quem devoret*;[15] the ritualism that impregnates the death of Mink—lying towards the East on the Earth, a voracious mother who calls the human dust back to her;[16] the affective problems raised by Linda's paternity,[17] in which those of *Light in August* or *The Possessed* are perhaps echoed; lastly the person of Miss Reba,[18] the buxom and garish madam of *Sanctuary*, that Faulkner was to introduce once more into the picaresque world of *The Reivers*.

Up to this point there is nothing clear cut nor very arresting: some vague reminiscences of earlier novels, scraps gleaned in the course of earlier readings or, quite simply, fortuitous analogies. *The Mansion*, finished in Charlottesville on March 9, 1959,[19] was, however, born during a period in which Faulkner spoke admiringly of Dostoevsky and the Russian novel in general. Already in *The Town*, Ratliff bore the names of a distant slavic ancestor, Vladimir Kyrilytch,[20] and as early as 1954, the name of Marya, the corporal's half-sister, endowed *A Fable* with an imperceptible Russian flavor. The slavic exoticism intensifies suddenly in *The Mansion* when Vladimir Kyrilytch Ratliff meets Myra Allanovna[21] in New York and receives from her—who sells them!—two neckties valued at the exorbitant price of one hundred and fifty dollars. The honest Ratliff intends to pay for them despite everything, and it is then that she seizes a lighter and threatens to burn the money, sketching Nastasya Filippovna's dramatic gesture in *The Idiot*.[22] The scene in some ways bears a greater resemblance and in other ways a lesser resemblance to that of Dostoevsky than the similar passage in *The Hamlet*. More, because it is a woman and a Russian to boot who conceives this extravagance; less, because she stops in time, because Ratliff does not have a passion for money and because, in any case, Myra does not wish to torture him. The coincidence could be simply accidental the first time; here it is all the more puzzling by virtue of the Russian context in which Faulkner situates the action. The repetition supports the hypothesis of a reading of *The Idiot*, or, as has already been suggested, of a detailed summary of its plot.

The Mansion is a sequel to *The Town*, the themes are similar or, rather, complementary. Flem Snopes reigns over Jefferson, and it remains only for him to disappear: at the pinnacle of his power, he allows himself to be killed by his cousin Mink, who dies in his turn. Thus the wolves eat one another, when they are not killed by the bullets of the townspeople. In *The Possessed*, we assist at the defeat of the forces of Evil: one confesses, another has himself arrested, Verhovensky flees after executing Shatov, Stavrogin commits suicide, the secret society is destroyed, and the town, purified of its parasites, is reborn. *The Town* and *The Mansion* retrace the same story: that of the rise and fall of the Snopeses, for, henceforth, the good no longer fears anyone. In addition to the general subject matter, several details can also be linked to *The Possessed*. Let us pass over the dirty photos exploited by Montgomery Ward Snopes:[23] they were present in *The Town*. The allusions to contemporary politics furnish more solid arguments. The communist party in Jefferson includes only three members or sympathizers: two Finnish refugees and Linda herself,[24] whose small meetings represent no menace to the established order comparable to the conspiracy hatched by Verhovensky nor to the Ku Klux Klan which Senator Clarence Snopes[25] first leads, and then combats out of pure opportunism. On the topic of Clarence, Faulkner hazards some opinions on despotism which recall those of *A Fable* and thus indirectly those of *Crime and Punishment* and "The Grand Inquisitor." On the other hand, by their specifically political context, the following three quotations evoke much more the chapters of *The Possessed*, entitled "A Meeting" and "Ivan the Tsarevitch" (II, chapters VII and VIII):

> not merely to beat, hammer men into insensibility and submission, but to use them; not merely to expend their inexhaustible numbers like ammunition or consume them like hogs or sheep, but to use, employ them like

mules or oxen, with one eye constant for the next furrow tomorrow or next year; using not just their competence to mark an X whenever and wherever old Will Varner ordered them to, but their capacity for passion and greed and alarm as well.[26]

to join things, anything, any organization to which human beings belonged, which he might compel or control or coerce through the emotions of religion or patriotism or just simple greed, political gravy-hunger[27]

with his own voice full of racial and religious and economic intolerance.[28]

The idea of bringing the masses into subjection is common to the three Dostoevskian novels; what changes is the objective to be attained. Raskolnikov believes "the vast mass of mankind is mere material,"[29] compares the "ordinary" man to "the cow"[30] and permits others to commit crime, but he and the Inquisitor lack Clarence's vulgar and narrowly selfish ambitions. The Inquisitor, like Clarence, raises human nature in order to dominate it, but also to assure the earthly happiness of humanity[31]—which Clarence mocks. Such are also the aims and methods of Shigalov:

He suggests as a final solution of the question the division of mankind into two unequal parts. One-tenth enjoys absolute liberty and unbounded power over the other nine-tenths. The others have to give up all individuality and become, so to speak, a herd, and, through boundless submission, will by a series of regenerations attain primaeval innocence, something like the Garden of Eden. They'll have to work, however. The measures proposed by the author for depriving nine-tenths of mankind of their freedom and transforming them into a herd through the education of whole generations are very remarkable, founded on the facts of nature and highly logical.[32]

Verhovensky, on the other hand, if he considers Shigalov "a man of genius,"[33] confesses unequivocally that he is himself "a scoundrel and not a Socialist."[34] He also wishes to reduce the crowd to "absolute submission"[35] and take advantage of its weakness:

Listen: I've reckoned them all up: a teacher who laughs with children at their God and at their cradle is on our side. The lawyer who defends an educated murderer because he is more cultured than his victims and could not help murdering them to get money is one of us. The schoolboys who murder a peasant for the sake of sensation are ours. . . . Among officials and literary men we have lots, lots, and they don't know it themselves. On the other hand, the docility of schoolboys and fools has reached an extreme pitch; the schoolmasters are bitter and bilious. On all sides we see vanity puffed up out of all proportion; brutal, monstrous appetites . . . Do you know how many we shall catch by little, ready-made ideas?. . . . But one or two generations of vice are essential now; monstrous, abject vice by which a man is transformed into a loathsome, cruel, egoistic reptile. That's what we need![36]

Verhovensky, however, aims only at destruction and, afterwards, at reigning over the ruins.[37] Faulkner rediscovers this nihilism[38] —young Flem is also called a "nihilist"[39]—among the racists and fascists of the South. There was no need to refer to *The Possessed* to denounce their attempts, but there is no doubt about the kinship of these texts.

The passage devoted to Clarence is not the only one which recalls *A Fable*. Now and again either the specter of Authority[40] or the person of Christ[41] reappears, vestiges of an idea caressed so long and assiduously that the author gives it up reluctantly. But none of this flows directly from Dostoevsky.

The characters include several maniacs. Flem, whose nest is now well feathered, no longer fits in this category; moreover, he rarely moves to the foreground in this story centered on Mink's revenge: at the most, he plays the willing victim.[42] Like Verhovensky, he does not hesitate to scuttle those who hinder him, but it matters little, for he will not escape his fate. Goodyhay, a World War II veteran turned preacher, is related to the fanatics and visionaries of *Light in August* and *The Brothers Karamazov*: Hines and Father Ferapont: "the coldly seething anchorite's eyes—the eyes of a fifth-century hermit looking at nothing from the entrance of his Mesopotamian cave—the body rigid in an immobility like a tremendous strain beneath a weight."[43] Meadowfill, who keeps close watch over his patch of ground, suffers an authentic alienation due to his mania.[44] They flank their master Mink, the pitiless and moving hero of *The Mansion*, like two disciples.

A killer tortured by an obsession, Mink often patterns his conduct on that of Raskolnikov. In his differences with Houston as well as with Flem—his two targets—he demonstrates his sense of honor and his intransigent pride.[45] Both times, he kills not out of personal interest but out of a principle:[46] the first time because Houston claimed an indemnity from him—unjustly, according to his account—for lodging his cow; the second, because his cousin Flem abandoned and, above all, ignobly betrayed him. The country bumpkin and the intellectual share an obstinate, blind pride which rests on a schematic and personal conception of the world. In addition, pride pushes them to crime and isolates them from their peers.[47] Mink, who wishes, in his own way, to be as shrewd as Raskolnikov, understands in his turn that there is quite a distance from *Kriegsspiel* to real warfare.[48] Like all of the monomaniacs modelled closely or distantly on *Crime and Punishment*—Quentin and Jason Compson, Joe Christmas, Thomas Sutpen, etc.—Mink believes in Fate, a force generally opposed to his designs, but which he expects will eventually deal justly with him. It is what he, quite summarily, calls "they."[49] Just the reverse of Raskolnikov, he does not knuckle under and finally beats Fate by sheer force of will. His views on fatality are, in fact, tainted with a very rigid Calvinism: his destiny, to be quite accurate, borders on predestination,[50] and his God is very much the one of Deuteronomy (32:35) "Vengeance and retribution are mine"—"*Old Moster jest punishes; He don't play jokes.*"[51] Mink also divides men in two classes: those who are born lucky and the others among whom he includes himself:

> He remembered how at first he had cursed his bad luck for letting them catch him but he knew better now: that there was no such thing as bad luck or good luck: you were either born a champion or not a champion and if he had been born a champion Houston not only couldn't, he wouldn't have dared, misuse him about that cow to where he had to kill him; that some folks were born to be failures and get caught always, some folks were born to be lied to and believe it, and he was one of them.[52]

We find here, in a Protestant abridgement, Raskolnikov's elucubrations on masters and slaves and his realization of his condition. In addition, Mink claims full responsibility for his acts and throws himself on his lawyer when the latter suggests that he serve his sentence in an insane asylum;[53] similarly, Rodya surges up with anger against those who accuse him of being delirious,[54] an attitude comparable to the attacks with which *The Brothers Karamazov*[55] crushes the new theory of the irresponsibility of the criminal. Mink will, therefore, go to prison unrepentant. Moreover, the freedom that Raskolnikov anticipates in vain from his crime—proof that he is "not a louse"[56] but a man—Mink can effectively enjoy, but on another level, stripped as he is of any intellectual refinement or moral sensibility.[57] As usual, the two characters alternately agree with and oppose each other. And, all things considered, Mink, whom Faulkner quite justly likens to a wild beast,[58] resembles the terrible Orlov of *The House of the Dead* (I, 4) as much as Raskolnikov:

> I can confidently say that I have never in my life met a man of such strength, of so iron a will as he. I had already seen at Tobolsk a celebrity of the same kind, formerly a brigand chief. He was a wild beast. . . . Korenev—that was the brigand's name. . . .
>
> . . . the man's (Orlov's) power of control was unlimited. . . . We saw in him nothing but unbounded energy, a thirst for action, a thirst for vengence, an eagerness to attain the object he had set before him. . . . I imagine there was no creature in the world who could have worked upon him simply by authority. He looked upon everything with surprising calmness, as though there was nothing in the universe that could astonish him.[59]

The murder of Houston and, in particular that of Flem, and their preparations are portrayed in considerable detail. Leaving the penitentiary, Mink arrives in Memphis in an atmosphere as suffocating as that fatal evening on which Raskolnikov first calls on the moneylender.[60] If it is the modern city rather than the climate that oppresses Faulkner's peasant,[61] all of Rodion's wanderings, used previously in the second part of *The Sound and the Fury*, are here again, in embryo: the flowered gardens, the walk along the river, the view from the parapet and the bridge, the stop on the bench, the encounter with the policeman who gives money to Mink (in Dostoevsky, it is Raskolnikov who gives the money), the nap after the wanderings, the solitude[62] and, the next day, the dealings with the self-proclaimed pawnbroker,[63] Quentin Compson before his suicide, Joe Christmas and Mink Snopes before their crime: all are fidgety, all obey an aimless movement, if it is to postpone only momentarily the fatal act. Despite their respective situations, the three heroes celebrate the same "rite" prior to the execution, a rite whose development derives, at least in *The Sound and the Fury*—that is, in the earliest case—almost certainly from *Crime and Punishment*. This novelistic form, fundamental to the Faulknerian universe, seems to owe its origin to a Dostoevskian reminiscence.

Linda, instead of preventing the murder of her "father," guides the avenging arm of Mink from afar. We are dealing here with the parricide by proxy of which Smerdyakov accuses Ivan Karamazov:[64] the one most guilty is not the one whom you would think. Toward Gavin Stevens, still impervious to sex although he finally marries Melisandre Backus, Linda takes the well-known attitude of matchmaker:[65] she tries to unite him to another woman. This behavior, we have said repeatedly, is common in Dostoevsky after *Poor People*, a work in Faulkner's possession since 1932.[66] Gavin never sleeps with Linda, nor does Dyevushkin with Varvara: love and sex remain irremediably separate. Let us note that at the moment when Gavin kisses Linda goodbye, he conceives an idea that would not be unworthy of *The Idiot*:

he thought with terror *How did it go? the man "whose irresistible attraction to women was that simply by being in their presence he gave them to convince themselves that he was capable of any sacrifice for them."*[67]

Do you know that she may love you now more than anyone, and in such a way that the more she torments you, the more she loves you? . . . Some women want to be loved like that, and that's just her character. And your love and your character must impress her! Do you know that a woman is capable of torturing a man with her cruelty and mockery without the faintest twinge of conscience, because she'll think every time she looks at you: 'I'm tormenting him to death now, but I'll make up for it with my love, later.' "[68]

With *The Mansion*, the Dostoevskian influence has a last revival before being extinguished.

The Reivers (1962)

In his last novel, Faulkner takes up once more the philosophical themes of the preceding period: freedom, choice, evil. Only the point of view is different: the insistence on the *ethos* of the gentleman and the humorous, indeed picaresque, tone with which the most serious problems are handled. Did the novelist feel that he had failed in the didactic genre? Was he tired of playing prophet? Did the creator of so many killers and damned souls want to breathe, at least once, a less polluted air? However that may be, there is no break of continuity between certain episodes of *The Mansion*[1] and *The Reivers*: the climate is the same despite the interest in the ethical. It is this latter aspect that is of interest to us: the final stage of an evolution begun under the influence of the Russian writer which must basically remain dependent on him right up until the end.

The hero, Lucius Priest, like young Chick of *Intruder in the Dust* is one of those noble-minded children that Dostoevsky loved so much. Like Chick and like Kolya of *The Brothers Karamazov* he does not quit until the enterprise has succeeded. *The Reivers* glorifies effort and perseverance in action much more explicitly— and much less Christianly[2]—than Dostoevsky does beneath the features of Alyosha.

The kinship with *Intruder in the Dust* and other works of that period deals primarily with the question of free will. Without saying anything new on this point, Faulkner finally specifies how he reconciles the aspiration to freedom with his innate sense of determinism: "assuming of course that you accept my definition of intelligence: which is the ability to cope with environment: which means to accept environment yet still retain at least something of personal liberty."[3] We will not dwell on the image—the cliché one might now say—of the individual bent beneath the burden of choice,[4] nor on the uncertainty which surrounds man's decisions,[5] but we will point out once more the opposition between the Southern nationalism advocated by Gavin Stevens in 1948 and the more federal convictions of old Lucius, the narrator of *The Reivers*. The South, regarded as cursed in *Absalom, Absalom!*, then transformed into a bastion of freedom, gives way to the United States, ceding to it its attributes: "our inalienable *constitutional* right of free will and private enterprise which has made our country what it is."[6] The evolution is triple because it leads from fatality to choice, from pessimism to optimism, and subsequently from the regional to the federal level. As ridiculous as it might seem to wish to connect this panegyric of liberal democracy with Dostoevsky, who in no way shared Faulkner's pronounced taste for banks and commerce—but who, nonetheless, realized the power of money—it is, however, to this that the philosophy of *The Brothers Karamazov* can lead when it is translated in political and economic terms. And, who knows, perhaps even the author's tardy love for the U.S.A., the interest he takes, in his last days, in the mission of the native land in the largest sense, came unconsciously from Dostoevsky's lyrical praise of the great Russian nation.

The attentive reader will perceive a good many other echoes, even if it is only the antinomy of the theoretical law and the individual,[7] but the most remarkable of these in our opinion deal with evil.

No further doubt remains about its final sublimation. *The Reivers* is, in substance, a novel about the temptation of evil, the initiation into evil, although the tragic theme of *Sanctuary* is here treated in rosy colors. As in *Requiem for a Nun*, evil finds itself rehabilitated. All experience is precious, we are told, even when it is acquired on the fringes of the straight and narrow path.[8] Inevitable because it is an integral part of existence,[9] evil is, nonetheless, capable of revaluation and, therefore, of resulting in good; thus, despite his indelicacies or rather because he has been led to commit them, Lucius causes the conversion of a prostitute:[10] "Nothing is ever lost. It's too valuable."[11] In addition, each person must accept responsibility for his errors: it is no use expecting others to condemn or absolve them, it is up to the individual to expiate them, and a gentleman—a variation of an old idea—is capable of bearing anything.[12] Evil loses even its name: the narrator never calls it anything but "Non-virtue,"[13] that is the contrary of good:

> You have heard—or anyway you will—people talk about evil times or an evil generation. There are no such things. No epoch of history nor generation of human beings either ever was or is or will be big enough to hold the un-virtue of any given moment, any more than they could contain all the air of any given moment; all they can do is hope to be as little spoiled as possible during their passage through it.[14]

We are here far from Popeye's satanism. The ideas expressed in *The Reivers*, or those which support its plot, are never copied directly from Dostoevsky. However, we find two of the primordial qualities of evil, as they are defined by Ivan Karamazov's devil: its utility and its innate character. On the other hand, the refusal to punish evil committed by another evokes Zossima's advice: "Remember particularly that you cannot be a judge of any one."[15] But much more than in *Requiem for a Nun*, the Russian doctrine is made subservient to an original thought. Momentarily tangent, the two curves begin to part company. Young Lucius is very much like Alyosha thrown into the sins of the world, but a defrocked Alyosha, emptied of his ardent faith, deprived of the luminous example of the saints, confronted with the enigmas of man.

NOTES TO CHAPTER X

The Town

1. *The Possessed*, pp. 469-71.
2. *The Town*, p. 106. See also p. 112.
3. *The Possessed*, p. XI.
4. *Ibid.*, p. 352.
5. *Ibid.*, p. 317.
6. *Ibid.*, p. 503.
7. *The Town*, pp. 74-75.
8. *The Possessed*, pp. 511-22.
9. *The Town*, p. 162.
10. *The Possessed*, pp. 327-28, 399.
11. See *ibid.*, p. 546, and *The Town*, pp. 201-2.
12. *The Town*, pp. 258-59.
13. *Ibid.*, p. 276.
14. *Ibid.*, p. 73. See also p. 75.
15. *The Eternal Husband*, p. 29. However, Tolstoy made a comparable remark in *Anna Karenina* (I, xvi), and Faulkner himself attributed "natural" celibacy to the Puritanism of the Frontier. See *Essays, Speeches and Letters*, p. 14.
16. See Cleanth Brooks, *William Faulkner: The Yoknapatawpha Country* (New Haven: Yale University Press, 1963), p. 194.
17. *A Raw Youth*, p. 520.
18. *The Town*, pp. 46-47.
19. See for instance Luzhin's astonishment when Raskolnikov tells him that he has presented Sonia, a prostitute, to his mother and sister. See *Crime and Punishment*, pp. 268-69.
20. *The Town*, pp. 322-26.
21. *Ibid.*, pp. 150, 341.
22. *Ibid.*, p. 175.
23. *Ibid.*, p. 115.
24. *Ibid.*, p. 133.
25. *Ibid.*, p. 307.

The Mansion

1. See *The Mansion*, p. 7, and *The Brothers Karamazov*, p. 111.
2. *The Mansion*, p. 21.
3. *Ibid.*, p. 309.
4. *Ibid.*, p. 223.
5. *Ibid.*, p. 365.
6. See *ibid.*, p. 307, and *The Brothers Karamazov*, p. 55.
7. *The Mansion*, p. 392.
8. *Ibid.*, pp. 367, 368, 370, 373-74.
9. *Ibid.*, p. 339.
10. *Ibid.*, p. 230.
11. *Ibid.*, p. 158. See also p. 397.
12. *Ibid.*, pp. 40-42.
13. *The Mansion*, pp. 92-94.
14. *Ibid.*, pp. 113-15.
15. *Ibid.*, pp. 111, 113.
16. *Ibid.*, p. 435. See also *The Possessed*, pp. 144-45.
17. *The Mansion*, p. 135.
18. *Ibid.*, pp. 72, 73, 79.
19. *Ibid.*, p. 436.
20. *The Town*, p. 323.
21. *The Mansion*, p. 167.
22. *Ibid.*, p. 176, and *The Idiot*, pp. 162-64.
23. *The Mansion*, p. 53.
24. *Ibid.*, p. 213.
25. *Ibid.*, p. 302.
26. *Ibid.*, p. 301.
27. *Ibid.*, pp. 303-4.
28. *Ibid.*, p. 306.
29. *Crime and Punishment*, p. 233.
30. *Ibid.*, p. 232.
31. *The Brothers Karamazov*, pp. 267-68, 271.
32. *The Possessed*, pp. 410-11.
33. *Ibid.*, p. 424.
34. *Ibid.*, p. 427.
35. *Ibid.*, p. 425.
36. *Ibid.*, pp. 427-28.
37. *Ibid.*, pp. 428-29.
38. *Ibid.*, p. 426.
39. *The Mansion*, p. 229.
40. *Ibid.*, p. 160.
41. *Ibid.*, p. 280.
42. *Ibid.*, pp. 415-16.
43. *Ibid.*, p. 279, and *The Brothers Karamazov*, pp. 172-73, 175.
44. *The Mansion*, 338.
45. *Ibid.*, p. 22.
46. *Ibid.*, p. 34.
47. *Ibid.*, pp. 392-93.
48. *Ibid.*, pp. 22, 415-16.
49. *Ibid.*, p. 6.
50. *Ibid.*, pp. 89-90.
51. *Ibid.*, p. 398. See also p. 406. On this point see Cleanth Brooks, *op. cit.*, pp. 231-32.
52. *The Mansion*, pp. 89-90.
53. *Ibid.*, p. 46.
54. *Crime and Punishment*, pp. 224-25, 305-6.

55. *The Brothers Karamazov*, pp. 64-65 and 790-91.
56. *Crime and Punishment*, p. 369.
57. *The Mansion*, pp. 432, 434.
58. *Ibid.*, pp. 373, 393.
59. *The House of the Dead*, p. 53.
60. *The Mansion*, pp. 283-84.
61. See *Crime and Punishment*, p. 49: "the huge houses that hemmed him in and weighed upon him."
62. *Ibid.*, pp. 41-55, and *The Mansion*, p. 285.
63. *Ibid.*, pp. 284-87.
64. *Ibid.*, p. 373 and 422 and *The Brothers Karamazov*, pp. 655, 661, and 665.
65. See *The Mansion*, pp. 241 and 252.
66. See *William Faulkner's Library—A Catalogue* compiled by Joseph Blotner (Charlottesville, Va.: University of Virginia Press, 1964), p. 82.
67. *The Mansion*, 424.
68. *The Idiot*, p. 347.

The Reivers

1. *The Mansion*, pp. 81, 317-18.
2. *The Reivers*, pp. 247, 279.
3. *Ibid.*, p. 121.
4. *Ibid.*, p. 66.
5. *Ibid.*, p. 58.
6. *Ibid.*, p. 215 (Our underlining). See also p. 234.
7. *Ibid.*, p. 243.
8. *Ibid.*, pp. 104-5.
9. *Ibid.*, pp. 174-75.
10. *Ibid.*, pp. 159-60.
11. *Ibid.*, p. 302.
12. *Ibid.*
13. *Ibid.*, pp. 62, 89.
14. *Ibid.*, p. 52.
15. *The Brothers Karamazov*, p. 336.

CONCLUSION

At the end of a study often more revealing about confluences than about influences, we must attempt to sort out the latter a little more clearly—a dangerous enterprise in view of the absence of external and positive proofs, but one which we have, nonetheless, already begun on the level of the phases or periods which take shape within Faulkner's oeuvre in relation to Dostoevsky. Isolated resemblances, vague for the most part when they occur in a particular novel or story, do not in themselves permit definitive conclusions. Only their multiplicity and the overall picture reveal a sufficiently clear and complex image of the influence exerted by Dostoevsky: the areas where it was manifested, its extent and nature according to the periods, its meaning for the study of the American author and, finally, the permanent principles which control its action.

Faulkner was not seduced in a constant manner by the Dostoevskian spell which, in addition, acted only through several texts and in rather well-defined areas. So we can immediately eliminate the period prior to *Sartoris* and *The Sound and the Fury*; if he read Dostoevsky around 1915-16, Faulkner began to be inspired by him only in 1929, when he conceived the great design that he was to pursue until his death. From 1929 to 1962, indeed, the fresco of Yoknapatawpha continued to flow more or less regularly and directly from that source. We know, on the other hand, that this novelist, who was also at times a poet, sometimes allowed himself short excursions *extra muros*. But certain literary genres, certain themes and milieux remained impervious to Dostoevsky.

We can detect no trace of him in the verse and rather little in the stories about the First World War (*Soldiers' Pay*, "Victory", "Crevasse", "All the Dead Pilots", "Turnabout", etc.). *A Fable*, to be sure, is an exception to the rule, but it is, above all, a parable on the human condition. The rare stories devoted to World War II ("Two Soldiers", "Shall Not Perish"), although from the same period as "The Bear", confirm the impression. However, it is not the war itself as a subject which repels Dostoevsky but its contemporaneousness and its reality; while the Russian fits without difficulty into the legendary framework of the Civil War (*Absalom, Absalom!*, *The Unvanquished*), it is apparently impossible to combine him with an experience as physical, immediate, "true" and as intensely lived as that of the R.A.F. pilot. Here we touch on a constant of this influence which was always linked to the world of imagination beginning in 1929 and was always excluded from purely autobiographical material, as *Mosquitoes* again shows. Whenever Dostoevsky enters the Faulknerian universe, he keeps clear of the area of private confession. Thus we never find him in the poetry. Another preliminary condition: if the influence assumes a gap between the life of the individual and artistic creation, even within the latter category it vanishes beyond certain limits. It does not impregnate, for instance, the evocation of a remote pass, known from hearsay or reconstructed by sheer imagination. This is the case with the customs of Indian tribes, a marginal theme which could not be said to be part of living experience. It is true that Faulkner attempts it only in his stories, and Dostoevsky hardly appears except in the longer works: note his accessory role in *These 13, Doctor Martino and Other Stories,* and most of the stories of *The Unvanquished, Go Down, Moses* and *Knight's Gambit.* One would say that, to work on Faulkner, Dostoevsky needs a space, a volume, an expanse that corresponds more or less to the range of his greatest novels: *Crime and Punishment, The Idiot, The Possessed, The Brothers Karamazov.* The short story, by definition brief and allusive, does not offer him a big enough field of operation. But we already sense that the freedom of movement he demands is not merely quantitative, it is measured by a good many other things than by numbers of pages. We have just said that there are subjects to which he is poorly adapted because they are too "real" or too fictitious. However, even in the intermediary area in which observation combines with imagination in the proper proportions, some sectors remain forbidden to him; at least his presence is only barely tolerated. This is the case with the world of the local chronicle, the hamlet where the Snopes confront the Varners, the provincial town which is the theater, first, of their triumph and then of their ruin. Can this be blamed on the limited scope of these novels? It is true of *The Town*, one of Faulkner's dullest novels despite Flem's demoniacal ambition. But *The Hamlet* does not lack for complexity; *As I Lay Dying*, which develops in a similar social sphere, counts among the most subtle constructions in literature; and Mink, the peasant of *The Mansion*, bears comparison with Raskolnikov. Despite the fact that Dostoevsky agrees ill with the picture of country life, the incompatibility cannot be imputed to a so-called poverty of the subject. This is an over-simple explanation—for the value of all subjects depends on how they are treated; besides, this hypothesis is given the lie by the texts. The reason is rather that the resources inherent in Faulknerian regionalism are situated on a wave length short of, or beyond, that of the Russian novelist: on the level of a dechristianized vitalism in *As I Lay Dying*, of a dithyramb on animality in Book Three of *The Hamlet* ("The Long Summer"), or that of the frozen inhumanity in the description of Flem's rise (*The Town*). Faulkner's Dostoevskian characters such as Joe Christmas, McEachern, or Nancy are far from being intellectuals: a worker, a farmer, a servant, in terms of intellectual curiosity they are not significantly different from the peasants of Frenchman's Bend. On the other hand, Faulkner can easily manage the perspective required by Dostoevsky in the country chronicle, as *The Mansion* shows. Nonetheless, he rarely introduces it into that genre, preferring other themes—often quite as comprehensive. Why is that so? Perhaps because Dostoevsky's novels are pre-eminently novels which take place in the city—Petersburg in *Crime and Punishment*, *The Idiot*, and *A Raw Youth*; a small town, probably about the size of Jefferson in *The Possessed* and *The Brothers Karamazov*—and which discuss questions dear to the urban intelligentsia. We pass easily, with a couple of minor changes, from Raskolnikov to Quentin Compson; we can imagine a theoretician like Gavin Stevens debating with Ivan and Zossima; and although Joe Christmas and Nancy do not analyze themselves as lucidly and relentlessly as their Russian counterparts, they at least find themselves confronting problems that are posed particularly in the context of the city. Christmas suffers from alienation, and Nancy's crime assumes as a background a young and well-to-do couple of Jefferson. It is, truly, more difficult to cross the moral, intellectual, and social gulf which separates the University of Petersburg from the isolated farms of *As I Lay Dying*, although the leap is not beyond Faulkner's forces. To open themselves to Russian influence, all that the chronicle and the pastoral require as a prior condition is an analogous manner of approaching the study of Man, a truism which is verified by the example of *The Mansion*. To summarize, the Faulknerian terrain conquered by Dostoevsky is limited as follows. Geographically, it coincides with Yoknapatawpha County: only *Pylon* and *A Fable* are at variance with this rule, but they are two failures, and the first, in addition, belongs to a transitional period. Historically, it extends approximately over the second half of the nineteenth century and the first half of the twentieth, thus including the period described by the Russian. Aesthetically, it ends at the frontiers of poetry and just barely crosses those of the short story; the genre to which it corresponds is pre-eminently the novel and, in particular, the novel which transforms the actual experience of life without lapsing into pure fantasy—the work which, being neither too close to, nor too distant from, the real, permits the artist to fuse the three ingredients of literature: observation, experience (which includes books read) and imagination.[1] Moreover, this narrative form requires, in addition to a mental disposition on the same pitch as the model—which is not always the case—a sufficiently ample framework and viewpoint. We think in this context of the famous definition of the novel formulated by Dostoevsky in his letter to Strachov of February 26–March 10, 1869:

> I have my own idea about art, and it is this: What most people regard as fantastic and lacking in universality, I hold to be the inmost essence of truth. Arid observation of everyday trivialities I have long ceased to regard as realism—it is quite the reverse. . . .

354

How paltry and petty is such a way of driving home actualities! Always the same old story! In this way, we shall let all true actuality slip through our fingers. And who will really delineate the facts, will steep himself in them?²

Faulkner has never spoken in public of any of Dostoevsky's works except *The Brothers Karamazov*. But we know that he possessed other novels as well and that he had read *Crime and Punishment* at least once. As for the other novels, he may have become aware of them either directly or indirectly. We have, in any case, constantly detected points of contact throughout his work with *The Possessed, The Idiot*, and sporadically with *A Raw Youth, The Eternal Husband, The House of the Dead, The Diary of a Writer, White Nights, The Insulted and the Injured*, and *Poor People*. Although we sometimes incline in favor of an influence, particularly in the case of the first two, the doubt remains on account of the scarcity or the imprecision of the analogies.

Nothing is more certain, on the other hand, than the action exercised by *The Brothers Karamazov*, a growing source of materials, and then of ideas, between 1929 and 1954. Faulkner was right to rank it among his favorite books: it is by this channel, rather than by the intermediary of *Crime and Punishment*, that Dostoevsky influenced his progress. The passages from these two masterpieces which the American remembers best and most often are rather numerous: Raskolnikov's preparations (I), "Rebellion" (V,4), "The Grand Inquisitor" (V,5), and the preachings of Zossima (VI). They correspond to the mental disposition, varying according to the period, of which we spoke earlier; they are situated at levels of sensibility which give easy access to the Dostoevskian world. Thus the reflections on the anguish of freedom, amplified in "The Grand Inquisitor", are met as early as *Mosquitoes*, before the contamination of 1929; and one of the heroes of *Soldiers' Pay* already defines property as the curse of our civilization. There is no need to go back to Dostoevsky to explain the origin of these ideas, although they are perhaps a residue of earlier readings. For the torments and difficulties which accompany freedom and ownership are, for a Southerner, nurtured on the history of the native land, raised in the memory of the emancipation of the blacks and the omnipotence of the whites, almost first hand observations. In this respect, Dostoevsky only sanctioned that of which Faulkner was already convinced. But we can assume that, at the same time, the Russian strengthened him in his opinions and encouraged him to define and proclaim them. The influence would have been impossible without the presence from the beginning of certain shared views. This is the door through which, around 1929, the Russian novelist's images surge in and, in their wake, his philosophical teachings. Starting from a fortuitous affinity in the ways of seeing, feeling, and thinking, we end up with a veritable impregnation and adoption of new elements which adapt and multiply easily in such a favorable climate. As a general rule, the process requires time for its accomplishment, for Faulkner does not appropriate without assimilating, that is, transposing. The borrowing is first timidly grafted upon the trunk and, nourished by foreign sap, it grows only at the price of mutations. Faulkner would need nearly ten years, from 1932 to 1942, from *Light in August* to "The Bear," to pass from Fate to free will and from evil to good. But he undergoes what is, in sum, a veritable spiritual revolution. Little by little, the influence increases and concentrates, carried by its own movement; the lines of forces, at first sparse and indistinct, converge and thicken. First, it is situations, motives, human types, constantly reshaped and coming principally from two books, whose spectrum is sketched; then, after the turning point of 1935-36, these elements find a more solid but also a more circumscribed foundation in the doctrine of *The Brothers Karamazov*, until the influence culminates in *Requiem for a Nun*.

The role of Dostoevsky can be estimated by the mere fact that we have been led to concern ourselves in these pages with most of the aspects of Faulkner and the most important problems he raises. Initially used as material, seen primarily as a creator of forms, as a novelist, Dostoevsky contributes a number of stones to the Faulknerian edifice, especially in *The Sound and the Fury*, *Light in August*, and *Absalom, Absalom!*. Then comes the desire to leave the wasteland, and it is more than ever to Dostoevsky that Faulkner turns, but this time it is to the thinker whose philosophy of atonement enables him little by little to lift the curse.

The instrument that Faulkner earlier used as he pleased is transformed into a means of salvation. In *Requiem for a Nun*, Faulkner transforms the model less than he conforms to it: Dostoevsky visibly draws him from his path, into countries where he is at the mercy of his guide.[3] In 1951-54, the impregnation loses the role of adjuvant first assigned to it; it is no longer friendship, but an invasion against which Faulkner soon reacts. His last three books show him retreating from temptations fatal to his talent, trying to revert to his earlier manner but without giving up the positions he had conquered. It is clear that the influence is felt each time the development of the work is modified and that it more and more determines this development. That is the case in 1929 when Faulkner laid the foundations of Yoknapatawpha and the phenomenon repeats itself, even more markedly, around 1935-36, when he began to weigh the chances of redemption, then again at the time of his conversion to the discursive mode. Beginning in 1938 and particularly in 1942, instrumentality, the principle which until then governed the relations of the two novelists, borders on causality, although the borrowings of ideas are not explained, in the final analysis, by the desire to imitate Dostoevsky, but by the will to solve a personal problem. It is due to a lack of dialectical resources that Faulkner turns to the Russian, who opens the gates of salvation to him but also draws him into an adventure above—or outside of—his means. Finally, the break of 1957 coincides with the rejection of an encumbering presence.

Thus, to detect Dostoevsky's traces in Faulkner's work is to write the history of this work, indicate its stages, and explain its evolution. But, on the esthetic level, it is also to estimate its value, and to reveal certain reasons for its success or failure. In this respect, we can say that Faulkner is best where he freely manipulates the Russian storyteller's images, and worst when he adopts the mannerisms of the thinker. Borrowings abound in the masterpieces as in the flops: in the first case they are primarily forms; in the second they are concepts. To be sure, one could hardly think of making Dostoevsky the only touchstone, the absolute criterion of Faulknerian studies. But such confrontations on the combined levels of literary history and criticism lead to results at least as clear as those provided by the usual approaches. The comparatist can only be delighted when his investigations corroborate those of other enquiries. The concordance of conclusions only reinforces his theses and confirms the extent of the debt contracted. And yet, comparative literature would be a vain occupation if it served only to confirm the discoveries of other disciplines or to track down beyond national borders the source of certain details. There is in literature, as in life, no magic masterkey. Methods are worth only what they tell us of the object to which we apply them; their excellence is measured only by their results. In the case with which we are concerned, the recourse to the comparative method leads to a less hesitant tracing of the Faulknerian curve, to a more comprehensive evaluation of the works than with the usual methods. It is in relation to Dostoevsky that the decisive turning points of 1935-36 and 1957, often overlooked previously, are identified; that the capital theme of choice, exploited between 1938 to 1962, emerges; that the failings of *Pylon*, *Requiem for a Nun*, *A Fable*, and *The Town* can be simultaneously explained. The advantage of the procedure consists in proposing a new division and evaluation of the Faulknerian *corpus*, in illuminating certain essential aspects, usually forgotten or underrated. Free will, for instance, has never received the attention it deserves, and placing Faulkner and its Russian prophet side by side is a particularly fruitful operation. Dostoevsky obviously provides an extremely active detector for the Americanist. A good many Faulknerian characteristics are set in relief by contact with him, while the dilemma which we have constantly come up against in this work—affinity or influence?—fades into the background, the comparison with Dostoevsky by itself furnishes an incomparable research tool. We will remember then, in addition to the influence exerted, the many benefits gained from this observation post. In the final analysis, it matters little whether *Pylon* is inspired by *The Idiot* or not, if the juxtaposition of Myshkin and the reporter enable us to understand the latter differently and better. It would be both tiresome and presumptuous to draw up an exhaustive inventory of the gains Faulknerian studies would derive from comparative literature properly understood; all the more so as we have just indicated the most obvious of them. Let us point out once again the elucidations of questions as crucial as the dialectics of the heart and mind, the political convictions, the social situation of the writer and, in particular, his nationalism and his attitude toward God. As for the details, they are legion: Quentin Compson's pride, Nancy's faith, the temptations of *A Fable*, the type of the monomaniac, etc. In short, thanks to Dostoevsky, it seems that we know better today—at least we hope so—how Faulkner's novels were born and what they mean.

In connection with the influence and its curve, we have spoken of impregnation and transposition.[4] Literal borrowings, we recall, are exceptional, and it is now imperative to examine the mutations undergone, to define their constants, if this is possible. Let us remark, first of all, that no matter how the gap between the source and the work diminishes, it always remains, even at the time of the most intimate relations. Sometimes appropriated virtually unchanged, sometimes manipulated beyond recognition, the foreign body is made subservient to an autonomous intuition. Faulkner, like most artists, acts just the reverse of the philologist: he ignores contexts, scorns the original meaning, isolates and reshapes images or ideas as he pleases. In addition, once absorbed into the novelist's experience, the borrowing, far from being regarded as such, develops in concert with other components; it is the same for situations that Faulkner invents and continues to adapt.[5] Very likely, Mink Snopes, in *The Mansion*, is not directly indebted to Raskolnikov: they are linked through the agency of Quentin Compson, Joe Christmas and other less important replicas. It is this sovereign scorn of mine and thine, the faculty of digesting another's work and making it one's own flesh and blood that makes the influence so difficult to identify, to say nothing of the fact that it is planted in congenial soil. At all times, one wanders in the no man's land between simple kinship and the authentic borrowing, one continually flounders in the shifting sands of metamorphosis.

There are, first of all, the transpositions in time and space: the long voyage which leads from imperial Russia to Sutpen's plantation and the Memphis brothel. In the process a host of picturesque details, too closely connected with the initial milieu, disintegrate. No more isbas, troikas, or samovars, but log cabins, automobiles, and whisky. But beneath this easily interchangeable costumery, man—a muzhik or a gentleman—remains the same. Adaptation to the environment is not an insurmountable difficulty and, in any case, it hardly affects the ideas. Dmitri's and Zossima's ideas about guilt and atonement are of universal significance: Faulkner can use them in diagnosing and curing the evils of the South.

The differences in focus are more interesting. The borrowed element, in consideration of the new meaning assigned to it, takes on a greater or lesser importance than in the source. Faulkner achieves intensification when he places a particular image under the magnifying glass (Quentin Compson's watch), expands the role of a character (Caddy), underlines the contrast of protagonists (Lena Grove and Joe Christmas), embroiders a situation (those of McEachern, Nancy), or generalizes an idea (the Fate in which only Raskolnikov believes). Exaggeration characterizes the realism proper to these novelists who willingly underline the unusual: excess, violence, horror. Quentin, Nancy and the corporal, Raskolnikov, Kirillov and Myshkin are extraordinary beings, fascinated by paradox. On the other hand, the borrowing is sometimes reduced to an echo: muffled, diluted or suggested, the Dostoevskian contribution is difficult to recognize. Attenuation, a procedure which consists in reducing the essential to the level of the accessory, is as common as the opposite type of distortion. What remains of Raskolnikov beneath the features of Labove or Henry Armstid, of the theme of the "little horse" in *Sartoris?* Nothing or practically nothing, to such an extent that one begins to doubt if there was an influence. The lessening, retrogression, summarization, and particularization correspond to the phenomena that we have just noted. Remember Raskolnikov's nightmare in *The Sound and the Fury,* Richard's story in *Sanctuary,* "The Grand Inquisitor" in *The Hamlet.*

One should not wonder at the divergence and amplitude of the changes. Imitation, annexation pure and simple, is not fashionable in an age which exalts surprise as a major artistic virtue. Let us not delude ourselves about the textual quotations of T. S. Eliot and Ezra Pound, for they are a response to a situation very different from that of, for instance, a writer of the Renaissance.

Faulkner shapes his materials on a pattern of his own with broad chisel strokes, and we know the polarity of his thought and his imagination.[6] In him, extremes meet; thus it is not rare that the remodelling goes as far as inversion.[7] Drusilla in "An Odor of Verbena" quotes arguments advanced by Dostoevsky against duelling to achieve the opposite purpose. Isaac McCaslin ("The Bear") does not accept the established order any more than does Ivan Karamazov; but, in his revolt, he wants to embrace what Ivan rejects. The corporal of *A Fable* is one of the "leaders of humanity" of which Raskolnikov speaks and yet he "is (not) guilty of terrible carnage," he desires only peace; this time, it is the "slave" who is the revolutionary. In passing from the Karamazovs to the Sutpens, Faulkner replaces one of the brothers by a sister and pushes family affection to incest. Quentin's hierarchy of motives in *The Sound and the Fury* reverses those presented in *Crime and Punishment*.

Faulkner does not work according to immutable and mechanical formulas. The operations described above are not calculated: their implicit rules can only be described by examining a number of borrowings, and they admit of a good many exceptions. This artist cares little for theory; an enemy of schools and programs, he limits himself to the practical—the exhausting struggle with language, the slow conquest of chaos by form. And yet, although spontaneous and guided by an empirical view of the situation, his attempts always carry him in the same direction. The most striking and frequent inversion, for instance, is the secularization of the work read. Faulkner was inspired only by the works Dostoevsky wrote after his "conversion": *Poor People* does not seem to have marked him. Nonetheless, his earlier books, although bathed in a puritanical atmosphere, virulently attack the American churches. The individual experience always opposes the official God of the community: we think of the contrast between the corporal and the priest, the faith of Dilsey or Nancy and the conventional reactions of their mistresses. Although drawing near to Dostoevsky on the topic of religion, Faulkner could never subscribe to the fervent convictions of Sonia, Myshkin, or Zossima. To pass from one to the other, the borrowing must be detached from the framework that gives it its meaning: by being inserted in a new context, it is distorted, it becomes, as it were, a metaphor and reflects its original meaning only by means of a rather inadequate comparison. In a good many cases, the metaphor antithetical: it takes the opposite position from the Dostoevskian idea and leads to heresy, indeed to sacrilege. To be sure, the Russian paints his heretics and demons with a more vigorous brush than his saints, and he also knew doubt. To be sure, Faulkner abominates a certain kind of materialism as much as Dostoevsky does. But between the nostalgic scepticism which devours Ivan Karamazov and the cold Reason of the conspirators, there is room for a revolt which Dostoevsky did not envision—Addie Bundren's rebellion which springs from the deepest levels of the flesh. In *The Wild Palms*, love, suffering, and life unite as in *The Brothers Karamazov*, but without converging toward a Creator: we remain on the strictly secular level of the passions. What would Zossima say in hearing Charlotte parody his teachings? Similarly, Faulkner limits the freedom, which Dostoevsky considered primarily as a philosophical principle, to the level of society, customs, the State: thus he can enlist the defender of the throne and altar in support of American liberalism. Faulkner secularizes the concepts of nation and immortality, the object of faith (*Intruder in the Dust, A Fable*), the dialogue of the Grand Inquisitor and Christ, the three temptations of the Gospels, the suffering of children (*Sanctuary*), the expiation of sin, etc. Faulkner's interest is not in religion itself, but in its social excrescences: fanaticism, intolerance and hypocrisy. And when he leaves the human, terrestrial, concrete level of the Church and its faithful to venture into ethics and theology, as he does during the period of *Requiem for a Nun*, he cuts himself off from a familiar field of observation, renounces the transposition which is natural to him, and inevitably fails. The frequency of this technique even allows us to put forward assumptions which might at first seem inadmissable on the origin of certain of his materials. One has only to recall the bear hunt in "The Bear", the detail of the bird in *A Fable*, the parallelism between Lucius Priest and Alyosha (*The Reivers*).

The manipulations studied thus far—intensification, attenuation, inversion and secularization—primarily affect the quality of the borrowing. In comparison others seem rather quantitative in nature. They concern, primarily images, situations, and psychological traits. Ideas are incorporeal and less easy to amputate or to juxtapose. Sometimes the Dostoevskian elements divide, scatter, and engender others in the Faulknerian world; at other times they agglutinate, knit together, and multiplicity is replaced by unity. The splitting and the combination of characters are evidenced in the passage of *Absalom, Absalom!* where the couples formed by Quentin and Shreve, Henry and Charles almost simultaneously stand out and blend together.

What we observe within the novelistic world we also find when we study its origin. As in *Absalom, Absalom!*, splitting seems less common than the reverse process. But one hesitates to generalize on examples as rare and controversial as those of Benjy and Dilsey (*The Sound and the Fury*)—derived from Sonia Marmeladov?— or Temple Drake and Narcissa Benbow (*Sanctuary*), distant descendants of Katerina Ivanovna of *The Brothers Karamazov*. If Faulkner had used this method more frequently, it would corroborate the conjectures advanced about *A Raw Youth* and *Absalom, Absalom!*, for Dolgoruky would indeed conform to the norm in giving birth to both Sutpen and Charles Bon. Unfortunately, we must be wary of an argument which rests on such fragile foundations. Let us add that the Dostoevskian heroes, in being divided, see their viability reduced proportionally and that they recover their strength, one might say, only because Faulkner plants them in rich soil. Benjy and Dilsey, to cite only two examples, are a good deal more than two aspects of Sonia. Some of our novelists' creatures resemble one another only distantly.

It is impossible to say how Faulkner interpreted Dostoevsky, for one can know the interpretation only through the work produced, that is to say, as it is mingled in the creation. Any observation based on the novels bears necessarily on this double process. Having made these reservations, we can state that Faulkner decomposes the model less often than he combines its details. His is not an analytical, discursive, objective mind. His outlook is based on a global apprehension of things, on the intuition of hidden relations, on the power to endow them with colors he alone can see. Corresponding to this tendency, which culminated in *The Sound and the Fury* and especially in the first part, is

363

the marriage of Dostoevskian characters. We might better say: the agglomeration. For if the paternity of McEachern (*Light in August*) is traceable to Fyodor Karamazov and Grigory, if certain acts of Labove (*The Hamlet*) result from the alliance of Raskolnikov and Svidrigailov, and if the reporter of *Pylon*, Sutpen (*Absalom, Absalom!*), and Mink Snopes (*The Mansion*) issue respectively from the couples Myshkin–Alyosha, Dolgoruky–Raskolnikov, and Raskolnikov–Orlov, it is three-sided, indeed even five-or-more-sided, relationships that give birth to Jason Compson (Luzhin, Ivan Karamazov, Smerdyakov), Isaac McCaslin (Alyosha, Dmitri, Ivan), the Temple Drake of *Requiem for a Nun* (Raskolnikov, Dmitri, Ivan), and mosaics like Joe Christmas and Nancy. The latter, we recall, is an extreme case: she appears when the influence reaches the zenith of its force. It goes without saying that all components are not equal in the final synthesis: there is always a base, a dominant chord that is inflected by the less important borrowings. In *A Fable*, for example, we find the resemblances between the Marshal and the Grand Inquisitor greater than those with Ivan Karamazov. The fundamental kernel does not always come from Dostoevsky; it can also emanate from life, imagination, or other books. The proportion, which is connected with the focus chosen by Faulkner, also guarantees the originality of the creation. Faulkner, not content simply to superimpose different portraits, submits situations and episodes to similar combinations. Moreover, he combines the ideas of nation and expiation which are totally unconnected in Dostoevsky. Even Dostoevsky's techniques are blended, as the composition of *Sanctuary* and *Absalom, Absalom!* perhaps testifies.

But, all things considered, the craftsman attracted Faulkner less than the psychologist, the image-maker, and the philosopher. Despite the fact that Dostoevsky announces the modern novel, he is, in this respect, too much the child of his own century to determine its evolution. Other aspects, however, easily pass from one period to the next. Whether pertaining only to Dostoevsky or to the Russian tradition, they invade the Faulknerian universe in which they usually scatter and atomize into tiny details. It has been necessary to identify these one by one, even at the risk of being criticized for over-ingeniousness, before defining their number, quality, meaning, and fertility.

NOTES TO CONCLUSION

1. *Faulkner in the University,* p. 172.
2. *Letters of Fyodor Dostoevsky,* pp. 166-67.
3. See Horst-Jurgen Gerigk, *Versuch über Dostojevskijs "Jüngling"* (München: Wilhelm Fink Verlag, 1965), p. 25: "Seine (Dosotevsky's) Nachahmer müssen künsterlich scheitern, wenn sie in seinen Werk in erster Linie die 'Ideen' sehen."
4. Richard P. Adams earlier arrived at similar conclusions. See "The Apprenticeship of William Faulkner," *Tulane Studies in English,* XII (1962), p. 155.
5. See Edward Holmes, *Faulkner's Twice-Told Tales* (The Hague: Mouton and Co., 1966), pp. 94-95.
6. See Walter J. Slatoff, *Quest for Failure* (Ithaca, N. Y.: Cornell University Press, 1960), pp. 79ff.
7. On this point see Victor Strandberg, "Faulkner's Poor Parson and the Technique of Inversion," *The Sewanee Review,* LXXIII, 2 (Spring, 1965), pp. 181-90.

BIBLIOGRAPHY

Quotations from Faulkner and Dostoevsky
are from the following editions:

I. Works of William Faulkner

The Marble Faun and *A Green Bough*. New York: Random House, 1965.
Soldiers' Pay. New York: Liveright Publishing Corporation, 1926.
Mosquitoes. New York: Boni and Liveright, 1927.
Sartoris. New York: Random House, 1951.
The Sound and the Fury and *As I Lay Dying*. With a New Appendix as a Foreword by the Author. The Modern Library. New York: Random House, 1946.
Sanctuary. With a New Introduction by the Author. The Modern Library. New York: Random House, 1932.
Light in August. New York: Random House, 1932.
Pylon. New York: Harrison Smith and Robert Haas, Inc., 1935.
Absalom, Absalom!. The Modern Library. New York: Random House, 1936.
The Unvanquished. New York: Random House, 1938.
The Wild Palms. Vintage Books. New York: Random House, 1939.
The Hamlet. Vintage Books. New York: Random House, 1931.
Go Down, Moses. The Modern Library. New York: Random House, 1940.
Intruder in the Dust. New York: Random House, 1948.
Knight's Gambit. New York: Random House, 1932.
Collected Stories of William Faulkner. New York: Random House, 1950.
Requiem for a Nun. The Modern Library. New York: Random House, 1950.
A Fable. New York: Random House, 1950.
The Town. Vintage Books. New York: Random House, 1957.
The Mansion. Vintage Books. New York: Random House, 1955.
The Reivers. A Reminiscence. New York: Random House, 1962.
Early Prose and Poetry. Compilation and Introduction by Carvel Collins. London: Jonathan Cape, 1963.
New Orleans Sketches. Introduction by Carvel Collins. New Brunswick, N.J.: Rutgers University Press, 1958.

Essays, Speeches and Public Letters. Edited by James B. Meriwether. New York: Random House, 1965.

Faulkner at Nagano. Edited by Robert A. Jelliffe. Tokyo: Kenkyusha Ltd., 1956.

Faulkner in the University. Class Conferences at the University of Virginia 1957-58. Edited by Frederick L. Gwynn and Joseph L. Blotner. Charlottesville, Virginia: The University of Virginia Press, 1959.

II. Works of Dostoevsky

White Nights and Other Stories. Translated from the Russian by Constance Garnett. New York: Macmillan, 1917. (Includes "Notes from the Underground.")

The Insulted and the Injured. Translated from the Russian by Constance Garnett. New York: Macmillan, 1915.

The House of the Dead. Translated from the Russian by Constance Garnett. New York: Macmillan, 1915.

Crime and Punishment. Translated from the Russian by Constance Garnett. London: Heinemann, 1964.

The Gambler and Other Stories. Translated from the Russian by Constance Garnett. New York: Macmillan, 1917. (Includes "Poor People" and "The Landlady").

The Idiot. Translated from the Russian by Constance Garnett. The Modern Library. New York: Random House, 1935.

The Eternal Husband and Other Stories. Translated from the Russian by Constance Garnett. New York: Macmillan, 1917. (Includes "The Double" and "Gentle Spirit").

The Possessed. Translated from the Russian by Constance Garnett. With a foreword by Avram Yarmolinsky and a translation of the hitherto-suppressed chapter "At Tikon's." The Modern Library. New York: Random House, 1936.

A Raw Youth. Translated from the Russian by Constance Garnett. New York: The Dial Press, 1947.

The Brothers Karamazov. Translated from the Russian by Constance Garnett. The Modern Library. New York: Random House, n.d.

The Diary of a Writer. Translated and annotated by Boris Brasol. New York: Charles Scribner's Sons, 1949.

Dostoevsky: A Self-Portrait. Edited by Jesse Coulson. London: Oxford University Press, 1962.

Letters of Fyodor Michailovitch Dostoevsky. Edited and translated by Ethel Colburn Mayne with an introduction by Avram Yarmolinsky. New York: Horizon Press, 1961.

The Notebooks of Crime and Punishment. Edited and translated by Edward Wasiolek. Chicago and London: University of Chicago Press, 1967.

The Notebooks of The Idiot. Edited and with an Introduction by Edward

BIBLIOGRAPHY

Wasiolek. Translated by Katherine Strelsky. Chicago and London: University of Chicago Press, 1967.

The Notebooks of the Possessed. Edited and with an Introduction by Edward Wasiolek. Translated by Victor Terras. Chicago and London: University of Chicago Press, 1968.

The Notebooks of The Brothers Karamazov. Edited and translated by Edward Wasiolek. Chicago and London: University of Chicago Press, 1971.

III. Works consulted

Adams, Richard P. "The Apprenticeship of William Faulkner." *Tulane Studies in English*, XII (1962), 113-56.

Anderson, Charles. "Faulkner's Moral Center." *Études Anglaises*, VII, 1 (January, 1954), 48-58.

Arban, Dominique. *Dostoievski par lui-même.* Paris. Éditions du Seuil, 1962.

Baiwir, Albert. *Le déclin de l'individualisme chez les romanciers américains contemporains.* Liège-Paris: Faculté de Philosophie et Lettres-Librairie E. Droz, 1943.

Balzac. *La comédie humaine.* Texte établi par Marcel Bouteron.
II. Paris: Éditions de la Nouvelle Revue Française, 1935.
IV. Paris: Éditions de la Nouvelle Revue Française, 1935.
IX. Paris: Éditions de la Nouvelle Revue Française, 1937.

Brenstock, J. W. "Dostoevsky and Balzac." *Mercure de France*, CLXXVI, No. 635 (December 1, 1924) 418-25.

Belperron, Pierre. *La guerre de Sécession (1861-1865). Ses cause et ses suites.* Paris: Plon, 1947.

Berberoff, K. *Étude sur le servage en Russie.* Grenoble: Allier Fréres, 1912.

Berdjajew, N. *Die Weltanschauung Dostojewskijs.* München: C. H. Becksche Verlagsbuchhandlung, 1925.

Blinoff, Marthe. "Dostoevsky et Balzac." *Comparative Literature*, III, 4 (Fall, 1951) 342-55.

Bloch, Marc: *La société féodale.* La formation des liens de dépendance. Paris: Albin Michel, 1939.

Bloch, Marc. *La société féodale.* Les classes et le gouvernement des hommes. Paris: Albin Michel, 1940.

Bouglé, C. *Essais sur le régime des castes.* Paris: Félix Alcan, 1935.

Bouvard, Loic. "Conversation with William Faulkner." *Modern Fiction Studies.* V,4 (Winter, 1959-60) p. 362.

Bowling, Lawrence. "Faulkner: The Theme of Pride in *The Sound and the Fury.*" *Modern Fiction Studies*, XI, 2 (Summer, 1965) 129-39.

Bradbury, John M. *Renaissance in the South.* A Critical History of the Literature, 1920-1960. Chapel Hill: The University of North Carolina Press, 1963.

Brierre, Annie. "Faulkner parle." *Les Nouvelles Littéraires*, No. 1466. October 6, 1955, pp. 1, 6.

Brooks, Cleanth. *William Faulkner: The Yoknapatawpha Country.* New Haven-London: Yale University Press, 1963.

Calmette, Joseph. *Le monde féodal.* Paris: Presses Universitaires de France, 1951.

Carr, Edward Hallett. *Dostoevsky (1821-1881).* A New Biography. With a Preface by D. S. Mirsky. London: George Allen & Unwin, Ltd., 1931.

Chamberlain, John. "Dostoyefsky's Shadow in the Deep South." *New York Times Book Review*, February 15, 1931.

Chase, Richard. *The American Novel and its Tradition.* Garden City, New York: Doubleday and Co., Inc., 1957.

Configuration critique de William Faulkner, I. Paris: Lettres modernes, 1957. II. Paris: Lettres modernes, 1959.

Conrad, Joseph. *Nostromo.* A Tale of the Seabord. With a General Introduction by Albert J. Guerard. New York: Dell Publishing Co., Inc., 1961.

Cuvillier, Armand. *Manuel de sociologie.* Paris: Presses Universitaires de France, 1960-62, 2 vols.

Dickens, Charles. *Great Expectations.* Harmondsworth: Penguin Books Ltd., 1955.

Doerne, Martin. *Gott und Mensch in Dostojewskijs Werk*, Göttingen: Vandenhoeck & Ruprecht, 1957.

Dostoevsky. A Collection of Critical Essays. Edited by René Wellek. Englewood Cliffs, N.J.: Prentice-Hall, Inc., 1962.

Dostojevskij-Studien. Gesammelt und herausgegeben von D. Cyzevśkyi. Reichenberg: Verlag Gebrüder Stiepel, 1931.

Dow, Roger. "Seichas: A Comparison of Pre-Reform Russia and the Ante-Bellum South." *The Russian Review*, VII, 1 (Autumn, 1947) 3-15.

Eaton, Clement. "Class Differences in the Old South." *The Virginia Quarterly Review*, XXXIII, 3 (Summer, 1957) 357-70.

Eaton, Clement. *The Growth of Southern Civilization 1790-1860.* London: Hamish Hamilton, 1961.

Evdokimov, Paul. *Gogol et Dostoievsky ou la descente aux enfers.* n.p.: Desclee De Brouwer, 1961.

Fanger, Donald. *Dostoevsky and Romantic Realism.* A Study of Dostoevsky in Relation to Balzac, Dickens, and Gogol. Cambridge, Mass.: Harvard University Press, 1965.

Faulkner, John. *My Brother Bill.* An Affectionate Reminiscence. London: Victor Gollancz Ltd., 1964.

William Faulkner's Library—A Catalogue. Compiled, with an Introduction, by Joseph Blotner. Charlottesville: University Press of Virginia, 1964.

William Faulkner. Three Decades of Criticism. Edited, with an Introduction and Bibliography, by Frederick J. Hoffman and Olga W. Vickery, East Lansing: Michigan State University Press, 1960.

William Faulkner. Two Decades of Criticism. Edited by Frederick J. Hoffman and Olga W. Vickery. East Lansing: Michigan State College Press, 1951.

Gerigk, Horst-Jürgen. *Versuch über Dostoevkijs "Jüngling."* Ein Beitrag zur Theorie des Romans. München: Wilhelm Fink Verlag, 1965.

Gide, André. *Dostoievsky.* Paris: Plon, 1923.

Girard, René. *Dostoïevski. Du double à l'unité.* Paris: Plon, 1963.

Grenier, Cynthia. "The Art of Fiction: An Interview with William Faulkner —September, 1955." *Accent,* XVI, 3 (Summer, 1956) 167-77.

Grenier, Jean. *Le choix.* Paris: Presses Universitaires de France, 1941.

Gwynn, Frederick L. "Faulkner's Raskolnikov." *Modern Fiction Studies,* IV, 2 (Summer, 1958) 169-72.

Hazendonck, Pieter. *De Aanranding van Eer of Goeden Naam.* Assen: Uitgave van Van Gorcum & Comp. N. V., 1946.

Hoffman, Frederick J. *William Faulkner.* New York, Twayne Publishers, Inc., 1961.

Hoffman, Frederick. *The Twenties.* American Writing in the Postwar Decade. New York: Collier Books, 1962.

Holmes, Edward M. *Faulkner's Twice-Told Tales.* His Re-Use of his Material. The Hague-Paris: Mouton & Co., 1966.

Howe, Irving. *William Faulkner.* A Critical Study. New York: Vintage Books 1962.

Ivanov, Vyacheslav. *Freedom and the Tragic Life.* A Study in Dostoevsky. Foreword by Sir Maurice Bowra. New York: The Noonday Press, 1952.

Jeudon, L. *La morale de l'honneur.* Paris: Félix Alcan, 1911.

Kampmann, Theoderich. *Dostojewski in Deutschland.* Münster in Westf.: Helios-Verlag G. M. B. H., 1931.

Karanikas, Alexander. *Tillers of a Myth.* Southern Agrarians as Social and Literary Critics. Madison-Milwaukee-London: The University of Wisconsin Press, 1966.

Klossowski, Pierre. *Sade mon prochain.* Paris: Éditions du Seuil, 1947.

Lampert, E. *Sons against Fathers.* Studies in Russian Radicalism and Revolution. Oxford: The Clarendon Press, 1965.

Lauth, Reinhard, *"Ich habe die Wahrheit gesehen." Die Philosophie Dostojewskis.* München: R. Piper & Co. Verlag, 1950.

Leavis, F. R. "Dostoevsky or Dickens." *Scrutiny,* II, 1 (June, 1933), 91-93.

Leroy-Beaulieu, Anatole. *L'empire des Tsars et les Russes.* I. Le pays et les habitants. Paris: Hachette, 1881.

Lévy-Bruhl, Lucien. *La morale et la science de moeurs.* Paris: Presses Universitaires de France, 1953.

Levinson, André. "Dostoevsky et le roman occidental." *Revues des Cours et Conferences,* XXVIII, 5 (February, 1927) 425-33; (March 15, 1927) 590-601; 8 (March 30, 1927) 686-97; 10 (April 30, 1927) 169-79.

Lloyd, J. A. T. *A Great Russian Realist* (Feodor Dostoieffsky). London: Stanley Paul & Co. n.d., (1912).

Lo Gatto, Ettore. *Storia della Russia.* Firenze: G. C. Sansoni, 1946.

Lubac, Henri de. *Le drame de l'humanisme athée.* Paris: Éditions Spes, 1945.

Magarshack, David. *Dostoevsky.* London: Secker & Warburg, 1962.

Malin, Irving. *William Faulkner. An Interpretation.* Stanford, California: Stanford University Press, 1957.

Mann, Thomas. *Ausgewählte Erzählungen.* Stockholm: Bermann-Fischer Verlag, 1945.

Matlaw, Ralph E. *The Brothers Karamazov. Novelistic Technique.* 's-Gravenhage: Mouton & Co., 1957.

Mayoux, Jean-Jacques. *La Profondeur et le rythme.* Grenoble-Paris: B. Arthaud, 1968.

Meriwether, James B. *William Faulkner: A Check List.* Princeton, New Jersey: Princeton University Library, 1957.

Millgate, Michael. *The Achievement of William Faulkner.* London: Constable, 1966.

Millgate, Michael. *William Faulkner.* Edinburgh-London: Oliver and Boyd, 1961.

Miner, Ward L. *The World of William Faulkner.* Durham, North Carolina: Duke University Press, 1952.

Mochulsky, Konstantin. *Dostoevsky.* His Life and Work. Translated, with an Introduction, by Michael A. Minihan. Princeton University Press, 1967.

Muchnic, Helen. *Dostoevsky's English Reputation* (1881-1936). Northampton, Massachusetts: Smith College Studies in Modern Languages, XX, April and July 1939.

Nathan, Monique. *Faulkner par lui-même.* Paris: Éditions du Seuil, 1963.

Neuschäffer, Walter. *Dostojewskijs Einfluss auf den englischen Roman.* Heidelberg: Carl Winter, 1935.

O'Connor, William Van. *The Tangled Fire of William Faulkner.* Minneapolis: University of Minnesota Press, 1954.

Portal, Roger. *Les Slaves.* Peuples et nations. Paris: Armand Colin, 1965.

Pouillon, Jean. *Temps et roman.* Paris: Gallimard, 1946.

Pritchett, V. S. "That Time and That Wilderness." *New Statesman,* September 28, 1962, pp. 405-6.

La profondeur et le rythme. Grenoble-Paris: B. Arthaud, 1948.

Proust, Marcel. *À la recherche du temps perdu,* XII, La Prisonniere (deuxième partie). Paris: Gallimard, 1947.

Russell, Bertrand. *History of Western Philosophy* and its Connection with Political and Social Circumstances from the Earliest Times to the Present Day. London: George Allen and Unwin Ltd., 1948.

Scheibert, Peter. *Von Bakunin zu Lenin.* Geschichte der Russischen revolutionären Ideologien 1840-1895. I, Die Formung des radikalen Denkens in der Auseinandersetzung mit Deutschem Idealismus und Französischem Bürgertum, Leiden, E. J. Brill, 1956.

Schulte Nordholt, Dr. J. W. *Het volk dat in duisternis wandelt.* De geschiedenis van de negers in Amerika. Arnhem: Van Loghum Slaterus, 1957.

Schwartz, Delmore. "A Fable by William Faulkner." *Perspectives USA,* 10 (Winter, 1955) 126-36.

BIBLIOGRAPHY

Le servage. Bruxelles: Éditions de la Librairie Encyclopédique, 1959.

Simmons, Ernest J. *Dostoevski. The Making of a Novelist.* London-New York-Toronto, Oxford University Press, 1940.

Slatoff, Walter J. *Quest for Failure.* A Study of William Faulkner. Ithaca, New York: Cornell University Press, 1960.

Le Statut des paysans libérés du servage 1861-1961. Recueil d'articles et de documents présentés par R. Portal avec la collaboration de T. Bakounine, M. Confino, C. Kastler, B. Kerblay, P. Péchoux, R. Philippot. Paris-La Haye: Mouton & Co., 1963.

Stepun, Fedor, *Dostojewski und Tolstoj.* Christentum und soziale Revolution. Drei Essays. München: Carl Hanser, 1961.

Strandberg, "Faulkner's Poor Parson and the Technique of Inversion." *Sewanee Review,* LXXXIII, 2 (Spring, 1965) 181-90.

Swiggart, Peter. *The Art of Faulkner's Novels.* Austin: University of Texas Press, 1963.

Taylor, William R. *Cavalier and Yankee.* The Old South and American National Character. Garden City, New York: Doubleday & Company, Inc., 1963.

Terraillon, Eugene. *L'honneur. Sentiment et principe moral.* Paris: Félix Alcan, 1912.

Tolstoi, Léon. *Anna Karénine. Résurrection.* Traductions et notes de Henri Mongault, Sylvie Luneau et E. Beaux. Introduction de Pierre Pascal. Index chronologique par Sylvie Luneau. Paris: Gallimard, 1951.

Trubetzkoy, N. S. *Dostoevskij als Künstler.* The Hague-London-Paris: Mouton & Co., 1964.

Van der Eng, Johannes. *Dostoevskij romancier.* Rapports entre sa vision du monde et ses procédés littéraires. 's-Gravenhage: Mouton & Co., n.d., 1957.

Varagnac, André. *Civilisation traditionelle et genres de vie.* Paris: Albin Michel, 1948.

Vickery, Olga W. *The Novels of William Faulkner.* A Critical Interpretation. Louisiana State University Press, 1961.

Vocabulaire technique et critique de la philosophie. Publié par André Lalande. Paris: Presses Universitaires de France, 1960.

Wasiolek, Edward. "Dostoevsky and *Sanctuary.*" *Modern Language Notes,* LXXIV, 2 (February, 1959) 114-17.

Weber, Robert W. "Raskol'nikov, Addie Bundren, Meursault. Sur la continuité d'un mythe." *Archiv für das Studium der neueren Sprachen und Literaturen,* 202. Band, 117. Jahrgang 2. Heft, pp. 81-92.

Westermarck, Edward. *L'origine et le développement des idées morales.* Édition française par Robert Godet. Paris: Payot, 1928-29, 2 vol.

Williams, T. Harry; Current, Richard; Freidel, Frank. *A History of the United States.* New York: Alfred A. Knopf, 1959, 2 vol.

Woodworth, S. S. *William Faulkner en France (1931-1952).* Paris: M. J. Minard, 1959.

Zander, L.-A. *Dostoïevsky. Le Problème du Bien.* Translated from Russian by R. Hofmann. Paris: Corrêa, 1946.

INDEX TO PROPER NAMES

INDEX TO CHARACTERS